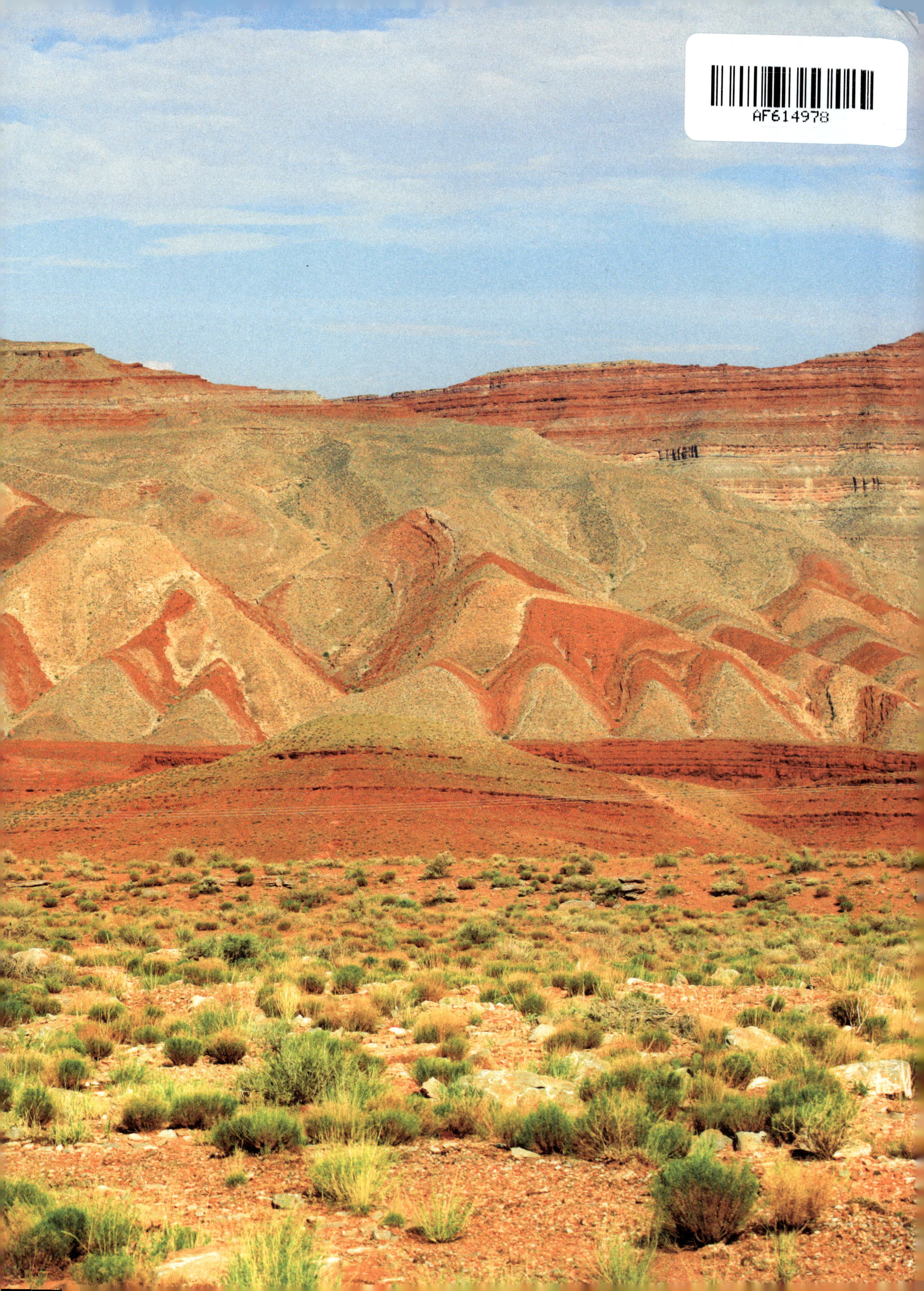

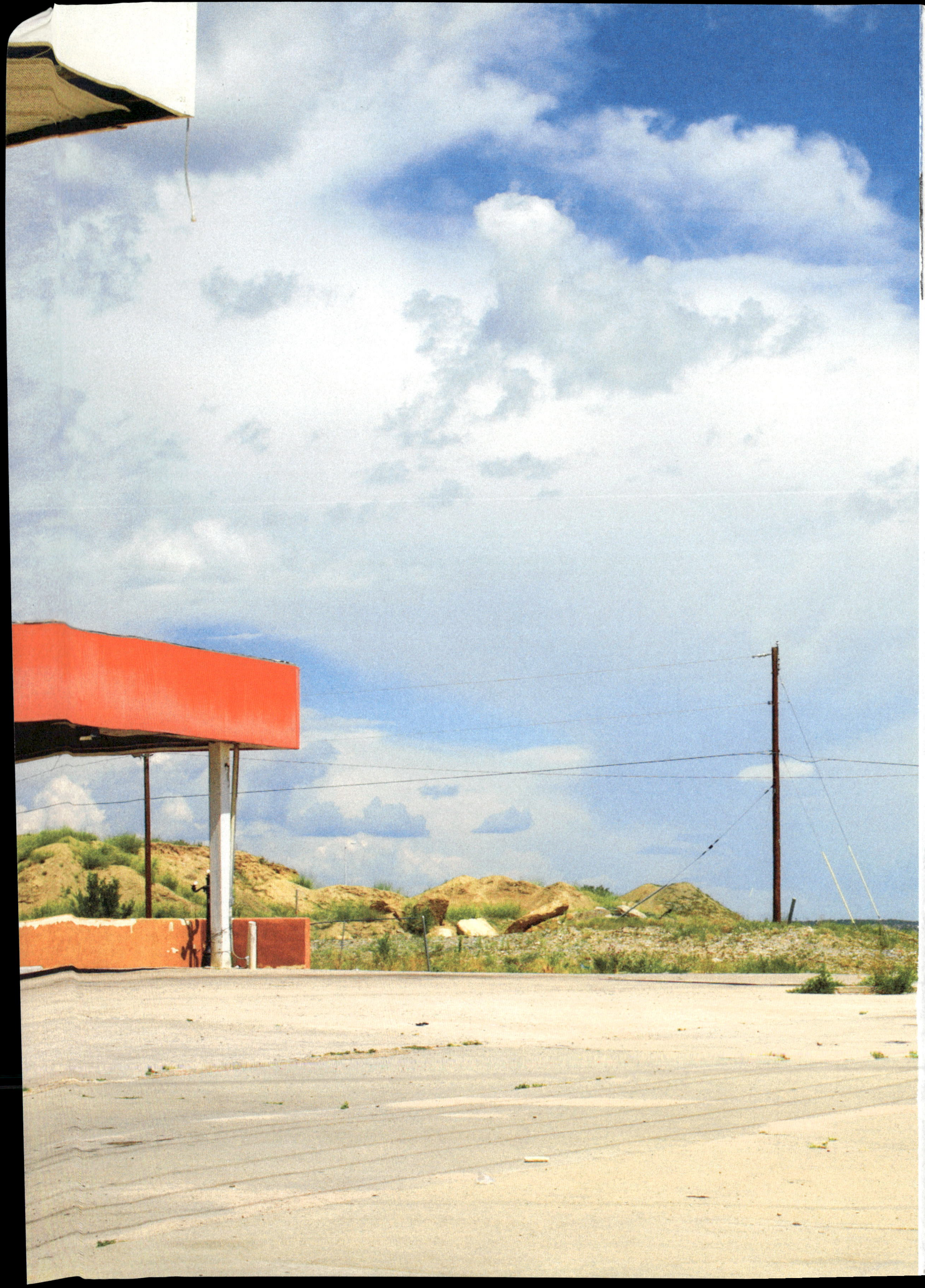

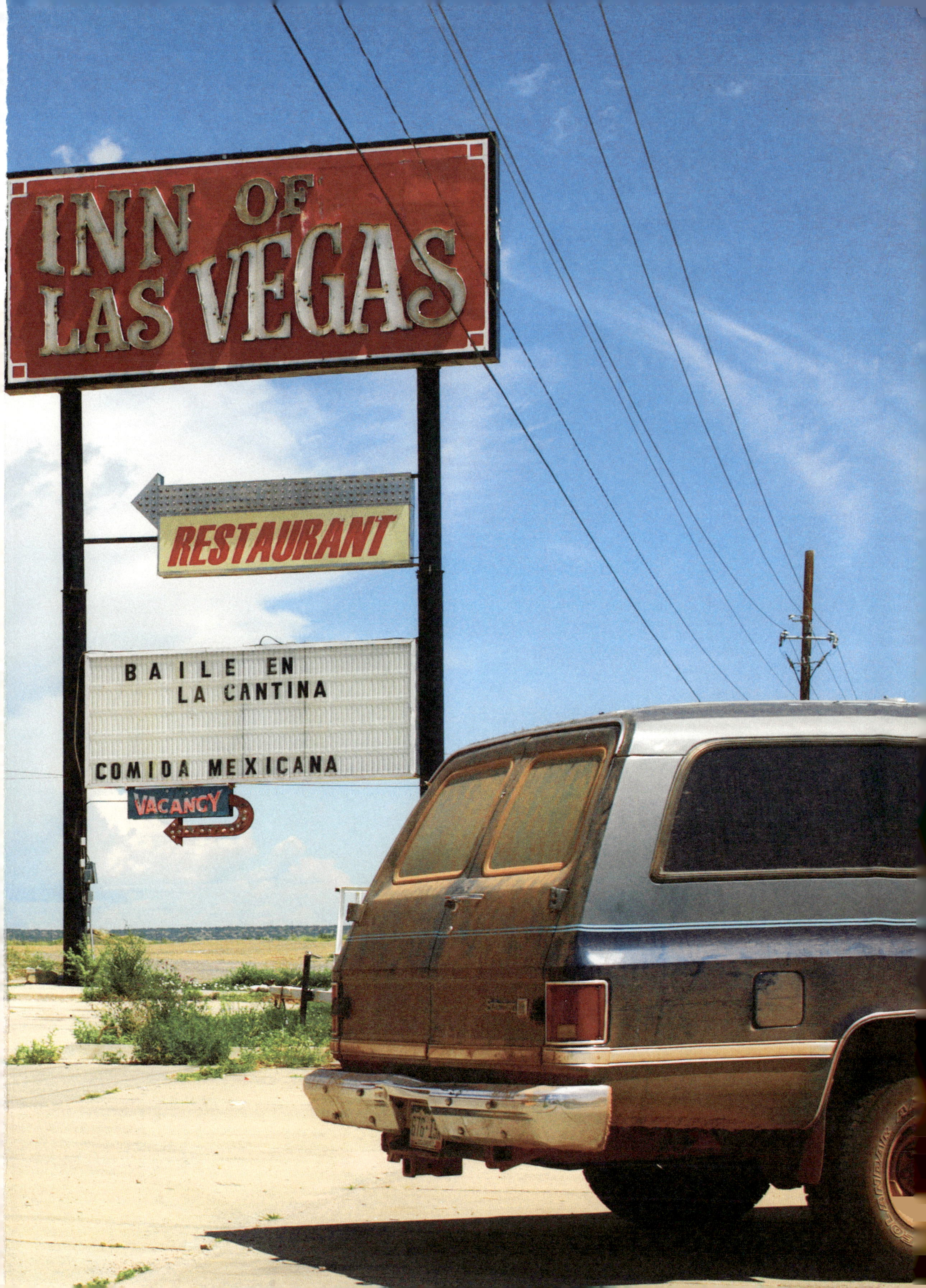
INN OF
LAS VEGAS
RESTAURANT
BAILE EN
LA CANTINA
COMIDA MEXICANA
VACANCY

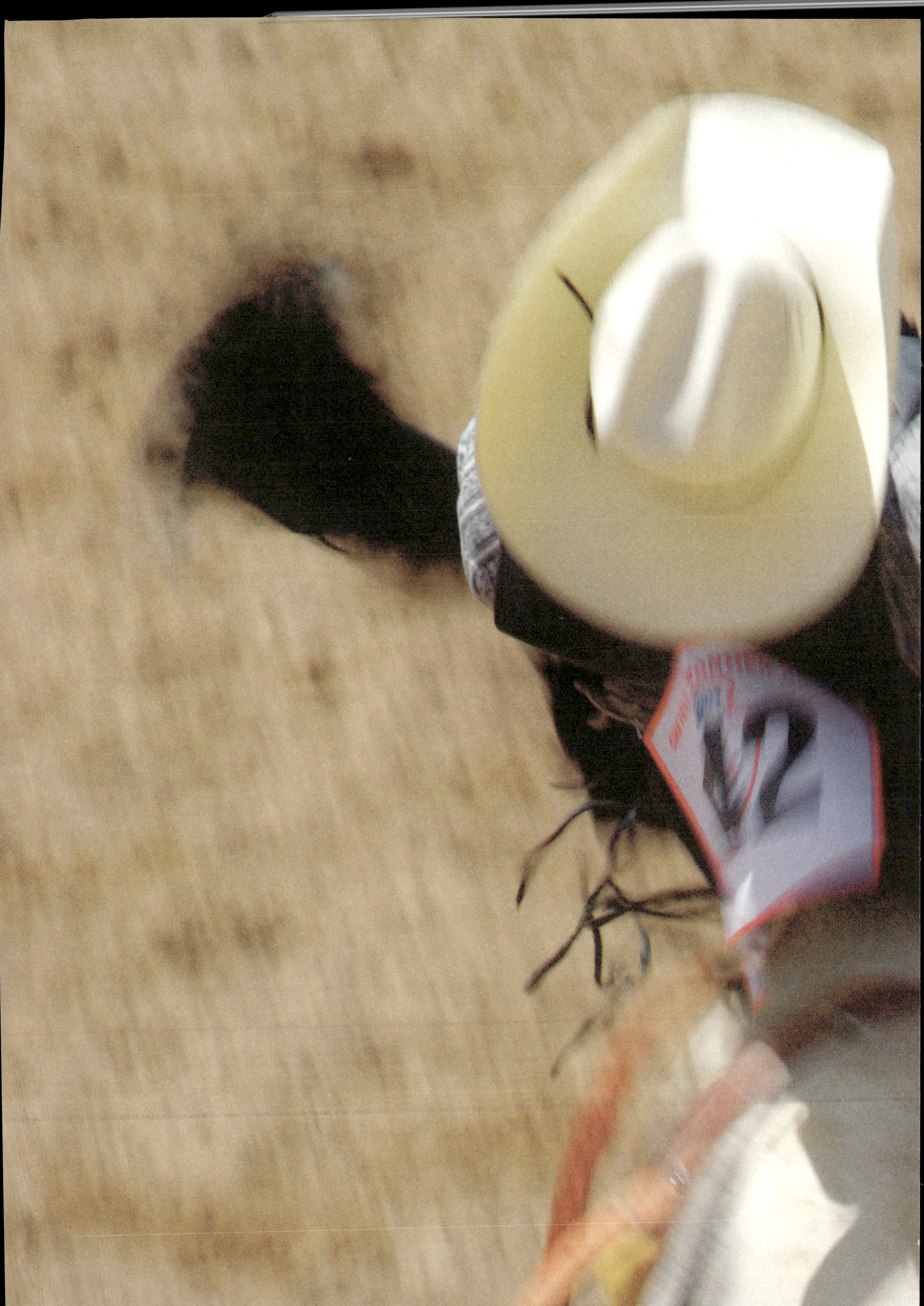

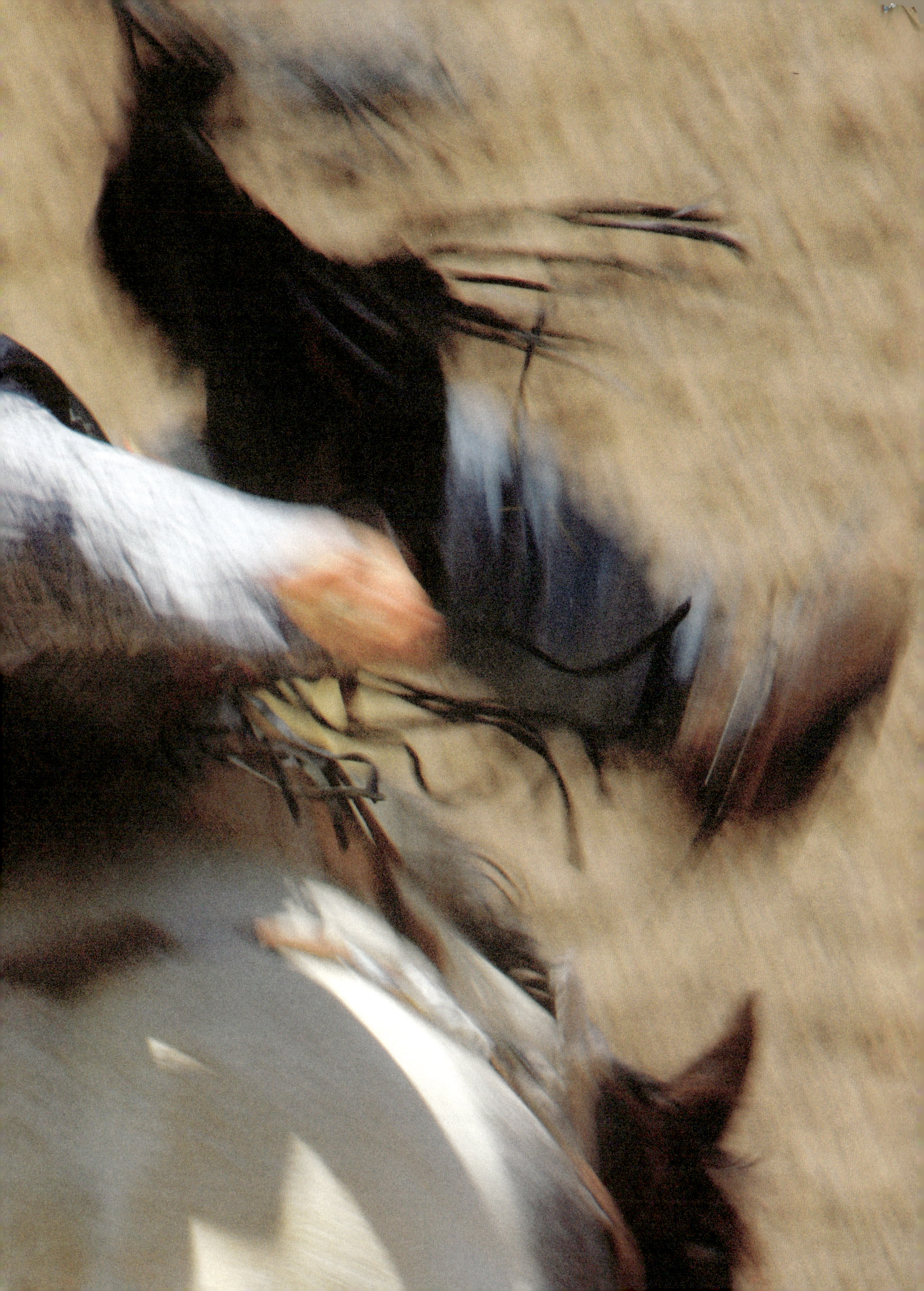

WEST

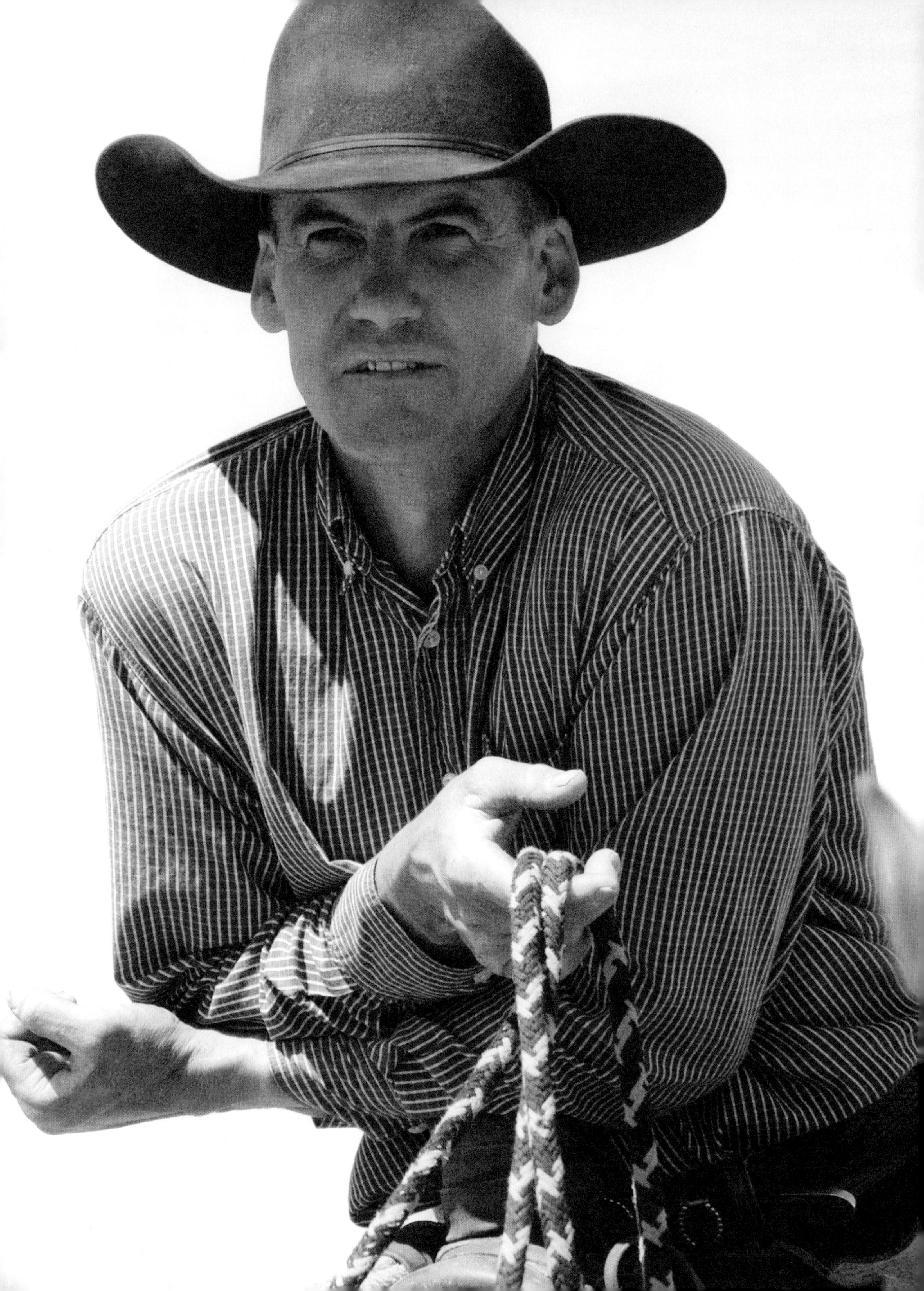

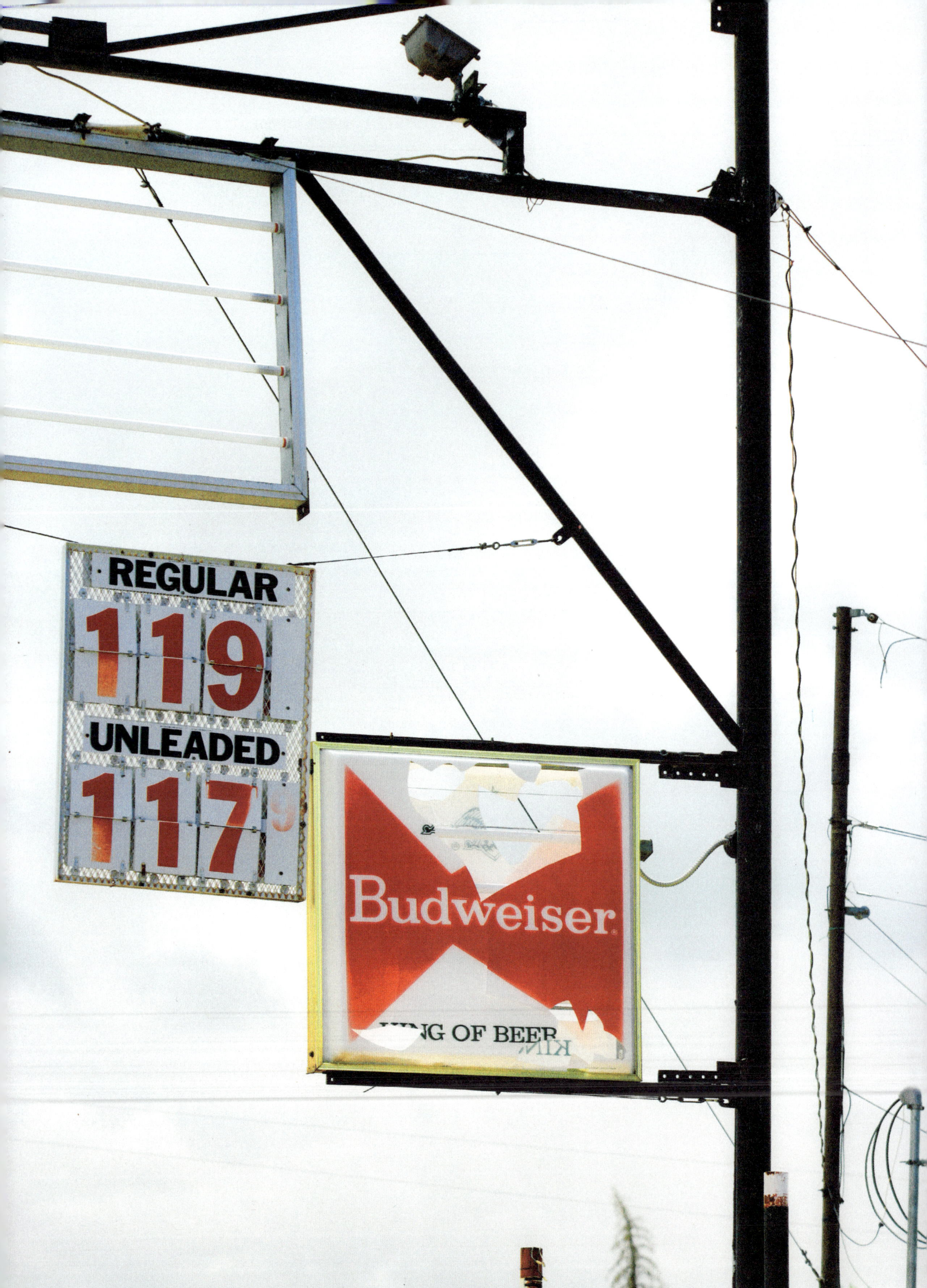
REGULAR
119
UNLEADED
117
Budweiser
KING OF BEER

PHOTO LARS STRANDBERG **TEXT** LARS ÅBERG **DESIGN** RONNIE NILSSON

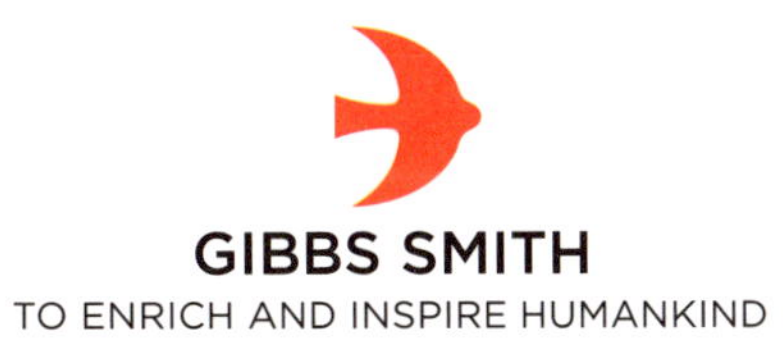

GIBBS SMITH
TO ENRICH AND INSPIRE HUMANKIND

CONTENTS

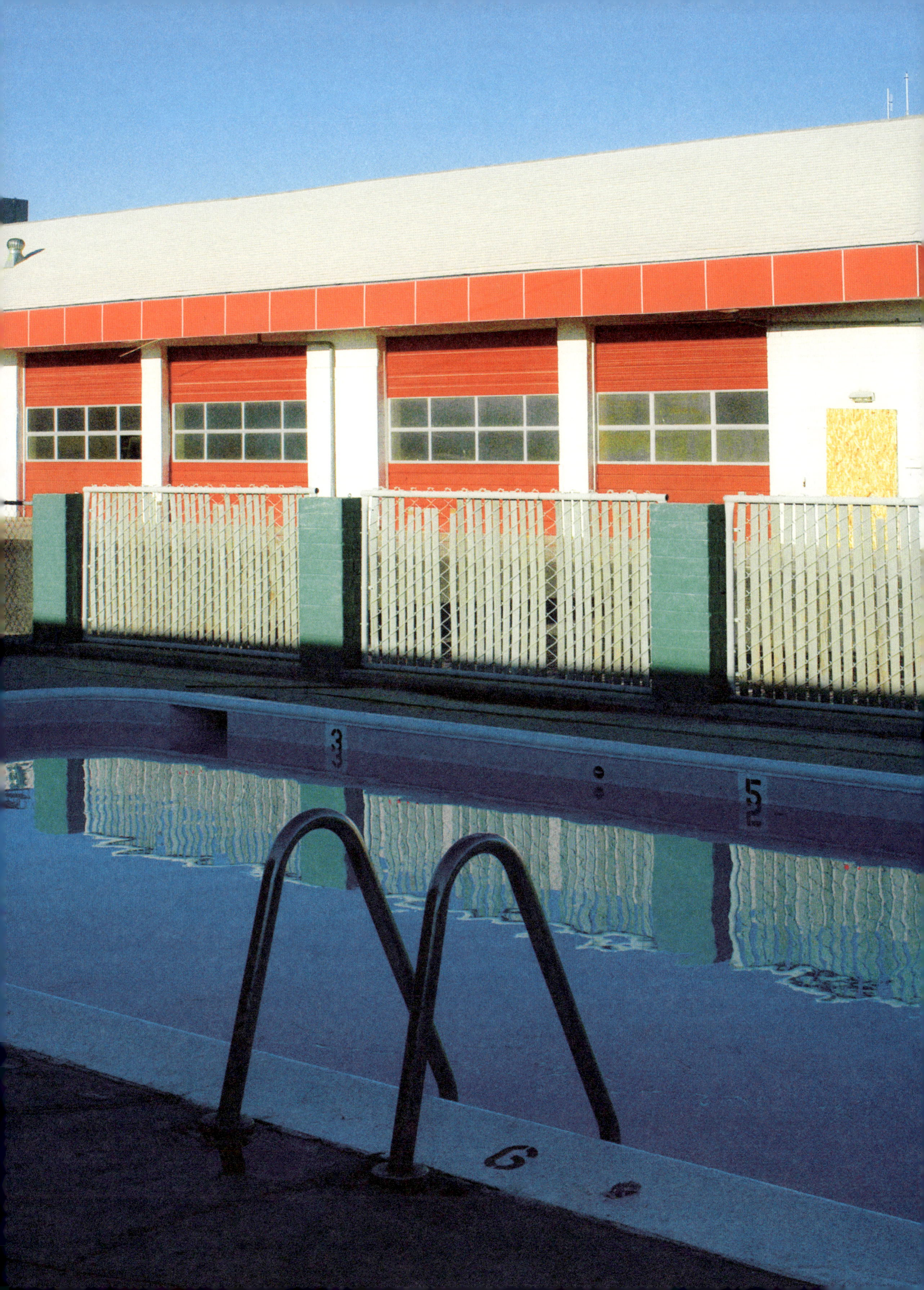
3
5
6

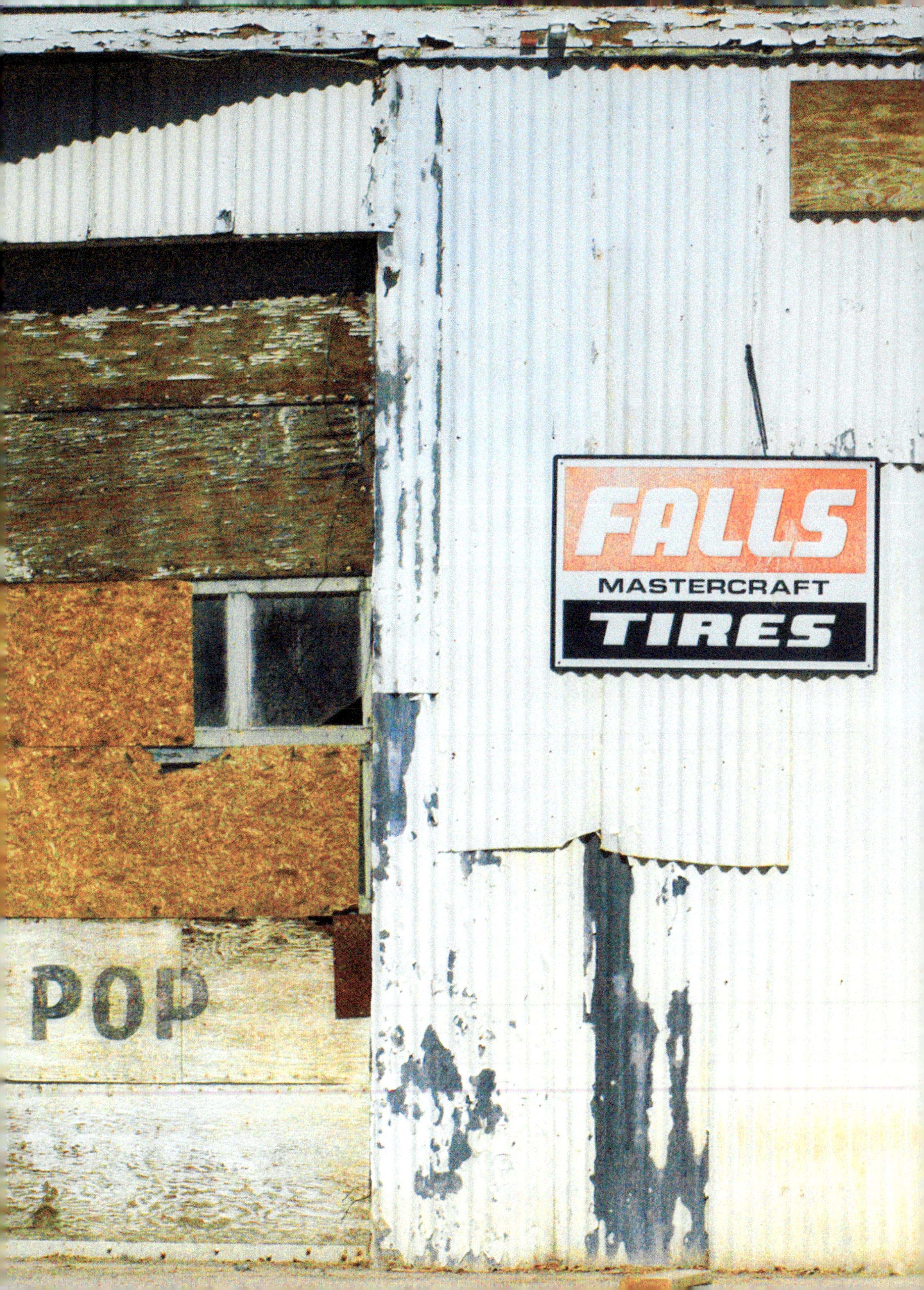
FALLS
MASTERCRAFT
TIRES
POP

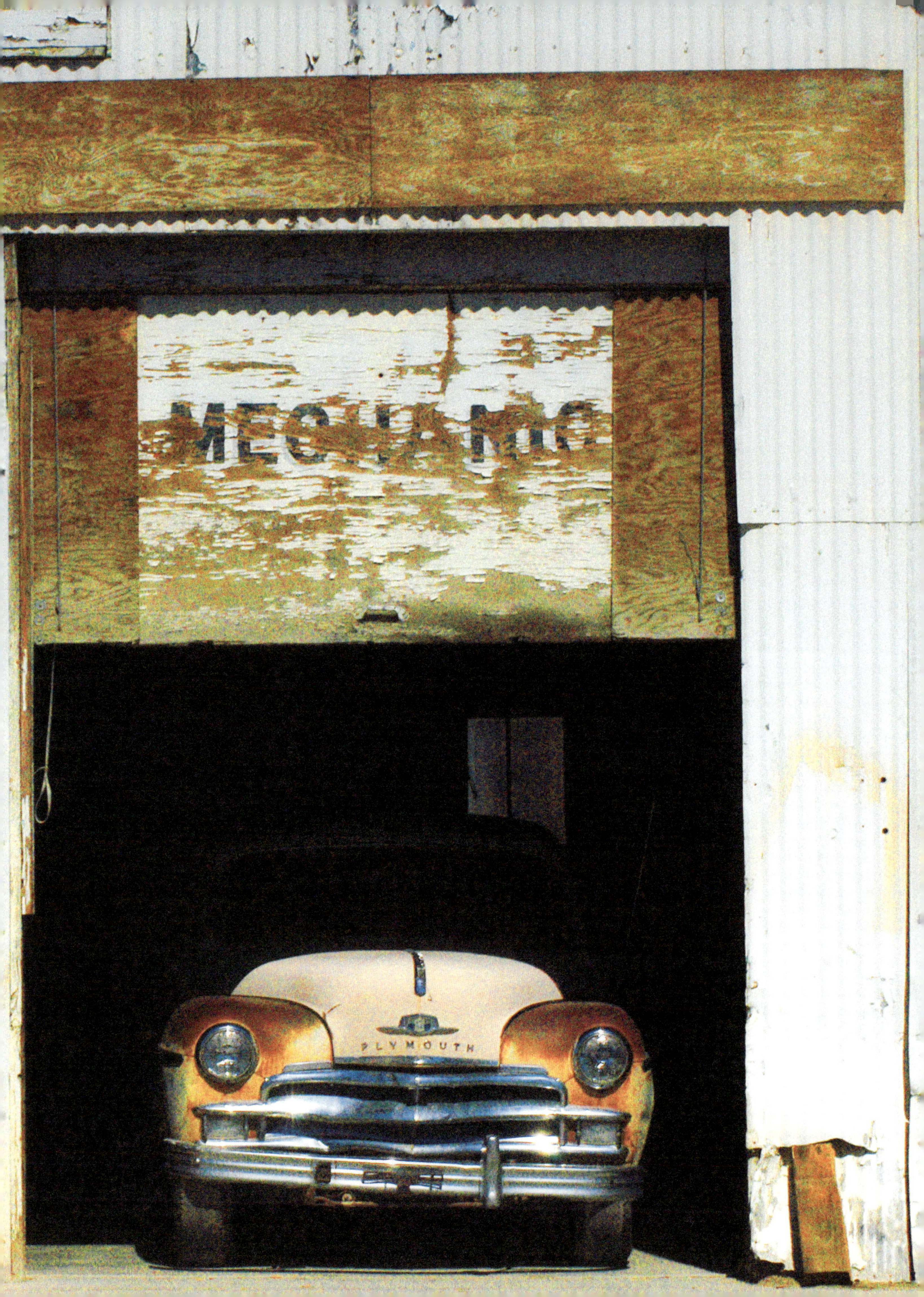
PLYMOUTH

WE WANTED TO GET AWAY, SAID THE WOMAN WHO HAD SETTLED ON A DIRT FARM BY THE OLD PONY EXPRESS

TRAIL. WE CAME HERE TO BE LEFT ALONE. THAT WAS THE WHOLE PURPOSE OF AMERICA.

LET'S CONSIDER IT A WORK IN PROGRESS. AS YOU ARE WALKING THE RED FIELDS OF DIRT OR GLIDING THROUGH THE COYOTE NIGHT YOU CANNOT HELP BUT BECOME ENTHRALLED. WHAT'S OUT THERE? WHERE'S IT ALL GOING?

MUSIC, BOOKS, AND MOVIES HAVE ALREADY TOLD YOU SEVERAL VERSIONS OF THE STORY – MORE THAN ANYTHING, THIS PLACE IS AN IDEA – AND THE WIND CARRIES THE SMELL OF DESPAIR AS WELL AS THE SCENT OF FREEDOM. IN THE LAND OF SEEMING PLENTY YOU ARE EXPECTED TO PAINT YOUR OWN MASTERPIECE.

The prevailing myth of the American West is also one of its truths: by traveling in this direction you could leave your old life behind – slavery, religious intolerance, a dysfunctional family, destitution, a prison sentence – and acquire a new name, creating the platform for a new beginning.

The English Puritans carried with them a vision of Utopia on their voyage across the Atlantic to the New World, and in 1630 their leader John Winthrop addressed his resolute fellow passengers: "For we must consider that we shall be as a City upon a Hill. The eyes of all people are upon us..." His vision has been interpreted as that of a beacon of light, a symbol for American expansionism. But it could just as easily be seen as a warning against the dangers of too much self-assertion: on such heights, everyone can see what you are up to.

With its wilderness and vast grassy plains the West is still disputed.

There are the issues of control over land and water, of urban thrust into rural values. Historical injustices are uncovered and fenceless territories condemned, their poetic magnetism gradually vanishing. Yet we continue to look this way with fascination. The scenery fills us with awe and wonder. We never seem to get enough of the idea of the place; there may be no more new frontier, but we won't mind getting lost in the visions nurtured by such surroundings.

The true spirit of this country is so often placed out West, close to a physical or imagined encounter with the forces of nature, that the republic should not be thought of as the center of the world but rather as the drifter that still tries to get away. In its conception of exceptionalism, America not only convinces itself of a holy mission, but also tries to keep this notion of morality and adventure to itself, as the sole bearer of its essence.

You can sell Western stuff as products. The soul of the West, however, can only be found under the prairie moon or in the shadow of the mesa.

The satisfaction of being special is part of one powerful American self-image. This also makes for a country of loneliness and loners and – despite the hustle and bustle of the metropolitan areas, where eight of ten citizens actually live – it is a retreat for those who want to be left to themselves. Out West, you will find the recluses, the departed, the refugees and desert voices, while just around the corner, only a stone's throw from Main Street with its parades, there are BBQ backyards where families grill and clean out their vans on Sundays. Americans export lifestyles and world views, but can themselves appear a bit like hermits in a global context.

So this big country is in many ways drifting on its own, by inner force. Trailer parks and shopping carts and roving carpenters and food coupon families and the newly divorced and the rejected and kids without a foothold; they are all in a state of flux, still moving westward, it is a gigantic, ongoing settler project, with beard-stubble and the understanding that all things, everything, ought to be different.

The nation wants to be a wall-to-wall carpet, but no one takes off his boots. Dirt will gather in the faraway corners, the wear and tear mercilessly exposed. Threadbare millions cast shadows into clean-cut swimming-pool communities. The road dust, coming from nowhere and everywhere, fills up most hotel lobbies, too.

Few live where they were born – each year a fifth of the population finds a new address. It is noticeable in the laundromats, in the dreary YMCA hangouts, the donut joints with free refills, the insanely mortgaged and consequently abandoned prefab homes, and in the number of anonymous letter boxes in the post offices. Ragged disbelievers, people with no real foundation beneath their feet. Tom Joad's ghost is roaming the infrastructure; the highway is alive tonight; as long as you move you are still in this world. If you stop, you'll be framed.

The stir, the commotion, the motion, they are all essential in America. But this movement also evokes its antithesis: although being self-made and independent is an ideal, there is a nostalgic, recurrent search for affinity, for community. Many dream of the timeless small town, the safeguarding of family, congregation, community, tribe, block, crew, of an identity manifesting itself in the make-believe terms of ethnicity. An eternal contradiction is at play: while longing for local kinship, a lot of people shun basic notions of society and the idea of public interference and collective responsibilities. There is nothing new here. Some of the Christian subcultures that moved or were driven from Europe to North America did not primarily look for regeneration, but more of the same thing, a stronger glue for the inner circle. The move was made to strengthen an inherent conservatism.

Simultaneously, the U.S. is constantly changing, rapidly displacing itself in time and space, where the remake is motivated by curiosity and improved prospects for the future. The train, and later the automobile and the airplane, sped up the motion. The vagabond ideal permits changes of identity, where you can leave your darkened hobo wardrobe to the rain and the wind and assume a new persona that will fit the new day. Ingrained in this movement, this drift through geographical and social landscapes, are other traits besides the financially prosperous ones. In a country this spacious, inquisitiveness often lives next door to seclusion and isolation. The realities of survival and the dominant lifestyle trends are centrifugalizing alternative views toward society's margins.

Utopia could never be shared with the majority. Keeping to yourself, you will be spared the questions of those who should mind their own business; this, too, has been a driving force in the great American move to the West.

Going West one escapes the dawn. If you journey fast enough, time will not only stand still but move in the other direction, making you younger for each mile traveled.

In the evenings, Western manliness is foaming at the pool table in the only bar in town while dusty boots pace through the Idaho two-step and steakhouse clouds sail off into the purpureal night, where the mountain silhouette has been drowned in black and the darkness is filled with cicada gossip. Gathered around a dried-up mining shaft in Silver City, men with glimmering spurs sit down to read homemade poems about white beans and coffee in tin mugs. The Santa Fe railroad is roaring through the valleys, and guys show up who look just like Gary Cooper on a fateful day, and they all know the names of every honky-tonk between Austin and Yuma. Thus, a westward journey may turn into an escape from aging and from the Old World, back to childhood and the joys of discovery.

At least one of those billboard cowboys smoked himself to death, but in the West the image of America is repeatedly reborn and recreated; man's successful struggle with nature, independence portrayed as weightless wisps of cloud against a sunset fragrant with expectations. While still young, the nation felt its way out here in order to draft its credo. Still, more than anything, the Western expansion was physical and on many levels brutal. Old-time greed and new-time colonialism were dressed up in fresh symbols and myths.

After the Civil War the wild notion of the West was established, with civilization's frontier running through deserts and rocky territories far beyond the Missippi waterway. The new borderline presented itself all over Western America, expressing emotional yearning and permanent state of conflict, its violent power games embedded in visionary prose and dreams of fortune.

But come the twentieth century, the West was no longer on the other side of those mountains. It was all around, located close to the core of people's imagination.

All these travels on never-ending backroads have taken me far out and deep down; beneath the surface, up into the screaming white light where no tracks can be obliterated. Far out is a word combination welded into an idea, both as identification of place and mental qualification. Out there. On the prairie, in the desert, among the mountains, beyond the woods. The open horizon, which widens even more as you come closer.

What is far out and outside is usually defined by those who live close to some kind of center, in itself a flexible term. Out there, in the sticks, are the derelict small towns, where the unseen becomes darkness, depressed and haunted by ruin ghosts and deformed, rusty farm machinery. Out there is where you'll find secret boundary marks; most things are different on the reverse, unknown side, possibly beautiful and picturesque, but increasingly complicated to handle as anything but a sentimentalized reserve for inner explorations.

Out there, too, an adventure lies waiting, an arena with no given rules of etiquette. But when modern people try to formulate the essence of the West, it often sounds a lot like homesickness. The passion for a cultural history still young enough not to have been set in a fixed mold corresponds to a certain rootlessness in the present, and to an uneasiness about a new world whose mergers and crossings of boundaries have become so difficult to grasp.

What is happening here is also an ongoing journey out of the cities, a continous, perpetual attempt by utopians and pioneers to create a new Eden on the outer fringes. Even though the old-time frontier mentality is lost, people still like to cling to that fantasy. Those who have continued to chase the Western sunset keep building out there, far out, and the need to start anew on virgin land has immediate consequences. On the outskirts of the urban West water resources are scarce and drying up. A former mayor in Albuquerque, New Mexico, a state which in many ways is truly far out, has declared that the greater the rate of expansion in new urban areas, the faster they will be deserted.

OUTSIDE IS AMERICA. ITS MOST EXCITING AND CAPTIVATING NOTION IS THE WEST.

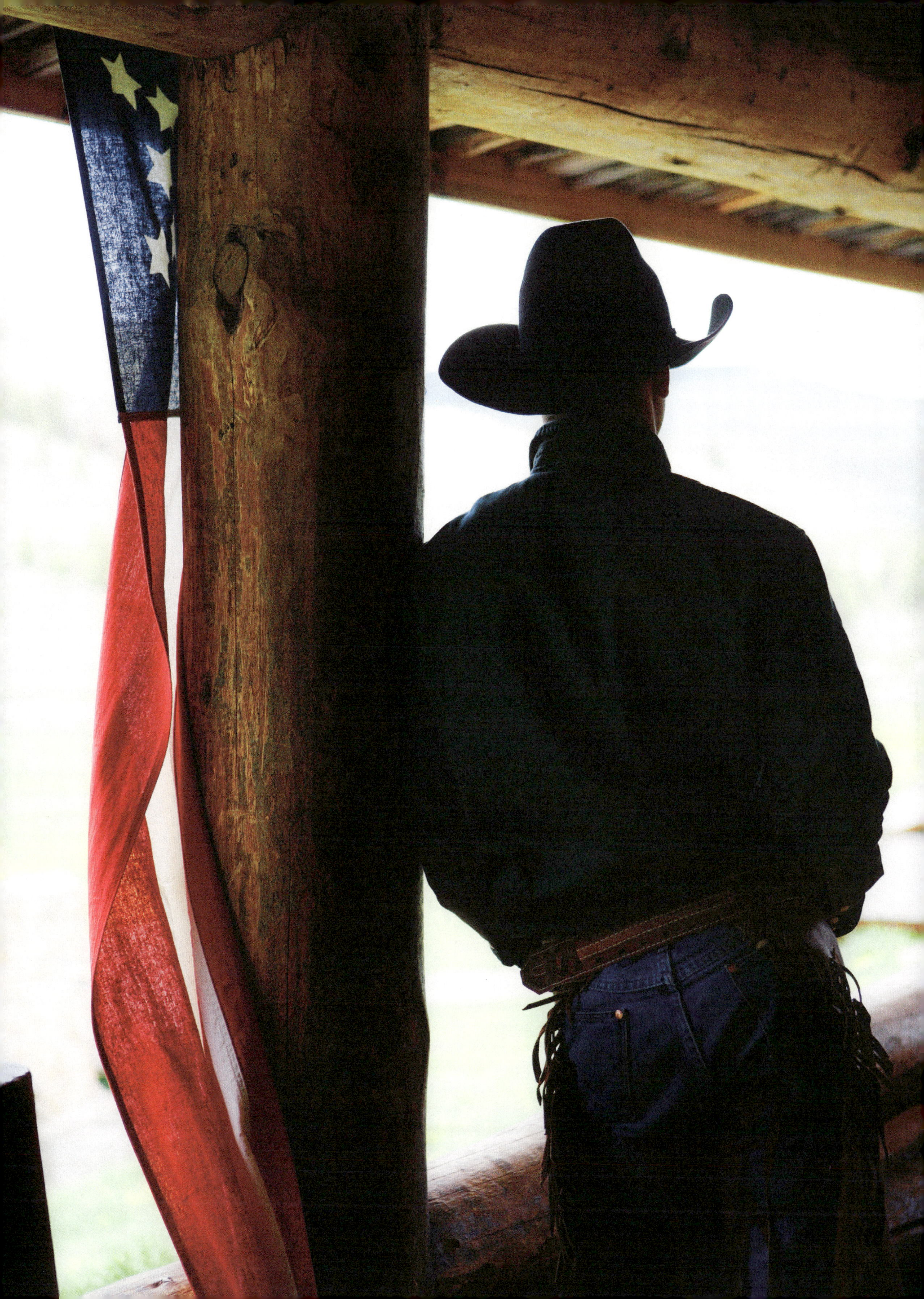

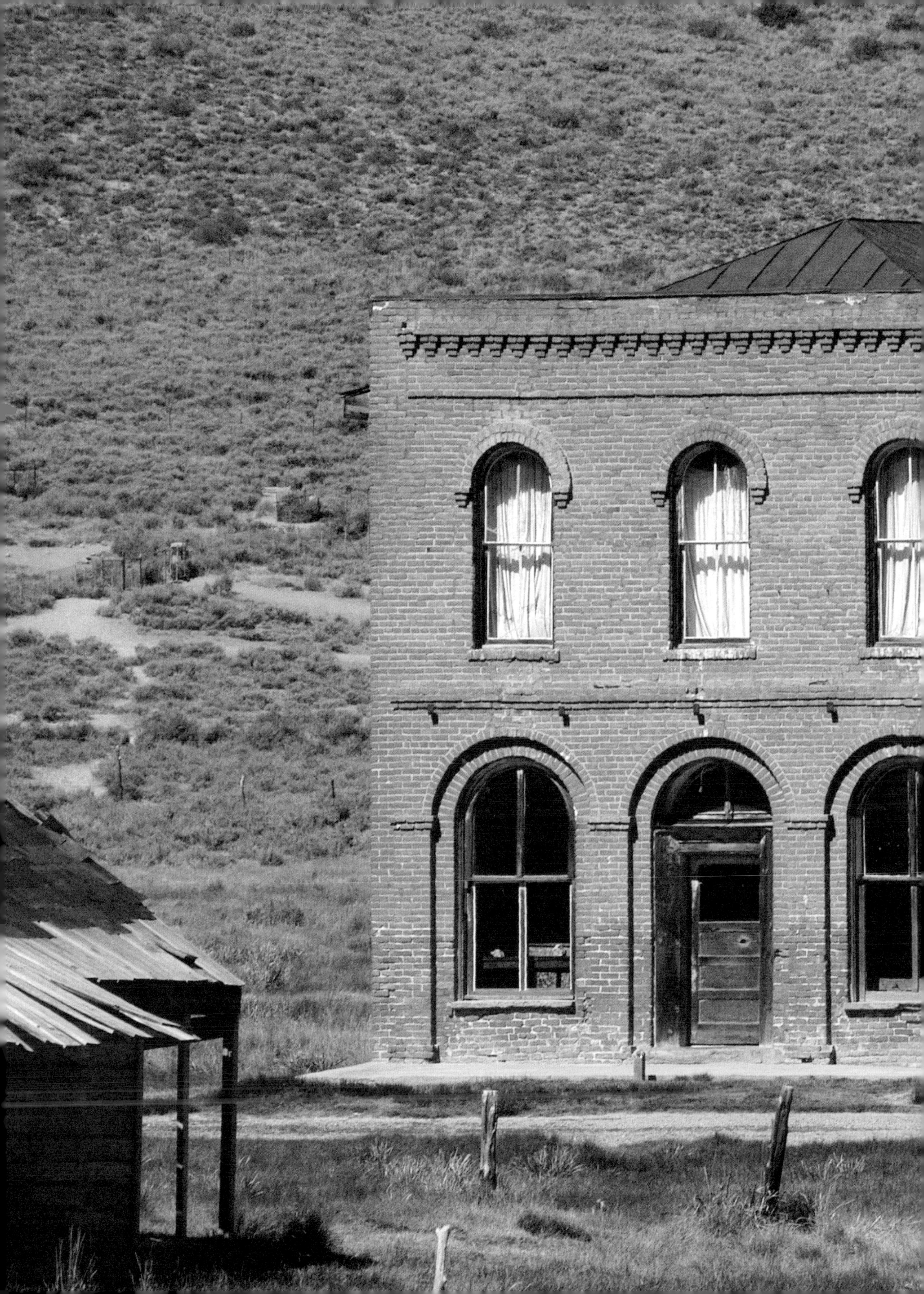

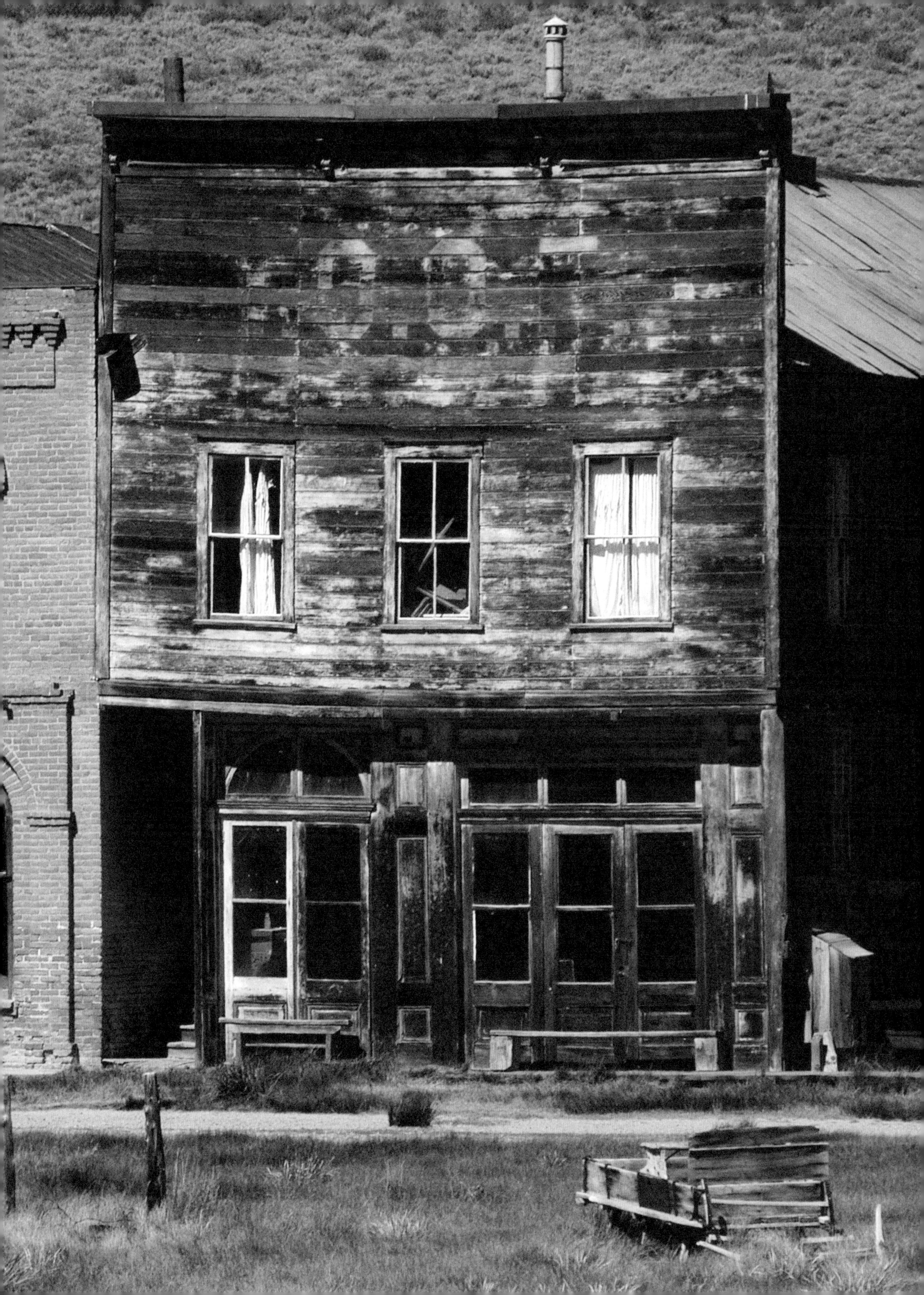

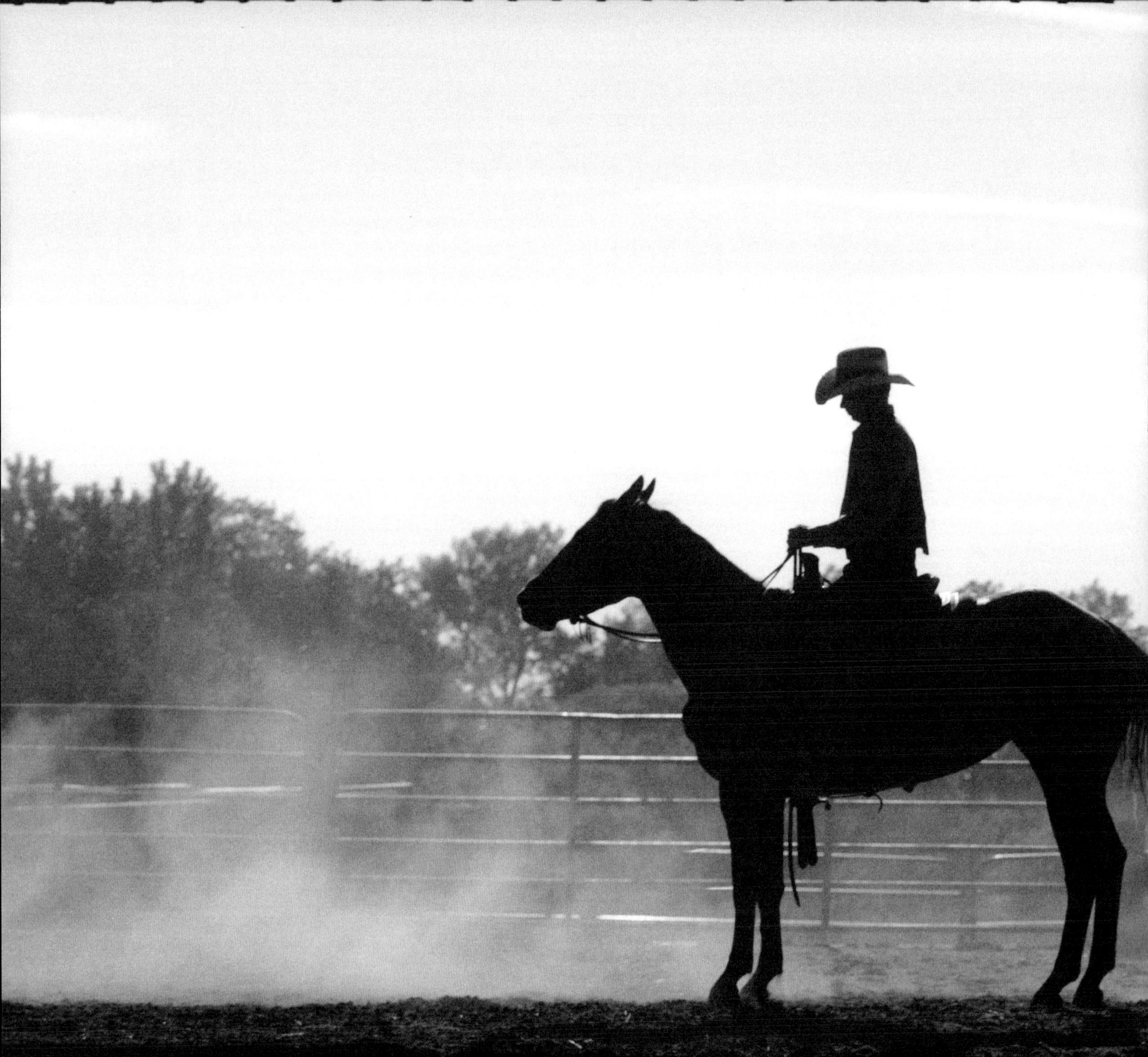

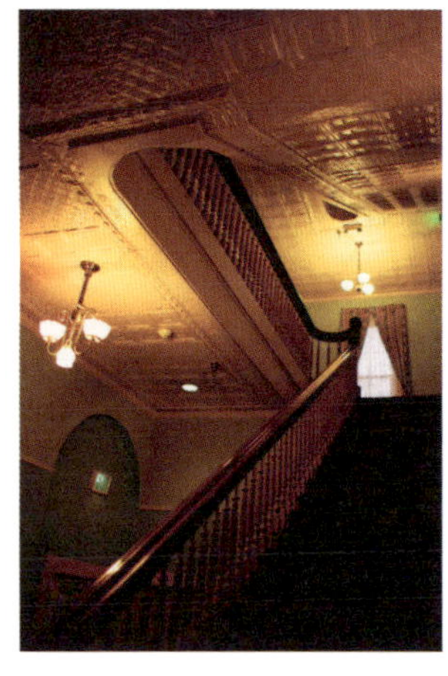
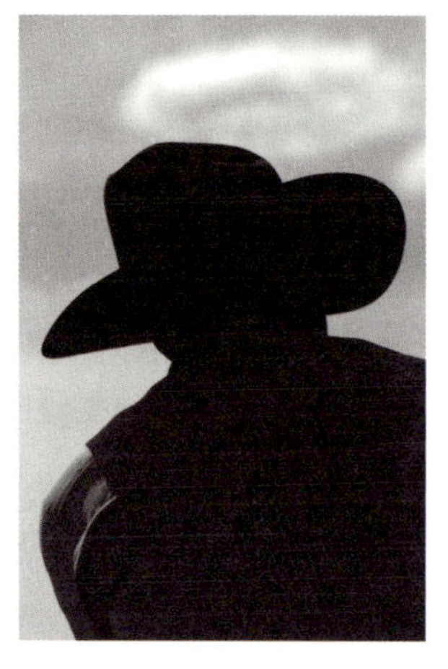
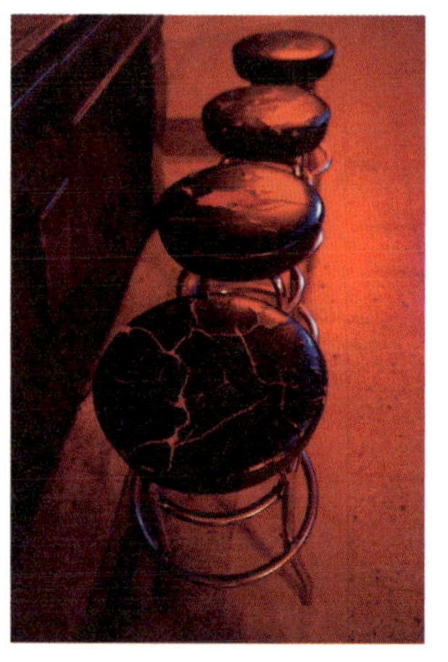
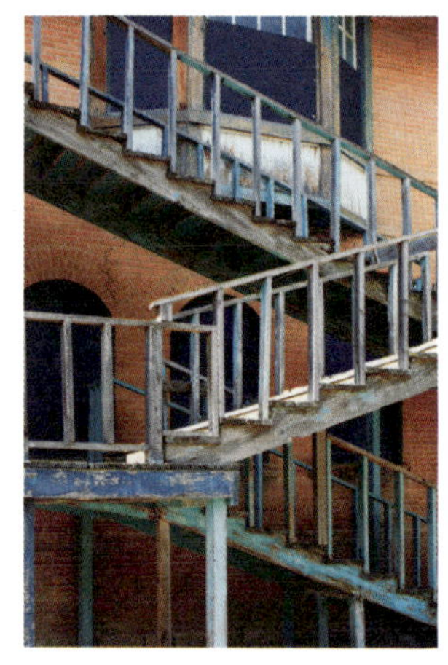
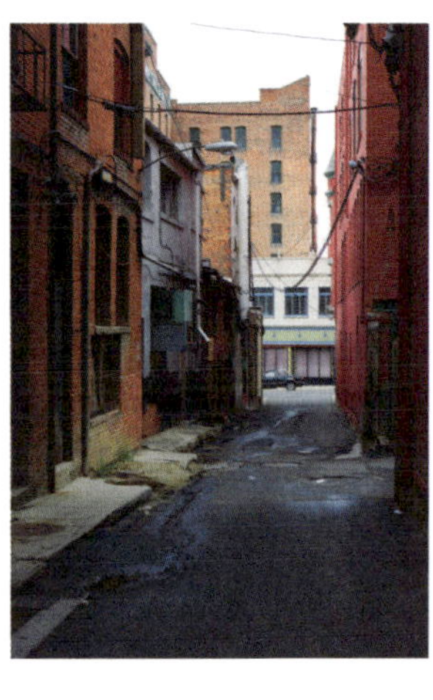
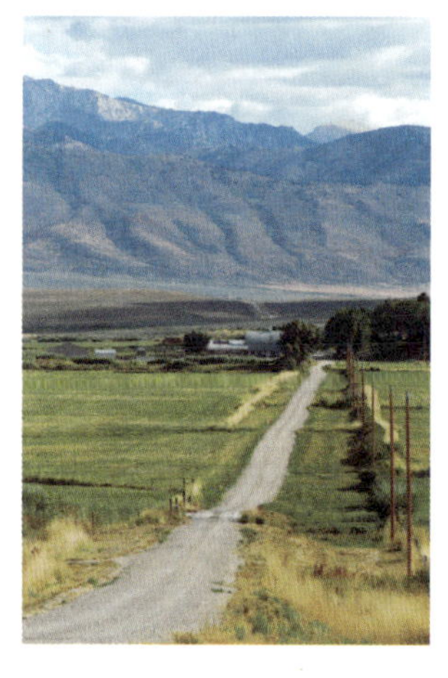
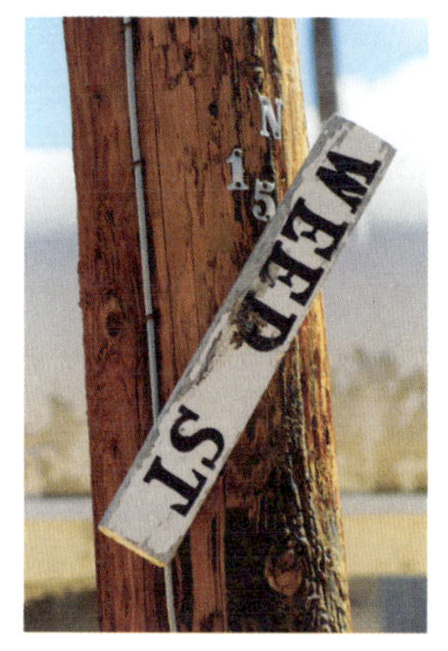
WEED ST
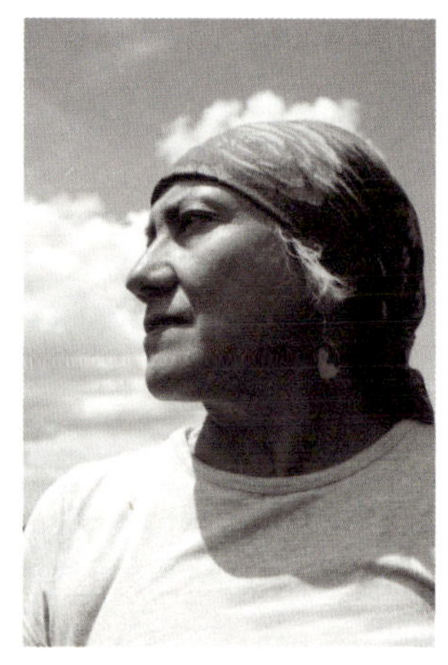
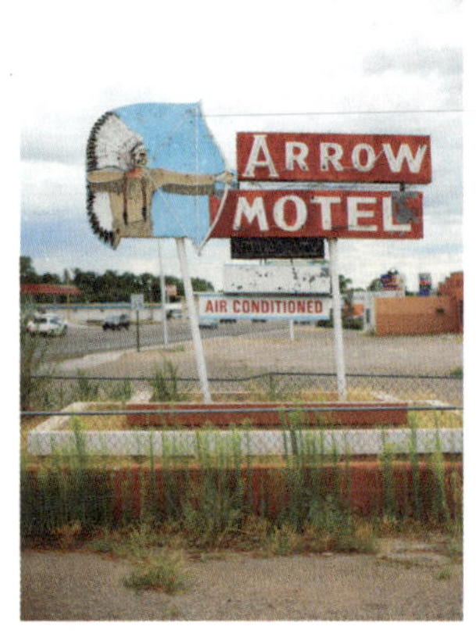
ARROW
MOTEL
AIR CONDITIONED
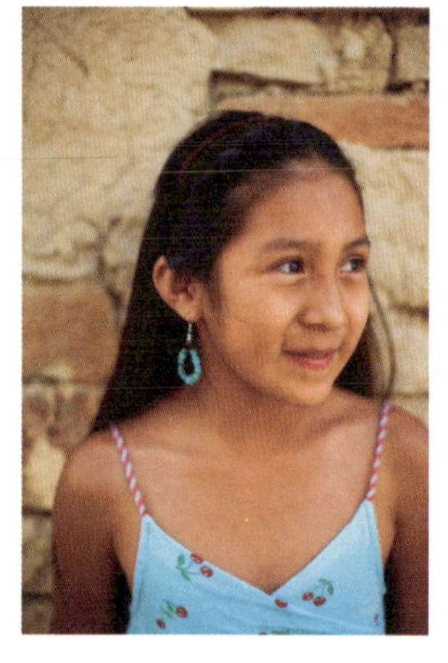
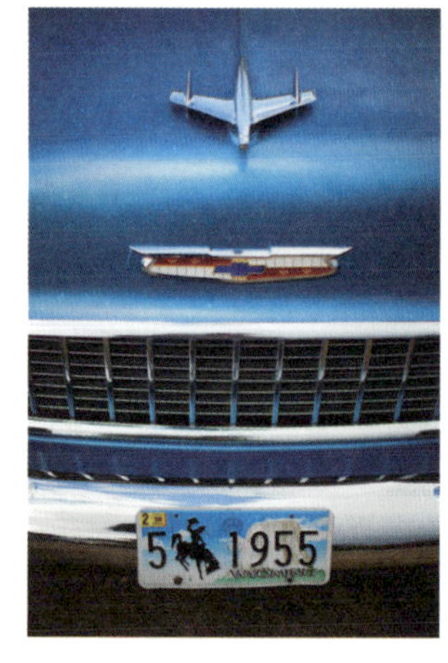
5 1955
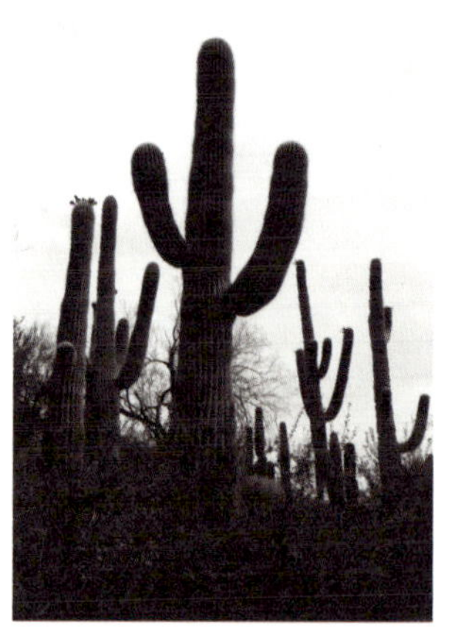
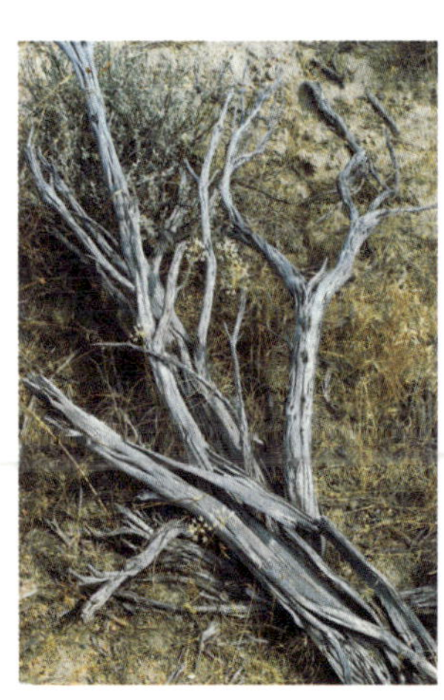
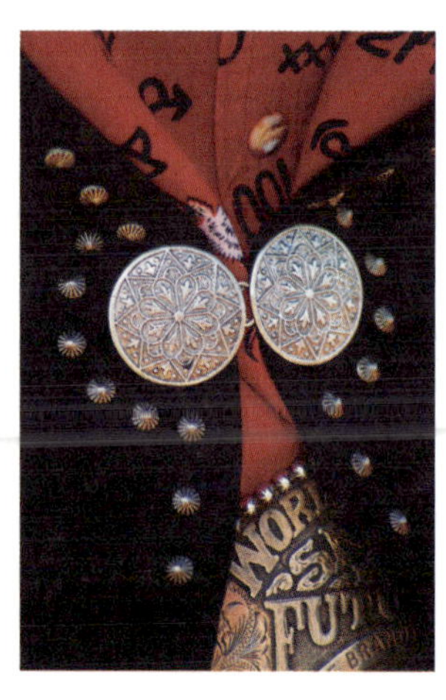
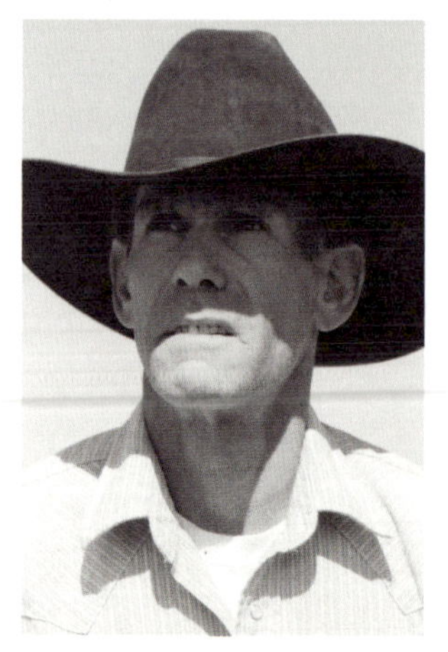
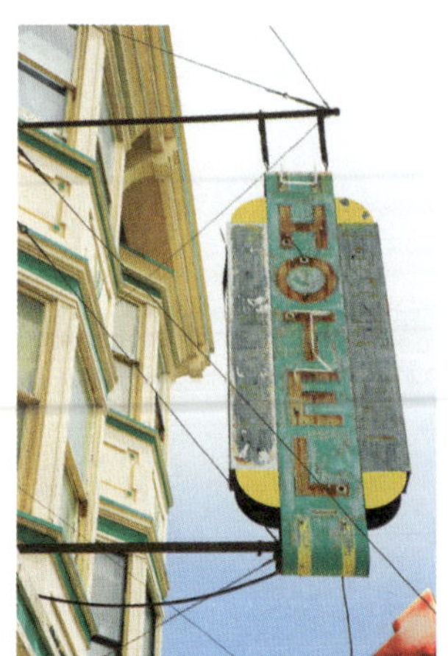
HOTEL

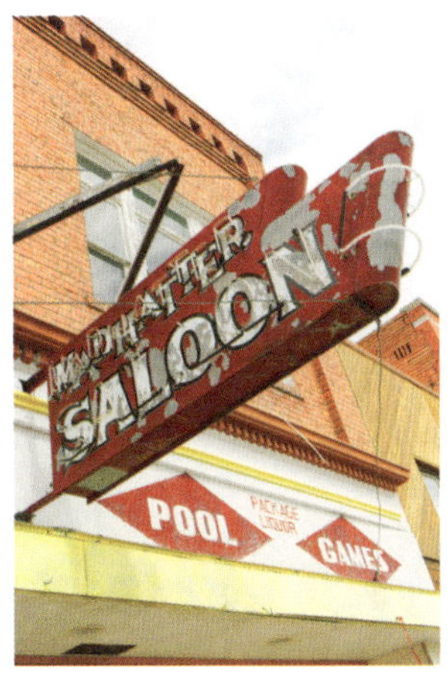
SALOON
POOL
GAMES

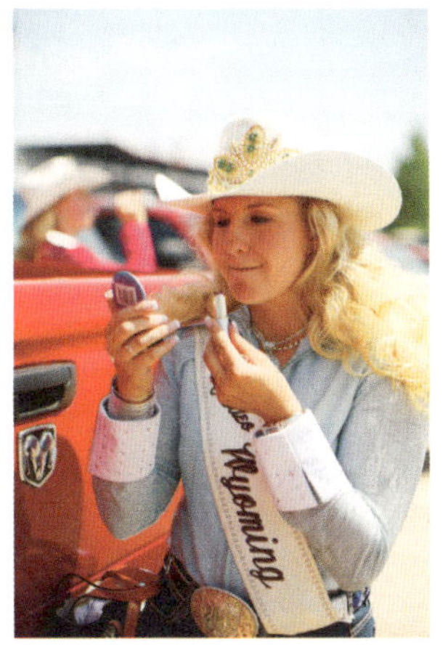
Wyoming

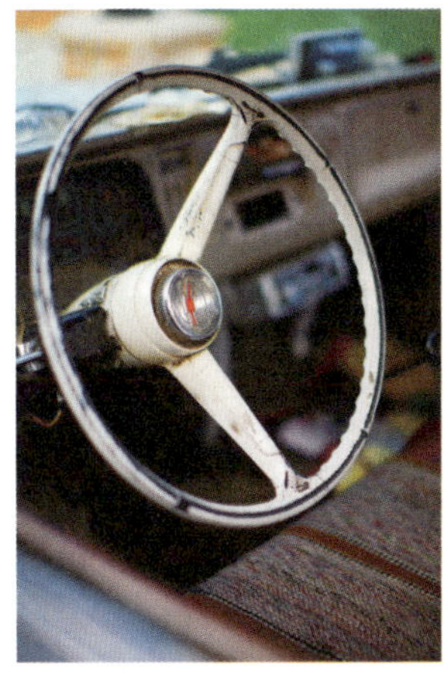

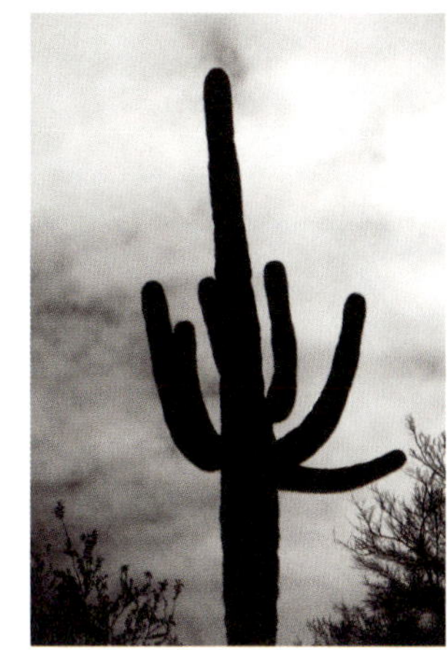

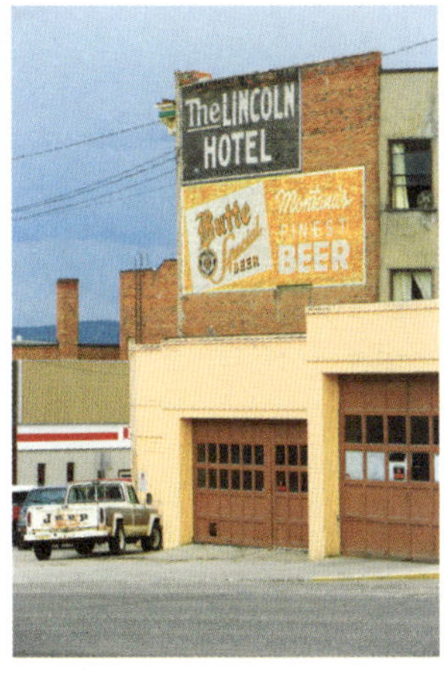
The LINCOLN
HOTEL
BEER

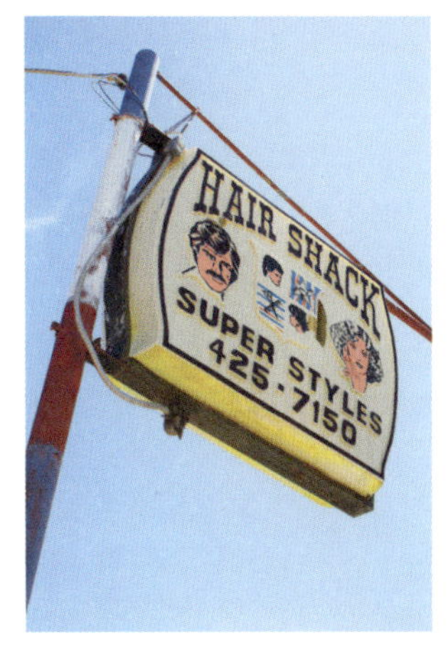
HAIR SHACK
SUPER STYLES
425-7150

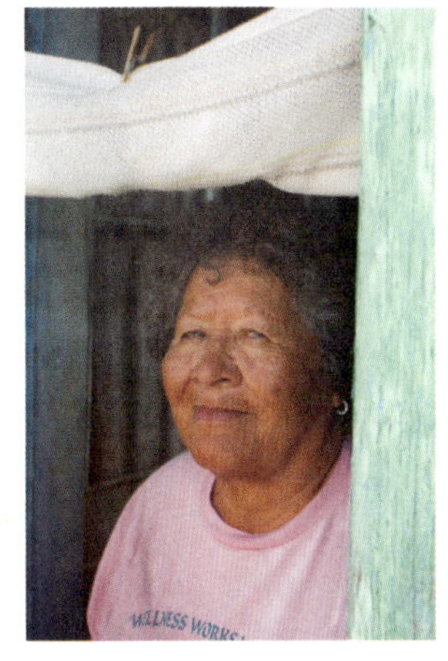

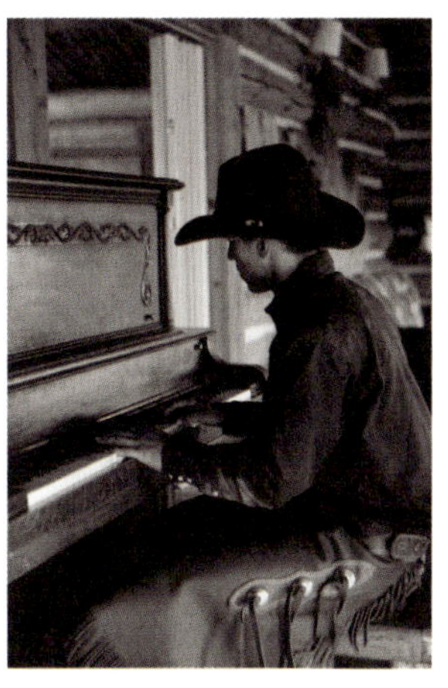

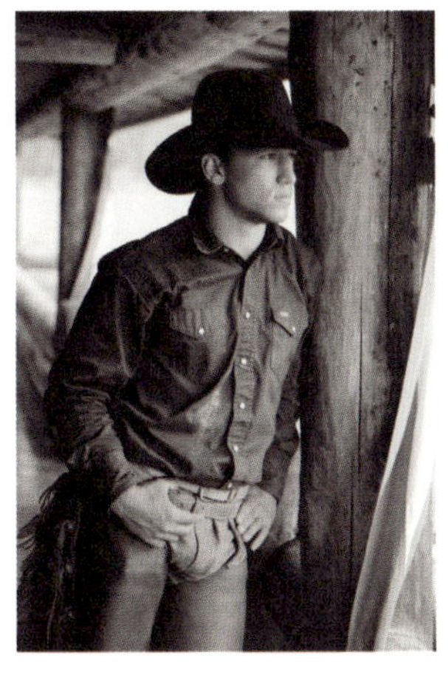

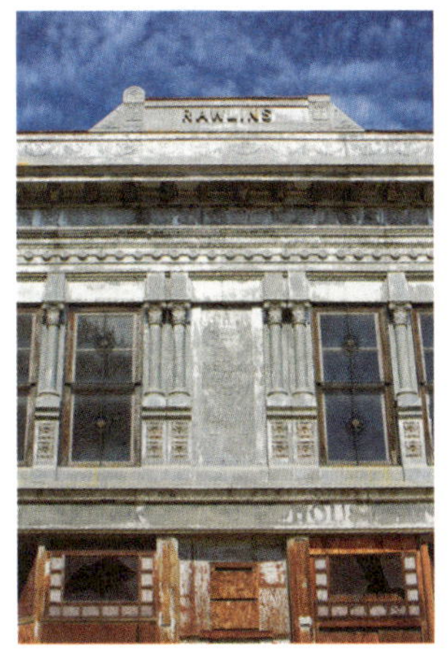
RAWLINS

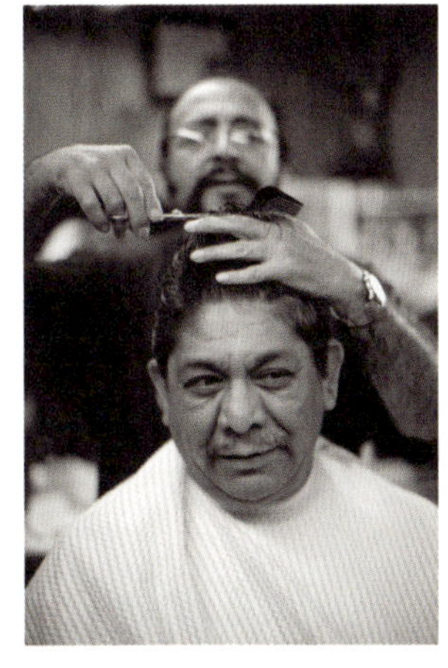

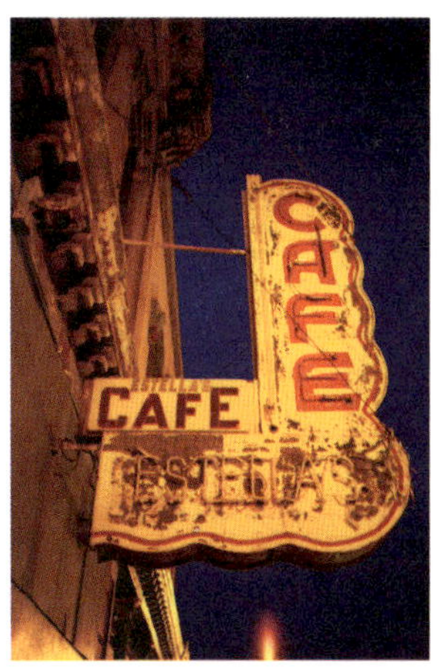
CAFE
CAFE

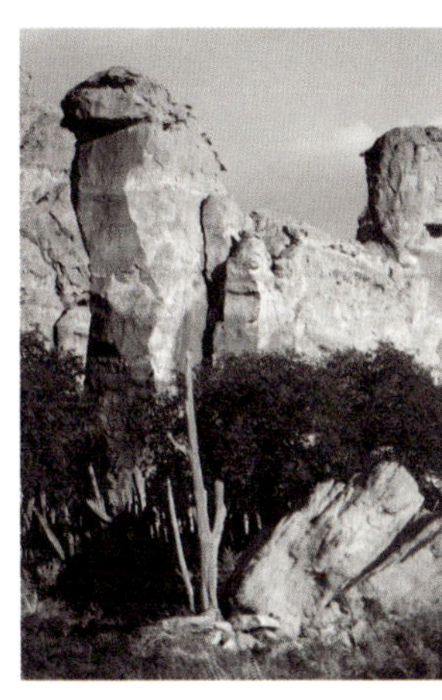

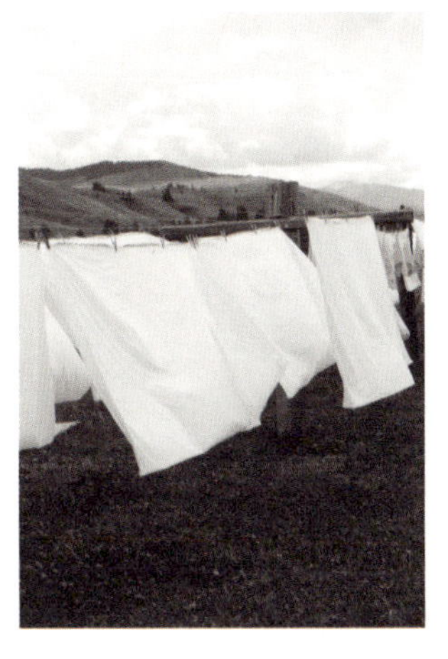

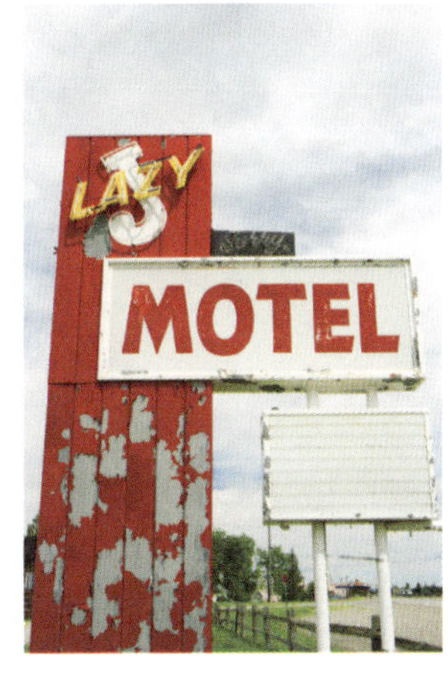
LAZY
MOTEL

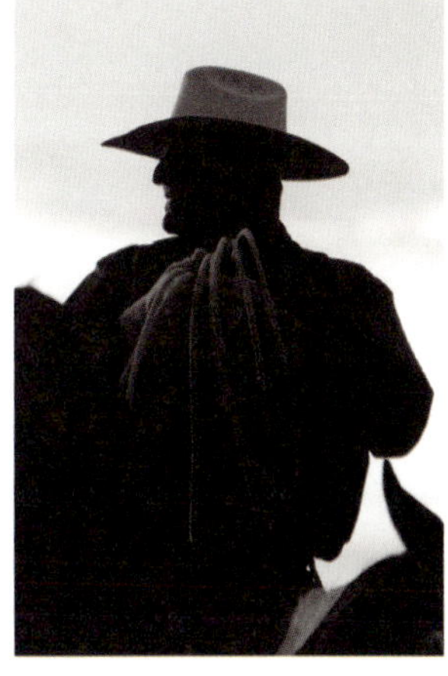

EVEN WITH THE MIDDAY HEAT POUNDING ON THE GROUND, THE WIND IS FREE TO MOVE THROUGH THE VALLEY; IT SLIPS BETWEEN THE SAGGING BOARDS, AND, NUDGING AT LOOSE SHEETING, LIFTS A COLORFUL MOUNTAIN BLUEBIRD ABOVE THE REMNANTS OF THE OLD MINING TOWN.

BODIE LEANS AND LIMPS, BUT BEHIND THE CURTAINS, ITS EVERYDAY LIFE IS STILL BRILLIANTLY DISPLAYED. IT IS AS IF EVERYONE IN TOWN JUST SIMULTANEOUSLY STOOD UP AND LEFT.

The place is striking in that you can picture exactly how the people once lived their lives. What they did, how they socialized, what they liked. During the second half of the 1800s, gold glimmered in the Sierra Nevada, the mountains of the high desert on the border between California and Nevada. Within a few years, ten thousand individuals made their homes in the no-man's land that was Bodie.

The road leading uphill appears to twist and wind all the way to where trails usually lie down to die. This could be an American concentrate; a bright dream on the darker side of freedom. The beauty is of a cinematic kind, a seemingly virgin wilderness open to everybody. Also, the notion that any individual can travel here, hide from his own past, create his own independence regardless of society, is quite obvious.

Gold had been discovered in California in 1848 and during the ensuing decade some 300,000 people ventured westward across the continent. Many were traveling along marked trails; others gambled and got stuck in unknown mountain areas, where those riding one way froze to death and those who chose another route around the cliffs became dehydrated in the desert heat, sand filling every pore of their poor lives.

Aiming for Bodie, straight into the sun-burnt mountains, people rode and walked to get rich, and to make a fresh start. Few of them succeeded. Most moved after a couple of years searching elsewhere for their Shangri-la. The last people to leave town piled their most precious belongings on horse-drawn carriages or pickup trucks.

The community founder was an exiled New Yorker named Waterman S. Body, who discovered gold in 1859 and was then killed by unforgiving winter temperatures, his life terminated on a slope where he had been hauling his equipment. However, the rumor was out and nineteen years later fortune struck as an impressive lode revealed itself in the area's deepest shaft.

It attracted people with arms full of hoes and hearts pounding with expectations. These were the years right after a divisive Civil War that pretty much defined how the young nation was portrayed in literature and movies. Beyond the Mississippi a Wild West was created. Cattle herds replaced the buffalo, the prairie was first declared open territory and then fenced in. The Native Americans were removed. Railroads pierced the silence of the valleys. And the long arm of the law never really reached out to the gold diggers' communities.

Soon it was an established truth that no mining town could be worse than Bodie in terms of bad men and foul weather.

The place did not seem particularly inviting, to say the least: the landscape was barren and wind-swept and the town itself sat at 8,300 feet with the mines another five or seven hundred feet farther up the hillsides. Initially, people would live in tents or dugouts. The cabins were simple shacks made from rough boards. During wintertime the cold was merciless, in the summers drought tumbled all around.

The attraction of gold forced the community to create an infrastructure. A street system was put in place, machines were dragged to the mines, hotels opened, and stores and a school were built. A narrow-gauge railway was constructed to carry lumber from the sawmill at the salty Mono Lake. Every day covered wagons with gold ingots would leave Bodie, guarded by forbidding men with sawed-off shotguns.

The period of glory was brief, as it was in most Western boomtowns. By 1883 people no longer got paid for their mining shares, the shafts were evacuated, and the workers moved on to the next glittering mirage. Introducing cyanide into the extraction process, Jim Cain, a banker and local businessman, managed to keep the town alive for a few more decades, but in 1932 some seventy percent of the wooden buildings went up in smoke after a young boy had been playing with matches. Cain loaded his safe on a carriage and left Bodie and his house with the glass veranda, which still stands at the corner of Green and Park Streets.

In the 1950s a monumental silence had established itself and no one would come out to shoo away the coyotes or the rattlesnakes. If a sound was heard, it was the wind.

The rusty colors and sun-bleached facades of the remaining 170 houses make them reminiscent of stranded ships. Behind the windows beds can be spotted, as well as skiing equipment, canned vegetables, pool tables, bar counters, a switchboard, and an advertisement for stockings with the season's new colors from Paris. The coffin lids are still open, waiting in semi-darkness at the undertaker's, and the cars that never got away continue to sink into the prickly grass.

Bodie still just sits there, looking back at us who wonder about the motive force of humans and how this country could turn out the way it is today.

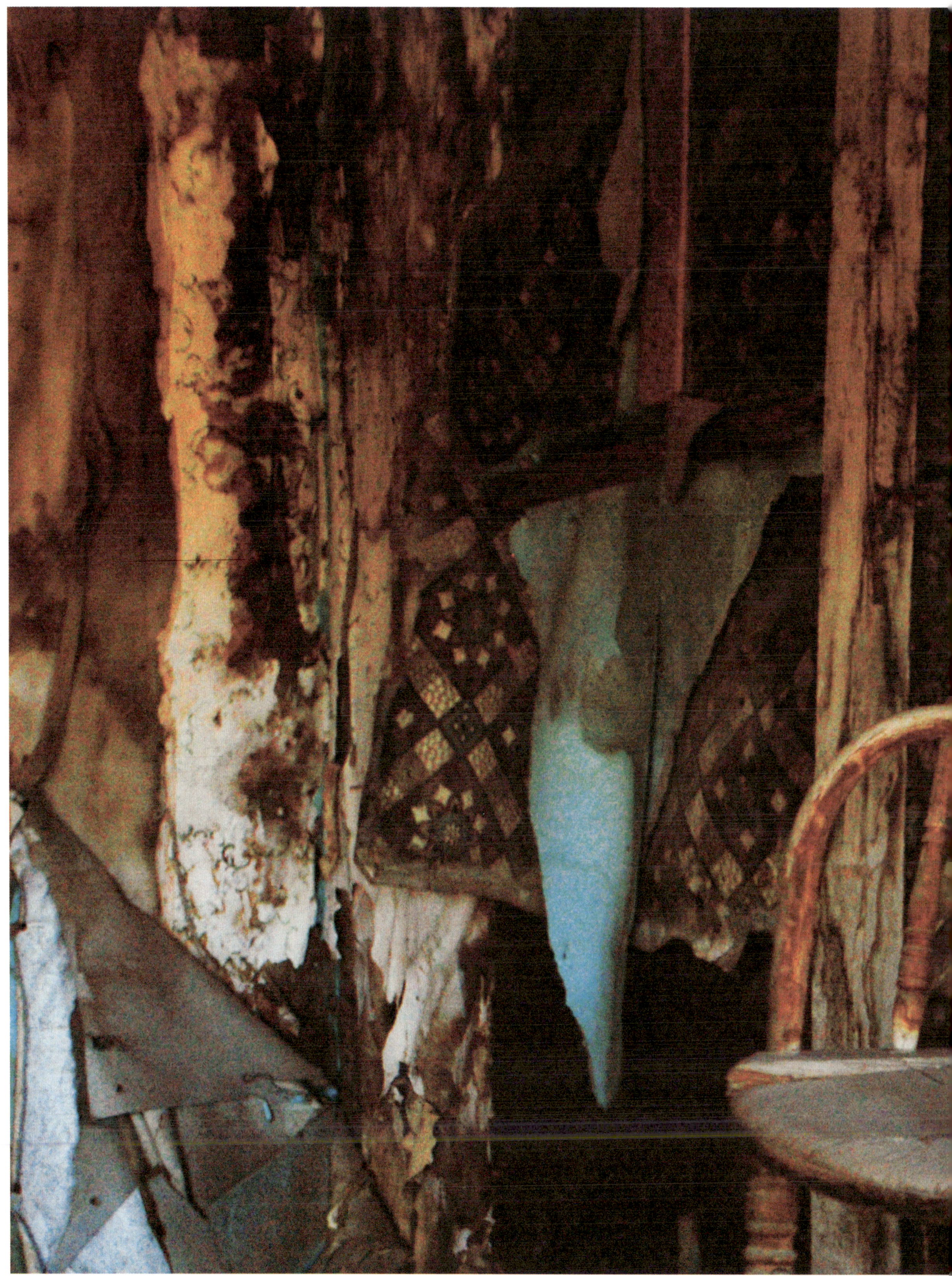

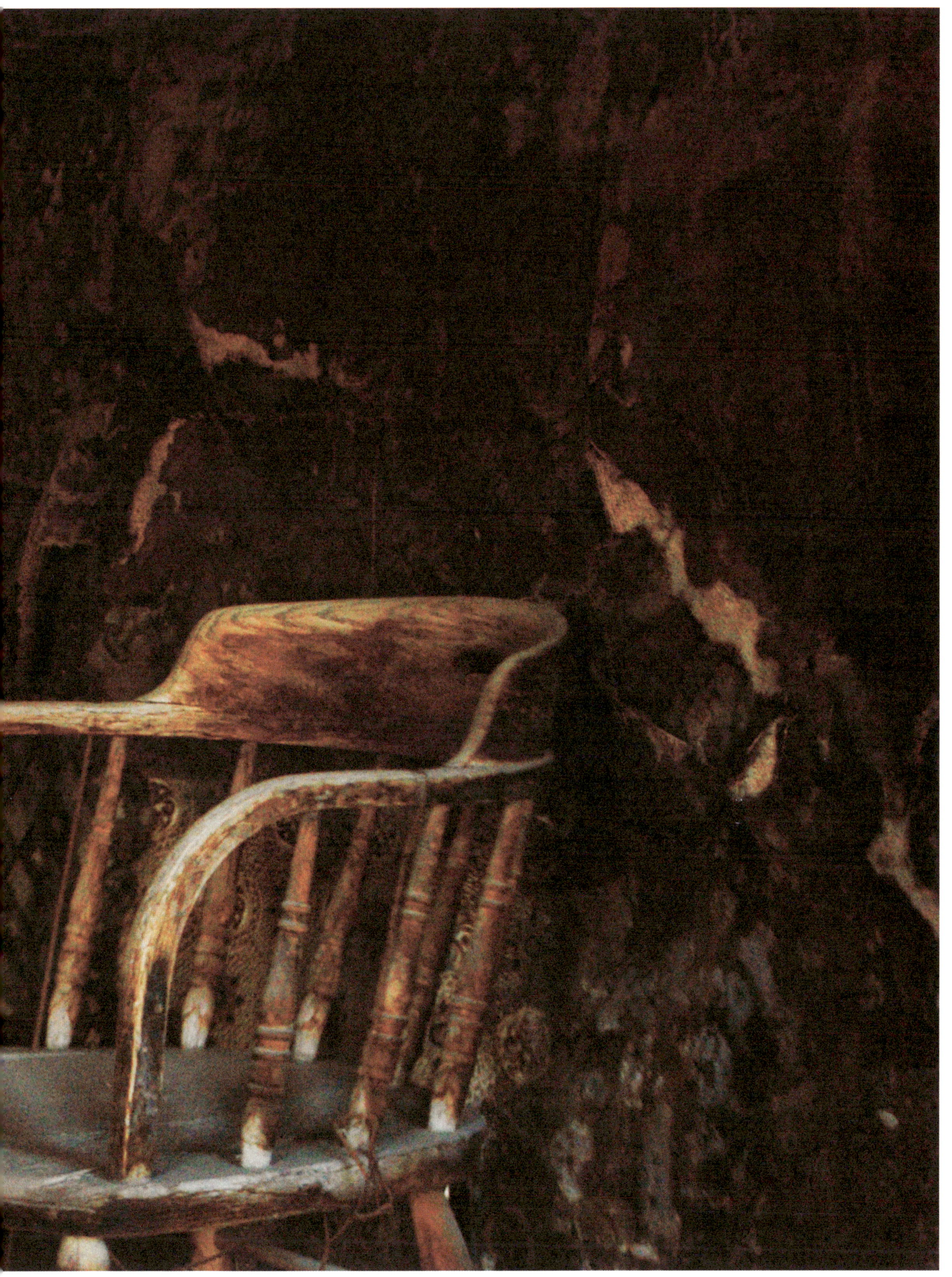

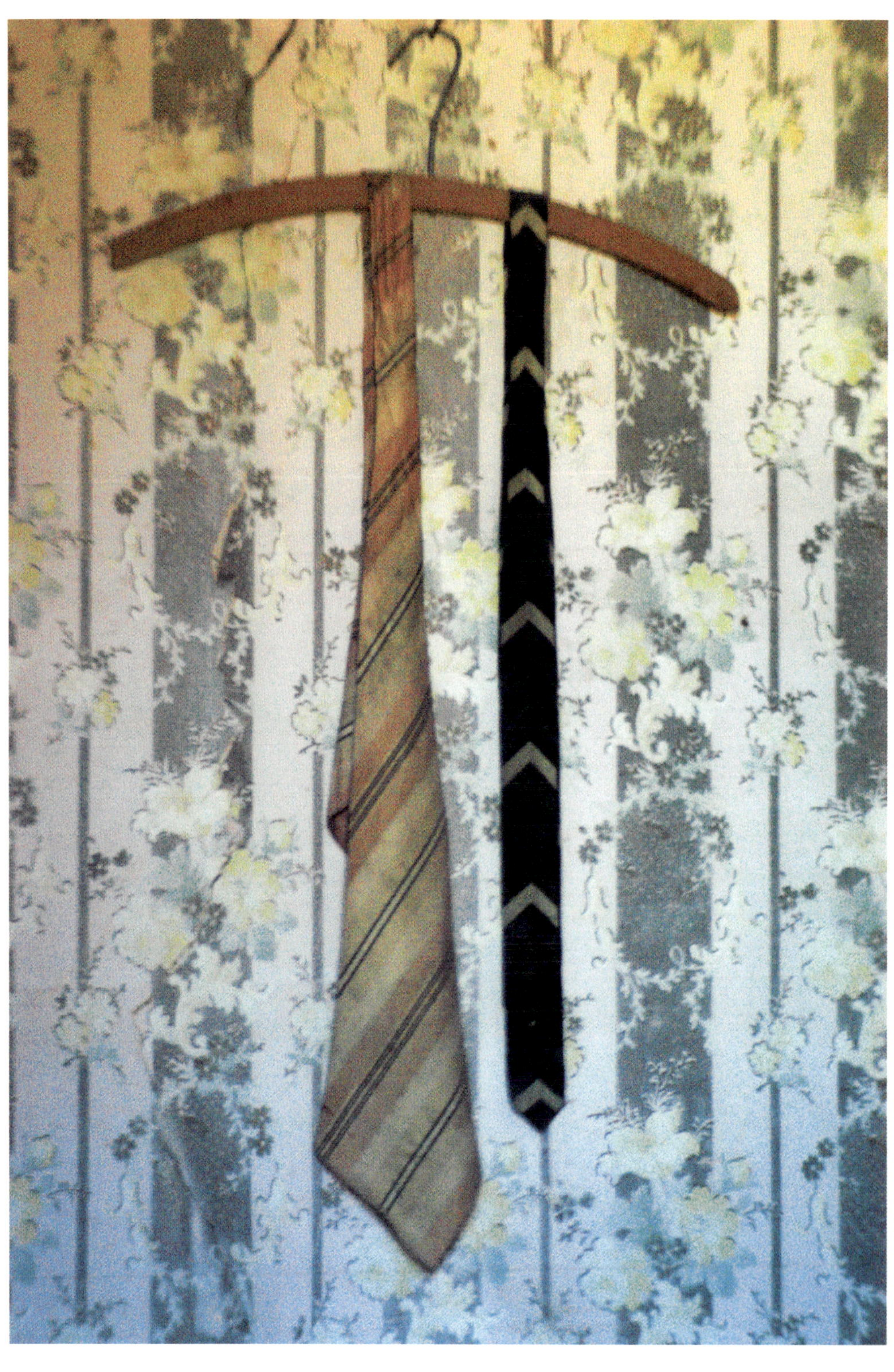

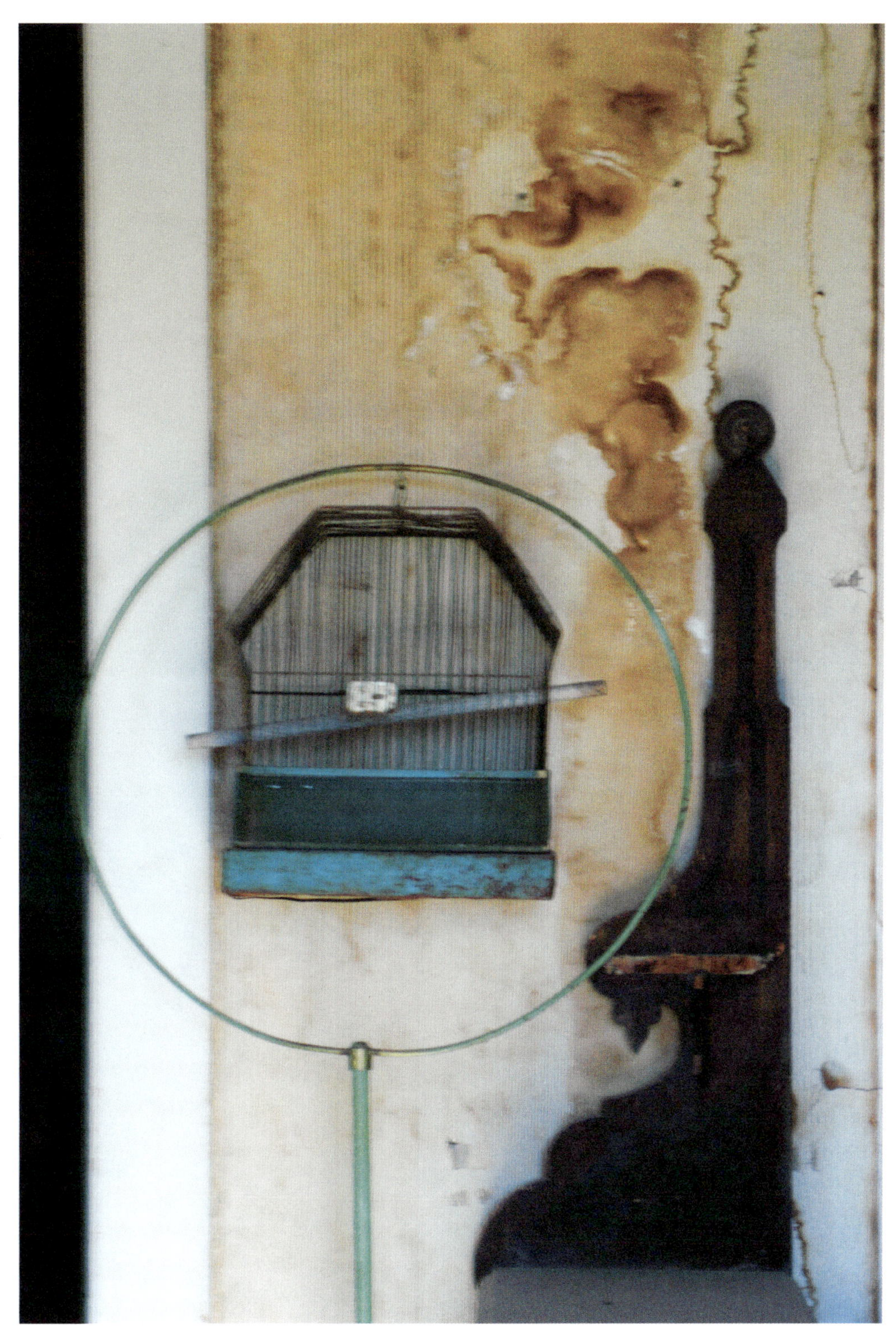

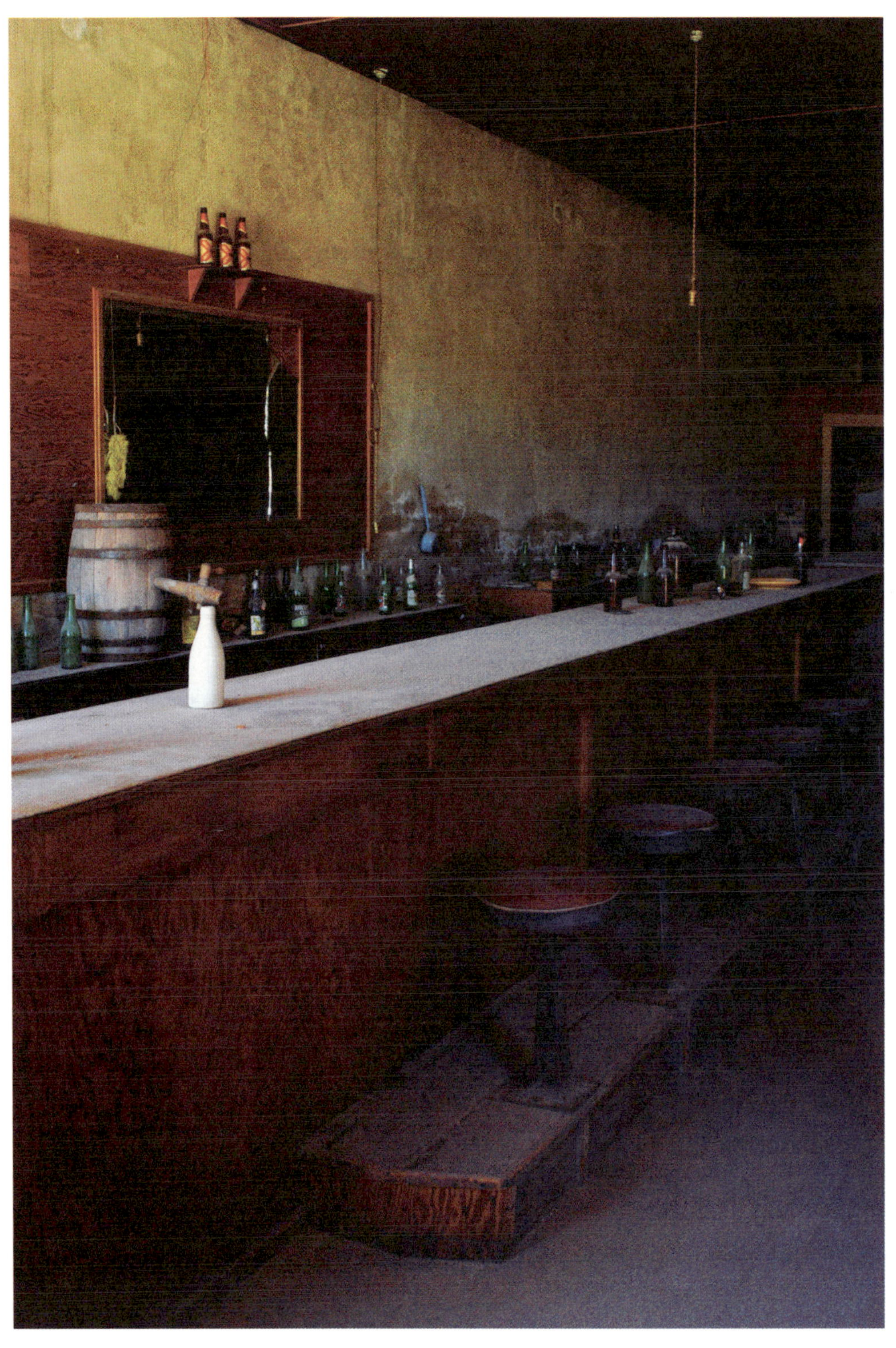

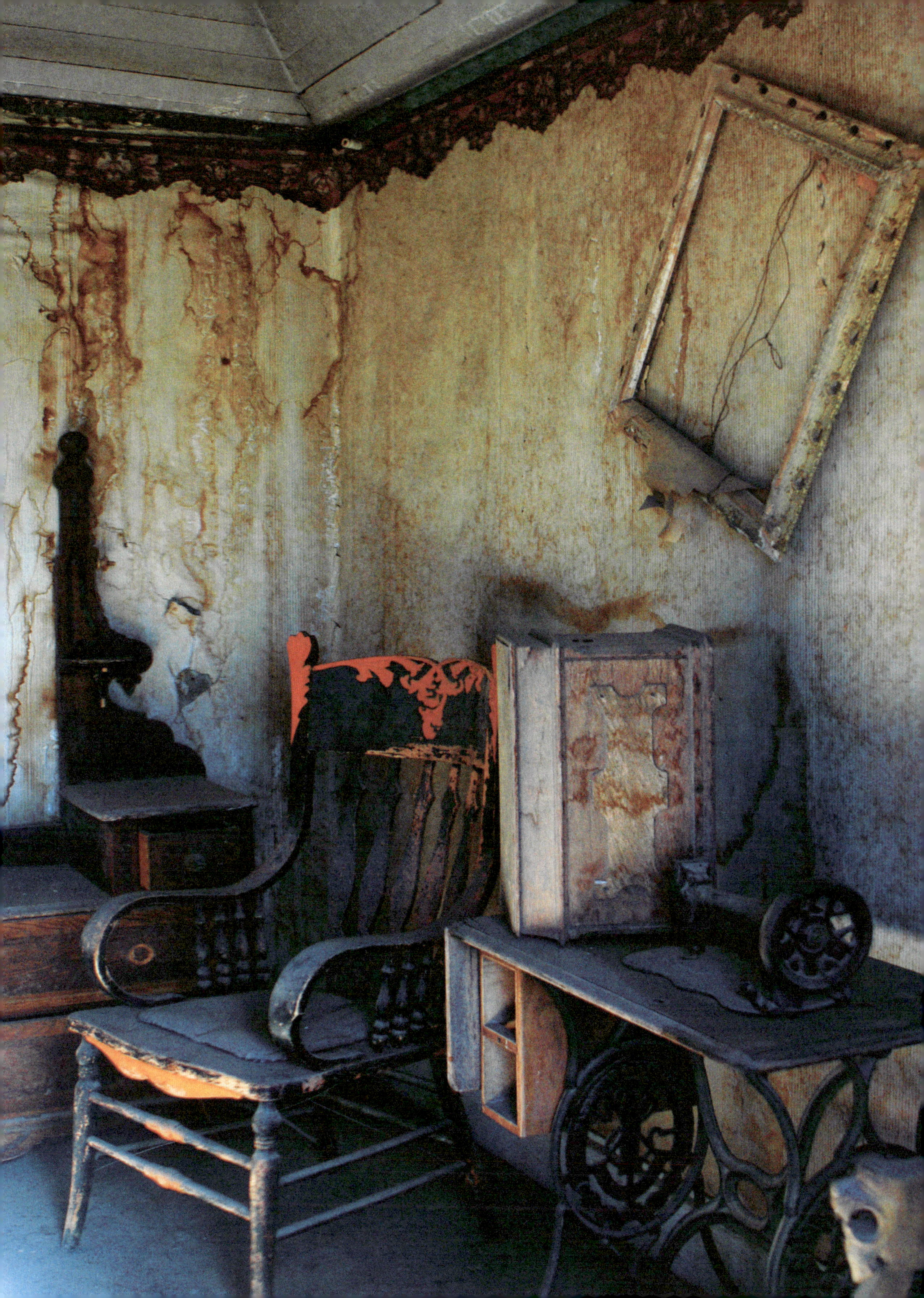

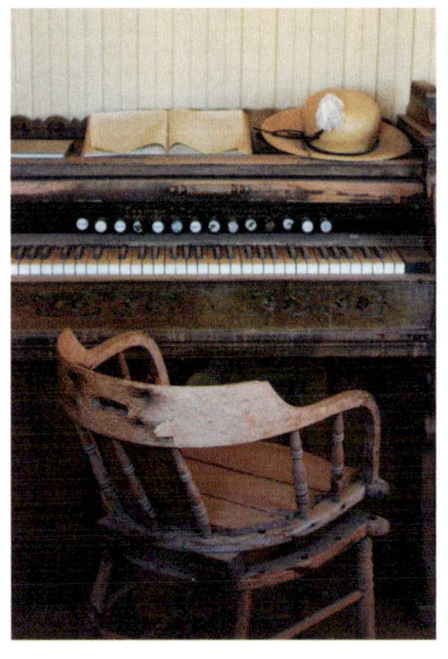

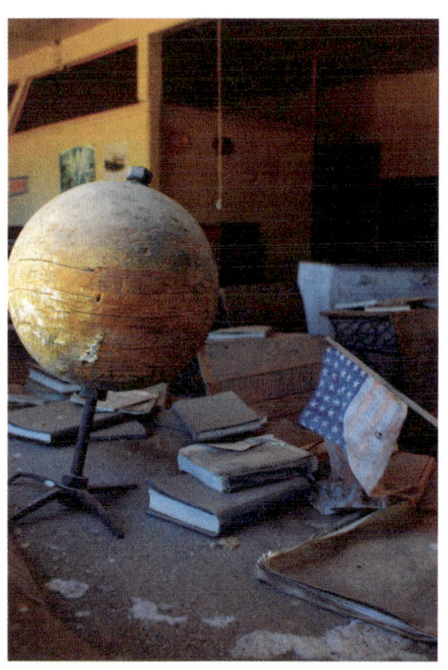

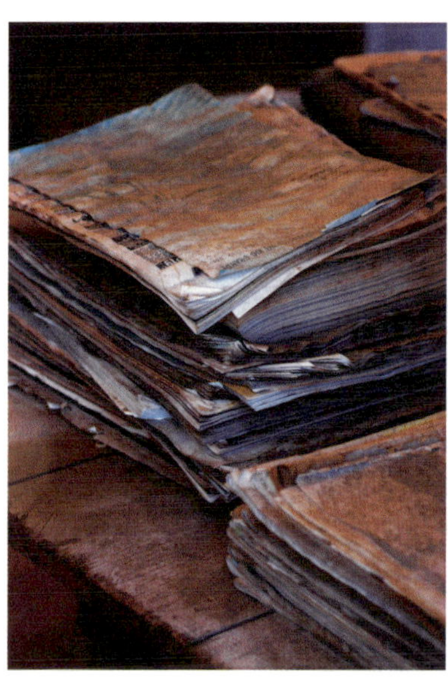

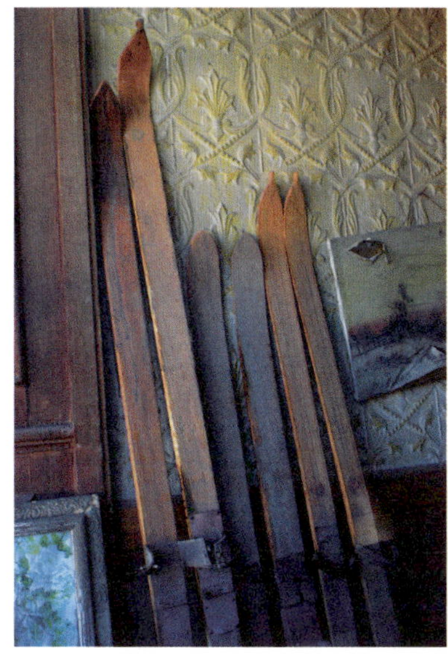

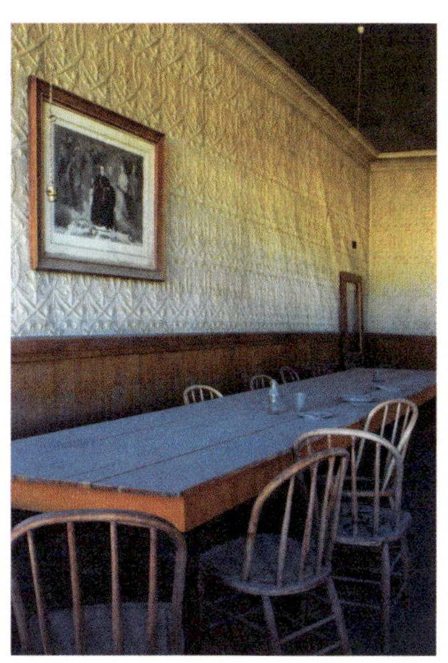

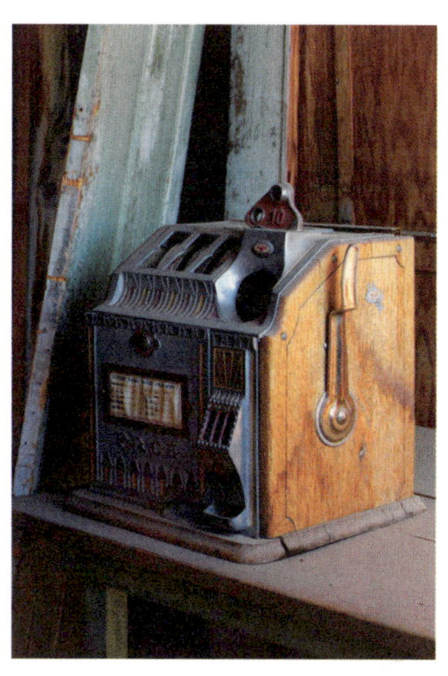

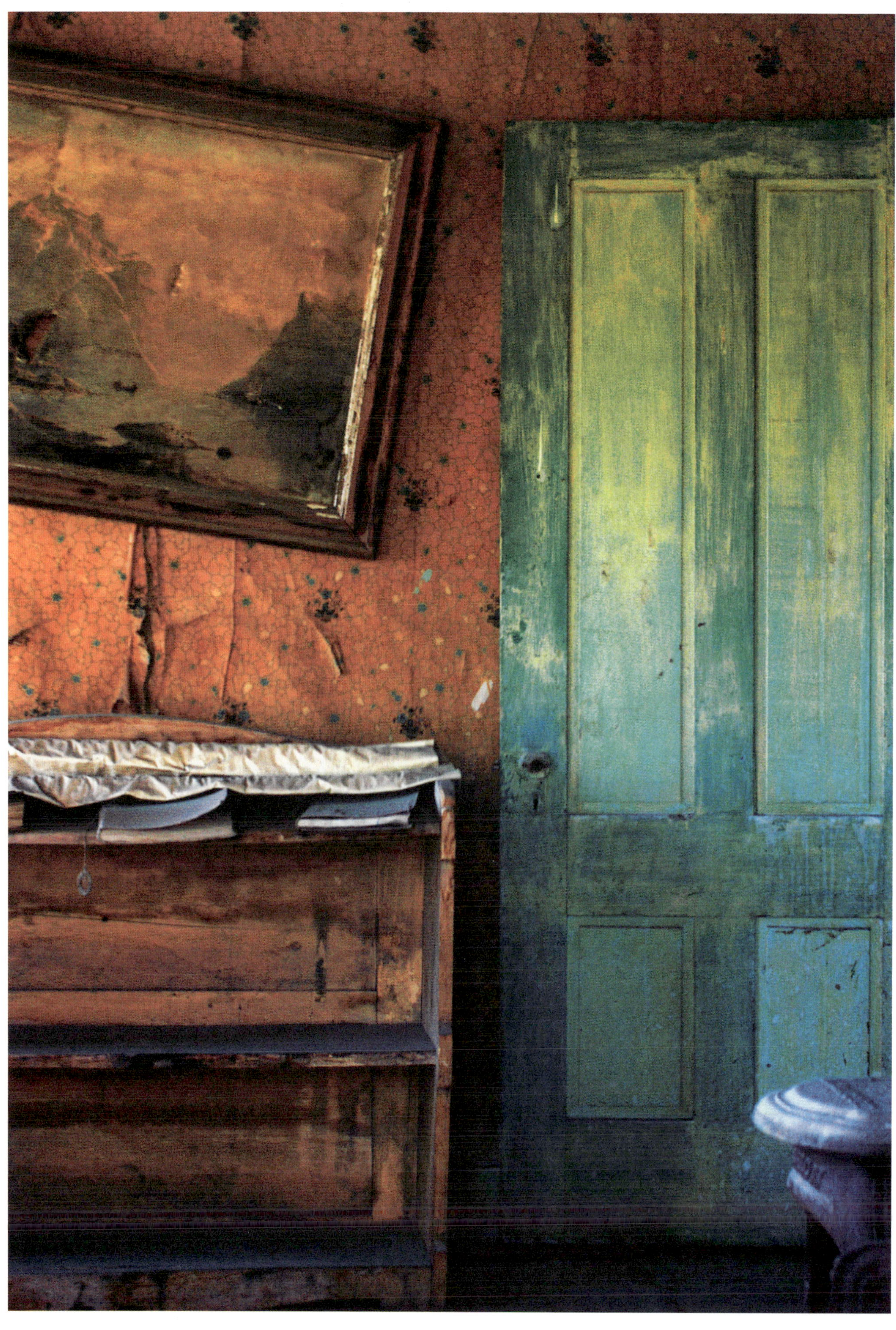

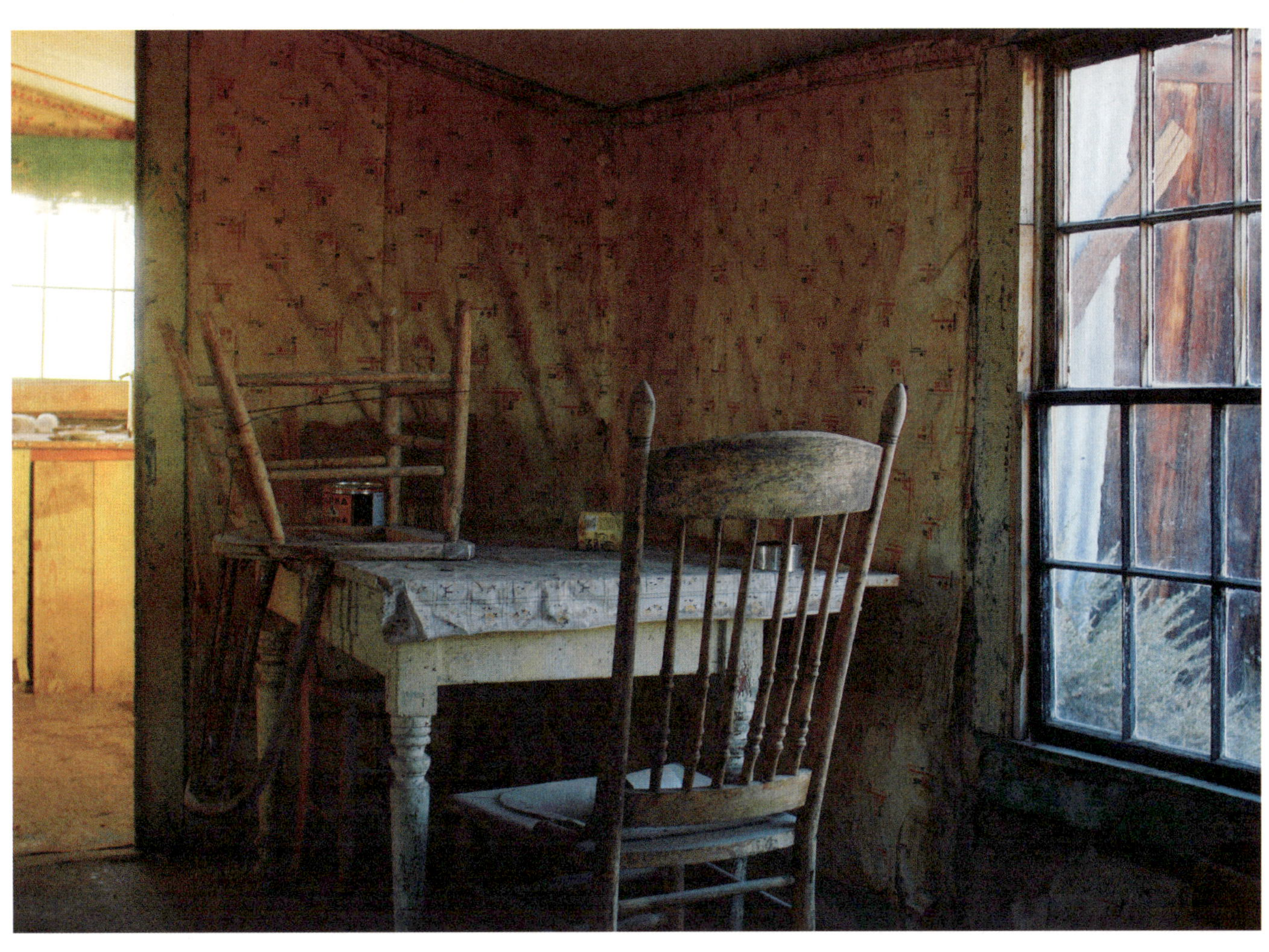

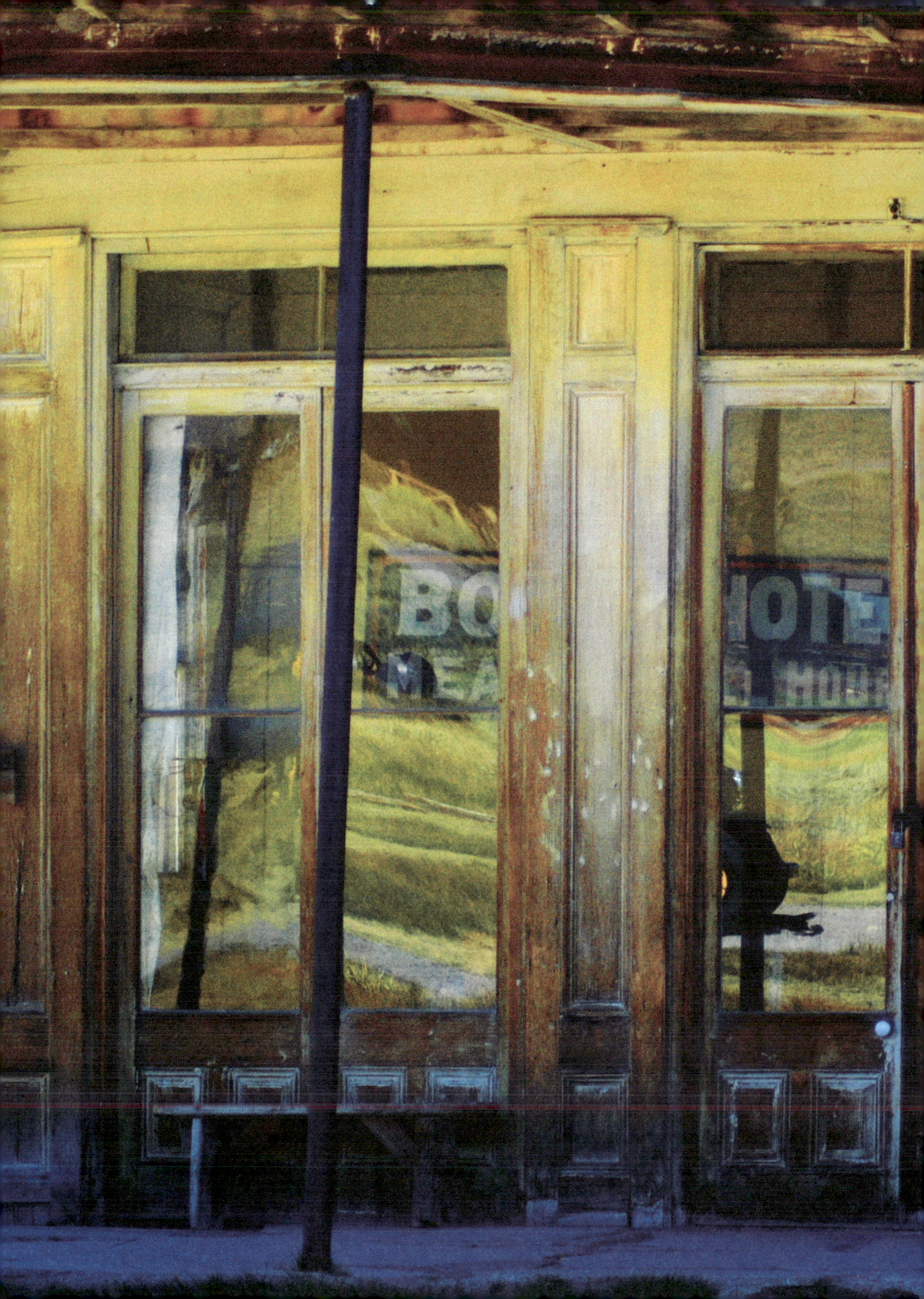
BO
HOTE

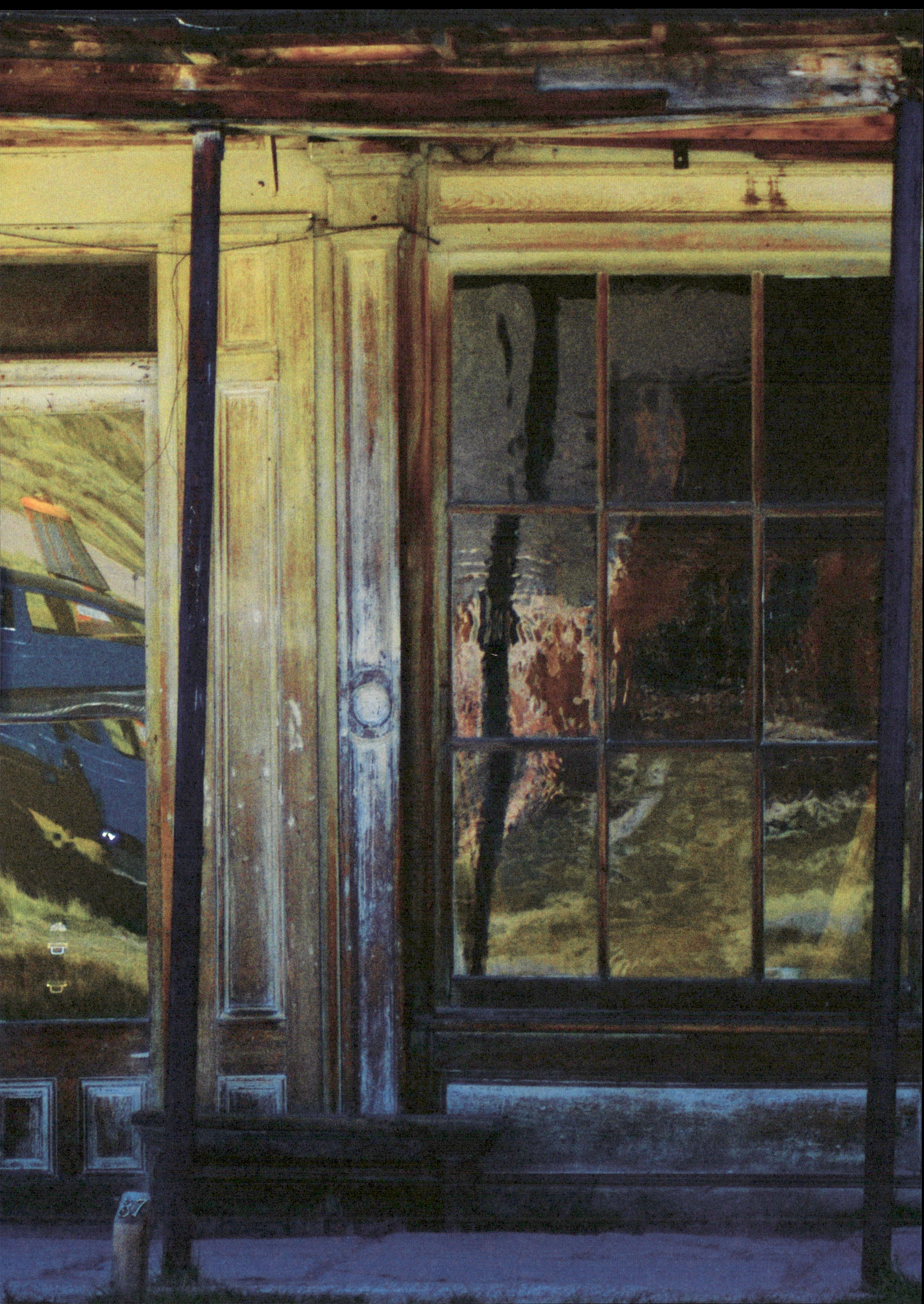
37

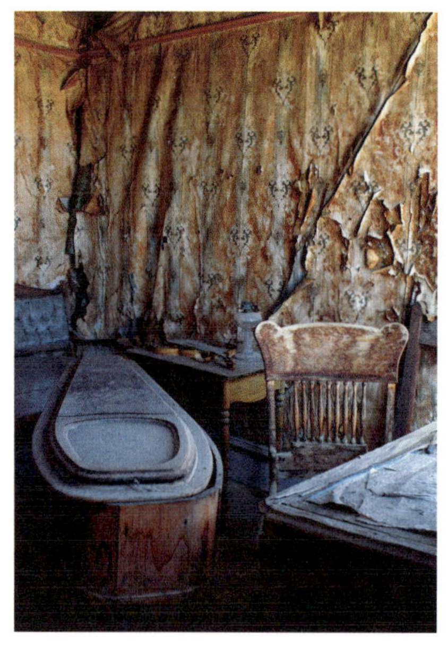

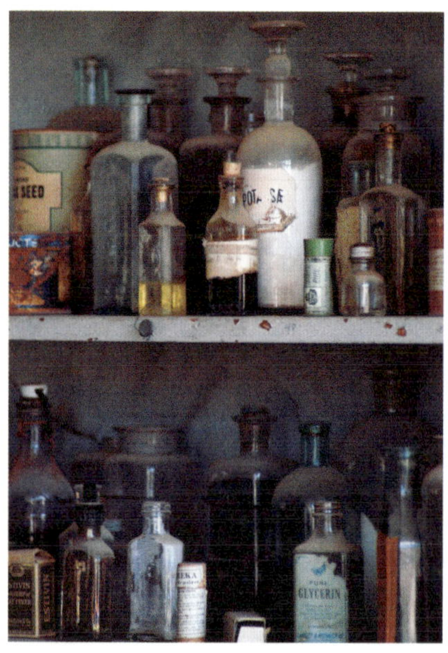
GLYCERIN

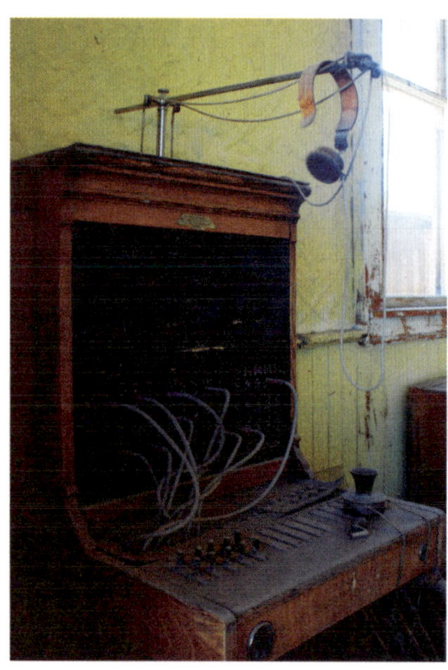

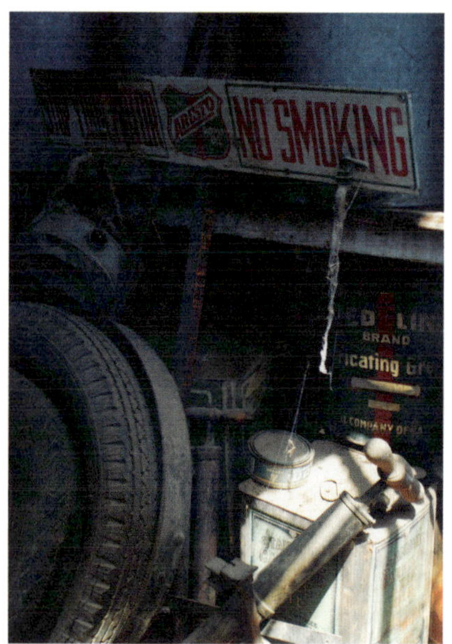
NO SMOKING

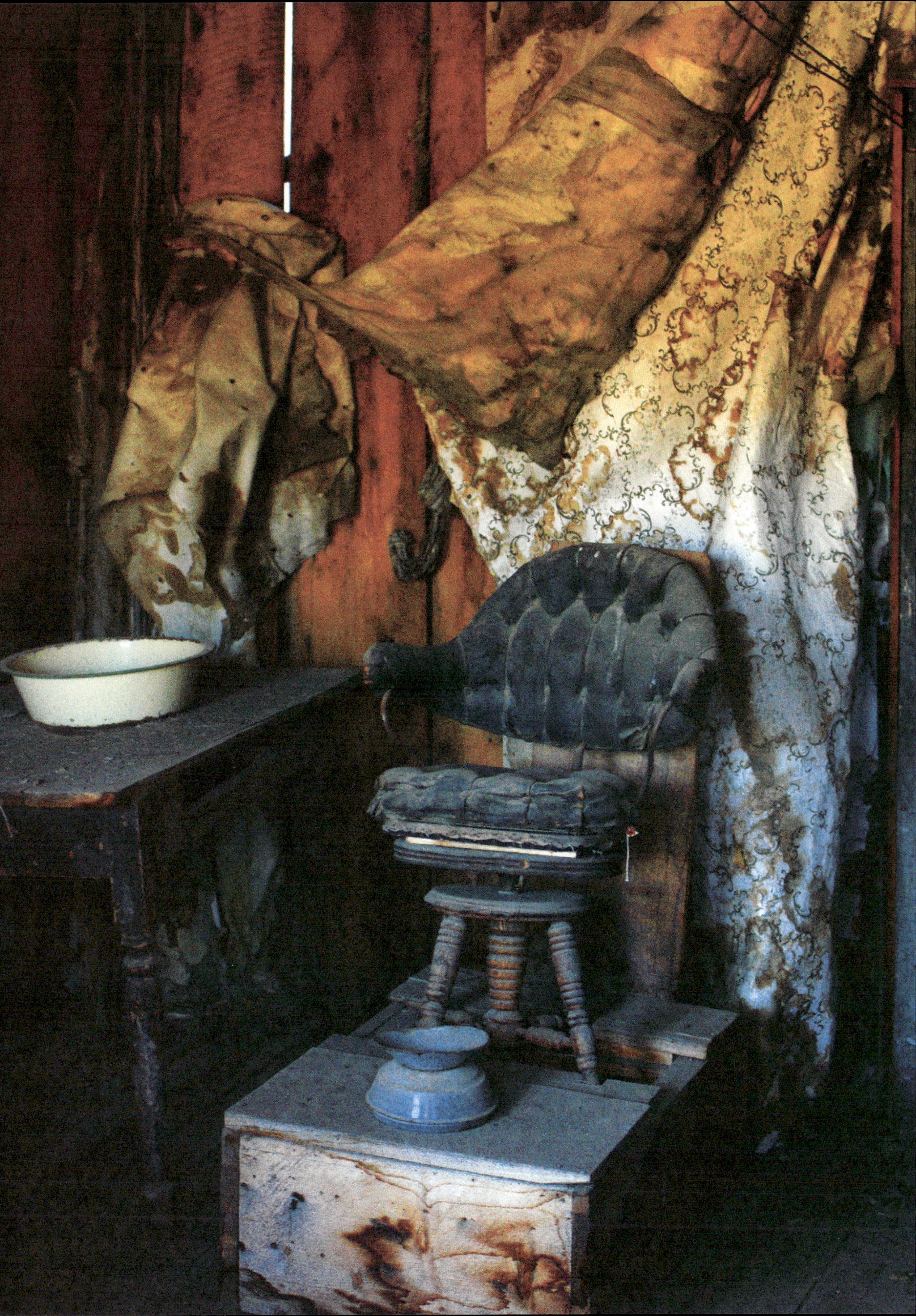

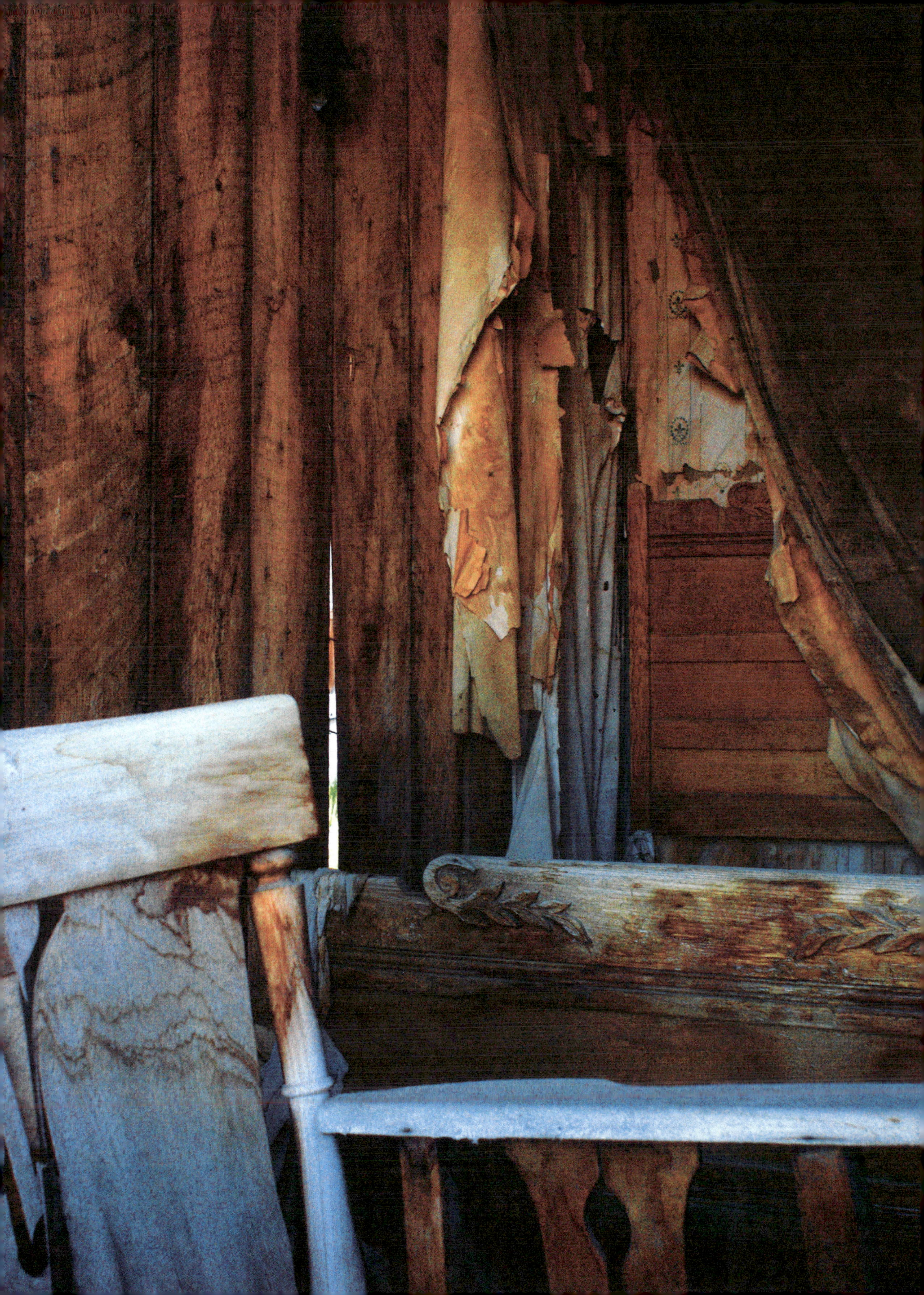

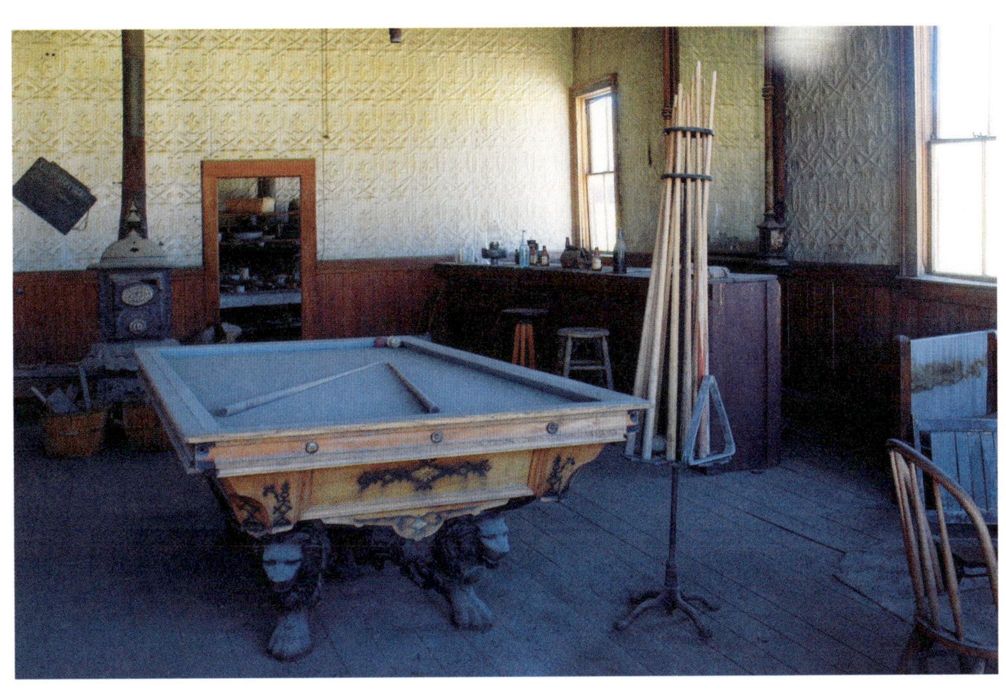

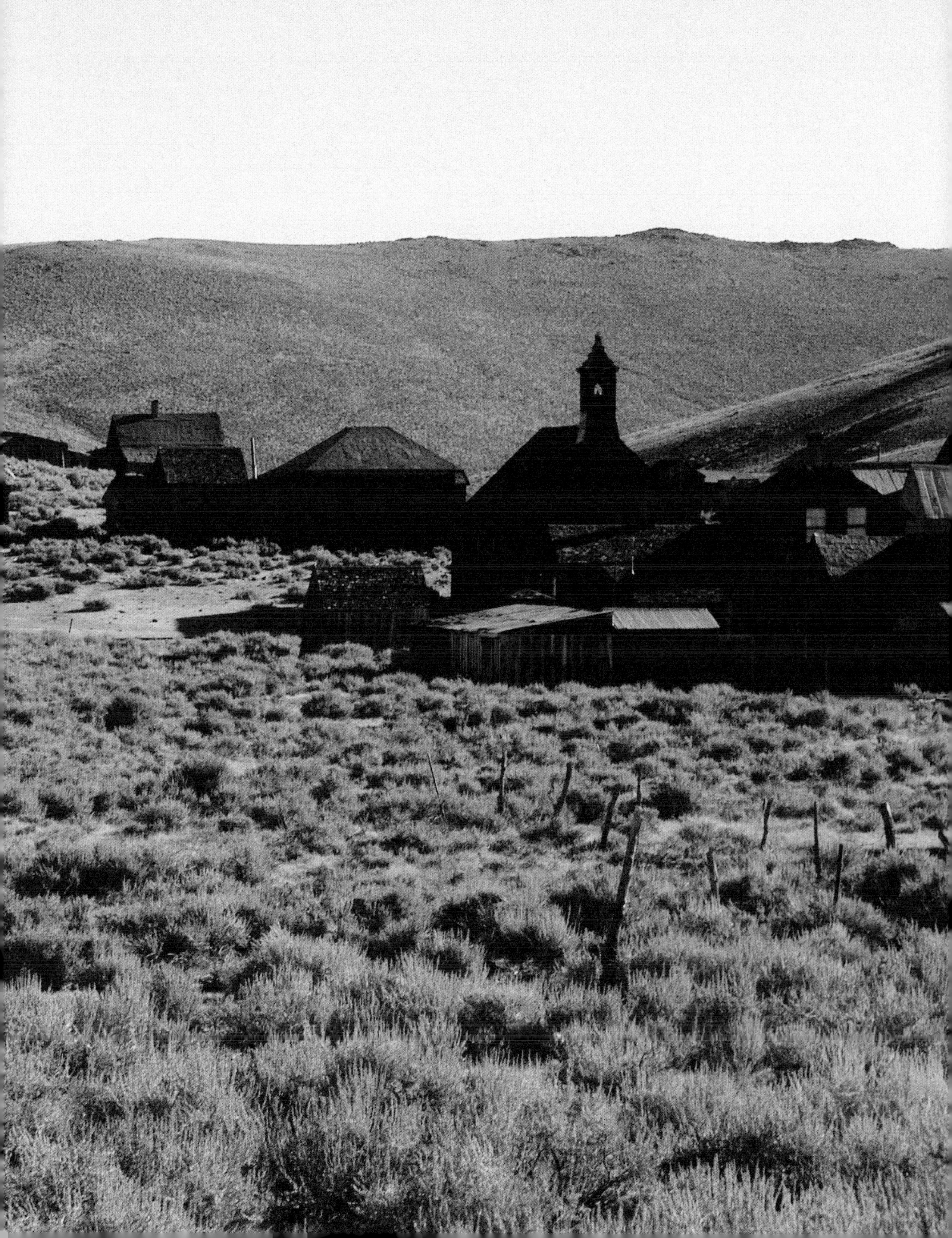

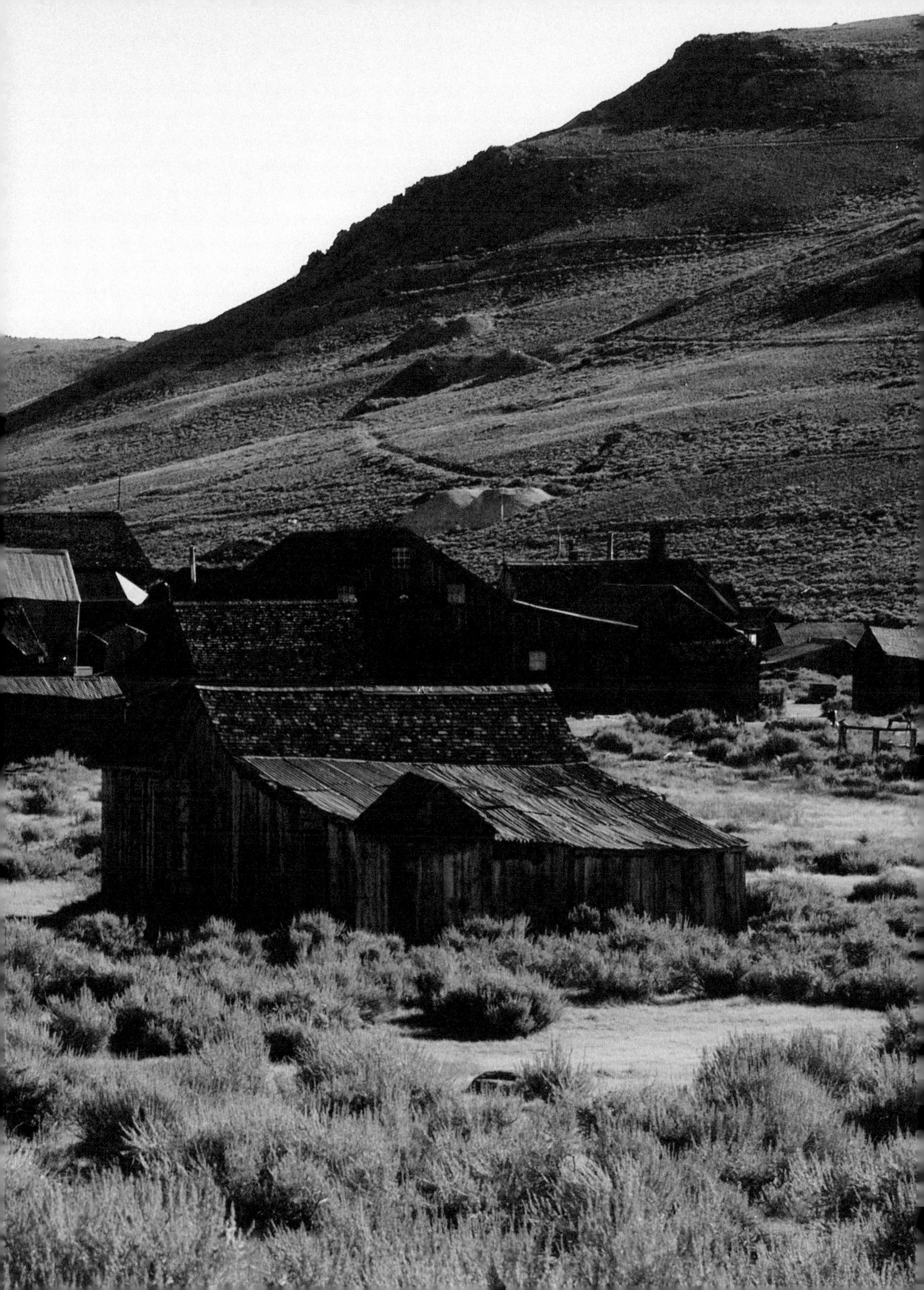

TAKE OFF

Before we take off, a friend provides us with water bottles and a detailed road map. The wilderness is not something she takes lightly. She doesn't trust it.

And, furthermore, you never get to be on your own out there; the more depopulated the place is, the more commercial shootings for new car models.

BORDER COUNTRY

The mosquitos are the only creatures disturbing the good spirits in the trailer camp. We open our mouths wide for burgers, sip at drinks, and watch the insects swarm around the lanterns beneath the plastic roof. At a distance the Mexicans stand smoking; glowing red spots in the approaching twilight.

Mister F sits in a folding chair with a soda. He is taking medication and has a bullet-like hole in his temple after an operation that just brought him back to life. While he drove us here in a van patterned with scratches from roadside cacti, he uninterruptedly spoke in Spanish over his CB radio. Around us, it was all Texas: pin-head grass, yucca, sun-bleached mesquite, traces of slithering reptiles, and diving hawks. His land, his territory.

He inherited the ranch from his father, a beef and game empire on whose land nocturnal smuggling caravans sneak northbound with their headlights turned off. Occasionally, beggars bang on the windows of the main building at awkward hours. Anyone persisting in this rattlesnake-laiden dust bowl must hold control over his finances and brains and trust the brittle species of grass to really hold their ground.

Mister F rules without ever raising his voice. He is way past the age of retirement. To his own great disappointment, he has fathered five daughters and no son. All of his Mexican laborers have swum or waded across the border and somewhere on the other side of those impressive blue mountains, those massive waves waiting to break, they have families and children who grow up much too fast.

RED DIRT

This dust; dirt being kicked up, filtering through the very existence and finding the remotest spot. Years with not a sign of rain have driven new species into the greener parts of the high sierra; tiny, alert-eyed monkeys, wild boar with rounded cheeks.

A bag of ice is the same price as a gallon of gas. You depend equally on both when you seek out the rocky landscape with tires covered in red dirt and speakers filled to the brim with vulnerable singer-songwriters and trembling corridos. It's a heat record out here, way past 100 degrees as we touched down; a dry heat sweeping the sweat away.

APPALOOSA

The sight is breathtaking in its perfection: 114 painted horses – white, grey, chestnut, black, spotted, speckled or striped, galloping down the slopes, first right at us and then down through a ravine and off toward the rising sun. They move in unison, thundering across the mute, still sleepy, landscape. In the cloud of dust torn up by their hooves, they pant, snort, stretch and almost disappear before making a U-turn.

It was Indians from the Nez Perce tribe who bred them and named them Appaloosa. As a boy, rancher Ken Kelsey would listen with fascination to his father's stories about how Chief Joseph and his people ran off to Canada and fought the cavalry from there. "The Indians needed small horses with stamina," he explains. "The cavalry had big thoroughbreds and they could never outride the Indians. White people hated the Appaloosa because of this and tried to eliminate them. The West would have looked different had the Indians won a few more battles. The whites fought over gold, the Indians over horses. They had another view on life."

HITCHHIKER

You are traveling on scorched, oil-stained rainbow asphalt with the electric sounds of the West in your ears: the pain and distress are seldom more than an inch away, they resonate in these songs, lurking beneath the thin surface of weather-beaten tableland. On the roadside, a tiny woman stands waiting, leaning somewhat forward in her sun-dried skin, a piece of cloth tied around her hair. She gets a lift. She sits in the back pointing at a distant spot. You speak English, then try a few words of Spanish, but she will not respond. You hold out a pack of cigarettes, she shakes her head. Her face in the rear mirror is dogged, her eyes on the lookout.

After a few miles you feel uneasiness creeping up from behind. Your clammy hands stick to the wheel, your shoes seem too big, your car too ostentatious. Your curiosity is about to become diluted. What are you doing here? Your friendly manners are a shitty excuse, a puny installment on a debt for which you, of course, are not responsible.

She then lifts a finger and steps out in a small village, nodding ever so silently. You drive your rental car westward, past painted horse herds, desert plateaux, silent Indian communities. You do not brake until you arrive in another galaxy: Las Vegas, Nevada, with free pink champagne in plastic cups for all gas station customers.

MOTEL MELANCHOLY

The motel room is sultry and on TV people kill each other and burn the corpses in a movie with a title you will not try to memorize. With the window wide open you listen to the last black crows fussing themselves to sleep in the crowns of the highway trees, and before daybreak, dreams have carried you far away, the wind in your hair and racing stripes on your cheeks.

This is a small valley town with four central blocks steeped in melancholy. Breakfast is served next door to the local hotel. Drowsy trumpets crawl out of the kitchen radio. The atmospheric beauty, once poignant, is now fading.

Later you drive past flat fields with leather-tanned farmworkers. A tractor pulls a harvesting machine through rows of cauliflower. At least thirty men and women cling to the monster-sized machine, or cut off the tops with broad, quick sweeps of knives that never hesitate.

FOG OF THE BAY

Like thin smoke, the mist rises from reddish blond cedar woods, with truckloads of timber grumbling by on muddy uphill slopes. The people tend to wear the stigma of isolation. The lumber jackets have become a second skin, the conversations are phrase fragments swishing about in smoking-hot coffee while the rain thuds on the ground.

You don't get any farther to the West than this: Cape Flattery on the Olympic peninsula, engulfed by a lead grey ocean and a steel-grey sky. The first indigenous encounter with American settlers in 1853 resulted in a smallpox epidemic, which wiped out more than half of the aboriginal Makah tribe and made the songs of the Pacific whales echo against the shoreline cliffs with a new kind of gloom. In 1913 the very last whale hunt took place, using canoes carved from the cedar.

Walking out on the breakwater, the enormity of the mist and greyness blurs your sense of time and borders. Closing your eyes you may hear the call of the hunter, and from the knotty jumble of the forest fog continues to drift across the bay like greetings from countless damp campfires.

BURNERS

Hollow-eyed locals from the reservation try to sell tacos to the caravan passing through the nondescript one-horse town of Nixon on its way toward the white desert peculiarly named Black Rock. A fading sun has painted the mesquite mountains pink and purple, and in one of the remote valleys Pyramid Lake displays a liquid mirror so intensely blue that it appears to be computer manipulated.

Another hour's drive to the north, the annual Burning Man village is beginning to make its mark. Many of the burners on the road surely think of this as hiking in another dimension. The cult that turned into a festival, attracting not only hedonistic castaways and alternative life-stylers but also corporate entities engaged in profit-enhancing team building, started when a heartbroken guy, incensed by his unhappiness, set fire to a wooden doll on the shore of the Pacific. The voodoo element grew as more desperate and jealous people showed up the next summer. Eventually, they were forced off of the beach. Now that tens of thousands gather each year in the Black Rock desert to burn a giant scarecrow, the symbolism is for everyone to figure out. A deceitful ex-lover? A musician who has sold out? A despicable politician? The whole damn system?

Watching the burners and their vehicles as they return to their ordinary lives one week later, covered in white desert powder, you cannot help but think how much they resemble a captured herd of wild horses being lead to the stables after a feverish attempt at escape.

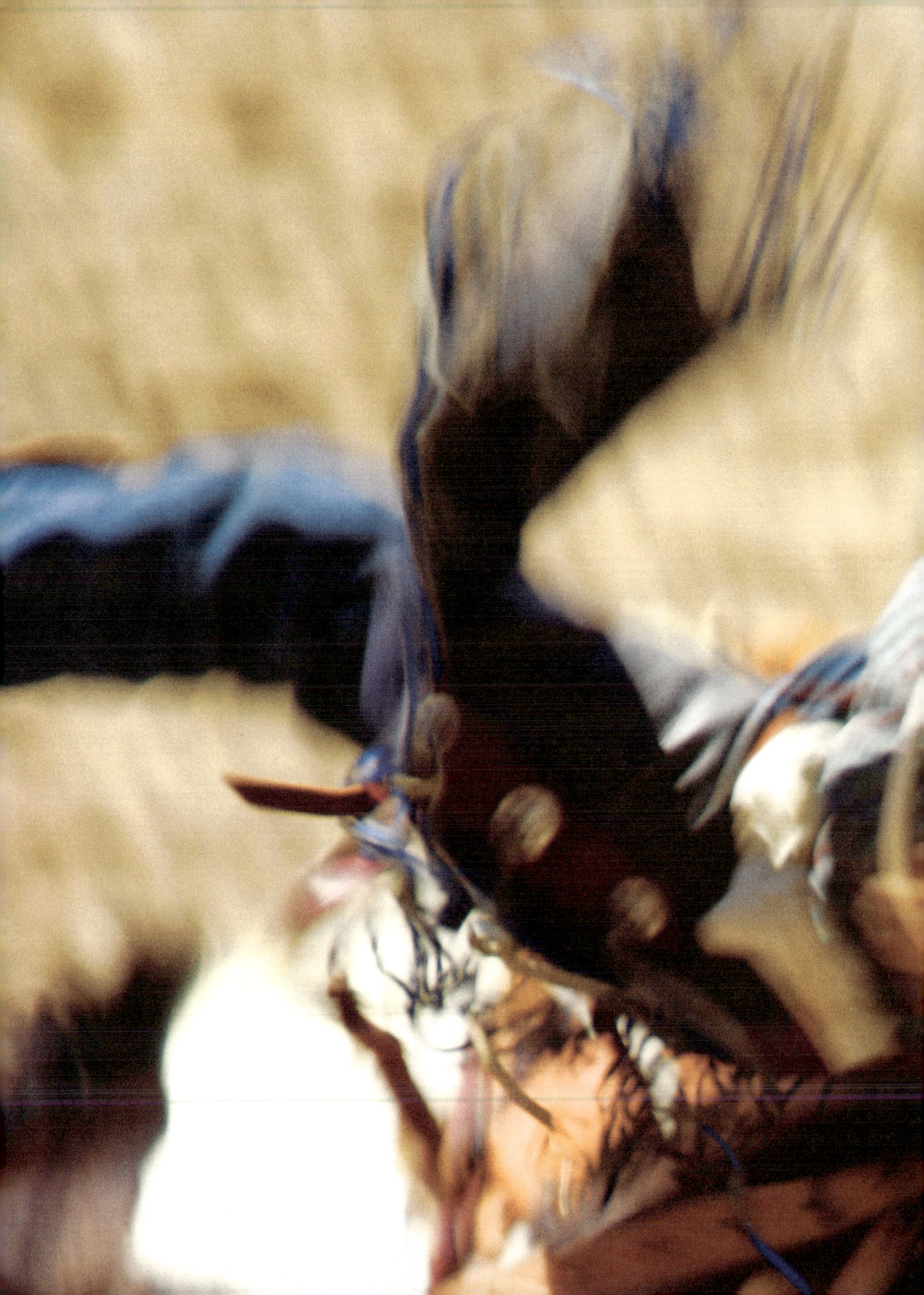

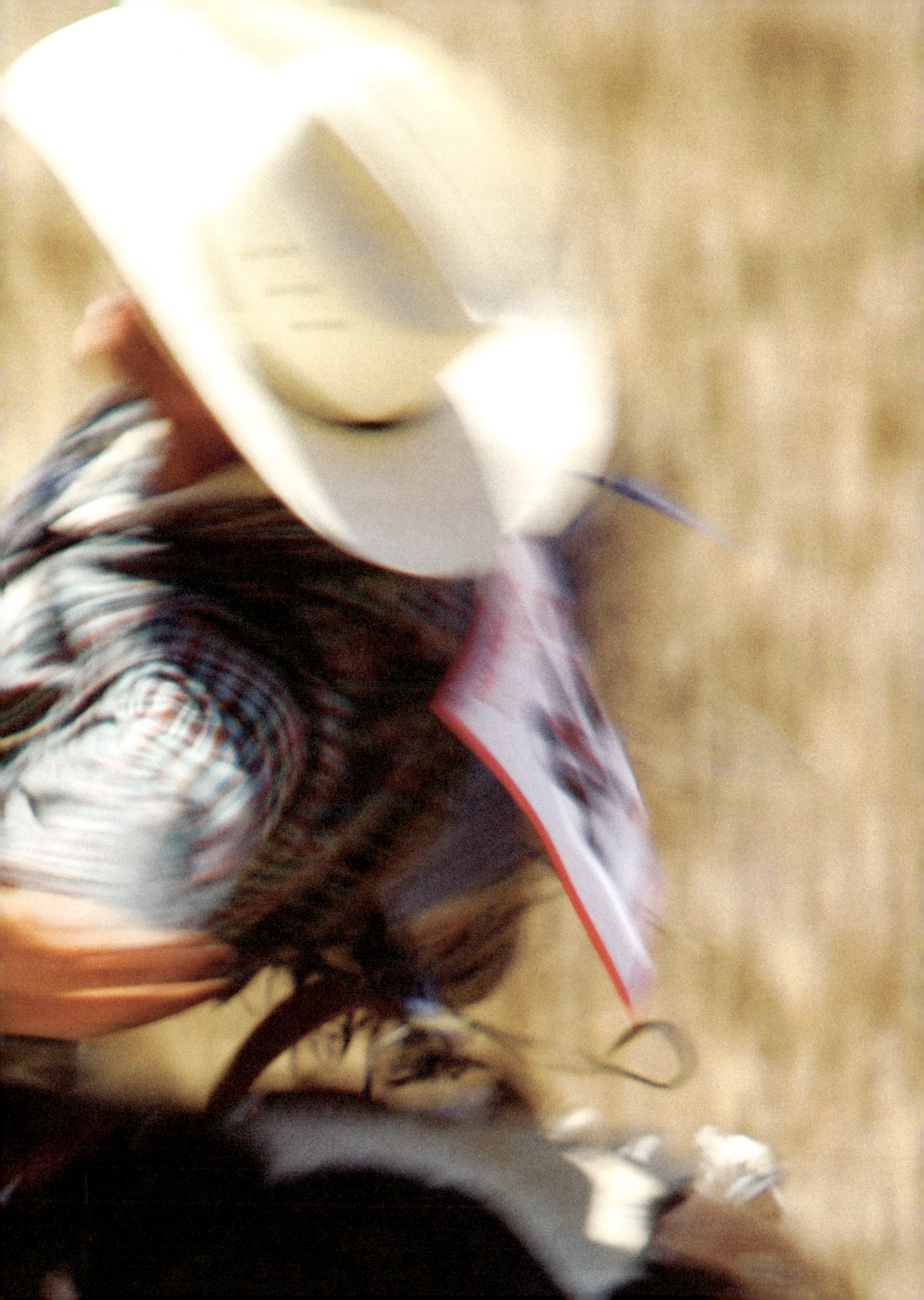

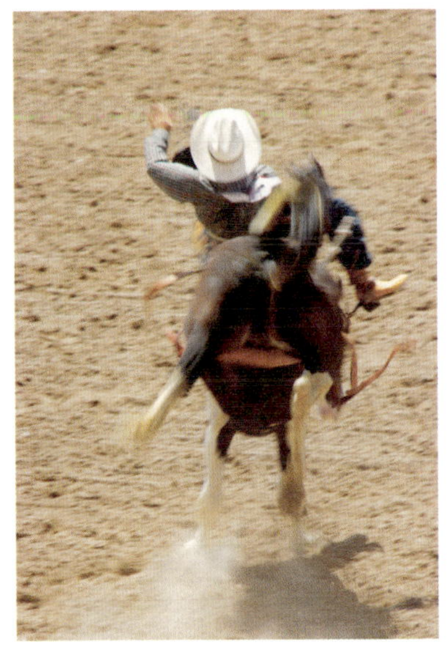

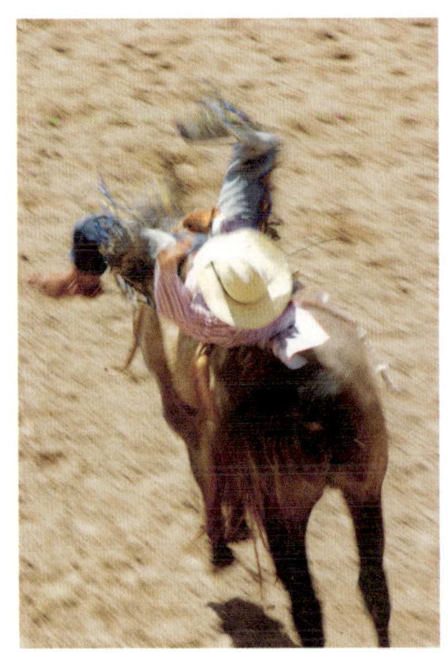

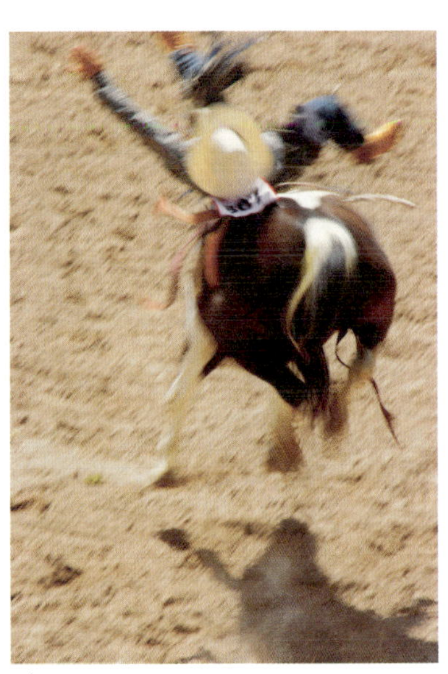

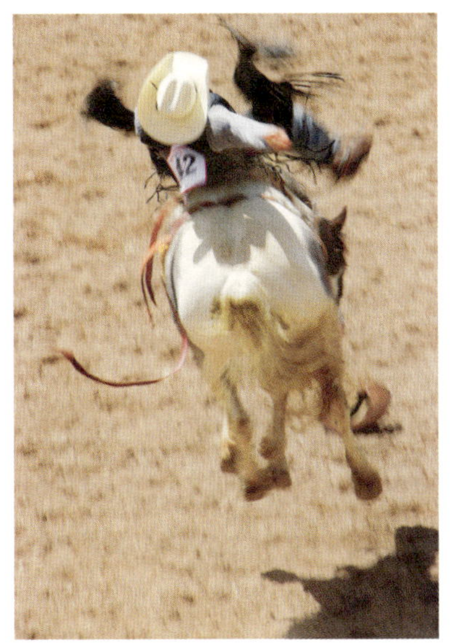
12

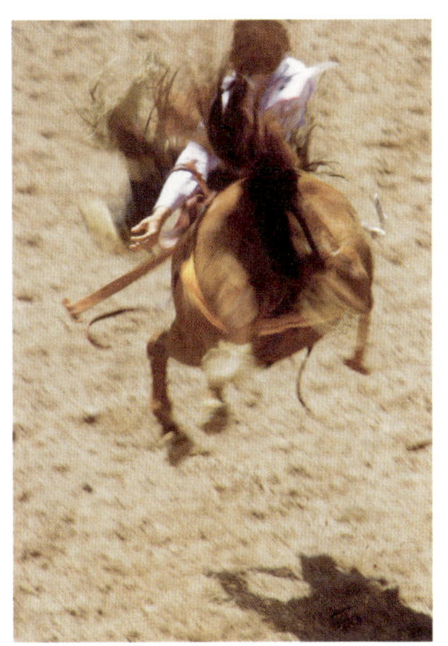

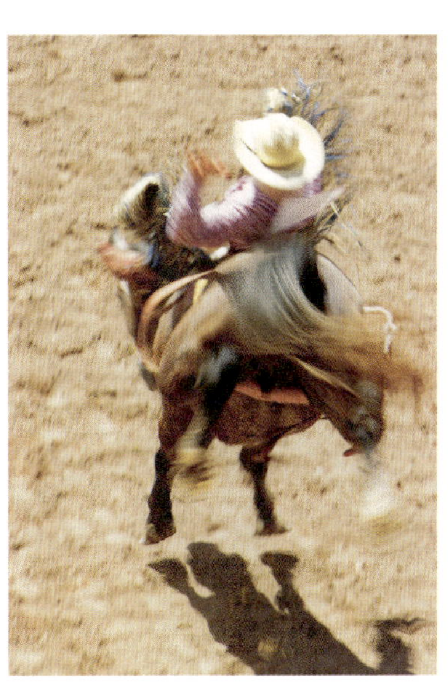

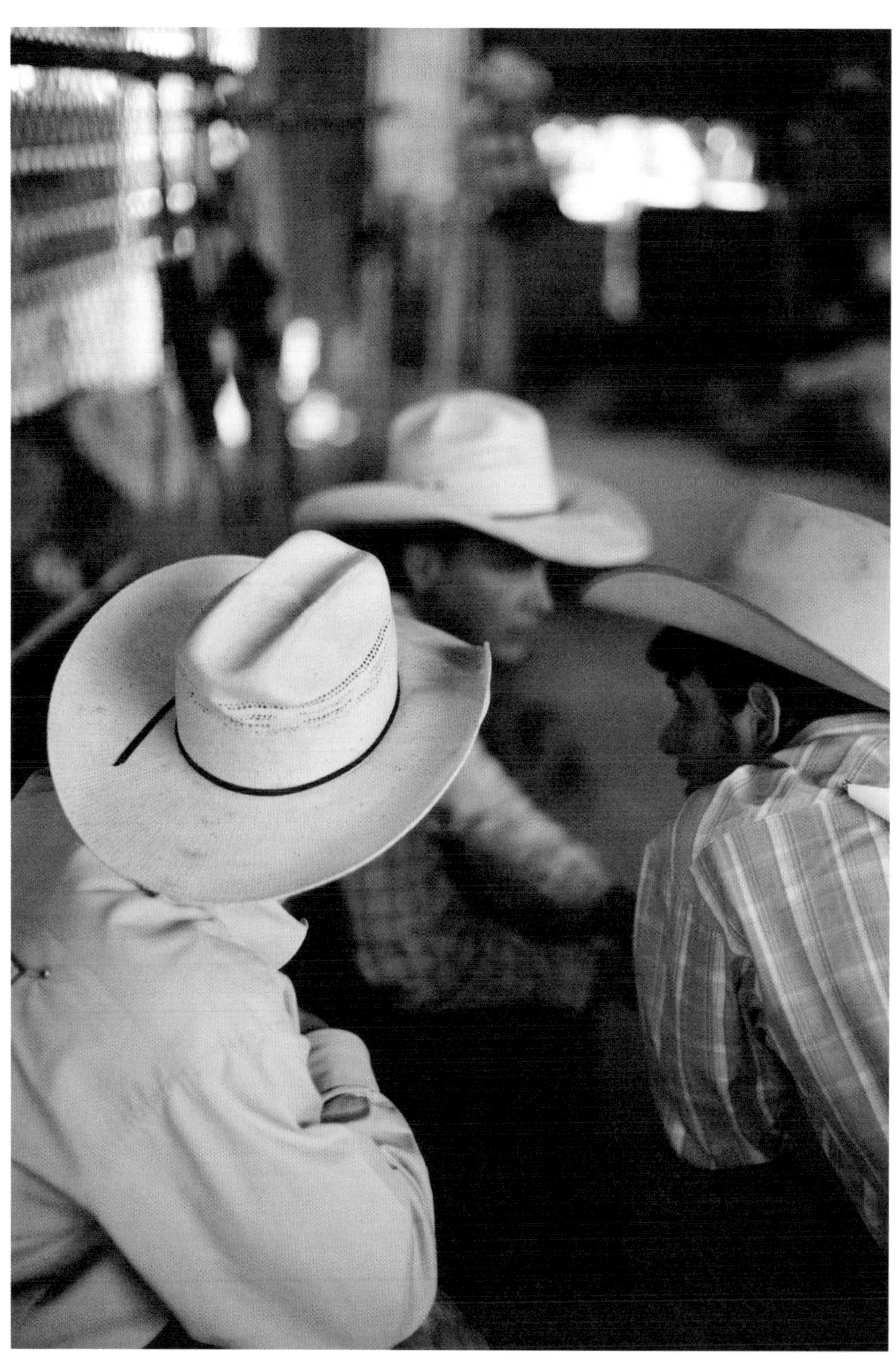

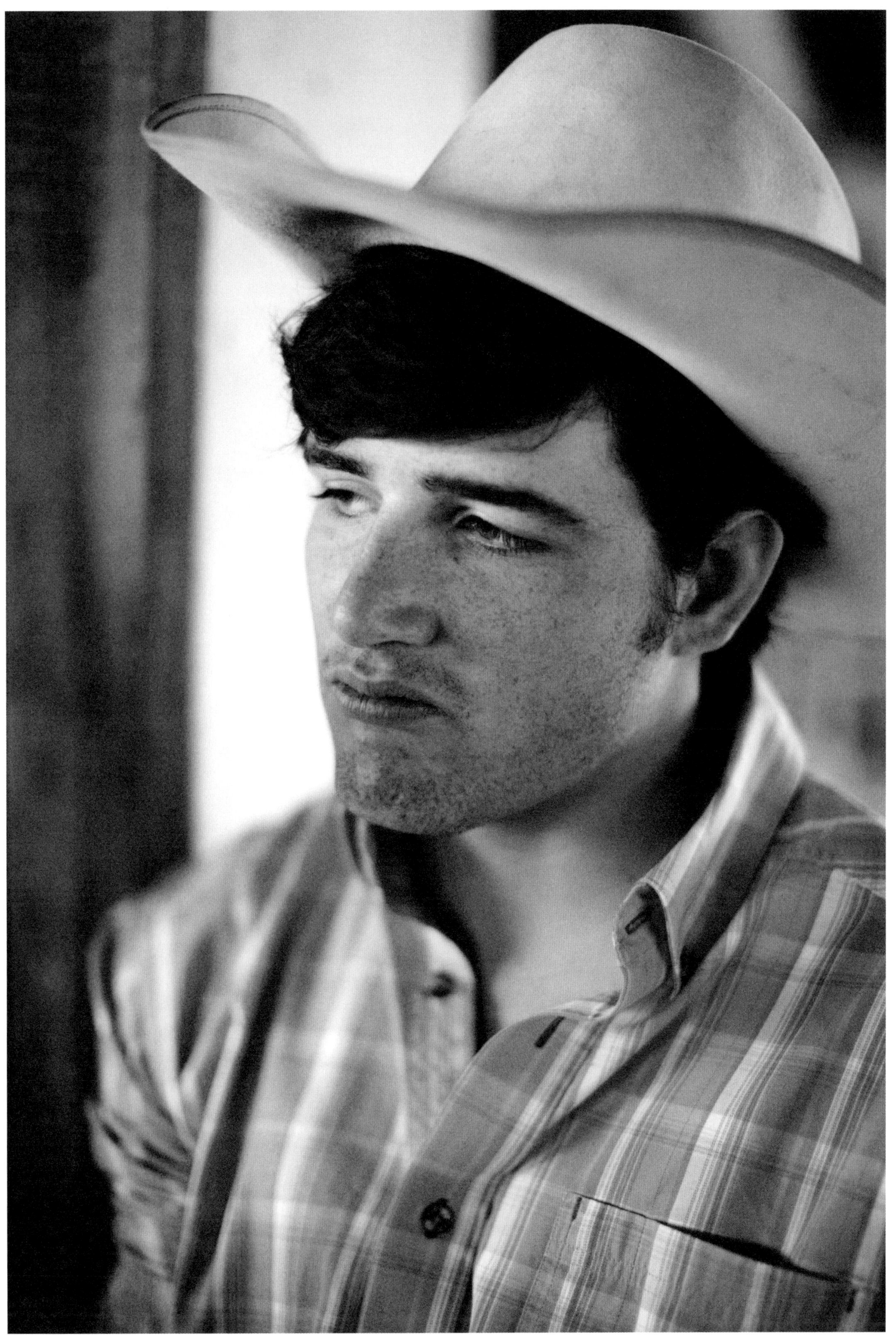

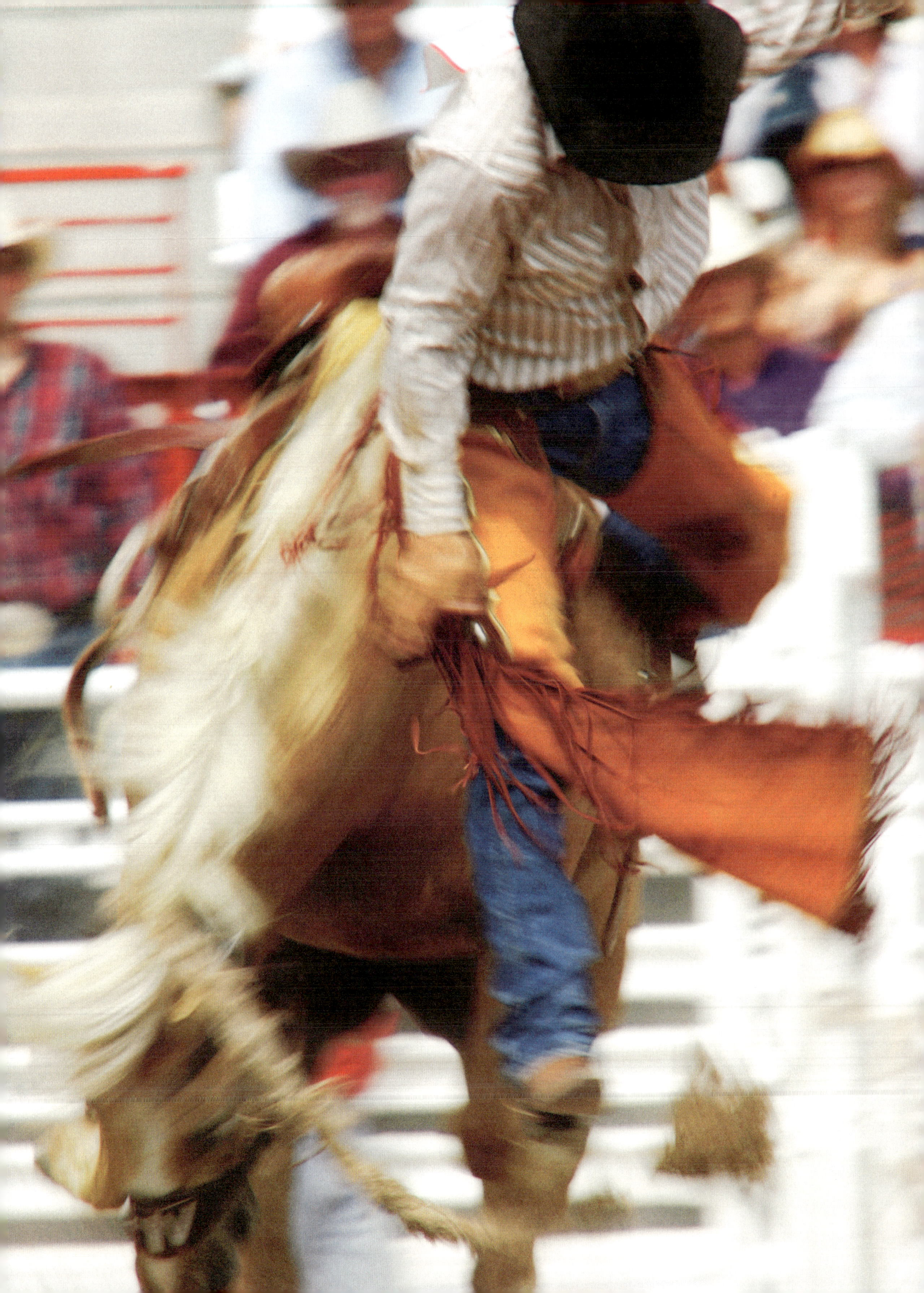

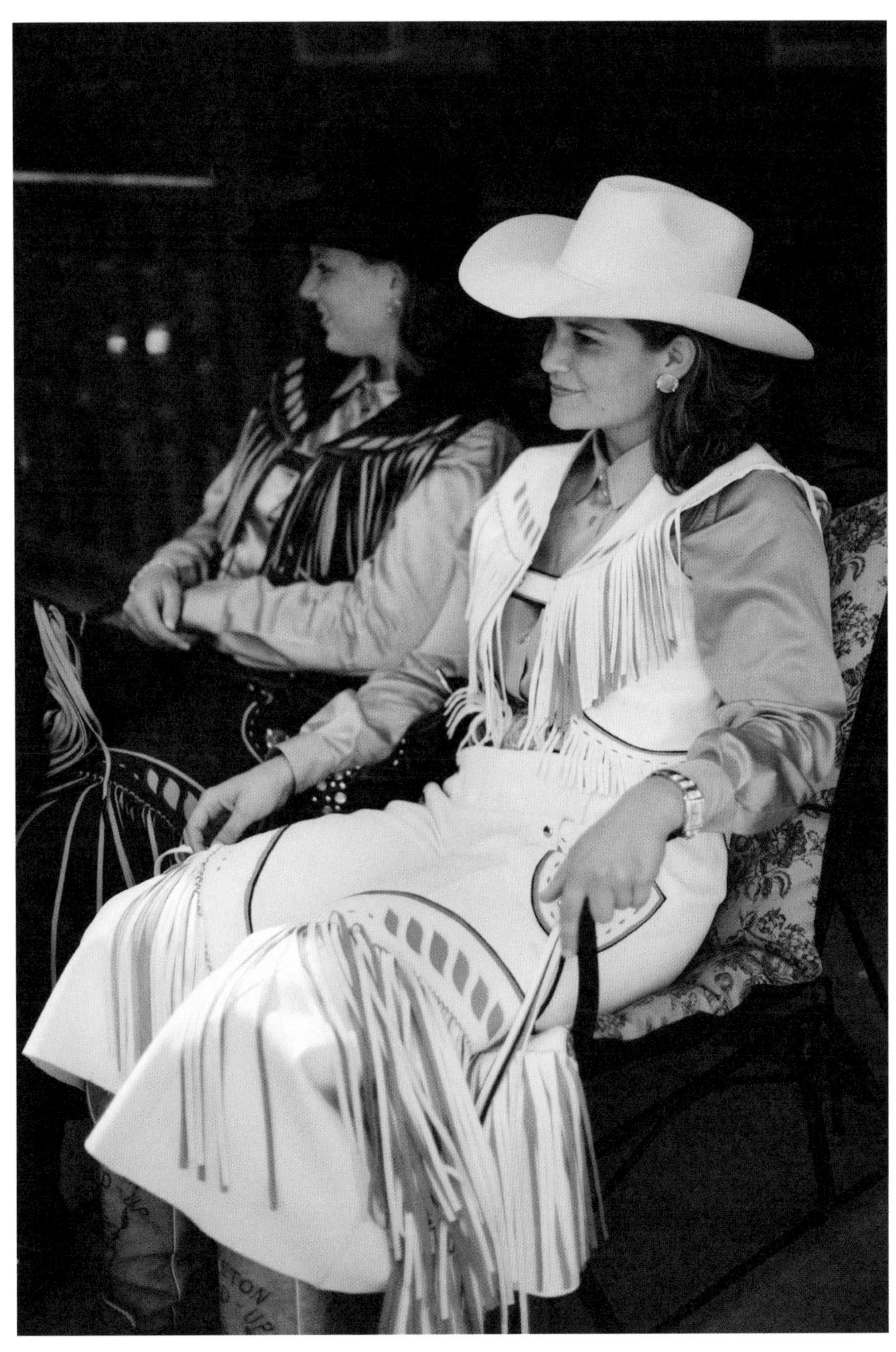

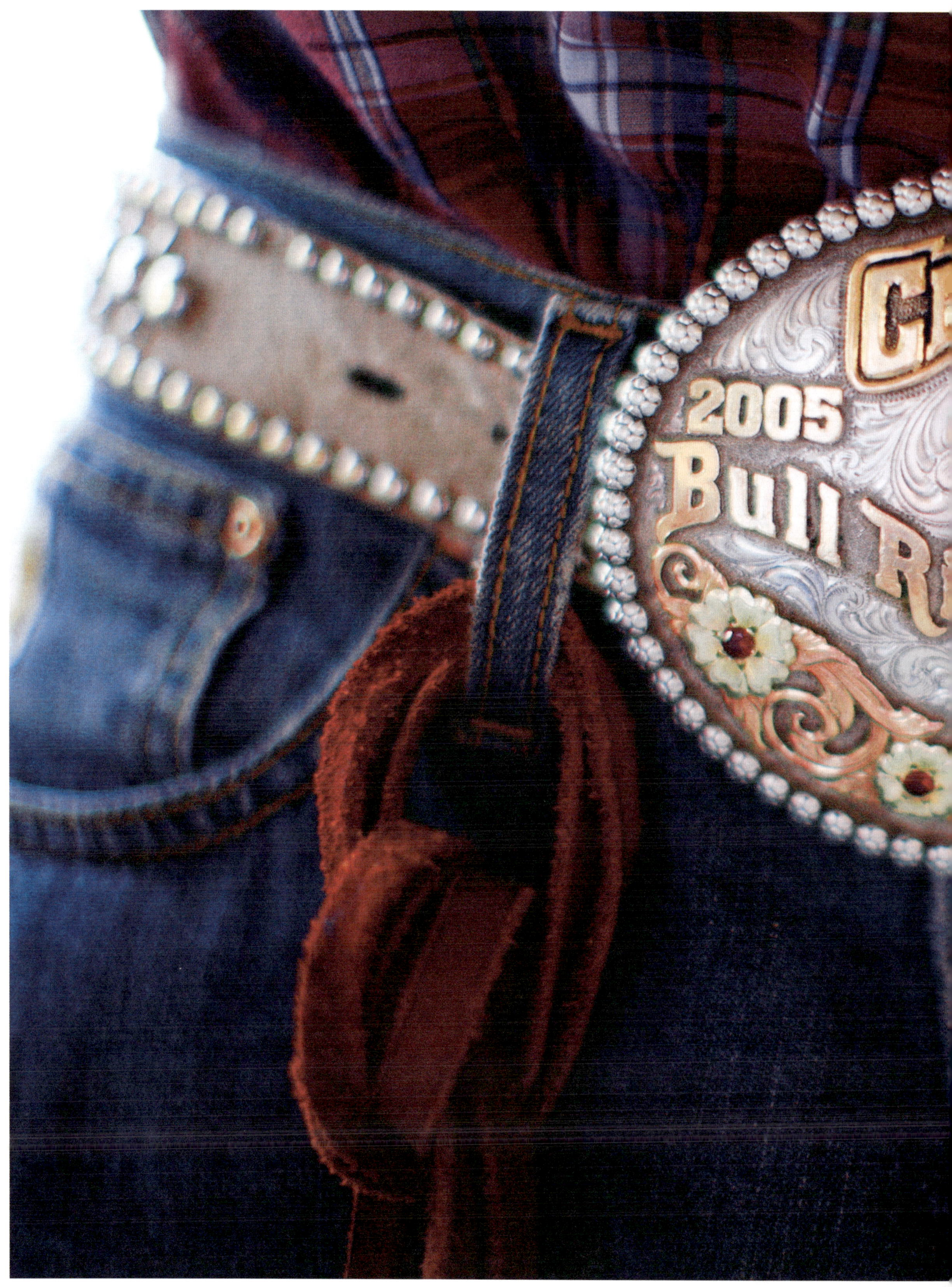
2005
Bull

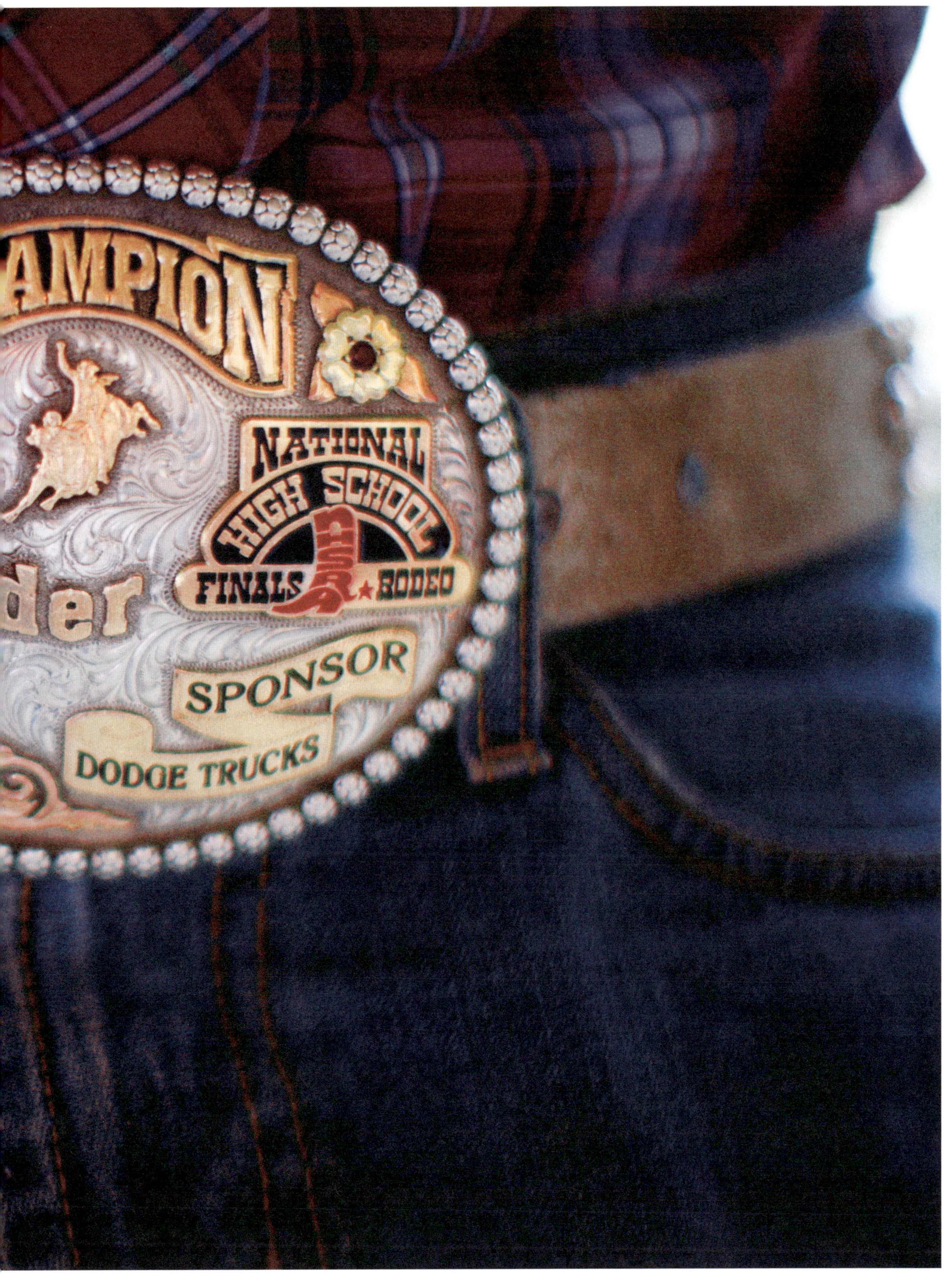
NATIONAL
HIGH SCHOOL
FINALS
RODEO
SPONSOR
DODGE TRUCKS

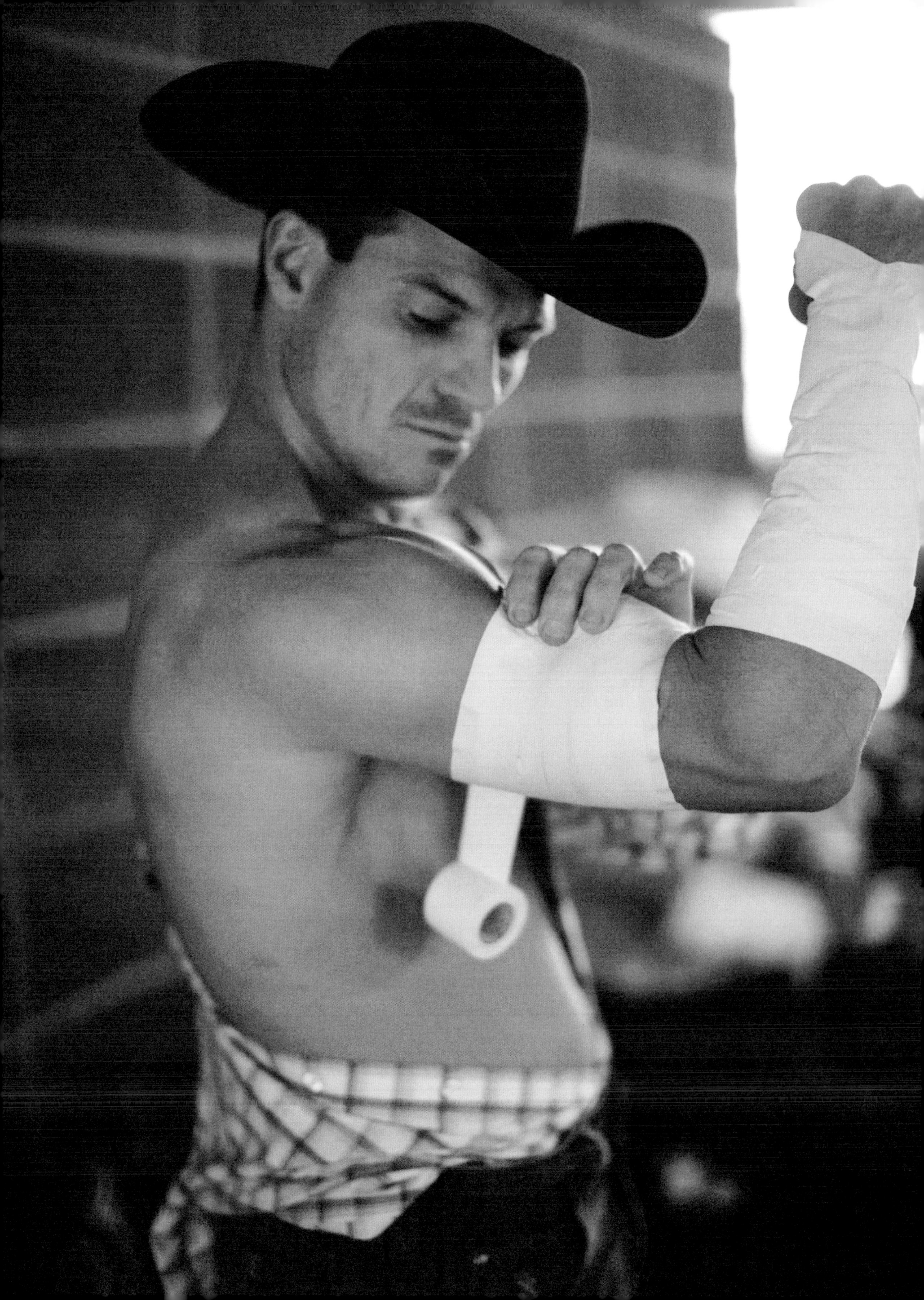

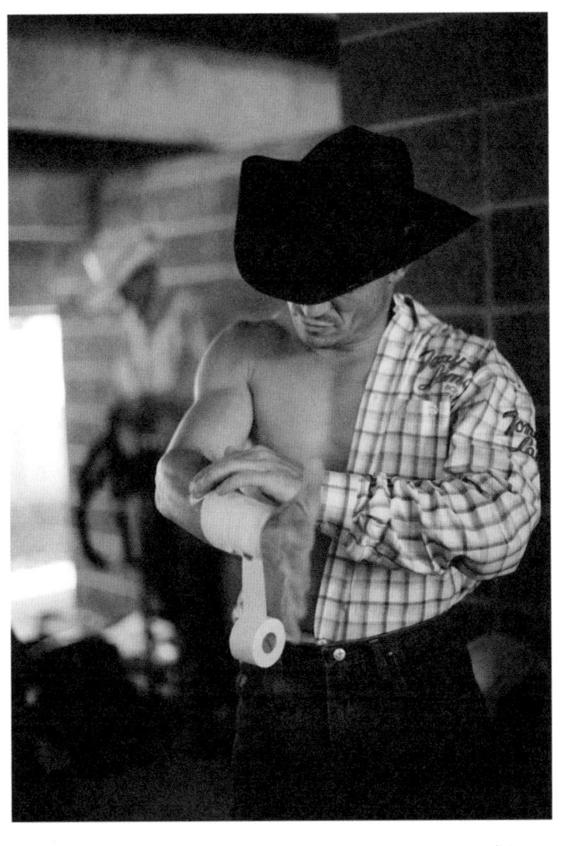

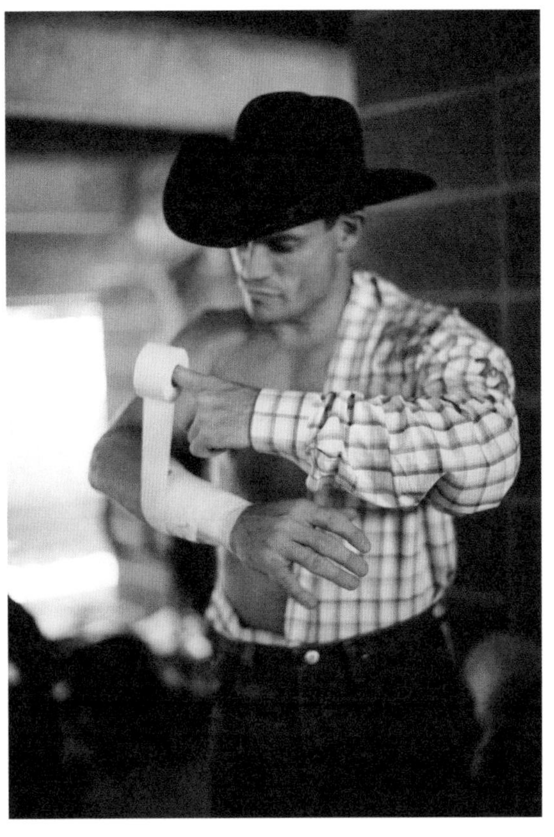

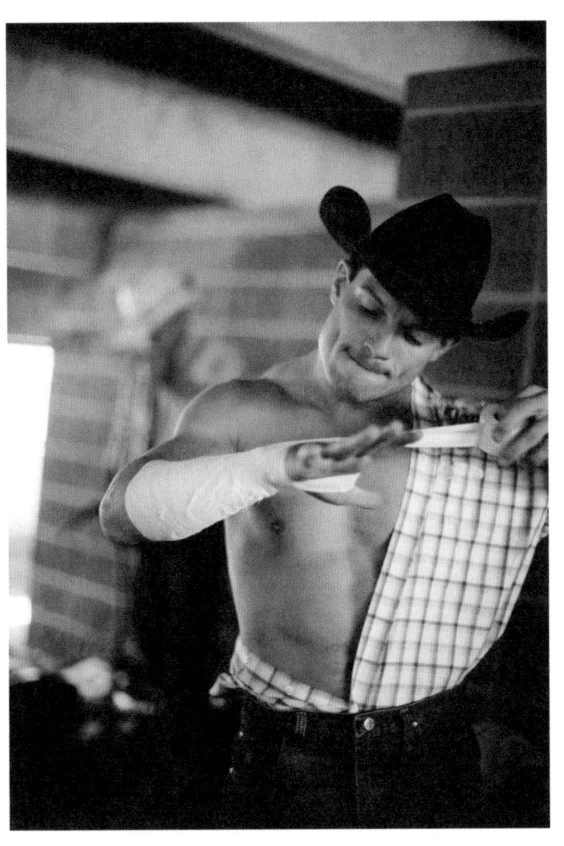

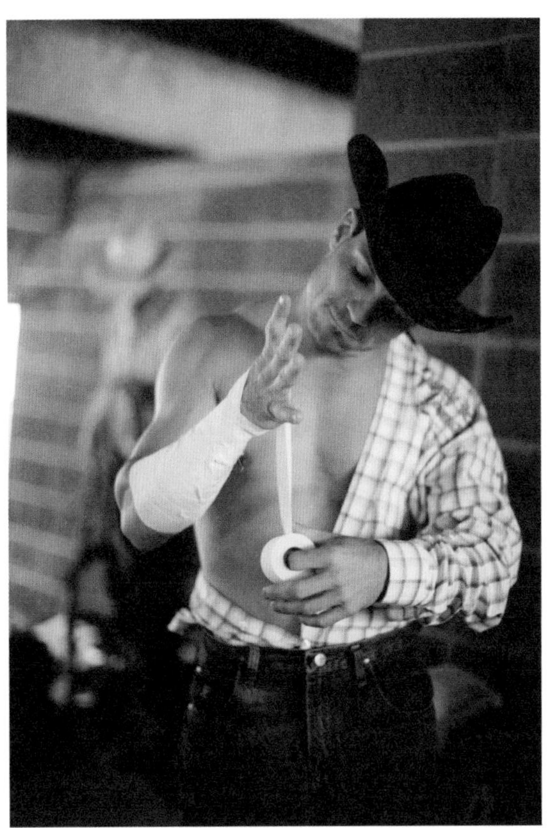

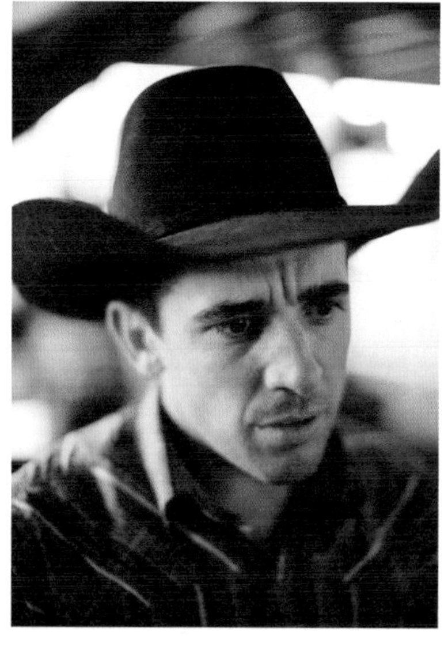
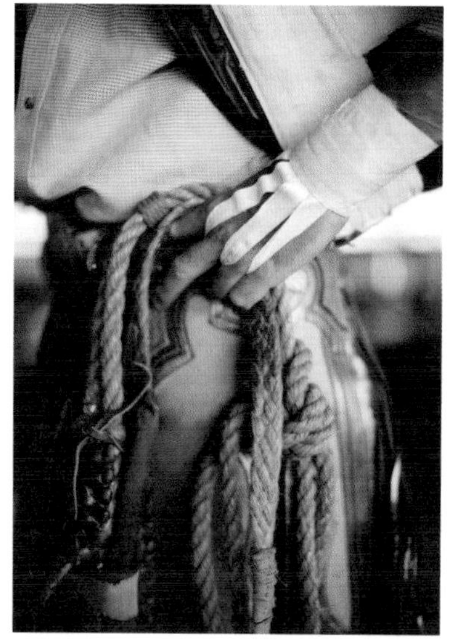
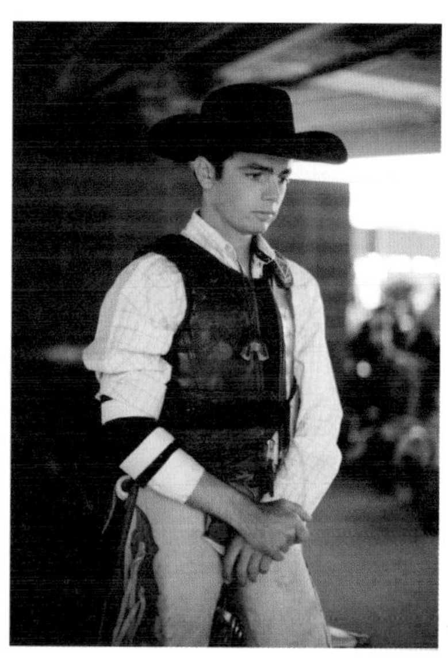
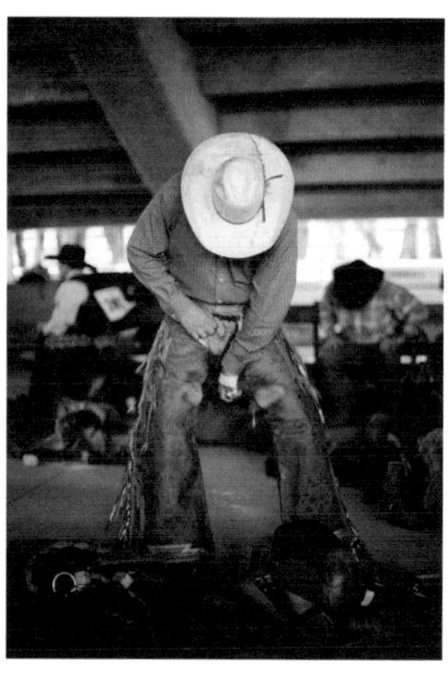
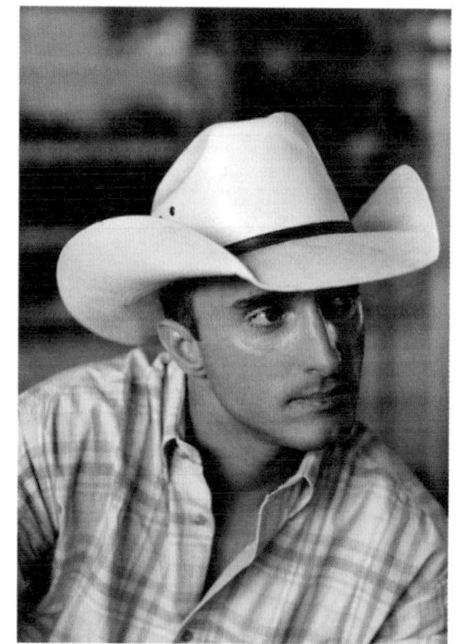
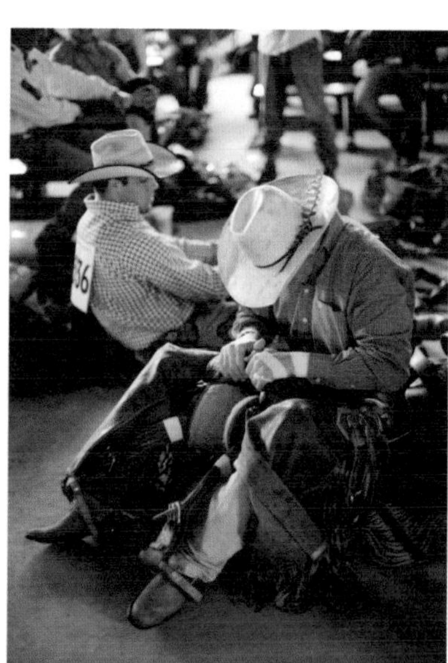

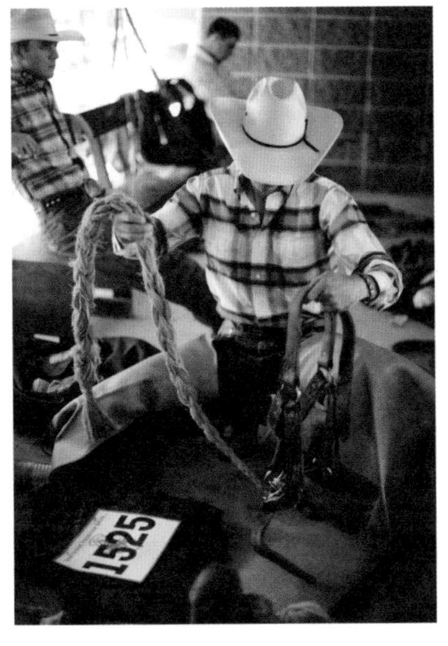
1525

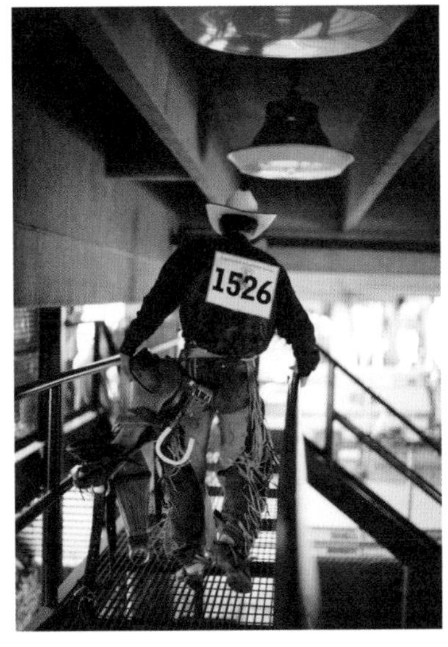
1526

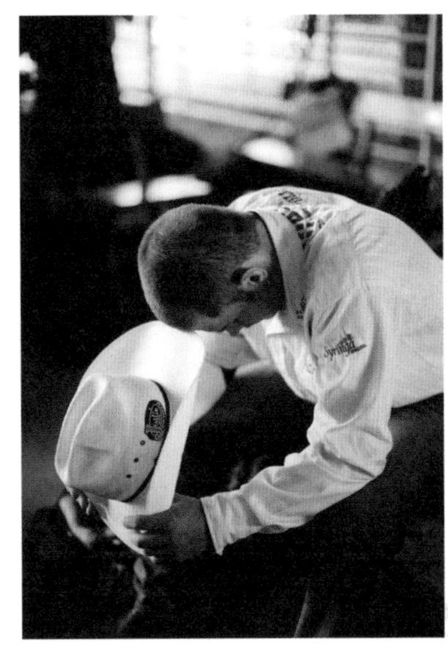

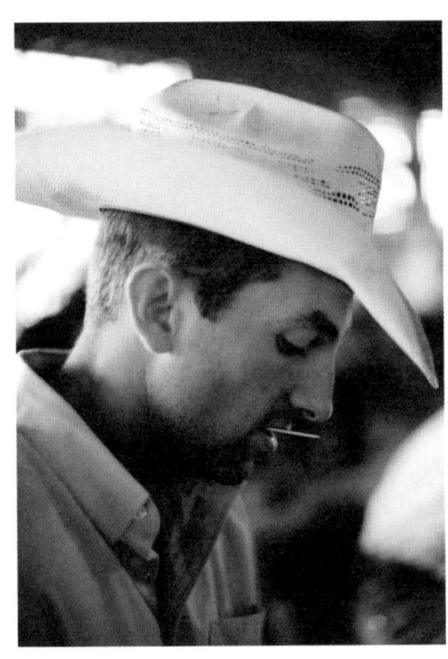

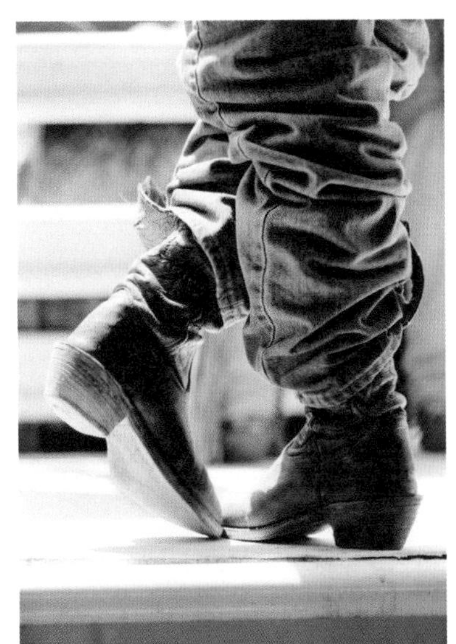

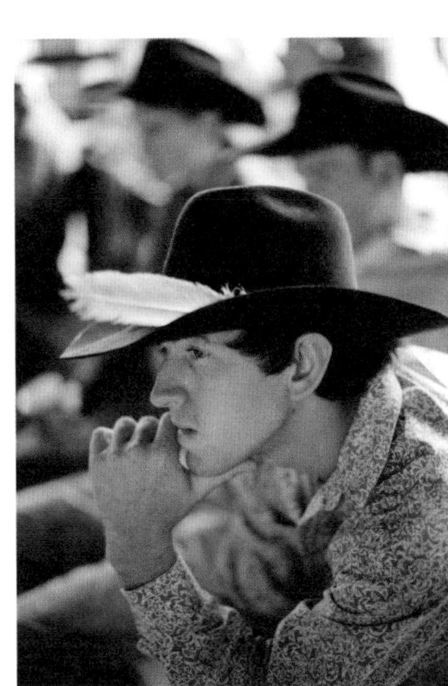

This world is defined by buckles, chaps, checkered shirts, vests, fringes, pearl buttons, battered hats, spurs, saddles, ropes – all this equipment and strong emotions have to be finely adjusted.

This is all adrenaline, beads of sweat, horses with rolling eyes and their hooves trying to climb the walls of the chute. This is dogged filing at saddle frames, this is stretching, snuff chewing, darkening eyes, concentration; profiles getting sharpened, straps tightened. These guys ride that very mythology, straight through American history. When they get thrown off, it really hurts.

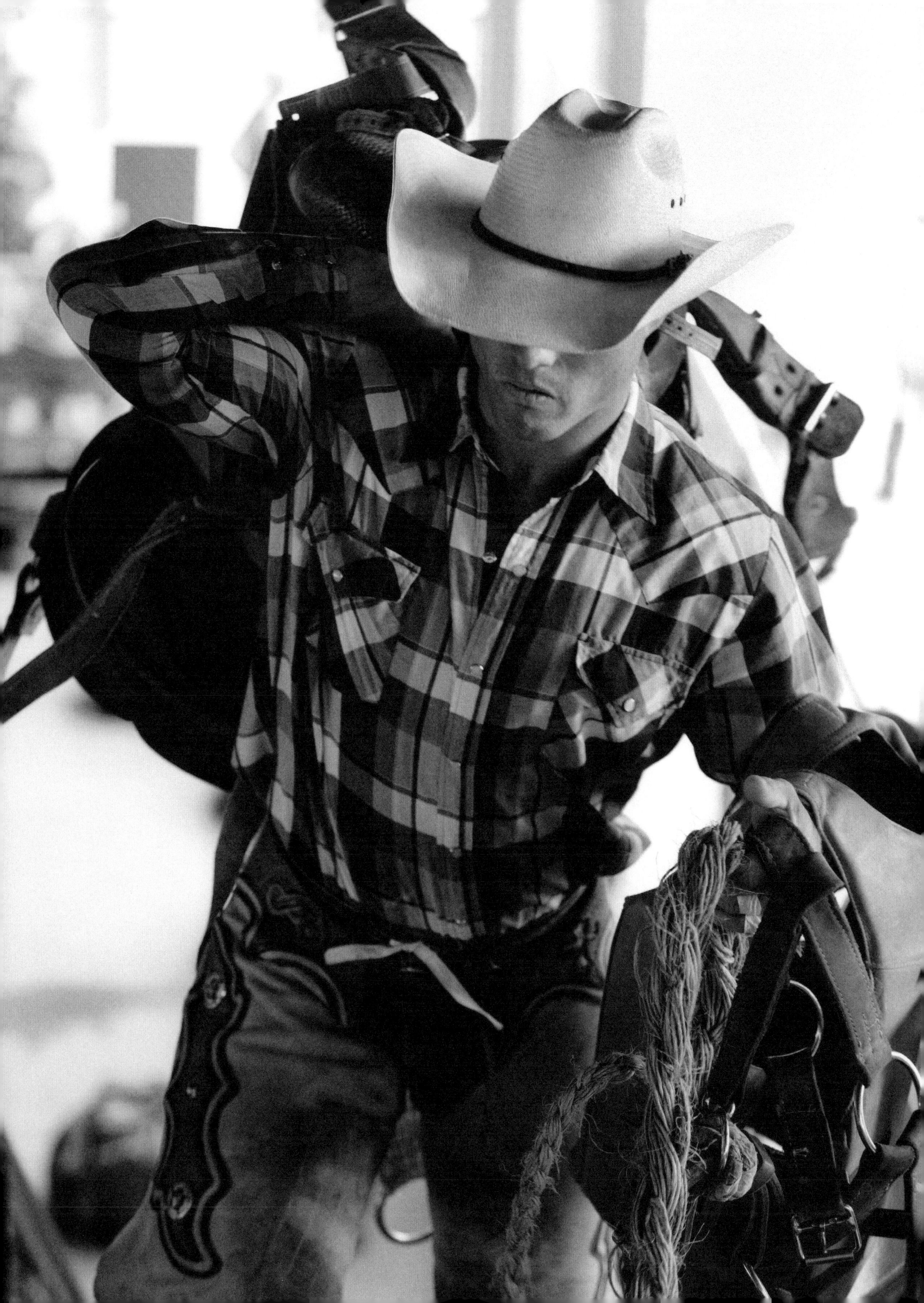

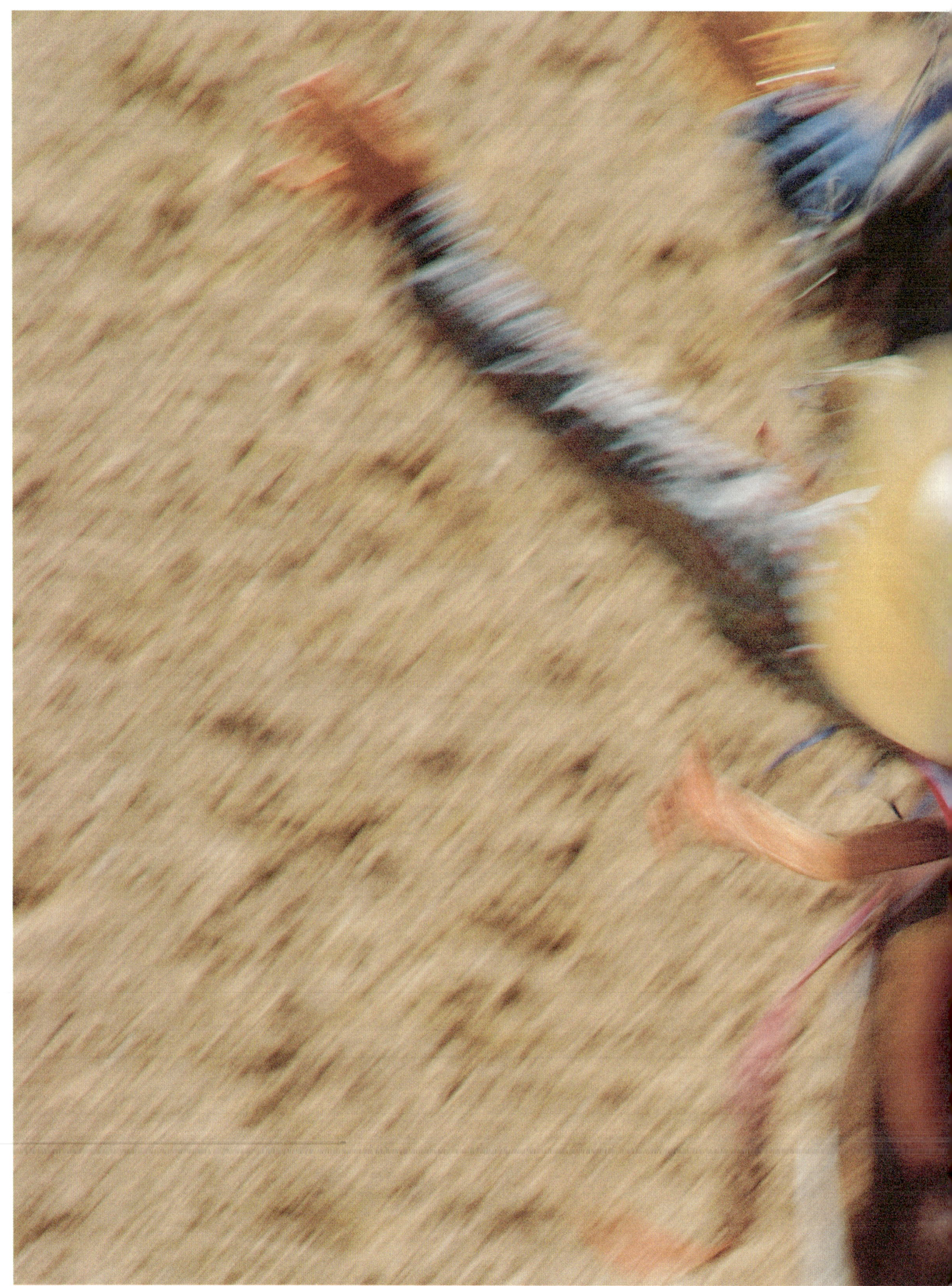

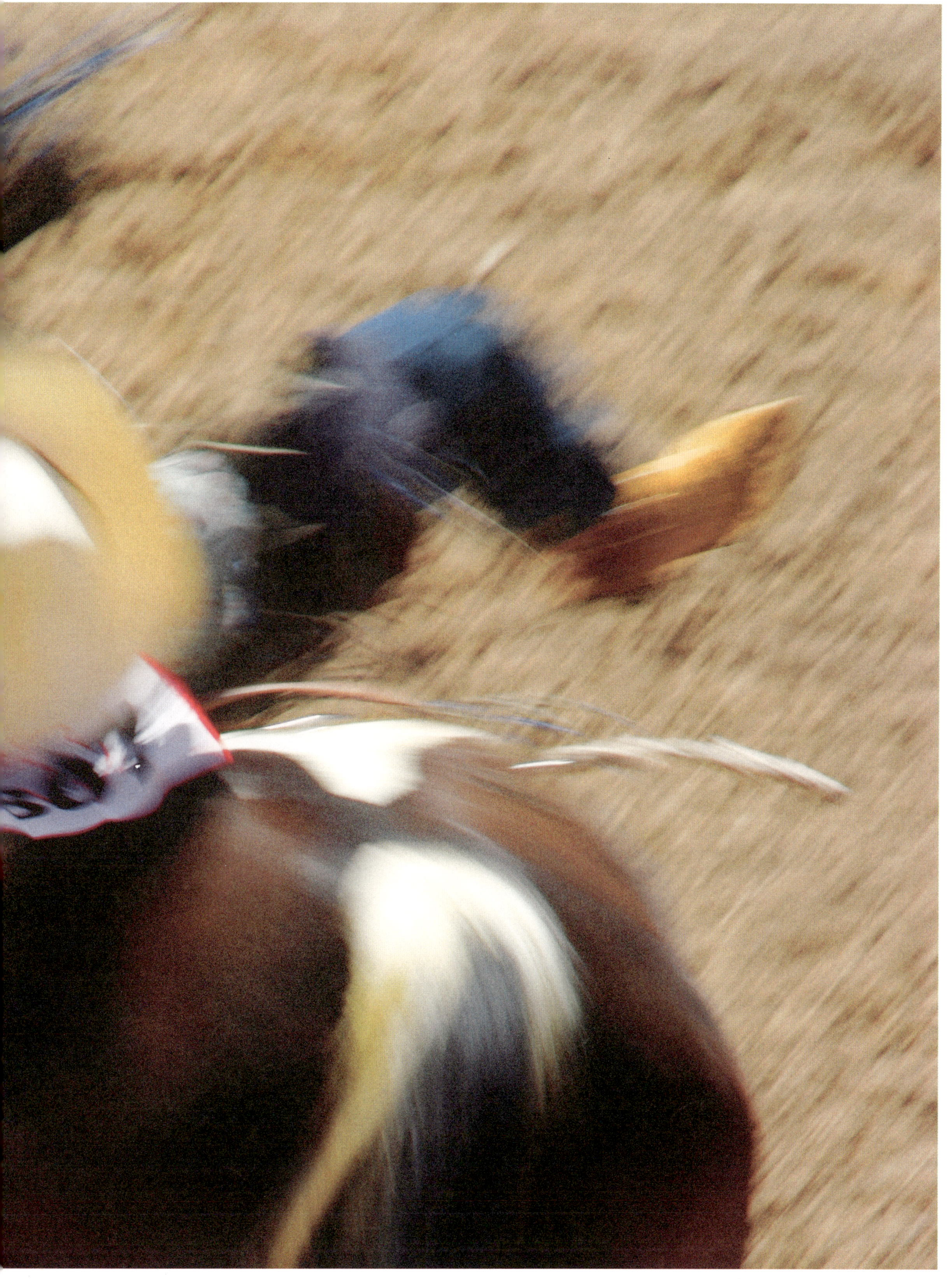

ON A MONUMENT VALLEY EVENING, BEFORE DISAPPEARING ALTOGETHER, THE SINKING SUN WILL TRANSFORM THE FAMOUS SANDSTONE SCULPTURES, BLIND THEM, COLOR THEM INTENSELY RED, WRAP THEM IN DARKISH BLUE AND FINALLY, AS THE VERY LAST RAY OF LIGHT TAPERS OFF TO A SIGH, GENTLY DRAPE THEM IN VELVET PURPLE.

That is when the wind arrives, a gusty sound from nowhere, from other mountains not visible in this desert. Moments later, a torrential rain, which seems completely out of this world, moves in. The Indians peddling turquoise and silver by the roadside hastily throw their goods into their backseats and roll up the windows. Red clay gushes over the roads. The next day, local papers report that two anglers have been washed away in a ravine ten miles to the south of here.

It was a doomsday experience, but soon the ground has once again become spider-dry with barely audible clicking sounds. The landscape in the Southwest raises existential questions; no one can spend a night here without incorporating the expanses and the wonders of space into her mindset.

Nora Naranjo-Morse's garden in Española exhibits a fluttering variety of hummingbirds. Crickets eat most of what is left on the ground. She has carefully placed the dirt and clay from her backyard in specially made wrappings and shipped them off to Washington, D.C. by plane. The material is dry, cracked, and full of historical memory. At first, the authorities seemed alarmed. What was she doing? Mailing poison? Spreading anthrax? They soon learned that these were ingredients for her tepee sculptures in front of the National Museum of the American Indian.

As an artist from a remote pueblo in New Mexico, Naranjo-Morse literally digs out her past. But who can tell what is authentic? When she was a young girl, groups of tourists were taken through her native village of Santa Clara and the guide would give advice to the local potters on which patterns had the most commercial appeal.

"Through the commodification of culture, this beads and feathers exploitation, you are rewarded for upholding certain notions about tradition. Native culture has become such an exotic phenomenon and it's all tied into the mystique of the West. I see that also with a lot of native institutions, where there is a very specific idea about what native should be and how that should be articulated to the world."

Uphill in Acoma, an extremely rural kind of skyscraper community where you can see for miles and the elevation provides an almost psychedelic kind of weightlessness, life goes on with America in the far distance, as if on another planet. The clay fronts and adobe walls and the nuances of the ground tend to blend and merge. Where the sun hits the flatland, its rays flow like orange juice. Palisades and sculptured figures of cracked rock reflect the light. Black birds rest on the gusts from the hollow land below where the conquistadors once appeared out of nowhere, like shimmering creatures, man and horse appearing as one body. The beauty of the landscape is singular, crumbled. History looms like Spanish armor; inspiration and brutal ruin are intertwined.

The absurdities of exploitation are many in this land of sandstone mythology. The mining, the radioactive leakage from the wounds of the earth, radiation in the building materials for homes and schools on the Navajo reservation, the water being flushed through pipelines from dry mountains to feed the production of electricity in faraway cities of glitter and glamour.

Once called the uranium capital of the world, Grants by the old Route 66 has now become a mere shadow of its old proud self. The signs have withered and paled and there is tumbleweed rolling down a main road lined with deserted garages. It used to be a boomtown when it was considered a civic virtue, if not a duty, to spend a family weekend in the desert with a Geiger counter. It's an irony of fate, often observed, that this barren land, rejected by settlers and thus deemed suitable for reservation purposes, should later turn out to be so profitable.

Now the young motel receptionist from India reveals her desire to join the others who have already left. She cannot understand how anyone can feel at home without crowds and traffic jams, in a town almost devoid of people.

Throughout history, human expectations have been a strong driving force; they transform societies, but may also exceed the limitations of nature's durability.

"With our consumerist culture we inhabit a dehumanized society," says Muskogee-born poet and musician Joy Harjo. "Along the way we lose respect for ourselves and the growing and living things that have been with us since the very beginning. We're losing the poetry."

Harjo lives in Albuquerque, in the midday heat of New Mexico. Since we met for the first time ten years ago she has tattooed her hands and arms in what could be interpreted as a physical reaffirmation of a certain way of seeing. Poetry is not an Indian thing; its emotional sign language is for all lost souls and for anyone born out of her or his time.

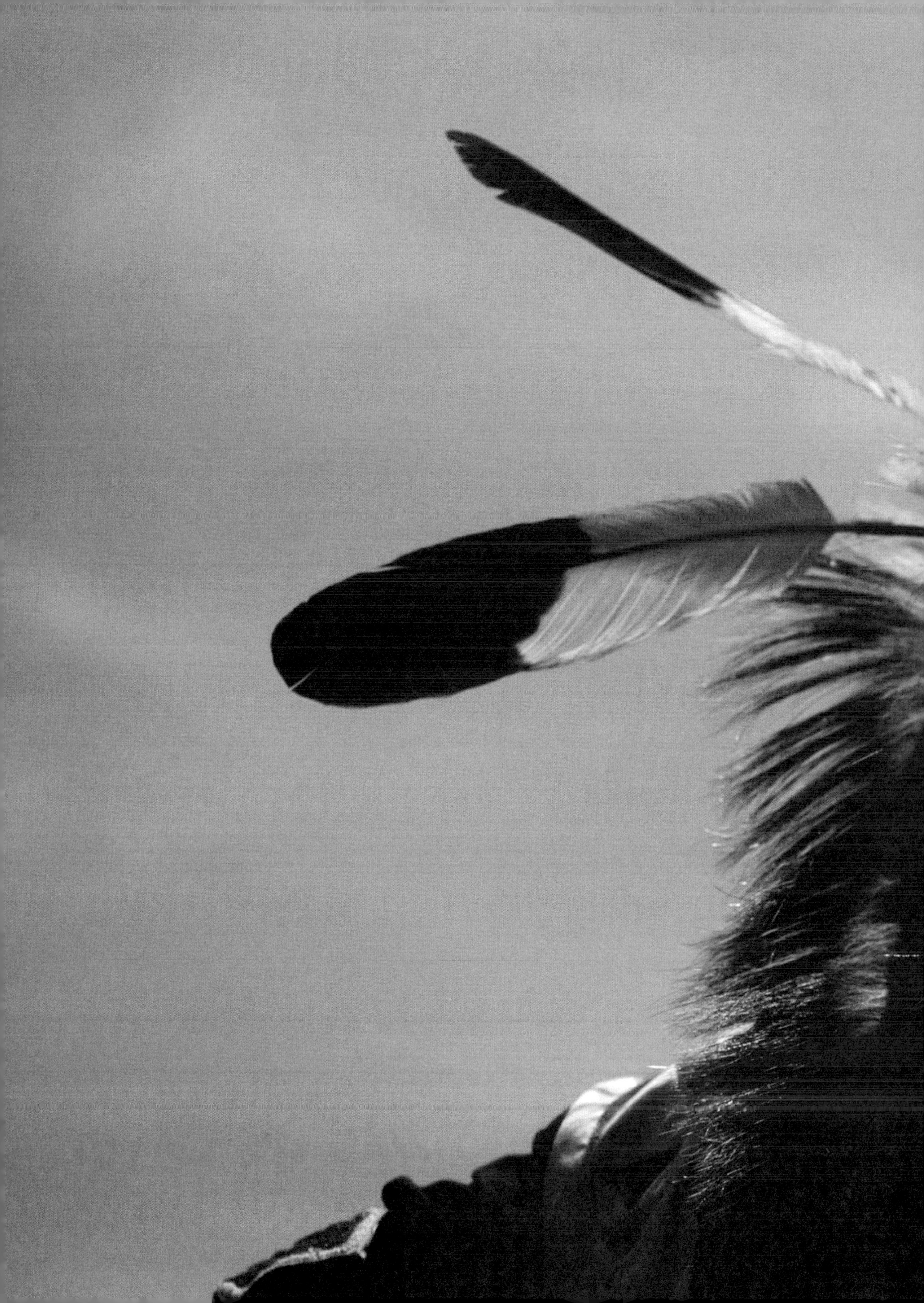

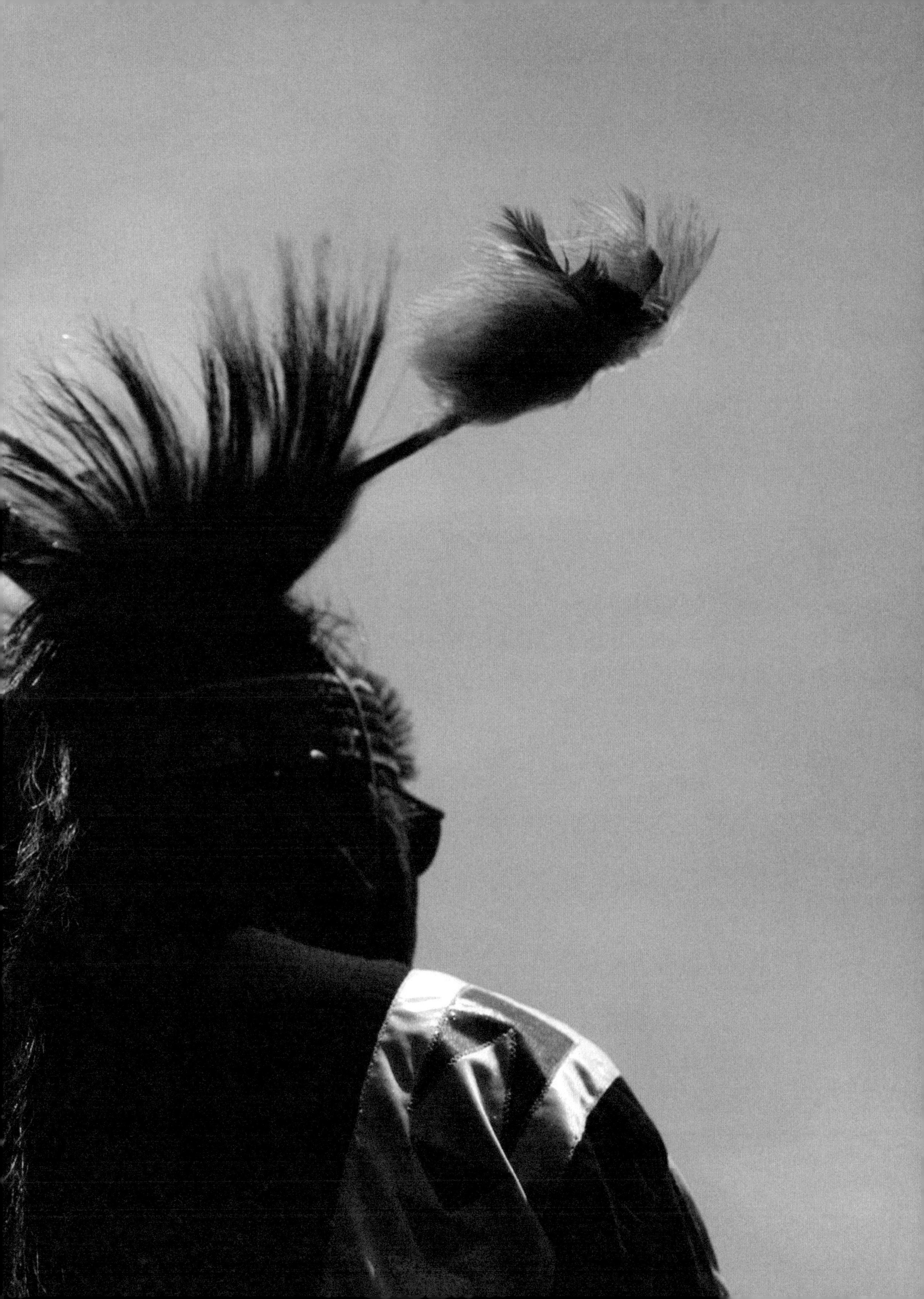

THE MIGHTIEST SONGS CAN MAKE ANYTHING HAPPEN. THEY EMANATE FROM THE EARLY DAYS OF CREATION AND ARE SO VERY ANCIENT THAT NOBODY KNOWS THE LANGUAGE. THEY HAVE NEVER CHANGED. DRUMS WILL THUNDER FOR DAYS IN THE UNDERGROUND; OUT OF SIGHT, SOMEHOW OUT OF THIS WORLD.

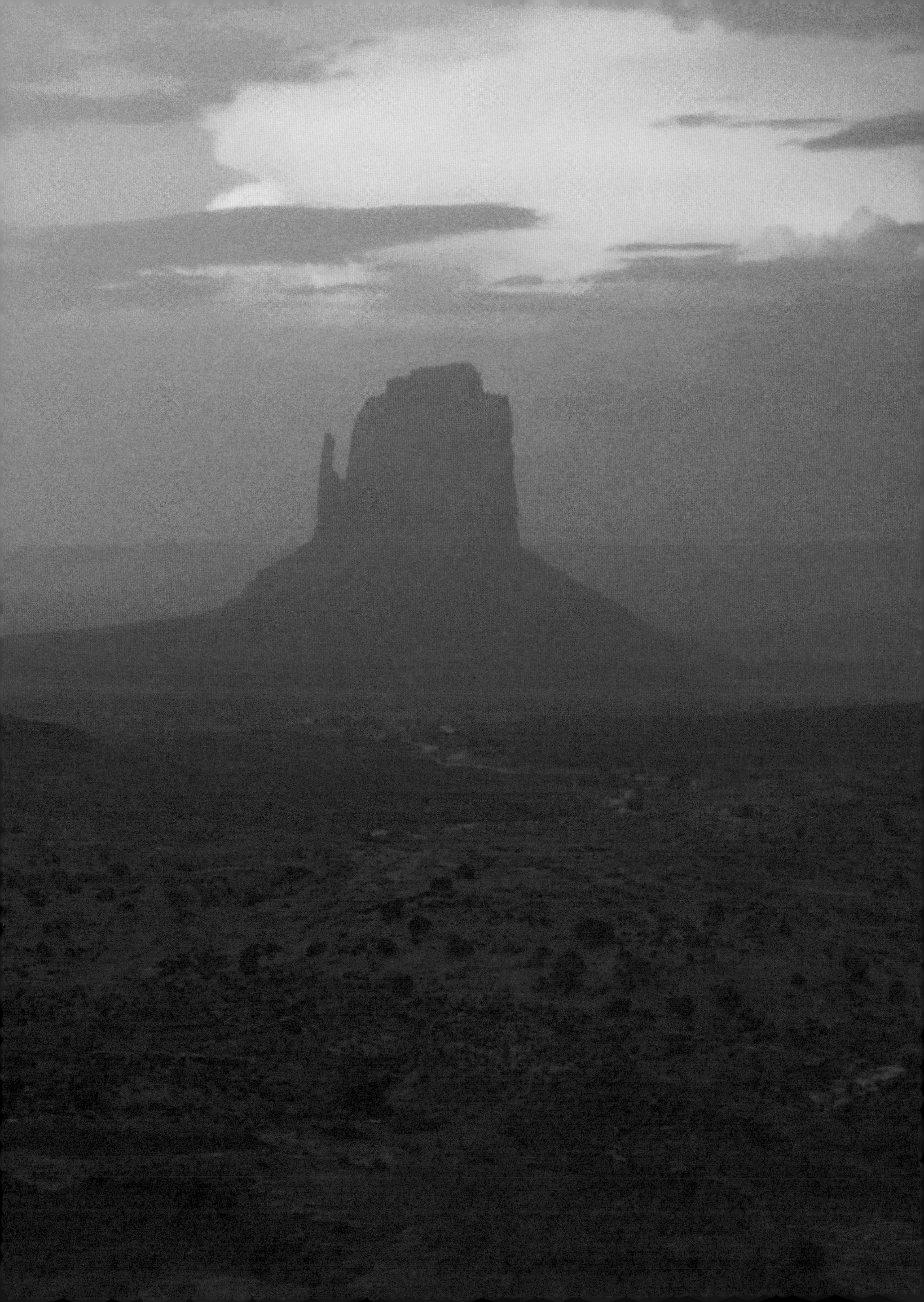

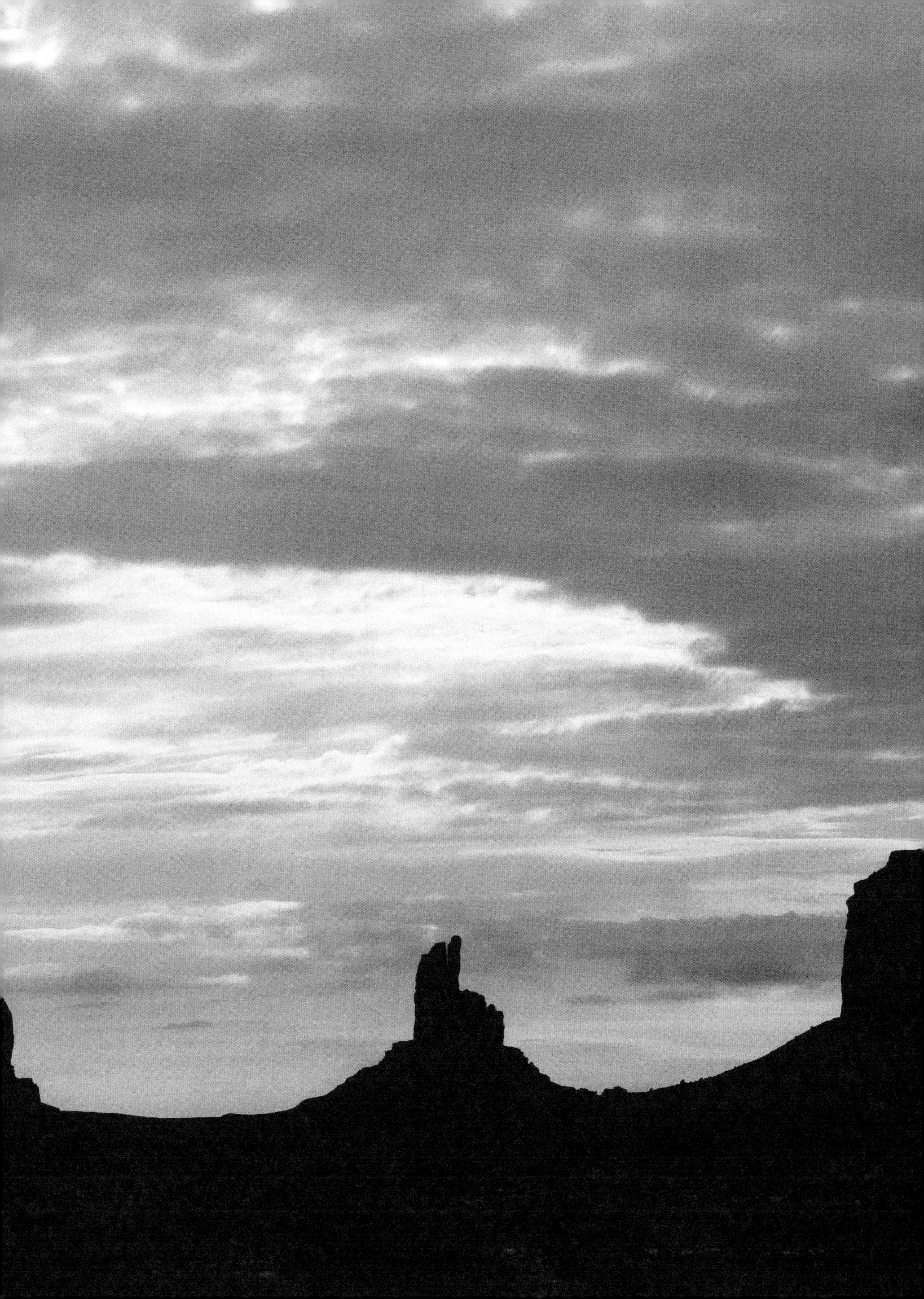

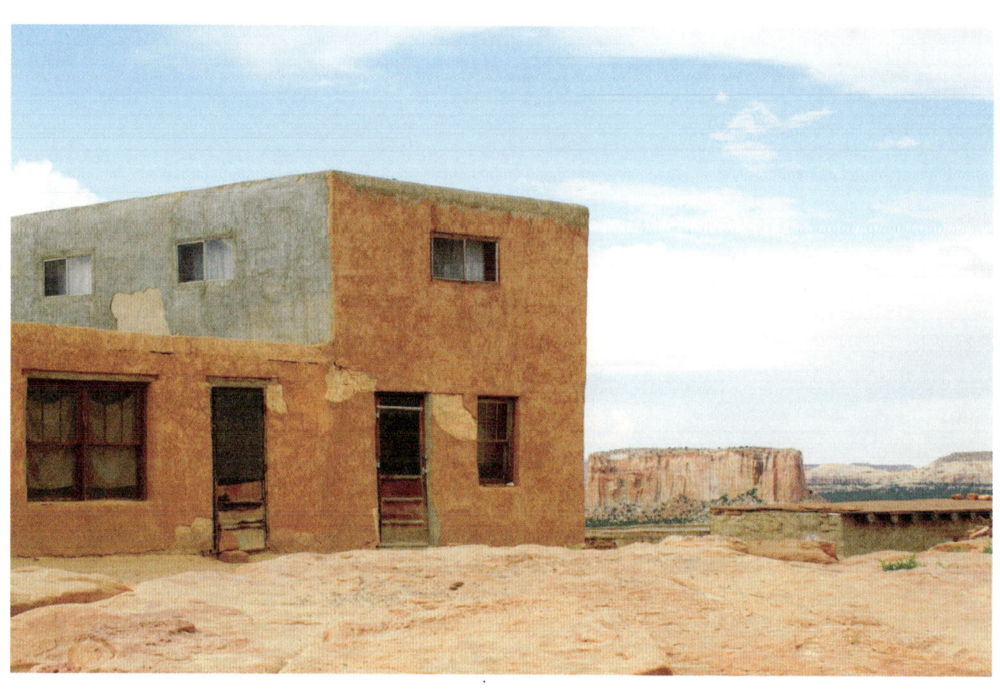

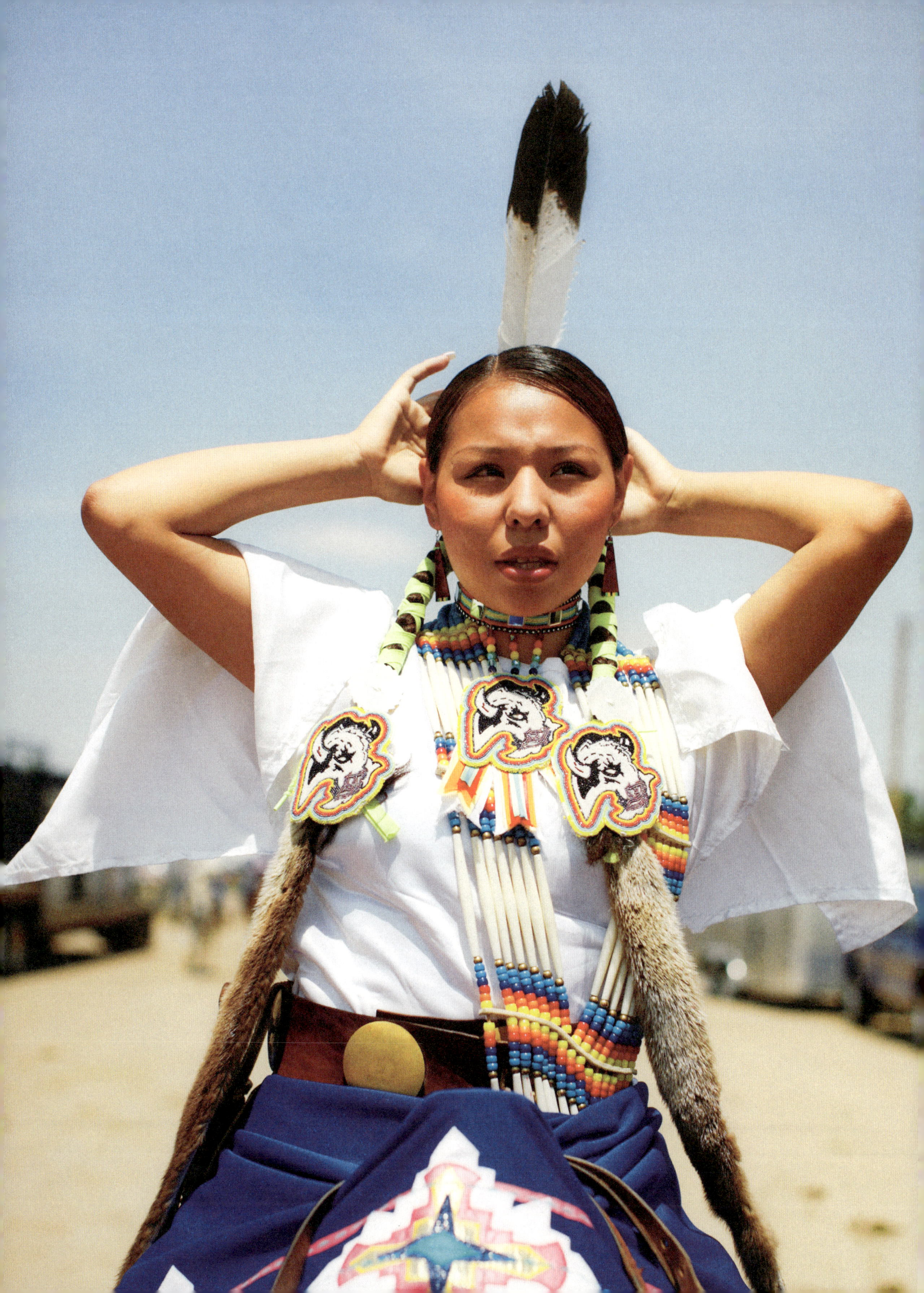

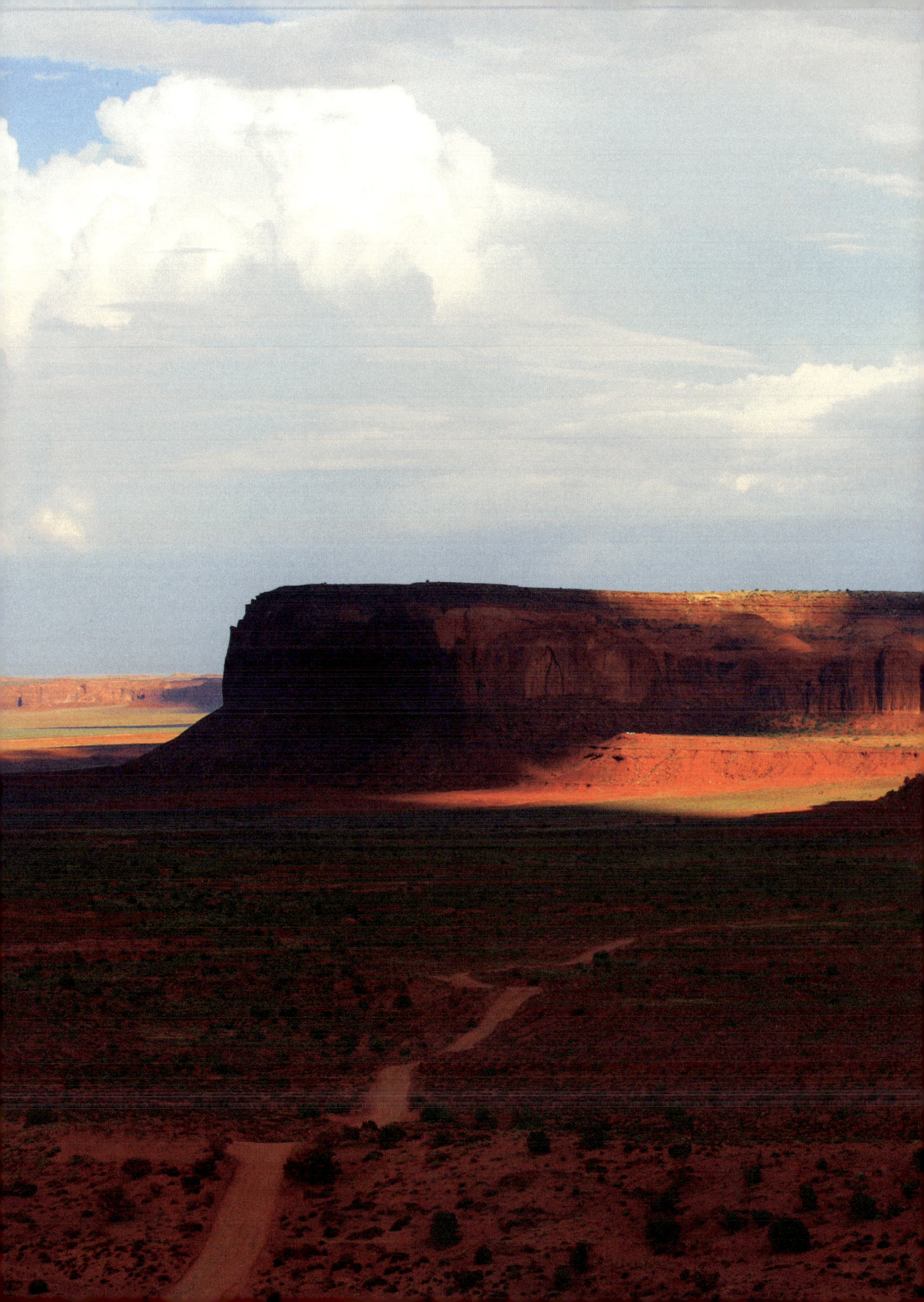

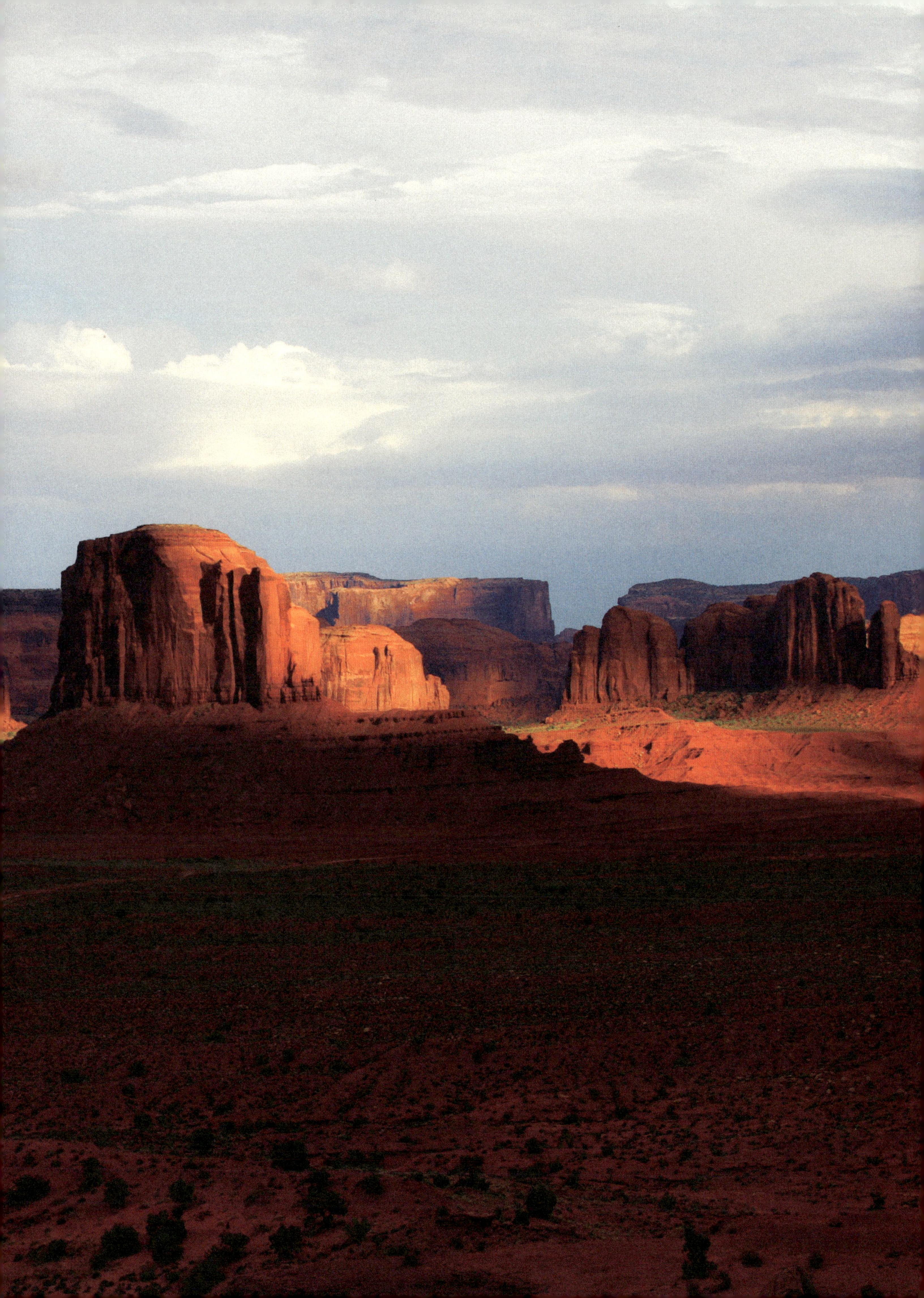

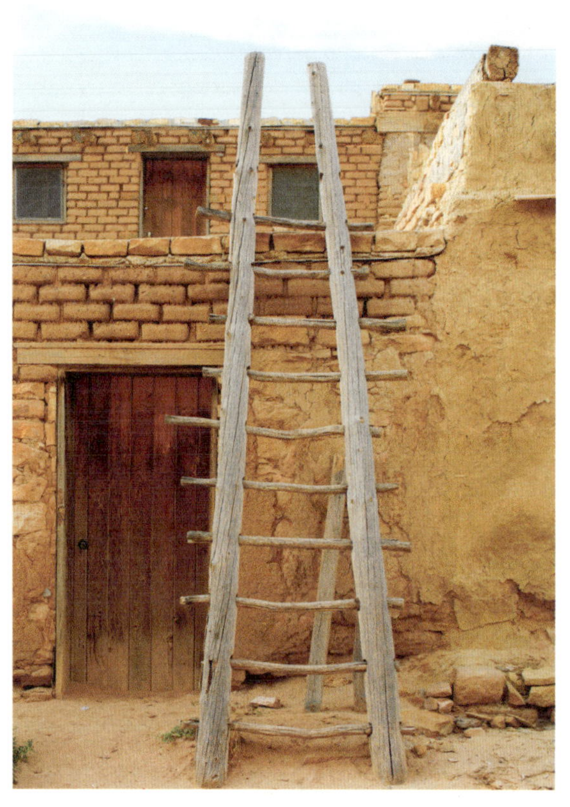

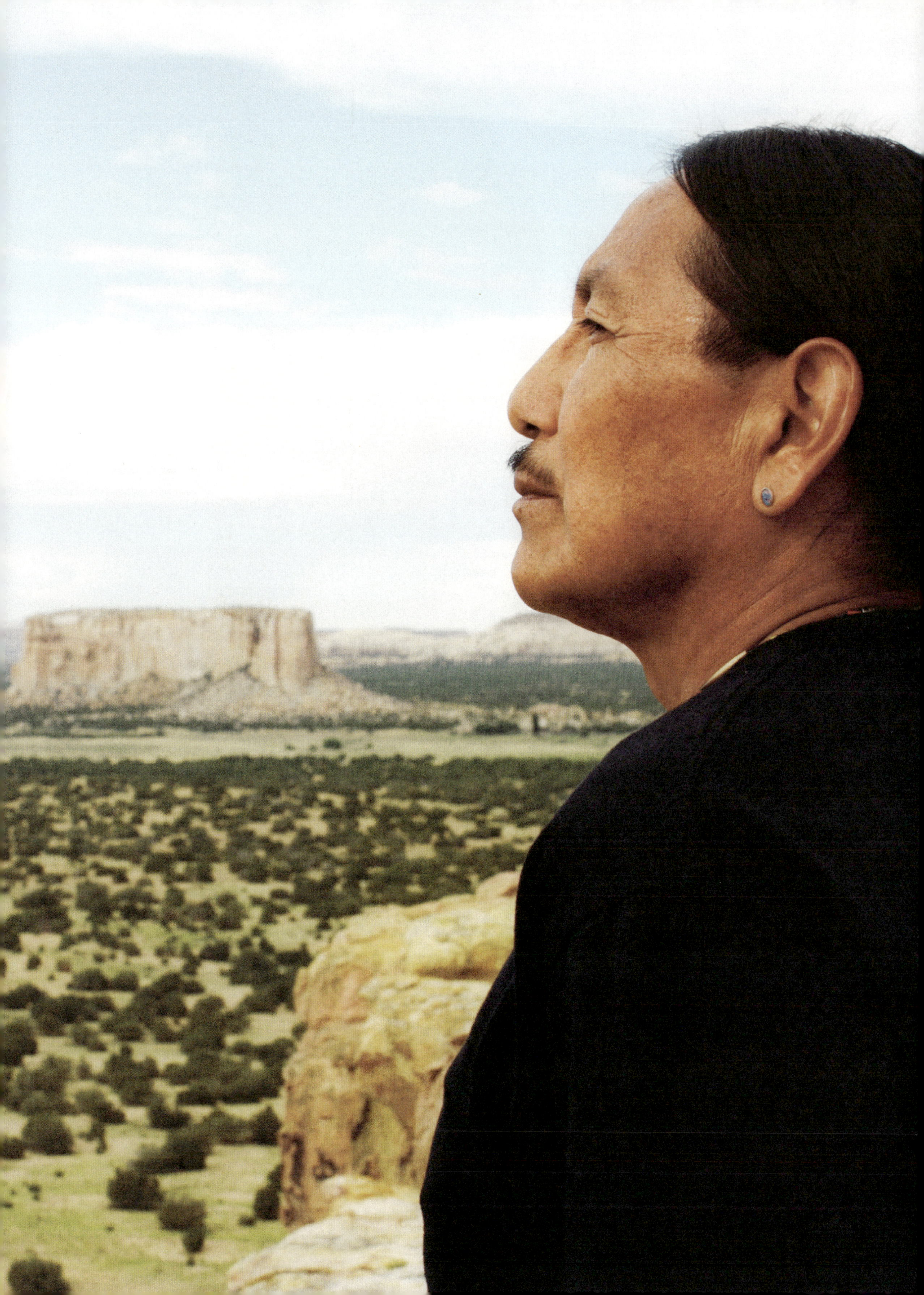

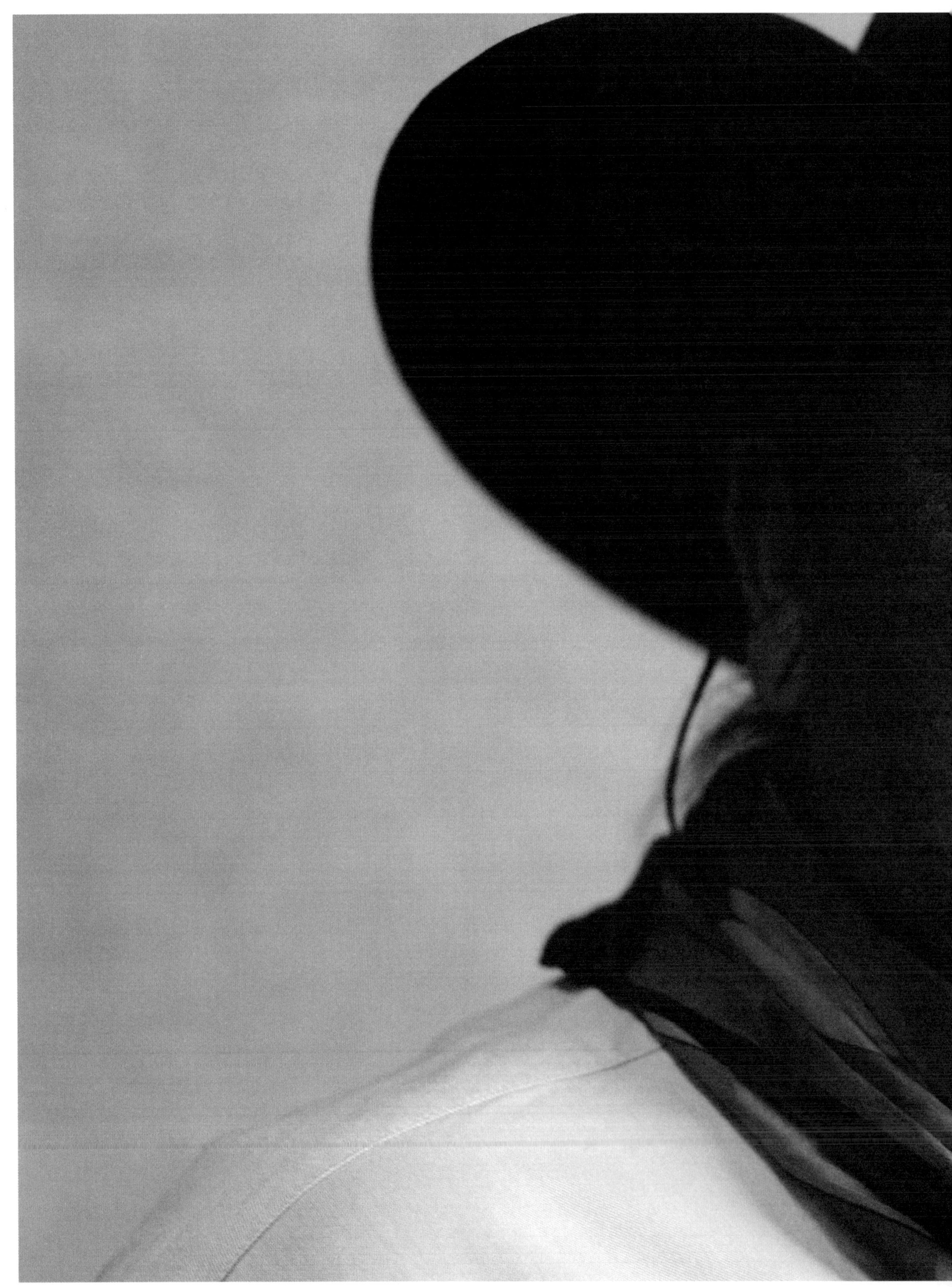

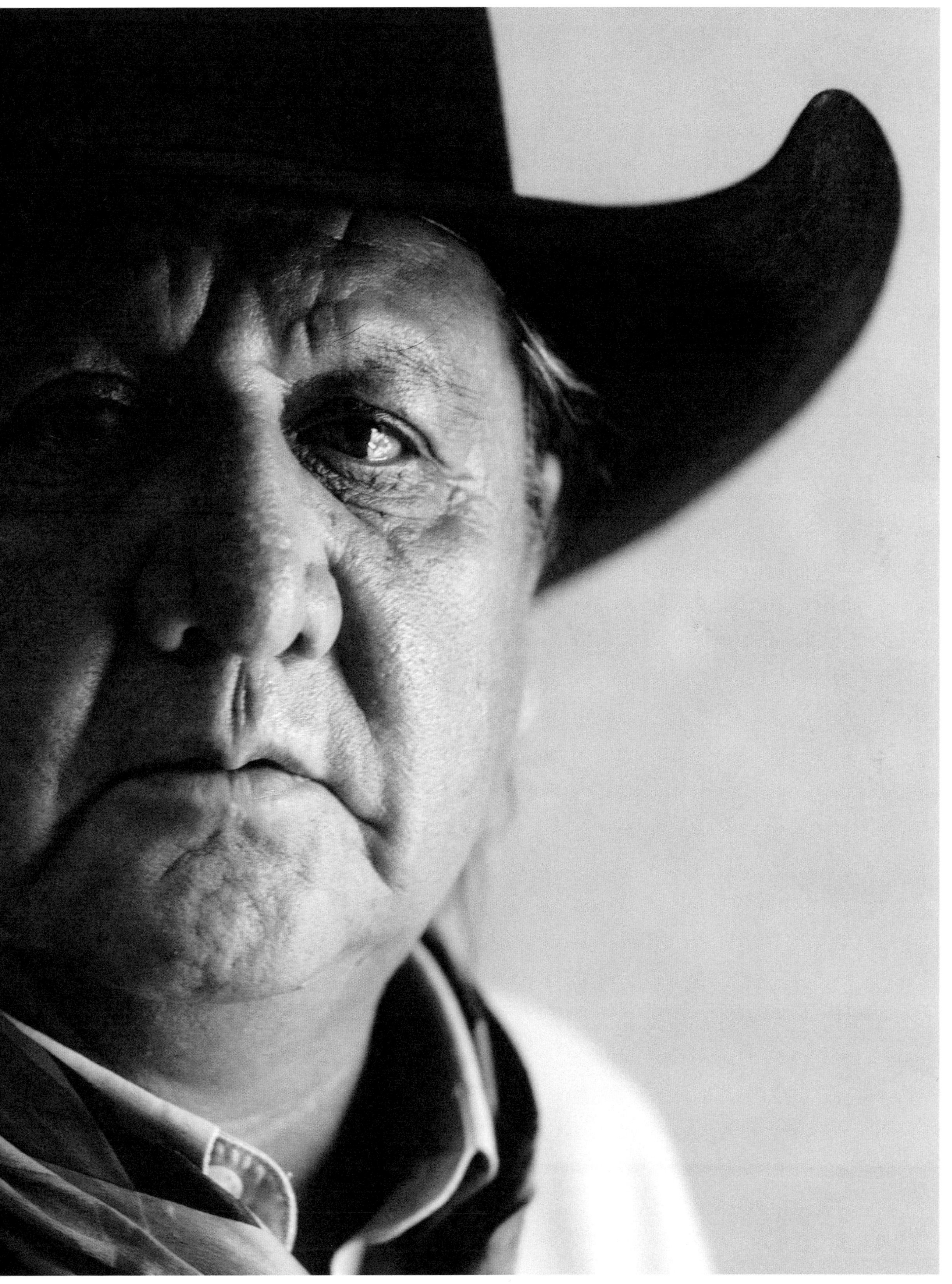

SOUND TRAVELS DIFFERENTLY. THE CONCEPT OF SPACE IS NOT THE SAME, AND NEITHER IS THE CHRONOLOGY; THE WATER SQUEEZED THROUGH THE SAND HAS BEEN TRAVELING FOR SO LONG THAT IT IS MEANINGLESS TO COUNT THE CENTURIES.

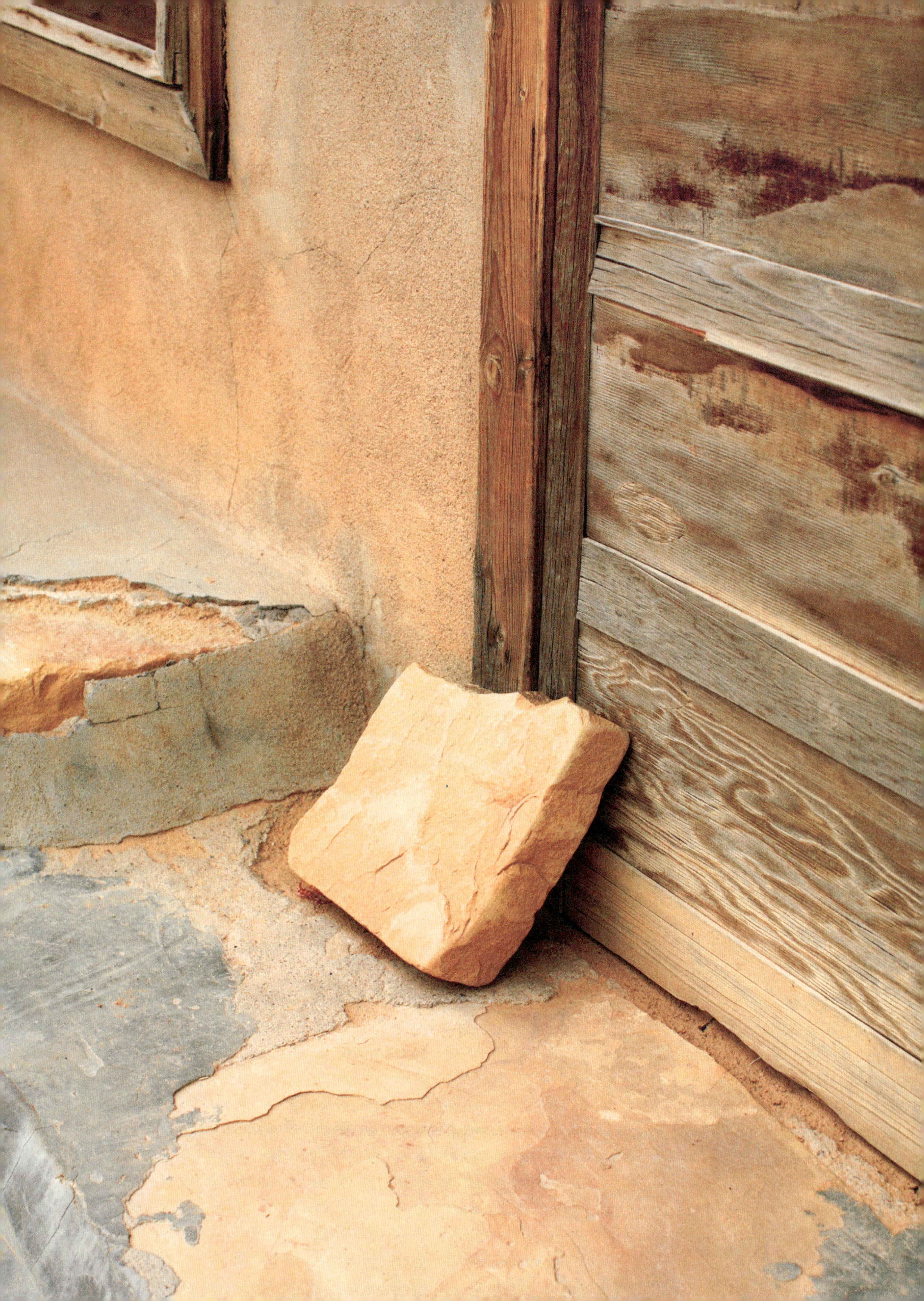

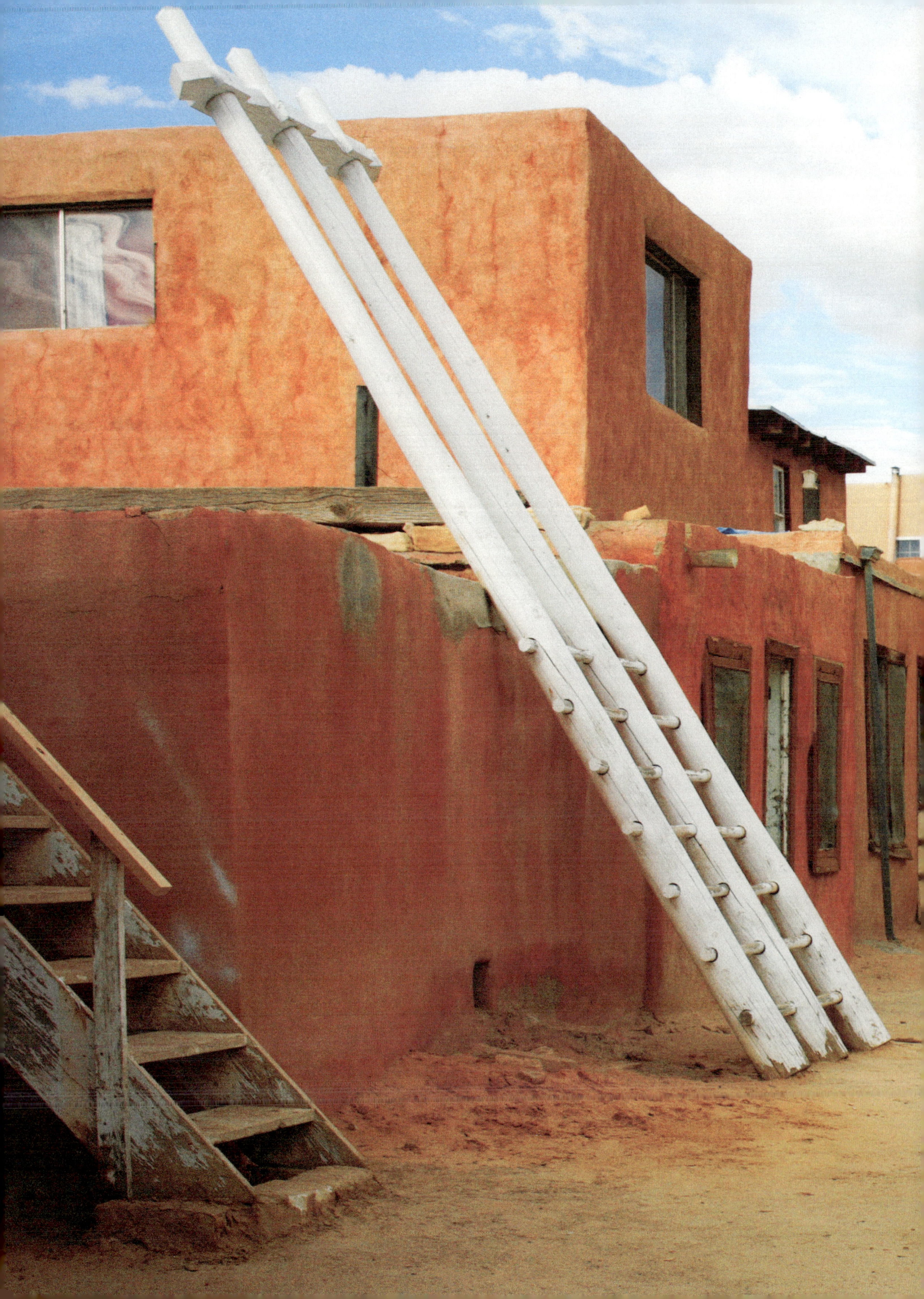

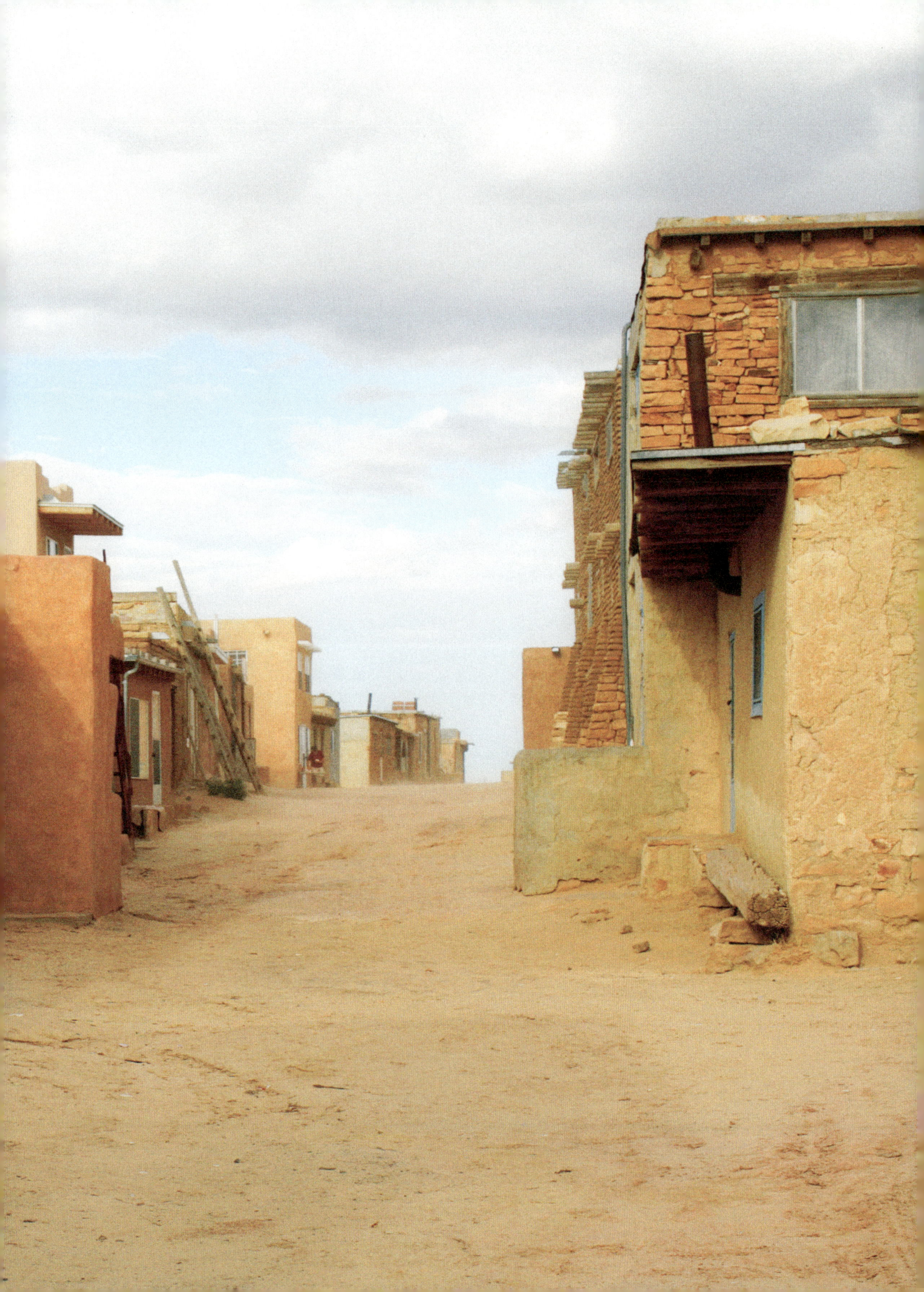

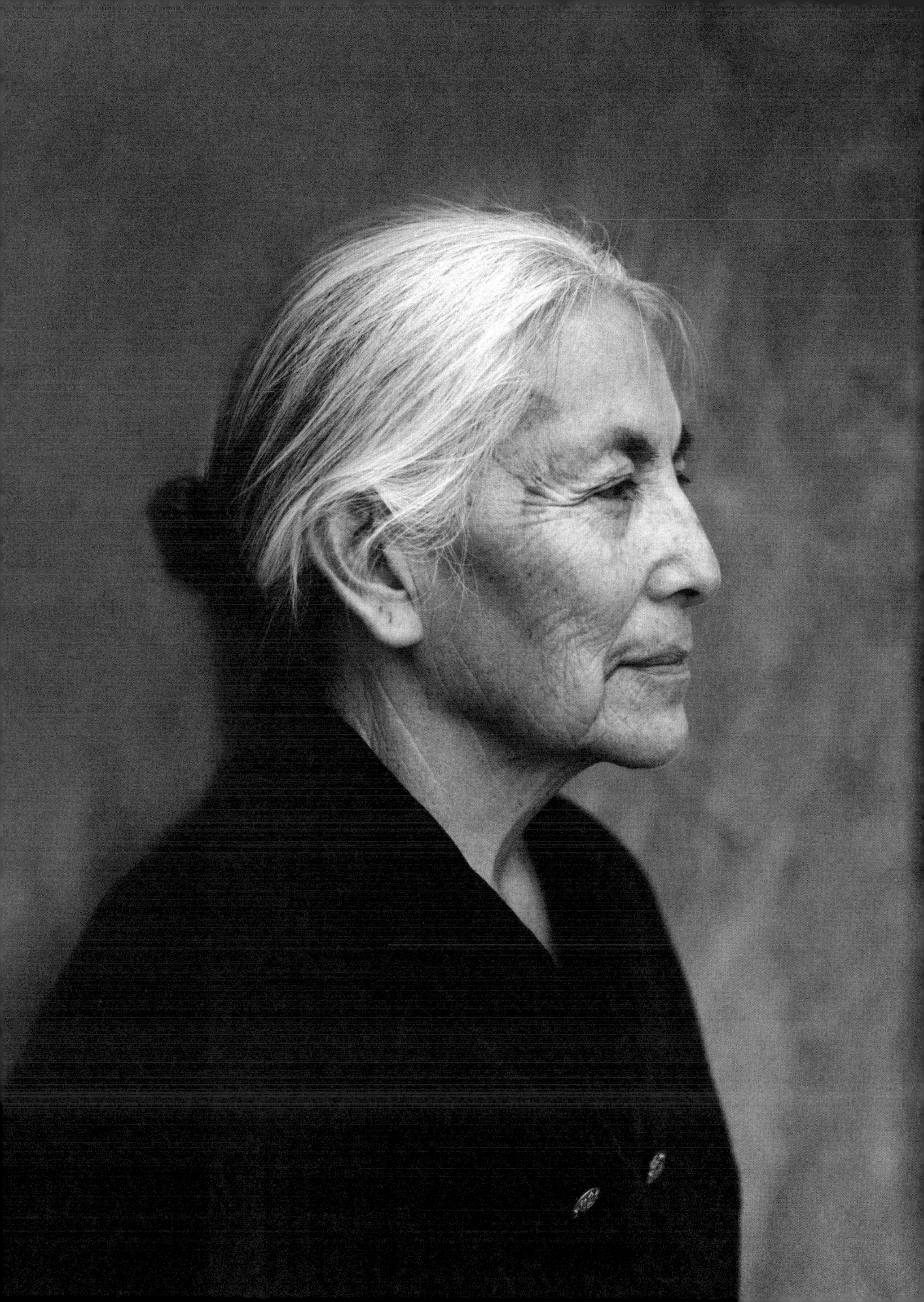

She drives an impressive, family-sized pickup truck. Her windows are open to the desert moon and she takes long walks every morning before sunrise just to get on the right track. She belongs to a local group that hopes to revitalize the Tewa language. The kids watch too much TV, she says, and thus they're losing the words.

As a child she would read by the light from a kerosene lamp. Now there are four casinos within a 22-mile radius with enough bulbs to light up the moon. Neighboring San Juan Pueblo has reclaimed its old name, Oke Oweenge, but also had a gaming-palace bestowed upon it; the Ohkay Casino, a quasi-Indian spelling, suggests that it's all right to gamble while tribal members with a sense of place and history consider it a disgrace.

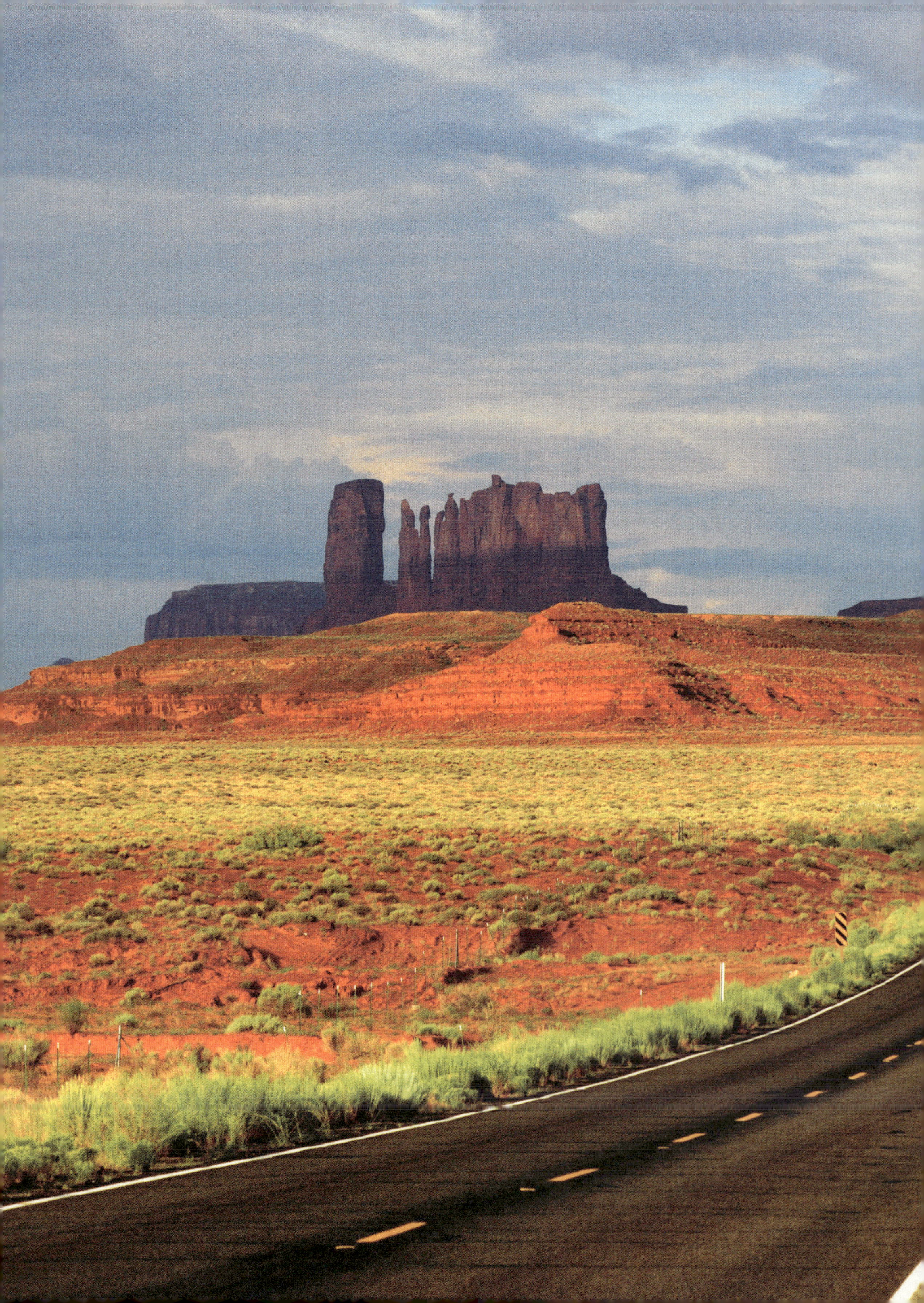

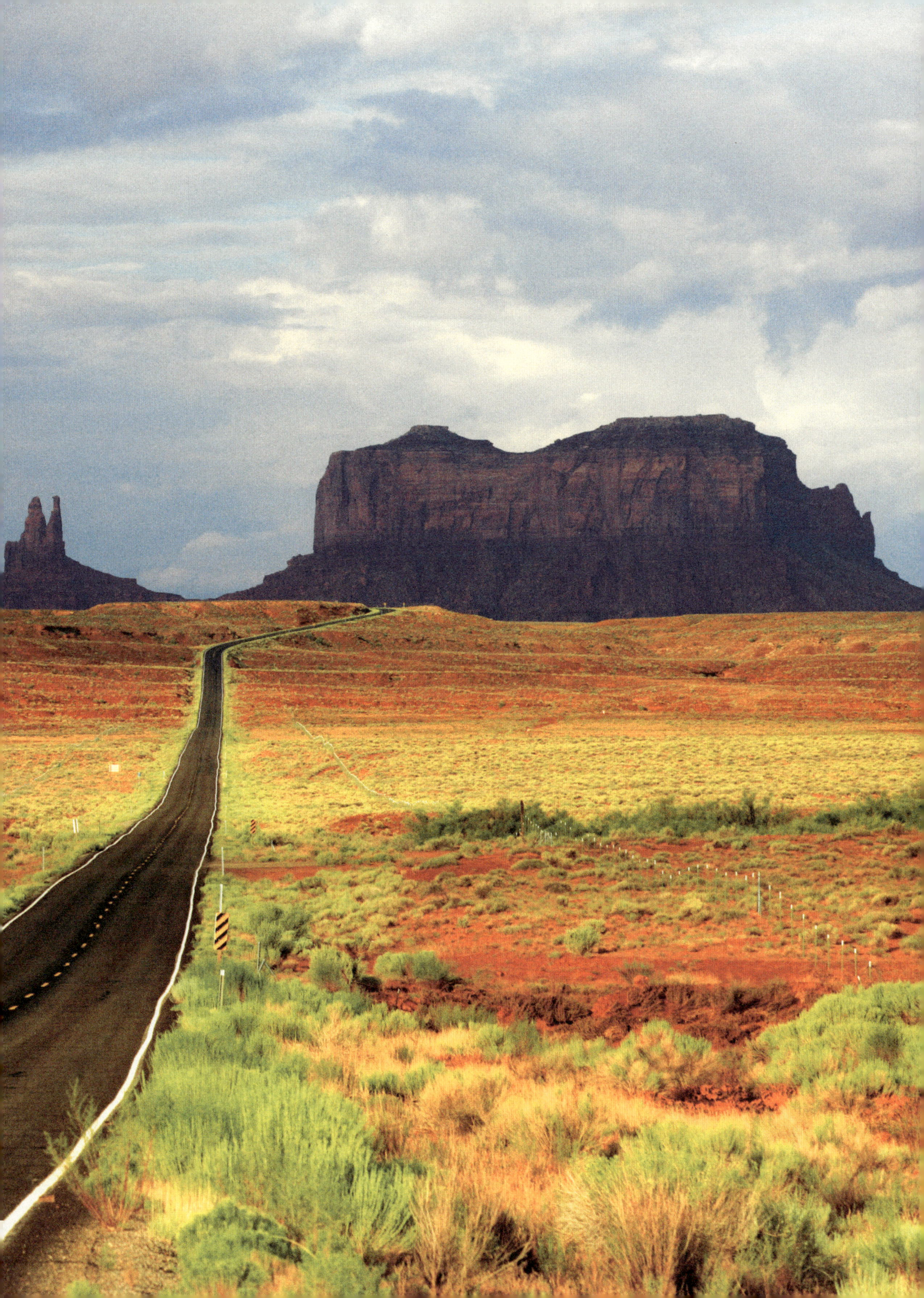

A SOLITARY MAN, THIN WITH A SLIGHTLY STOOPING POSTURE, IS STANDING ON THE SMALL STAGE IN THE MIDDLE OF THE VILLAGE AS THE RAIN BEGINS TO FALL.

HE IS A SETTLER WITH A WANDERING MIND, NOT A SURVIVALIST. HE DIDN'T JOURNEY HERE ON WAGON WHEELS; INSTEAD, HIS VEHICLE WAS FREE-SPIRITED, A VISION OF PRESENCE WITHOUT DESTRUCTION OR BOREDOM. HE IS NOT ASKING FOR APPLAUSE, JUST WISHING THAT THE ORCHESTRA HAD BEEN AROUND AT THIS MOMENT, THAT MORE PEOPLE WOULD LISTEN TO HIS IDEAS.

We will leave him there on his own for a while, Paolo Soleri. He is more than 90 years old by now and has a few things on his mind. Soon enough he will tell us about them.

Loneliness is a feeling that easily sneaks up from behind in the Arizona high desert, but it quickly blends with wonder and fascination before the barren beauty of the landscape; everything that grows out here exists almost on charity and at dawn you may hear invisible birds calling from the mesquite-covered heights of crushed sandstone. The sky arches all the way down to Mexico. In the desert you become an adventurer, footprints are erased overnight, and it is not difficult to imagine yourself as the very first human being ever to walk the land in this particular place.

Yet, it is only an hour's drive to the multi-million metropolis of Phoenix, whose explosive development with garden pools, golf courses, and stolen saguaro cacti in the driveways has been sucking up groundwater from the surrounding dirt plains.

Paolo Soleri's small experimental village of Arcosanti is located to the north of the city, on a rocky shelf that is impossible to discover from the freeway. This is the defining project of his life. With almost unbearable slowness his dream is cast in small-scale concrete, a car-free community with its functions held together by airy arches and a visionary arcology, the idea of an architecture expressed in ecological terms. He likes to call Arcosanti an urban laboratory. It may come across as a fusion of a space station and a dug-out Indian pueblo; a village that is also an art exhibition. Imported Italian cypress trees stand erect in the Mind Garden. Out on the edge of a cliff, his own cabin hangs adventurously, its windows facing the first morning light.

With an architect's diploma from his hometown of Torino, Italy, Soleri arrived in the U.S. after the second World War and came to Arizona to work for Frank Lloyd Wright, the modernist legend. Outside of Phoenix the newcomer settled with his family in a partly dug down house, later expanded with a studio and a series of rounded concrete rooms with cubist-inspired pueblo patterns.

Nowadays this place, named Cosanti, is right in the middle of Suburbia and has become part of the American sprawl that Soleri so detests.

"By adopting the dream of the suburban city we are filling the earth with hermitages," he says. "Hermits never developed any civilizations, as far as I know. I would rather have people living on top of each other than giving them boring views, where all they can see is their neighbor's clothesline."

He has come in from the rain with a few drops on his bushy eyebrows. Once, he tells us, someone from the Disney corporation showed up intent on buying his creation.

"In a way that's the last thing I would like to see – a resort, catering to a lifestyle that is becoming more and more vulgar."

The piano behind the stage is the worse for wear and in this casual light, grey and sort of joyless as the final heavy rain clouds pass by, we notice that the urban laboratory could do with better maintenance, too. It is not so much an issue of peeling paint as it is the lack of a sense of caring, the feeling that people do not engage enough in order to embody the dream. One instrument is not sufficient; it will, as Soleri points out, be useless without a good composer, good musicians, and a good audience.

What he probably means is that if the creative flame is not kept alive, someone like Disney will drive through and buy the whole lot: the instruments, the musical copyrights, the audience, all of it.

The adventure of somebody building an idealistic and lean model city in the American desert tickles one's fancy on many levels. As a utopian project it is overwhelming. As a personal bid, it is encouraging and even touching. Paolo Soleri has designed ceramics factories, space communities and imaginative bridges. His work has been exhibited all over the world and he has written numerous books, filled with architectural philosophy. But in the end, nothing has been more important than to show, in this very resolute fashion, that another world is possible.

The physical work is done by visiting students, many of them from architecture and construction schools. Some stay for years, but most of them are on an expedition, pursuing meaningfulness in life, leaving behind the tiring demands of commerce. According to plan this will eventually become a town for five thousand people, while at the moment there are only one hundred. Vegetables are grown in solar-driven greenhouses. Construction began in 1970 and is snailing its way forward on a microscopic budget based on the sales of Solari-designed pots and ceramic windbells, whose frail sounds reflect perfectly the fragility of both the project and the landscape.

When the rain has been chased off, light is flowing through Arcosanti.

It falls on the small squares, sneaks into the curved arches, and bounces off the projecting ramps and out-of-the-way angles. A black-and-yellow tarantula suddenly appears beneath a couple of fig trees. The moisture is evaporating on the ornamented tiles of the walking paths, where reliefs and discrete patterns have been inserted. The more you look, the more you see: everywhere there are tiny, decorated Indian pots or square pieces of ceramics, artistic impulses etched into the raw face of concrete.

In a peculiar but also well thought-out way the entire village is held together as one single body, connected through facing stairways and communal spaces on double levels. The apartments overlook half-open patios. With its terraced and climbing, clinging structure, the environment might be more fun for children than for senior citizens with aching joints. This is also a place that requires sunscreen with a high protection factor, and cowboy boots should you want to go hiking out on the land.

Cars are parked outside the housing area. During a concert years ago almost one hundred vehicles were destroyed in a fire, an apocalyptic accident which may have been symbolically interpreted by the many who saw the flames blaze against the star-spangled night sky.

"Our lives must become leaner, simpler, more frugal," stresses Paolo Soleri. "Most organisms lead a very lean life. A small heap of leaves can sustain animals eternally. If the whole world adopted the wasteful lifestyle of the Americans, we would need twelve earths in order to survive. I compare the crisis that we are locking ourselves into with a tsunami. It is invisible, but irresistible. We are spreading a traumatic consumerism across the globe and soon enough the tsunami will wash against reality."

In Arcosanti, mountain bikes lean on the front doors and from a slightly distorted cd player in the bronze foundry the instrumental voice of Sonny Rollins can be heard blowing across the rocky desert. Sweaty backs are pouring the glowing metal into molds that will turn into windbell details. In the ceramics workshop, which is also outside underneath a generous arch, a new recruit receives her first instructions. The pot patterns, simple, pregnant,and decorative in the way of indigenous art, continue to follow us everywhere we go; on steps, in a window bay, on the discarded plaster tiles left on the ground. They create an installation on their own.

Paolo Soleri never strays far from his sketchbook. If something has been strengthened through the years, it is his visionary profile – the philosophical element in his architectural thinking, which hopes to bring people closer together, condense cities, shrink distances between production and consumption and between body and soul.

In one of his books, Soleri describes how future cities must become three-dimensional instead of two-dimensional and simply rolled out in a field. In everything, from the tiniest bacteria, there are three basic conditions one has to consider: duration, complexity, and miniaturization (complexity demanding that all resources be used in a clever way). Of course, this is all highly applicable to most human spaces.

"We worship gods that we have created ourselves," the old architect sighs. "One such god is technology. The market is another. Our tolerance for theology should be transferred to aesthetics," he argues.

This may sound a bit pessimistic, but Soleri believes that things will grow better in the long run.

"Oh yeah, because if you think of where we came from you cannot be anything but optimistic. We came from little cells, and, you know, here we are. The evolution has been formidable, beyond understanding."

And what have you learned yourself from all these years with Arcosanti?

"I have built the piano. I try to enable the musicians to play and to live. I am elated that reality is so fantastic, but pessimistic because so little has been achieved. Our future will be incredibly fantastic, but also extremely dangerous."

At this point the desert sun is all over us and he walks away to stand in the shadow of an Italian olive tree. Some of the ceramics students are splashing in the swimming pool beneath the Solerian overnight cabin by the ledge. Behind us, a conveniently small-scale crane is lifting a concrete block for an addition to the restaurant building.

Everything moves slowly, it is hot. It is a new world in the middle of nowhere. This is how ideas grow. Moving forward. Soon the orchestra and the audience will need to take over.

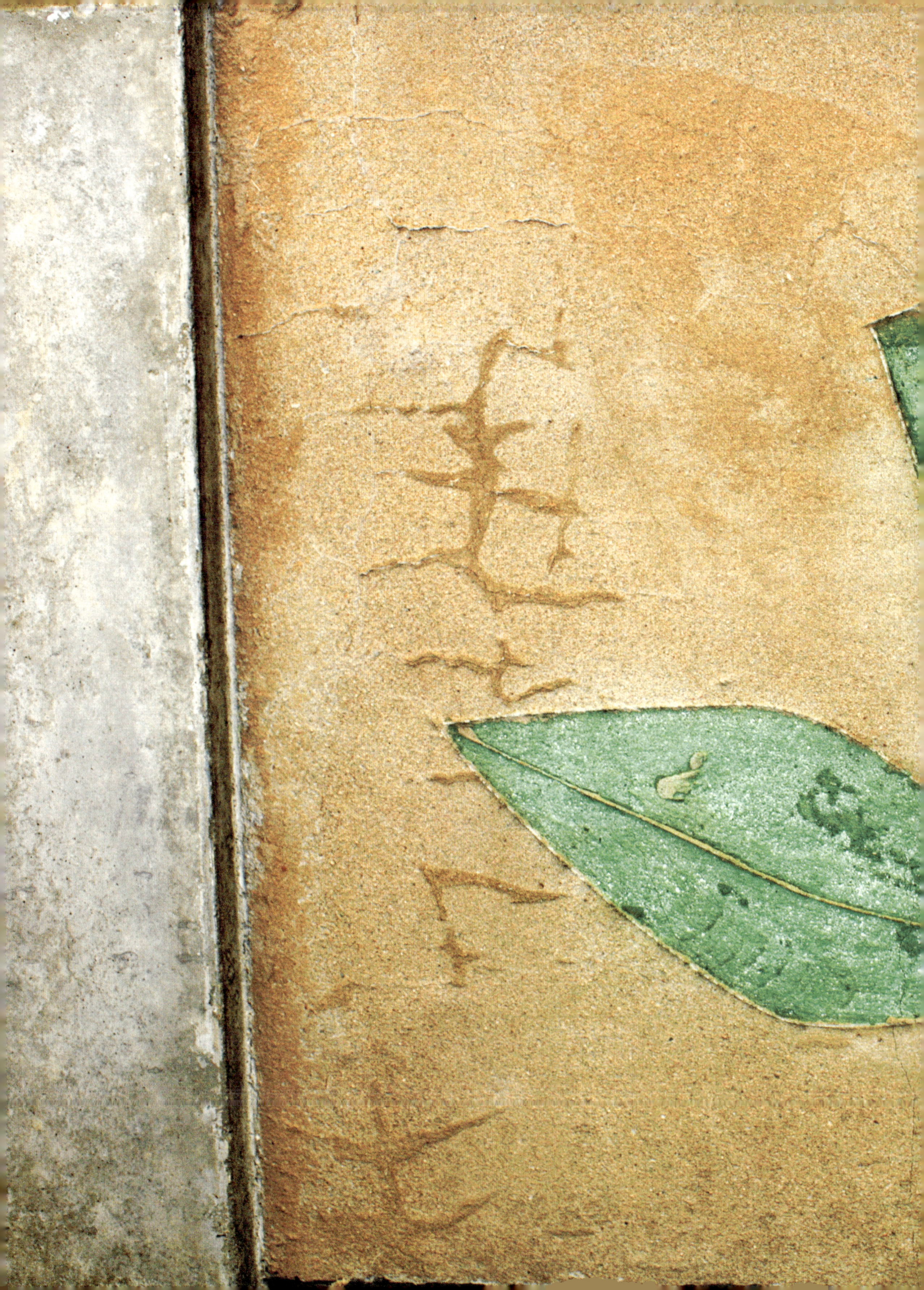

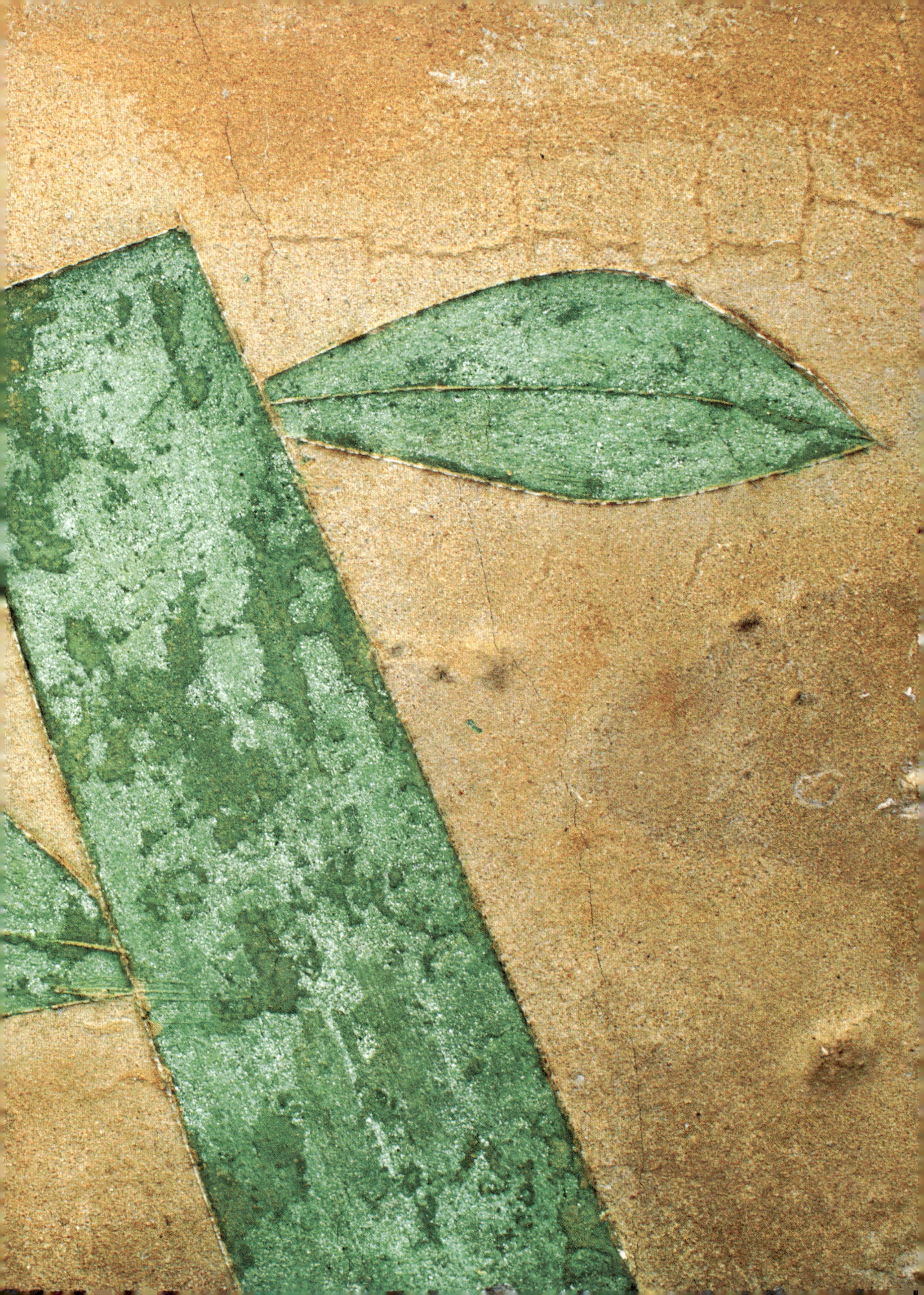

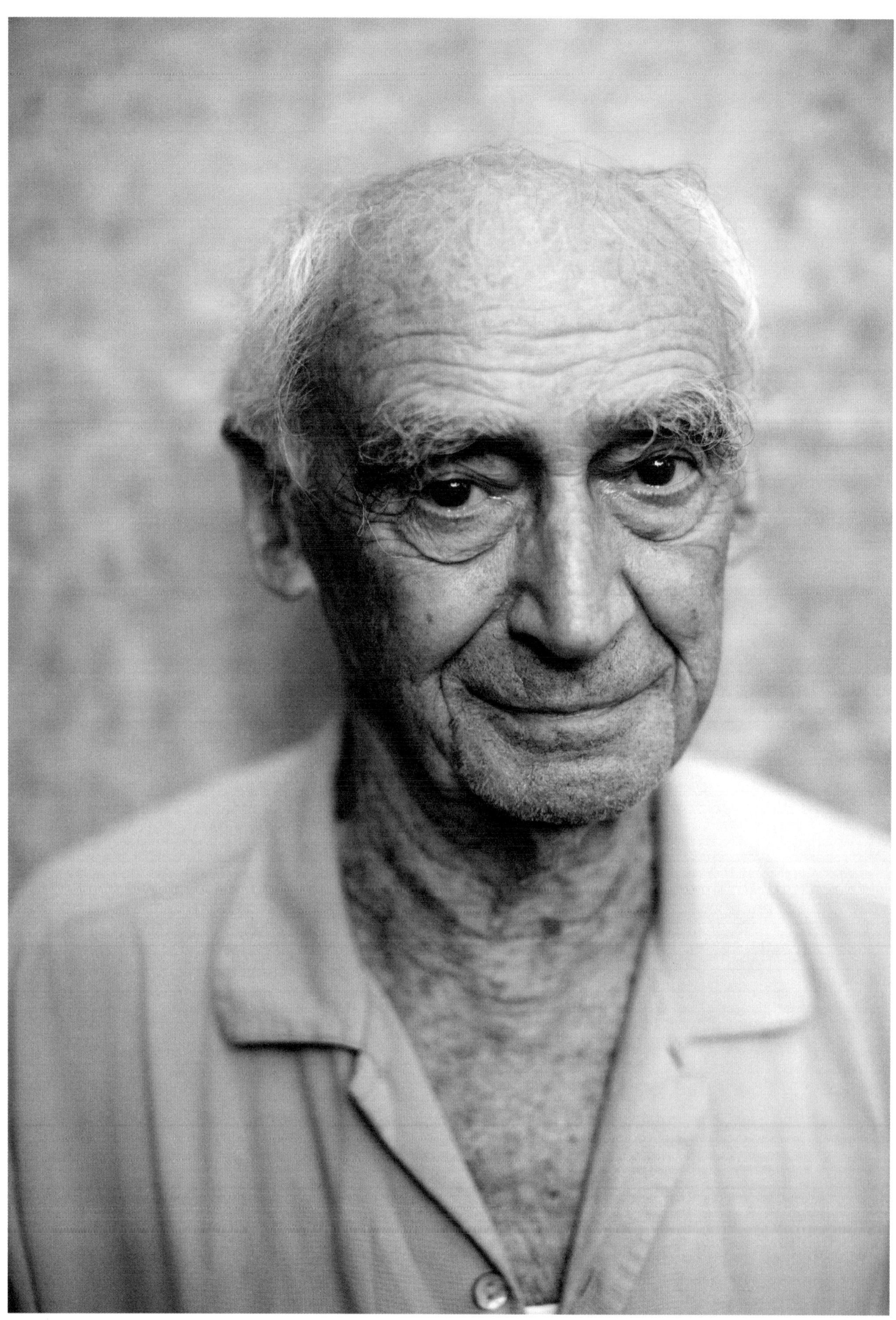

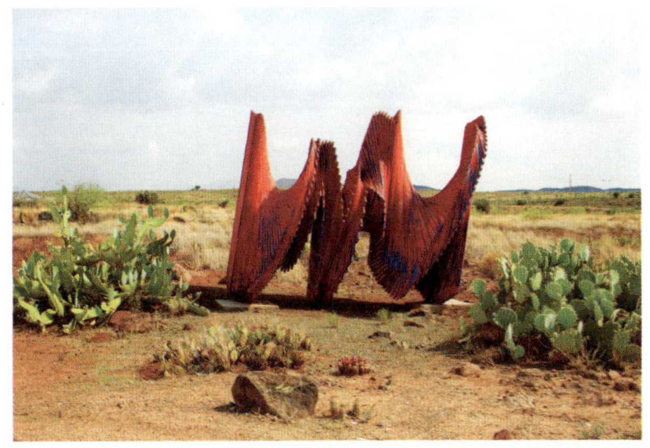

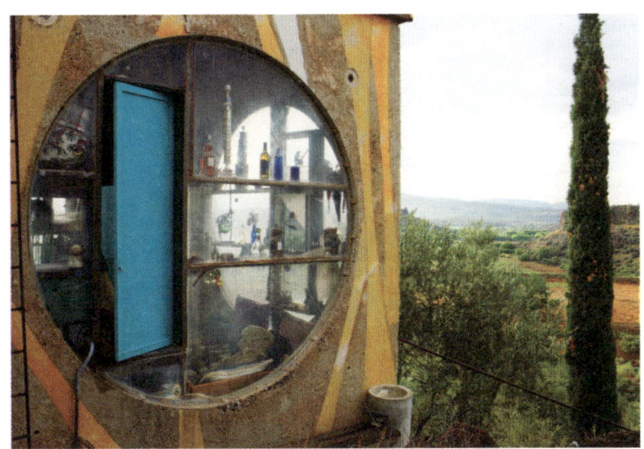

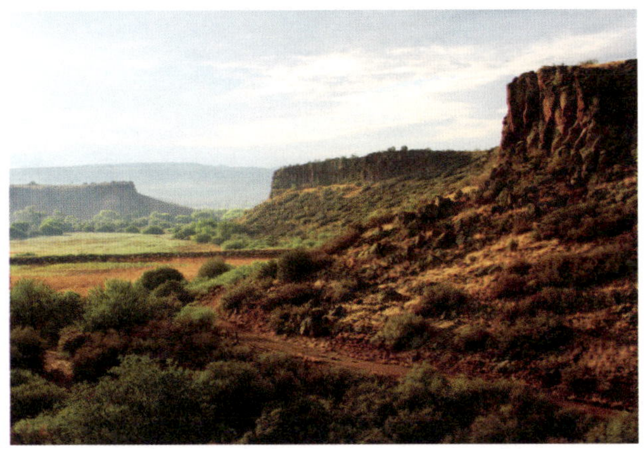

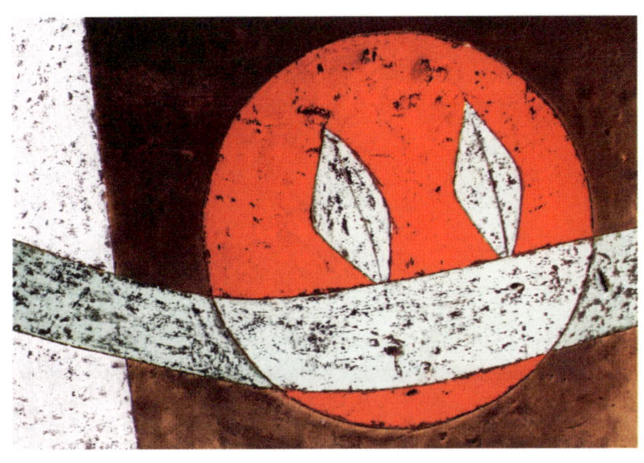

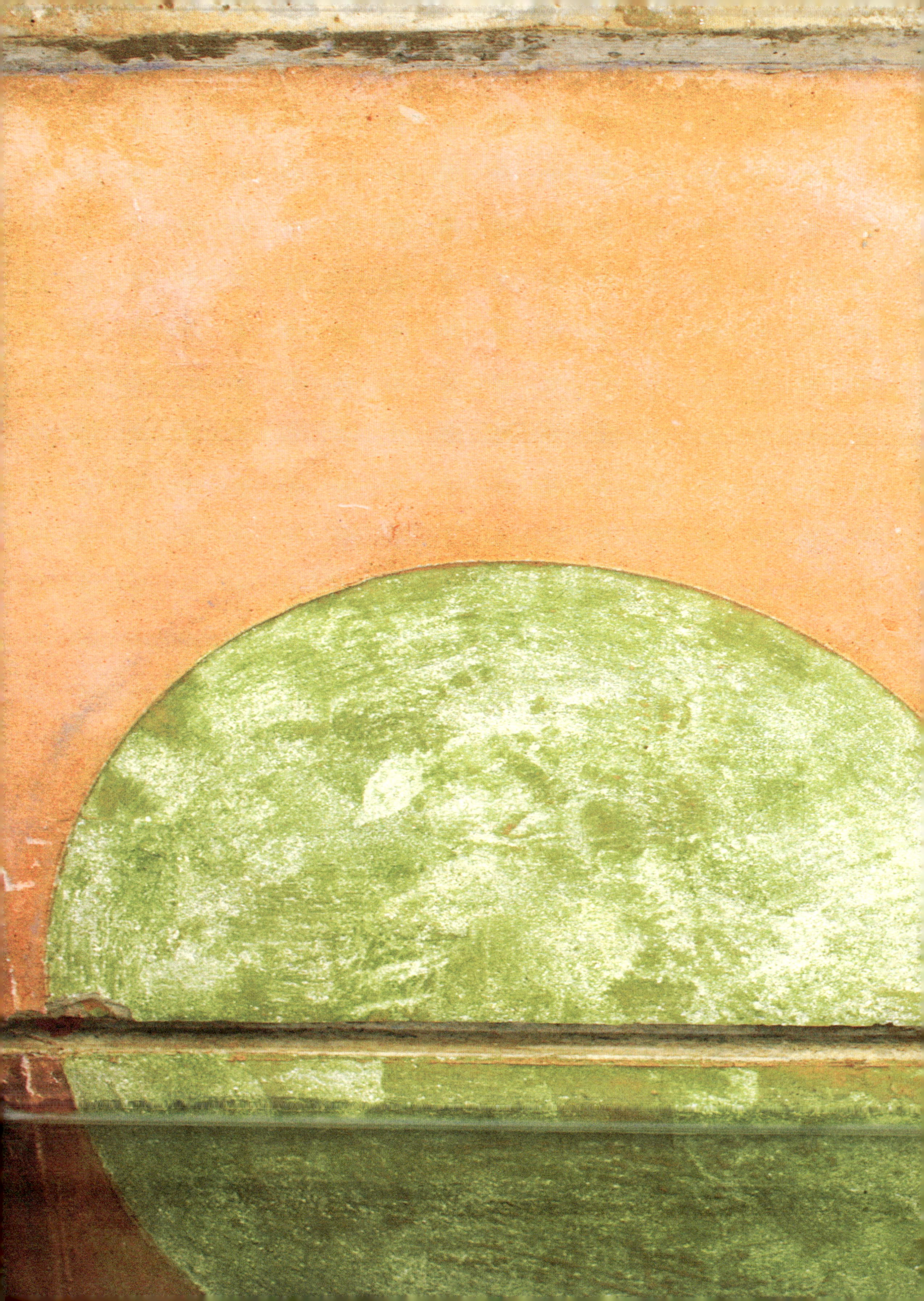

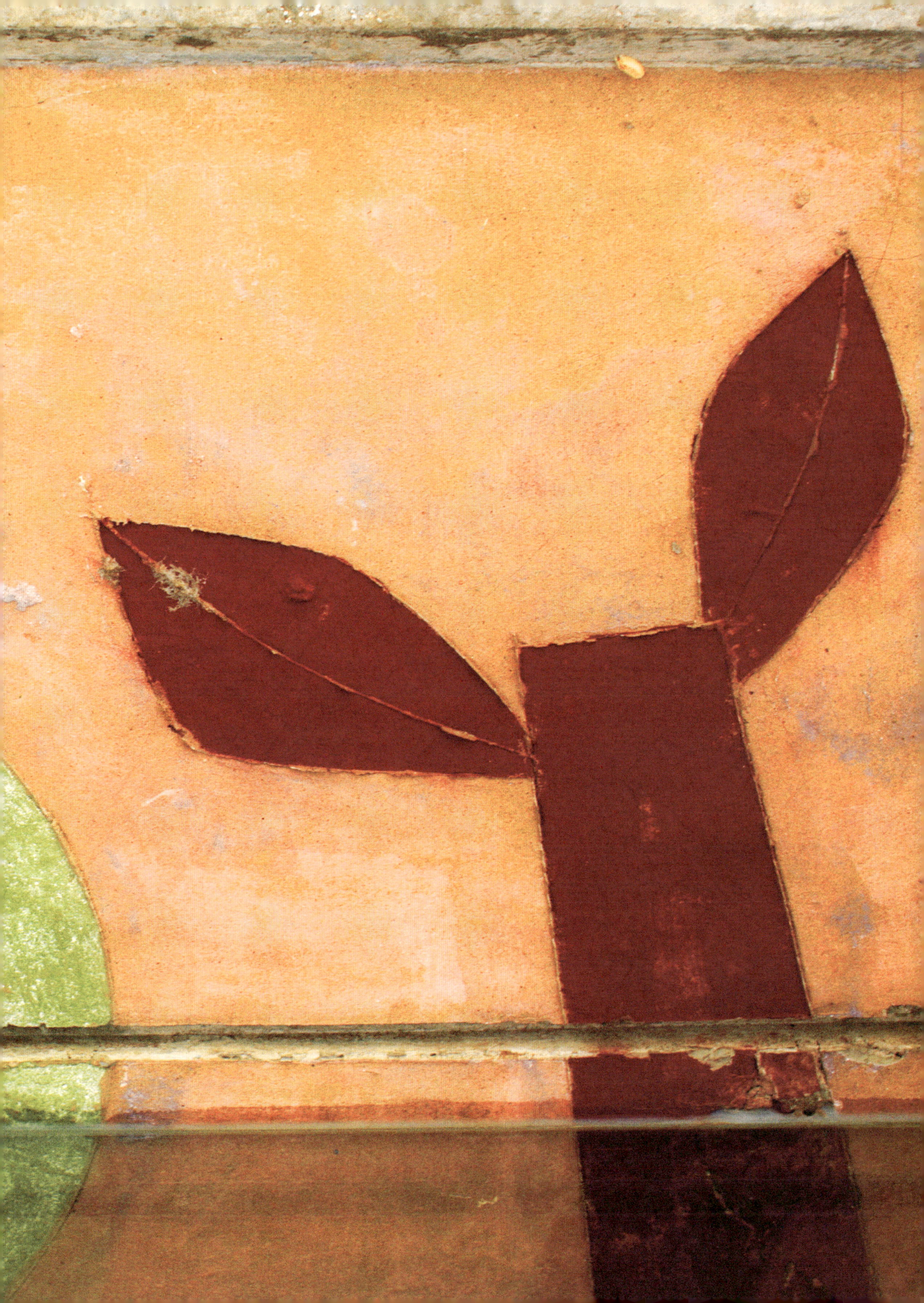

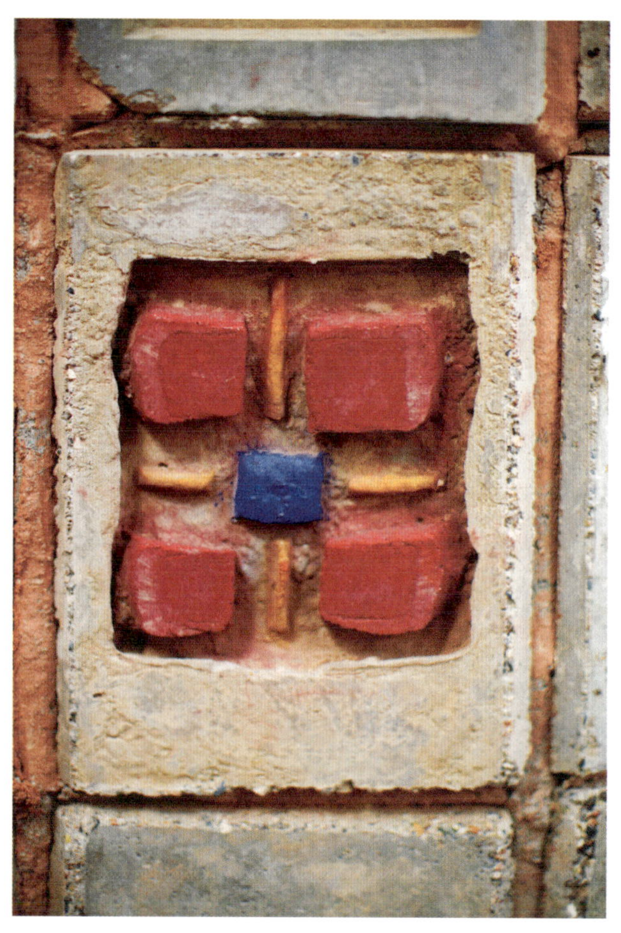

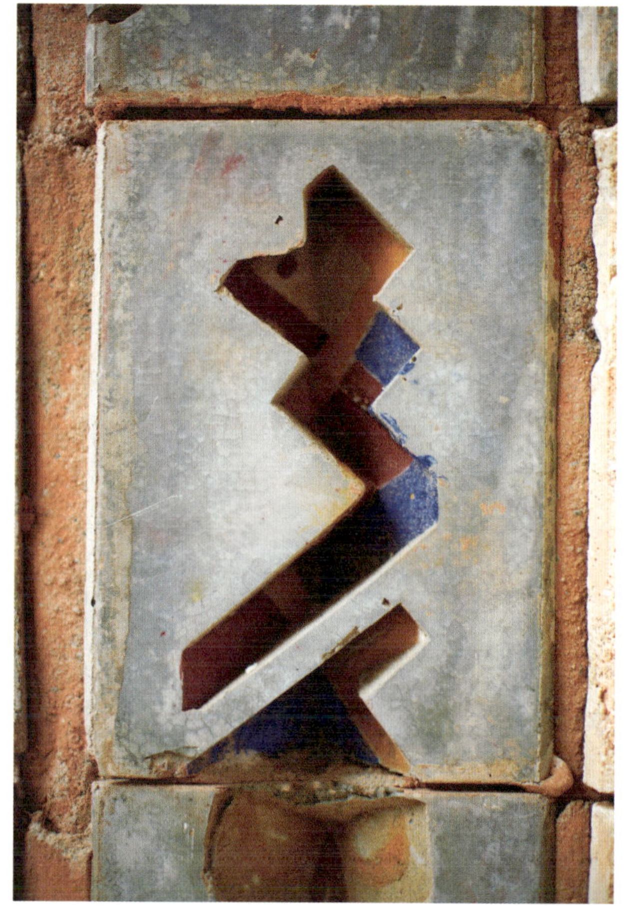

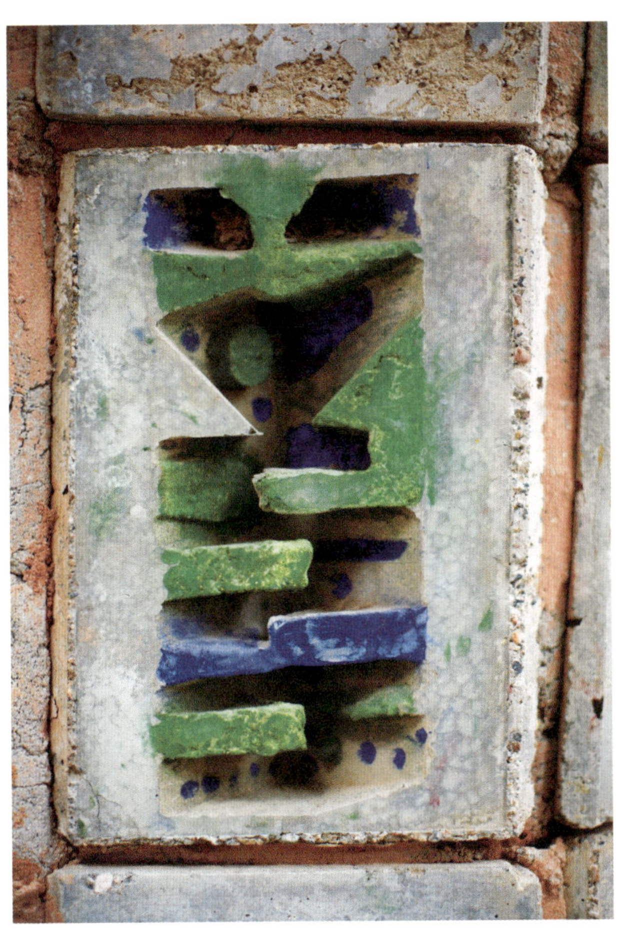

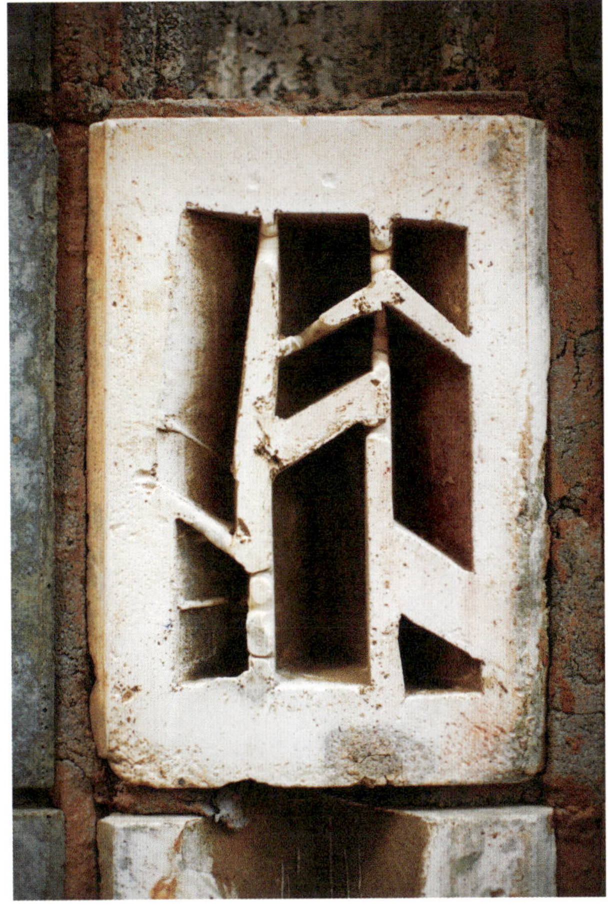

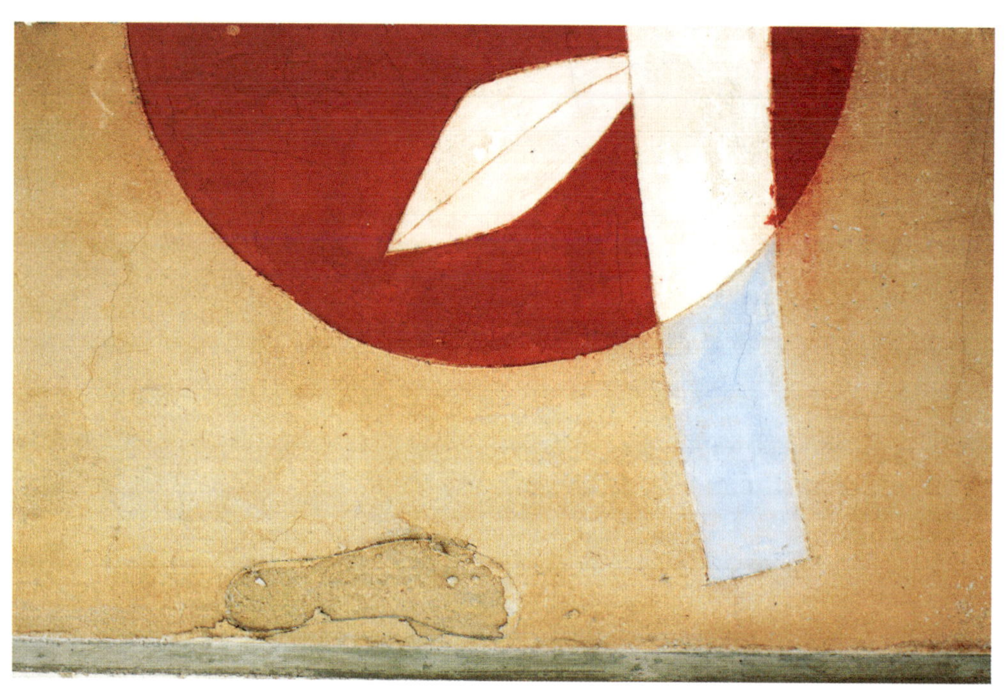

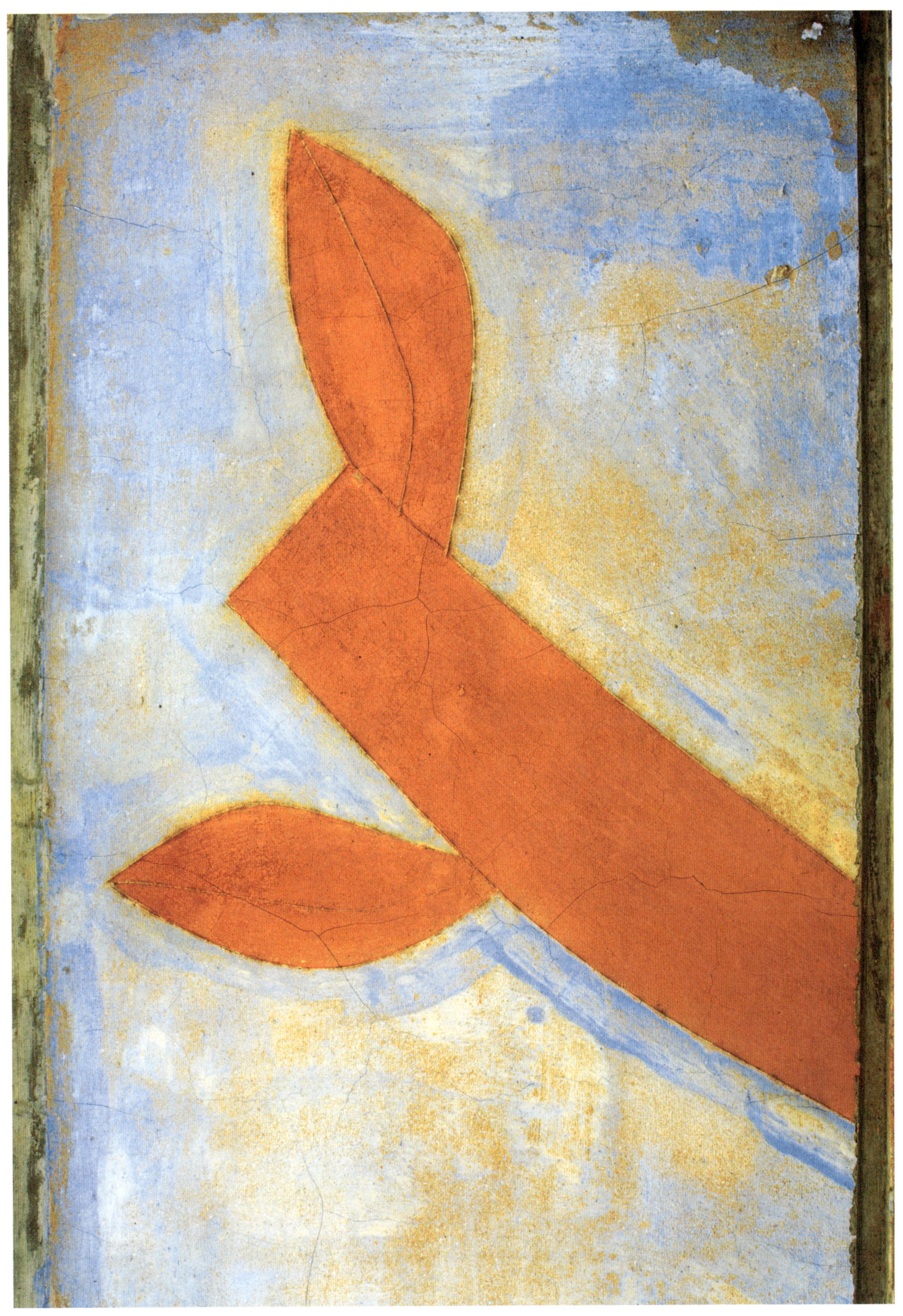

WILD HORSES

THE MUG BETWEEN THE HANDS OF THE MAN; ALL THESE YEARS OF DIRT AND SAND, OF DUST FILLING THE PORES, ETCHED IN UNDERNEATH THE SKIN, OF TORN AND SNARED FINGERS, OF BREATHLESS SWEAT AND TAUT MUSCLES AND RIGID LEATHER AND TIGHT REINS AND THE WILD GALLOP IN AN ALMOST CENTURY-OLD CLOUD OF FLYING WESTERN PARTICLES. ALL THESE DEPOSITS OF BLACK BEVERAGE AND IMPREGNATED TOBACCO.

It has been a long time since Darrell Winfield dismounted and quit being the Marlboro man, settling on his Wyoming horse ranch. He is now trying to come to terms with his cancer and the only treatment he would ever accept is the regular sweat lodge sessioning with a medicine man from the Wind River reservation.

Winfield secured the cigarette deal in 1968, when the wannabes from Hollywood were replaced by the real thing, and he has since been in more films and commercials than any other Marlboro man. Now that he is too old to drive cattle he still needs the snorting of horses around him; the smell, the body heat. It is not even a choice: you either like them or you don't.

The northbound road to the country town of Riverton loses itself in a hazy semi-desert. Behind every curve lies a new sensation of astonishing cliff formations. Touching the outskirts of Wind River we lose our car radio signal.

More than anything America remains a matter of discussion; without that debatable document, the philosophical contradictions of the nation's constitution, it would be a mere supermarket. And what better symbol of independent spiritualism than the wild horse?

One late afternoon, with the sun slowly setting beyond the undulating mountains to the West, we join Kent Stockton and Joe Crofts for a brief expedition into the wild horse territory near Riverton and its neighboring reservation. It will be a few hours before we are embraced by darkness and the pale ground turns a deepor ohado of purplo. Stookton ic at tho whool, Crofts in the back with his loudspeaker-like voice, fine-tuned at his job at the local penitentiary, cursing the shyness of the elusive horses.

The four-wheeler bounces up the rocky slopes and pushes its way forward on narrowing paths between cliff walls and dry creek furrows; the higher we climb, and the farther from the presence of others we get, the more breathless the view. The long valleys draw green lines in the folded panorama terrain and every now and then we run into small groups of impala antelopes, who immediately turn their dazzlingly white behinds at us and take off into the falling light.

"We're not a vanishing breed," says Stockton while stroking his drooping yet happy-looking moustache. "Someone has to gather those cows and somebody has to brand and castrate them, make sure that they're well. I don't think you can do that on the internet."

He studied to become a doctor in Kansas City, but kept nagging at his girlfriend about how he wanted to move out West.

"Ever since I was a little kid I wanted to be a cowboy," he confesses. "It just looked like such a glamorous kind of life. There was no cowboying in our family, but in 1973 I brought Mary Margaret with me to Wyoming and became a country doctor."

That was not the whole story, however. He bought horses and cattle, real longhorns. He placed two saddles in his waiting room and filled the basement and the shed with many more. He learned to be a connoisseur, a man with detailed knowledge about spurs and chaps with fringes.

"At first I laughed at him, I thought his dream was funny," Mary Margaret Stockton later confides. "The first six months we lived in Riverton, he was in heaven and I was sure I wasn't in the same place. But I did discover the uniqueness and the beauty and the romance that he was looking for. People are genuine out here. In the West the relationships are more honest, whereas in a big city they are more... complex."

We can feel a mild evening breeze moving up and down the hillsides and it looks as though half a continent stretches out before our feet. Joe Crofts's voice is roaring across the land as we pause for a pee and a snack:

"It is deceptive as hell, you can get lost out here at any time. But I'd have to tell you, Doctor Stockton, I could stay here for weeks, it soothes my soul. This sage, this smell, Doctor Stockton, is like a dream for a true cowboy."

We listen to the doctor echo coming back at us from the northern heights and it then bounces down the more level plains of the Wind River reserve.

"But where are the darned horses?"

Crofts grew up close to the foot of the mountain, and he describes how in his childhood a swift stream of settlers would arrive hauling water across the ridges and how an immigrant from Spain would live in a cave with his wife and a few sheep until loneliness and the grim obstinacy of winter got the better of them and made them move on.

Kent Stockton is about to liquidate his family practice in Riverton; now that he is retiring he wants to dedicate himself to the horses and the longhorns, and to poetry. As we fill ourselves with beenie weenies from his tin can and wash them down with black cherry vanilla coke, he reads his own twilight poem "The long shadows time" to us. It is quite an amazing scene: four guys inside a jeep in the wilderness, gulping down crap food while immersed in verses of literature.

But the desert moon is up and darkness hangs its curtain all around us, so Joe Crofts urges on:

"Doctor Stockton, when night arrives up here it's like playing chess with a blindfold."

It is estimated that 4,500 wild horses live scattered across Wyoming and soon we spot a couple of them, silhouettes on a hilltop. Fifteen minutes later a herd of maybe forty animals creates a minor dust bowl a hundred yards away. They thunder into the last remainder of sunlight and the dry cloud places a floating dreamlike film between us and the myth of the untamed America.

In the gravel surrounding Highway 789 between Creston Junction and Baggs, where Butch Cassidy once dug down to escape the law, there are small oil and natural gas pumps scattered all over the place. Down at the Salisbury Ranch, the O'Toole family is constantly at work with the creek and the canals that draw off water and divert it into the alfalfa fields. Everybody in cowboy territory, from California to North Dakota, talks about the drought. The winters produce less snow on high altitudes which is reflected in the lower levels in the streams.

"So far, the first guy to come here has claimed the water. What happens now that the expanding cities want to take that water from the ranch folks?" asks Pat O'Toole. "How many people can this land handle?"

A major western problem is its popularity. People migrate this way, looking for peace and quiet and unpolluted air or a fresh start with a new job. The precious drops of water are sucked into the boomtowns of the New West.

"There are so many romantic notions," sighs Sharon O'Toole, "but truth be told, this is a dying culture. When my dad was young, food production was seen as something positive. Now there's a whole movement to get rid of the cattle on federal grazing lands and substitute them with deer and wilderness. But the wild is a myth; the land needs to be taken care of, otherwise it'll be overgrown with weeds or wrecked by mindless four-wheel tourists."

Her grandmother came here as a little girl in a covered wagon from Missouri. She learned to fish and hunt and when she got married the couple cleared some land by the river and worked their way through the depression years. Most neighbors were Indians. Now their son, George Salisbury, Sharon's father, is white-bearded and limping and when the cattle are driven to their new pastures he comes riding behind in his old Cadillac.

The air is crisp, as if filtered through the mountain tops. Several of the cowboys come from Peru and have worked on the ranch a couple of years; a few of them stay on the mountainside in simple prairie wagons, where they keep an eye on the sheep herds that drift like clouds up and down the hilly slopes.

Identity by way of horses is what you will encounter even in the penitentiary outside Riverton. Here, the wild creatures gathered from the mountains where Joe Crofts's thundering voice echoed through the stillness of dusk become the therapists for young kids run wild in the impasses of drugs and assault. Nervous and eager to jump the fence, the hooves kick up dust as we walk into the corral. A sudden, collective tension is spreading among the animals as they prepare to take off. In just a few weeks, the inmates will be able to put saddles on them. When they have been broken, they will be auctioned off. Mike Buchanan explains:

"In America we have two big problems. What should we do with all the wild horses? And with all the inmates?"

He has found the answer: put them together and let the horses train the criminals. With his thin, scraggy cowboying body he is responsible for the prison's wild horse program and no other treatment has shown better results. Perhaps for the first time in their lives, the locked-up guys must try to create a functioning relationship with another living soul.

"The wild horse life is never romantic, that's a delusion. Their lives are crap. Really tough. They're constantly fighting to survive. The horses and the inmates have a lot in common. They have no freedom. They don't have a life. It's all about survival."

Unwilling to completely accept Buchanan's unsentimental analysis, we continue our journey through the West. As travelers we quite enjoy the thought of 4,500 healthy horses leading unrestrained outdoor lives in the backwoods of Wyoming. We pay the Marlboro man one final visit and drink more coffee from stained mugs while watching his grandchildren ride in clouds of light dust.

Afterwards, driving toward the northwestern corner of the state, we pass Shoshoni with its dusted down motels and a biker bar with loud music before taking a break in the settler town of Meeteetse and entering Yellowstone. The scenery here is indeed amazing with its many faces and facets, including smooth lakes and violent falls through canyons. The naked rock has turned yellow and orange from fumes from the thermic interior of the earth. Where wildfires have raged, trees are left standing like singed toothpicks.

A surprisingly large herd of buffalo grazes at Blacktail Deer Creek near the northern end of Yellowstone. The twilight provides their disproportionate bodies with a bluish Friday night color. One bull is rubbing up against a tree trunk to get rid of what is left of his old coat. A coyote moves hastily across a meadow toward a single unknowing antelope.

This is the great silence before the railroad, before the onset of civilization.

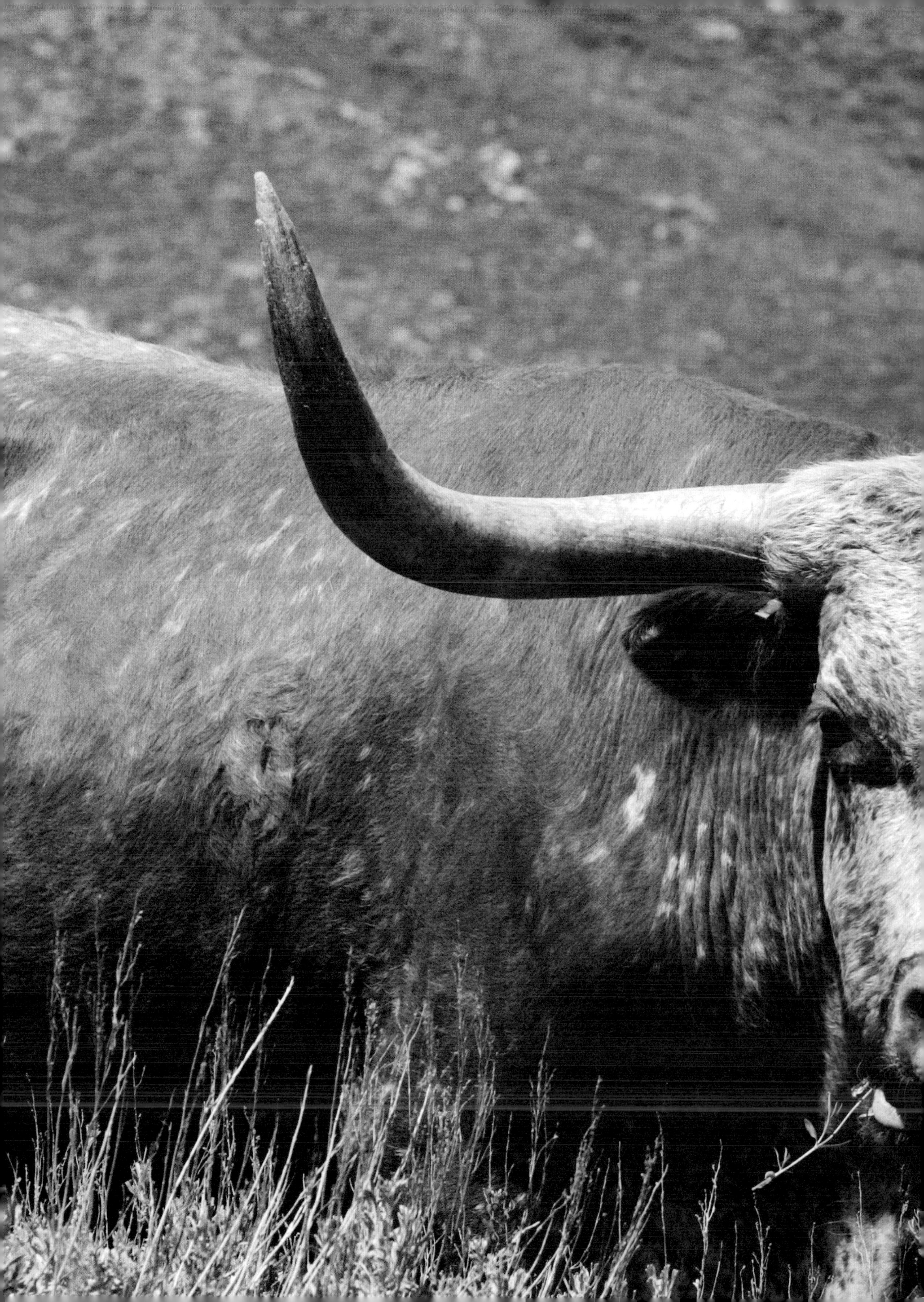

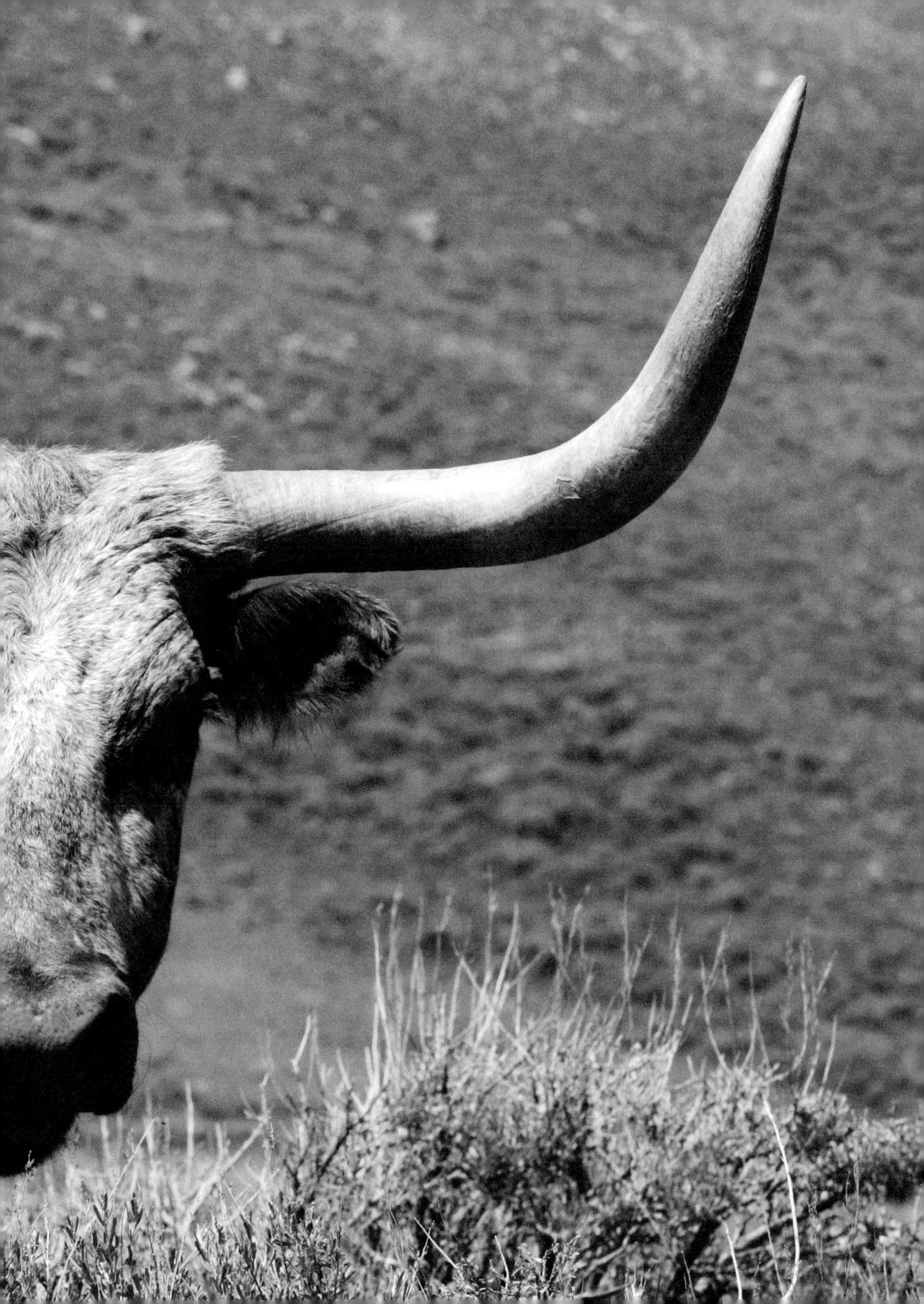

"I'm a first-generation rural American. I guess it's about romance and moving toward honesty and simplicity; the possibility to shake hands and make a deal and know you don't have to have it on paper. When we moved out West I wore cowboy clothes and I was the only doctor in town that did that. All the others had traditional white coats. And suits. I was an oddball."

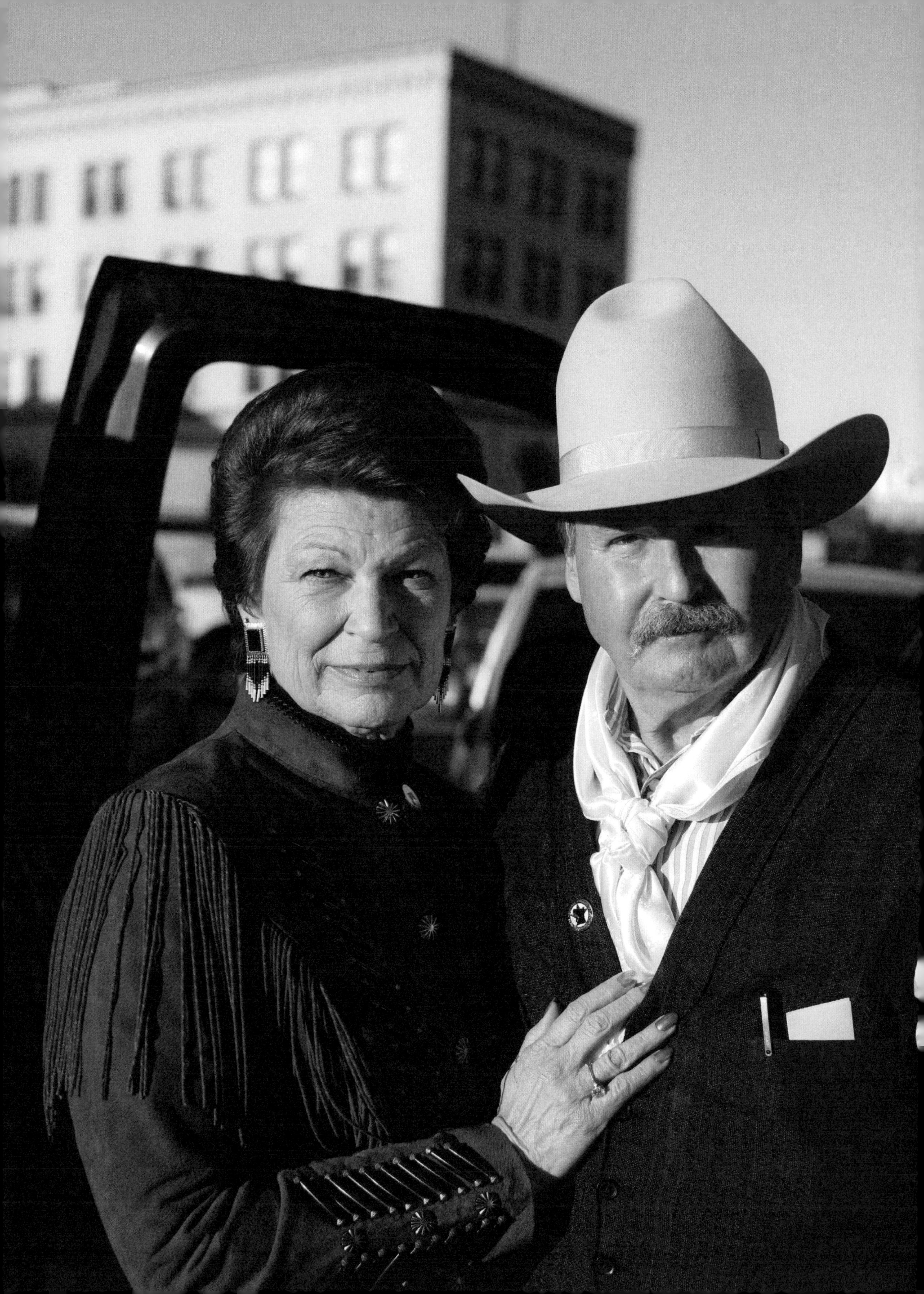

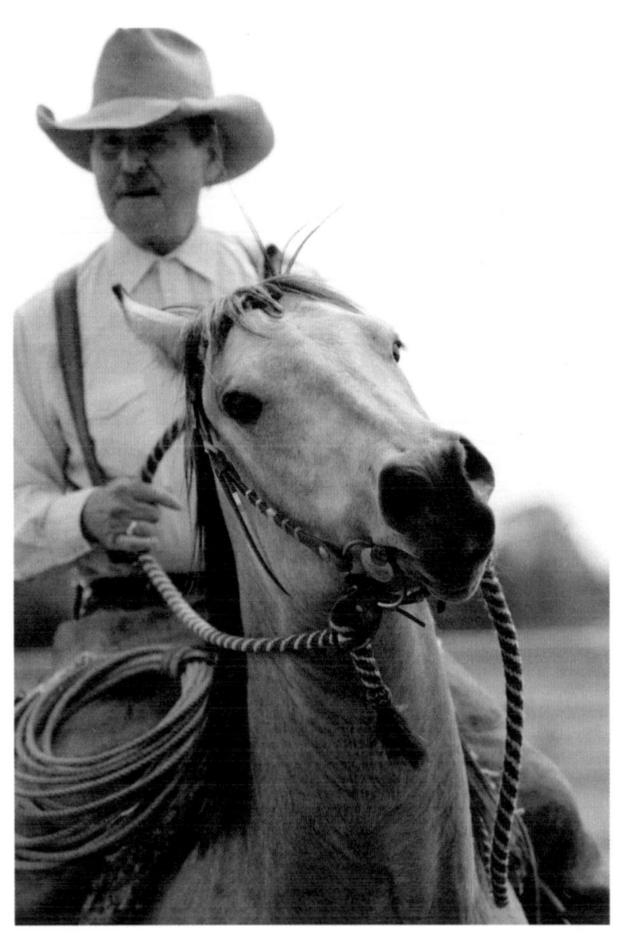

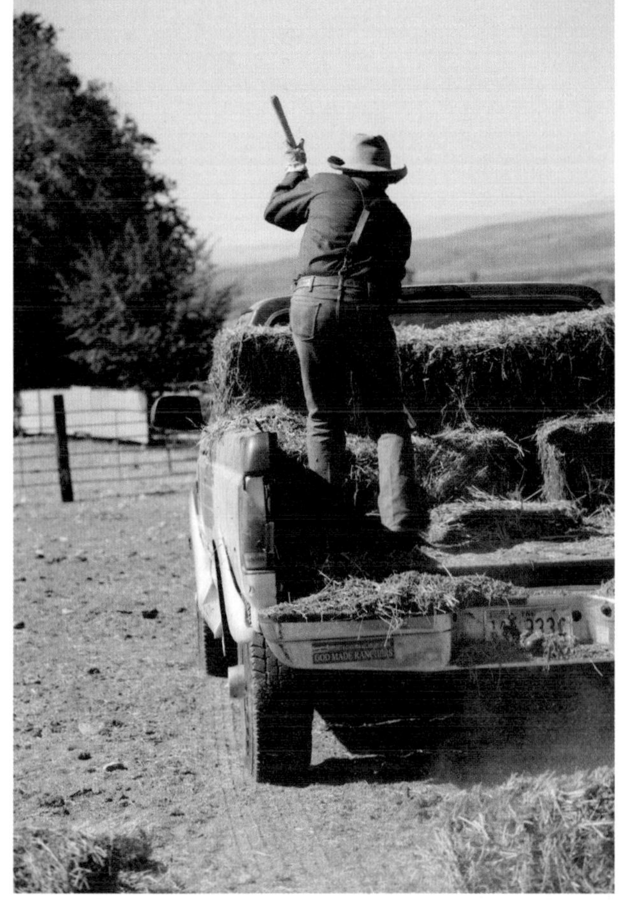

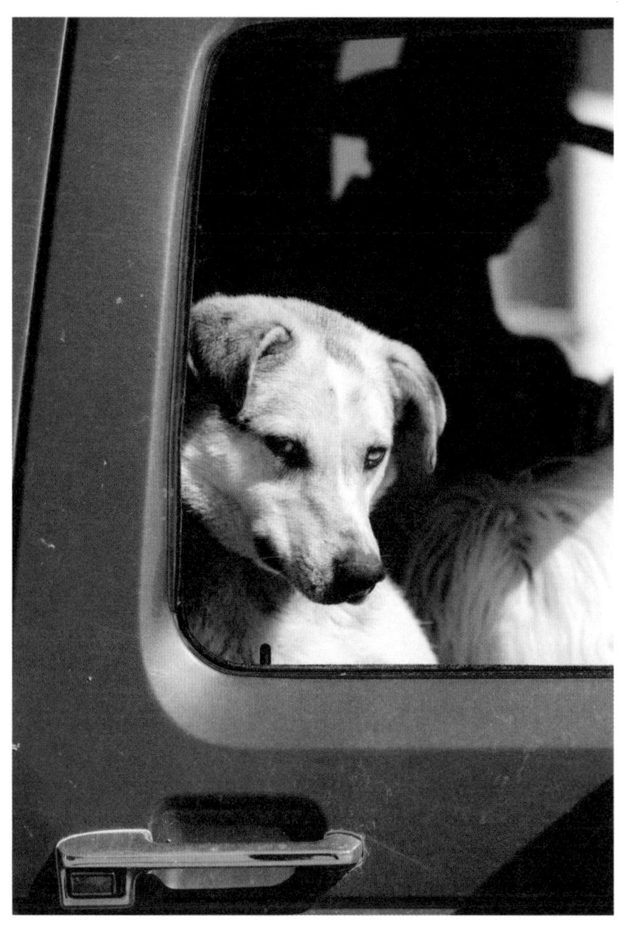

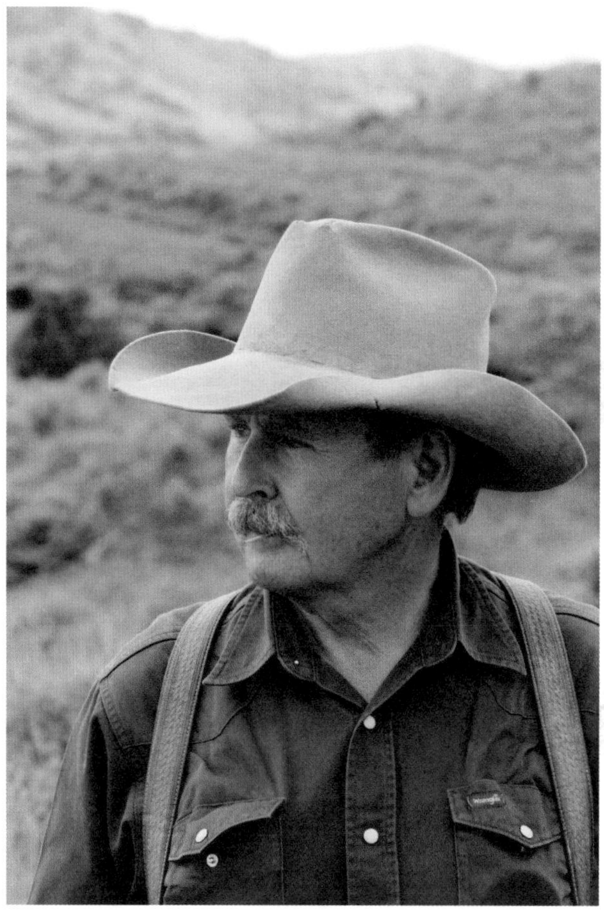

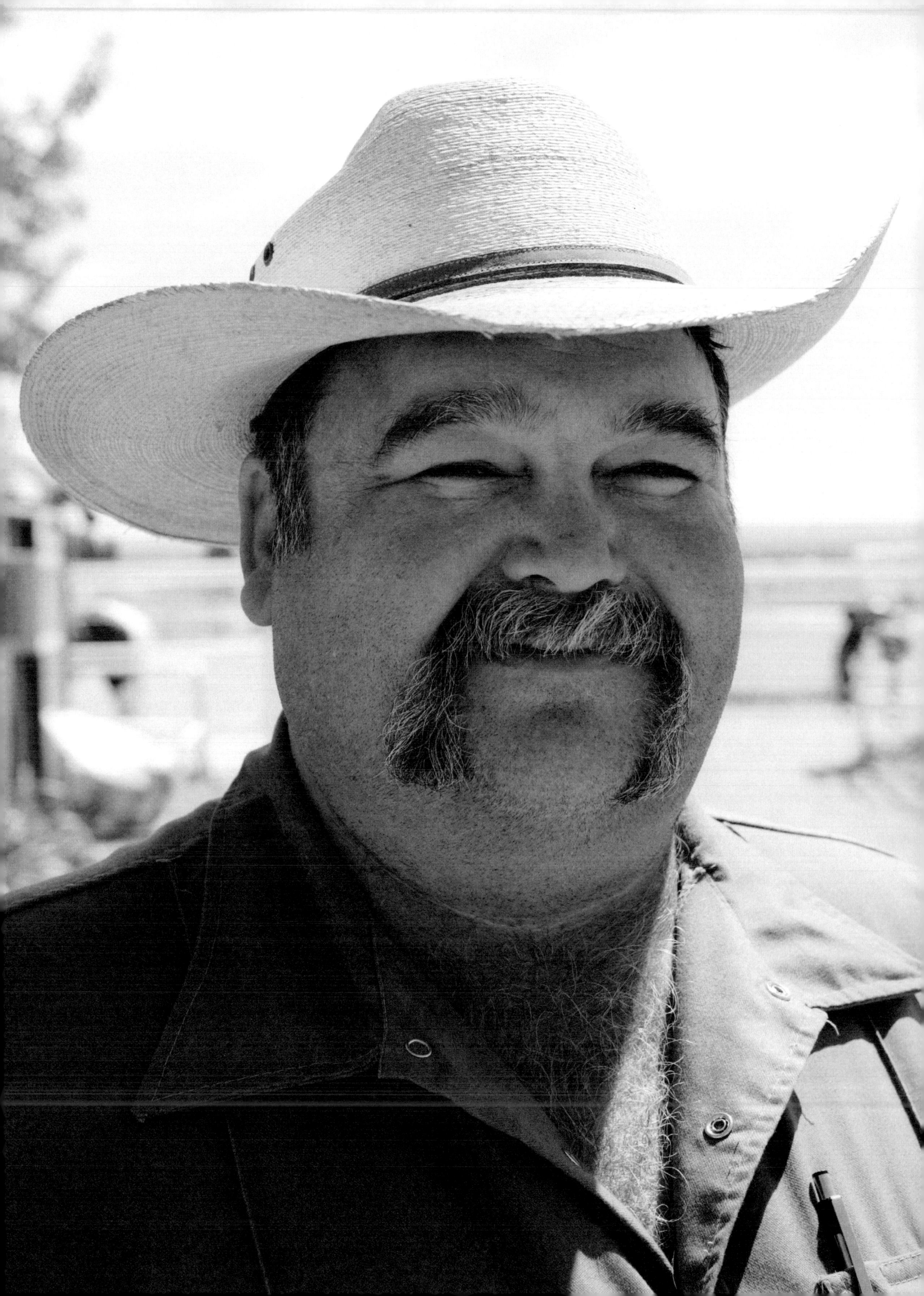

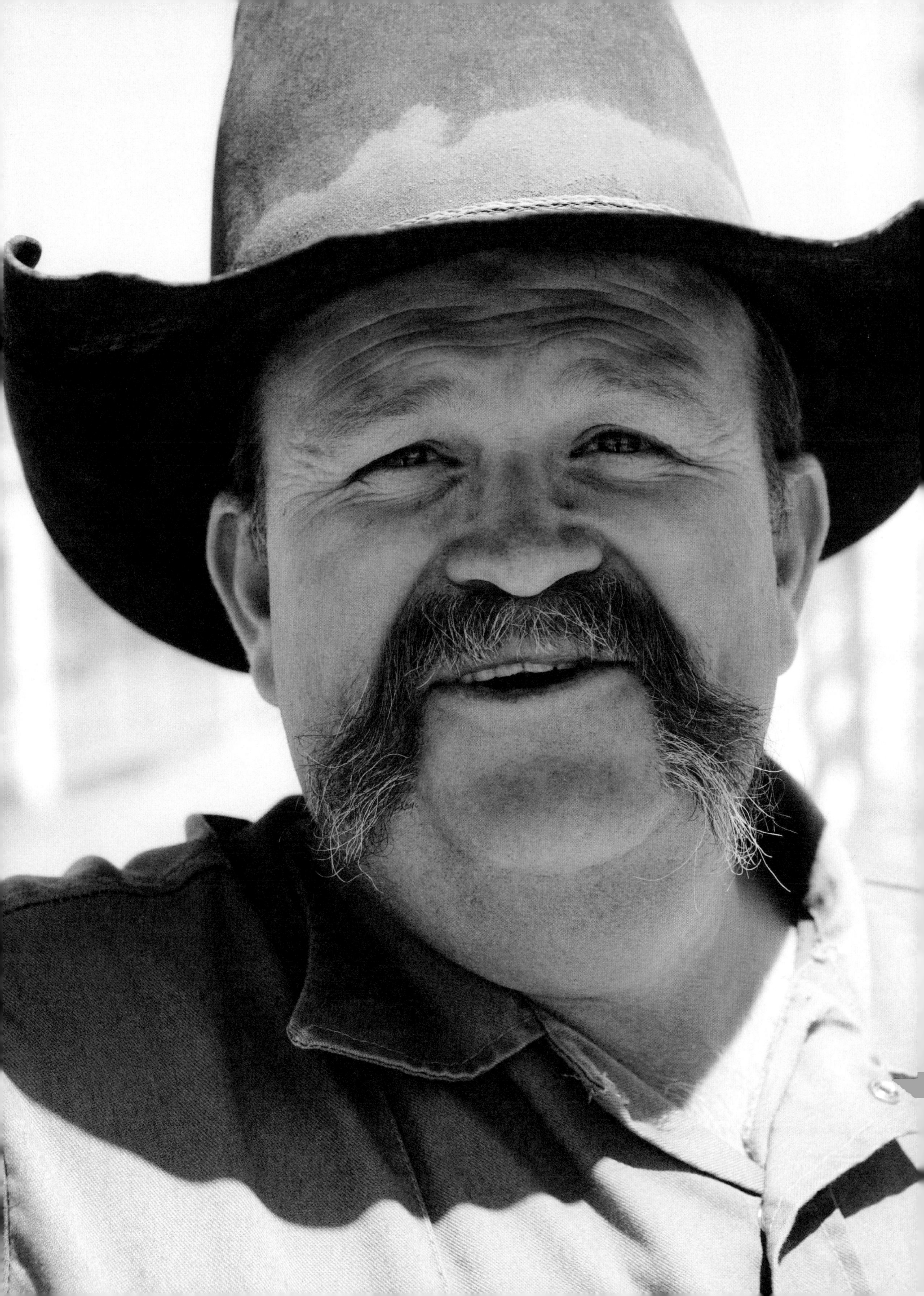

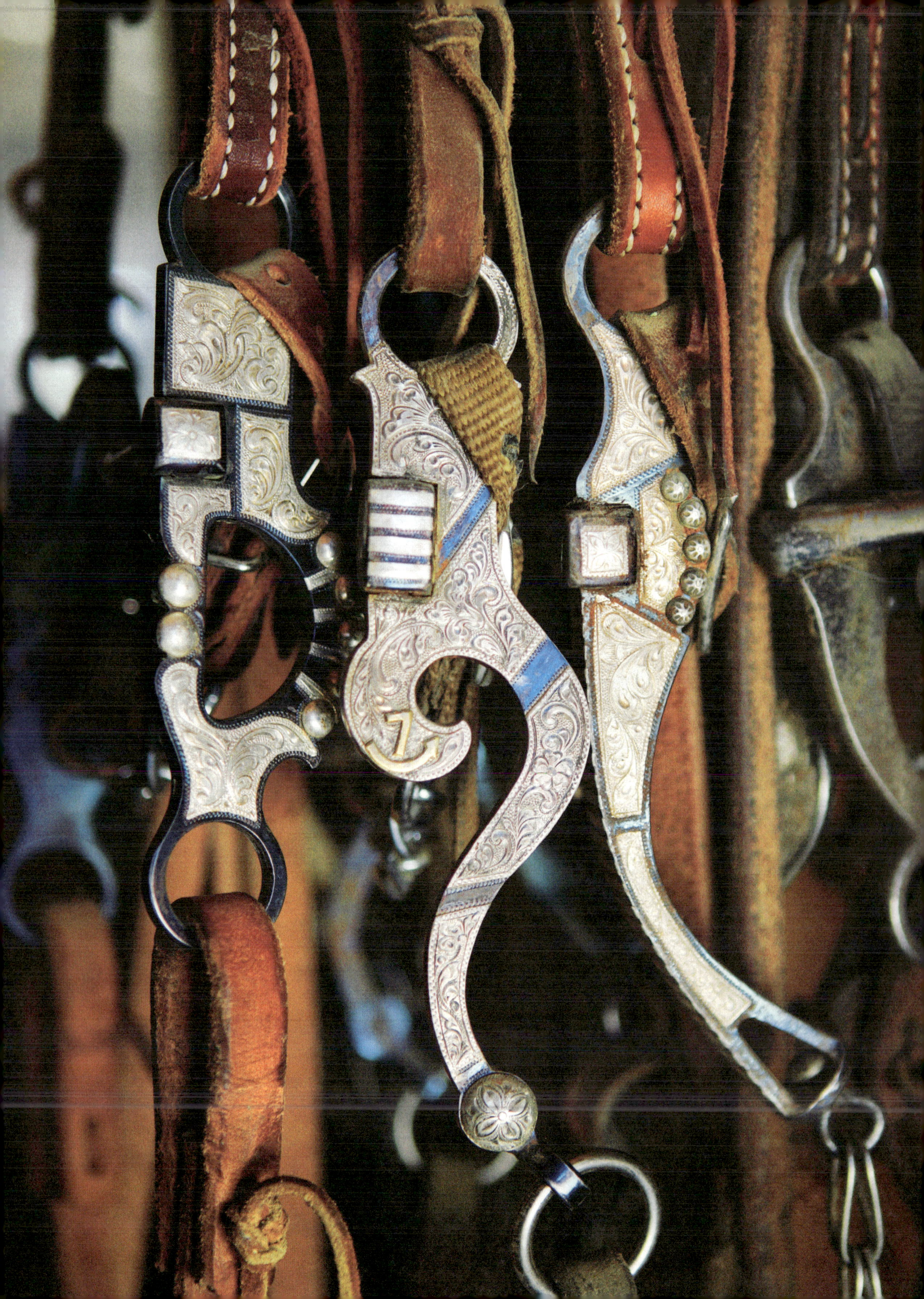
7

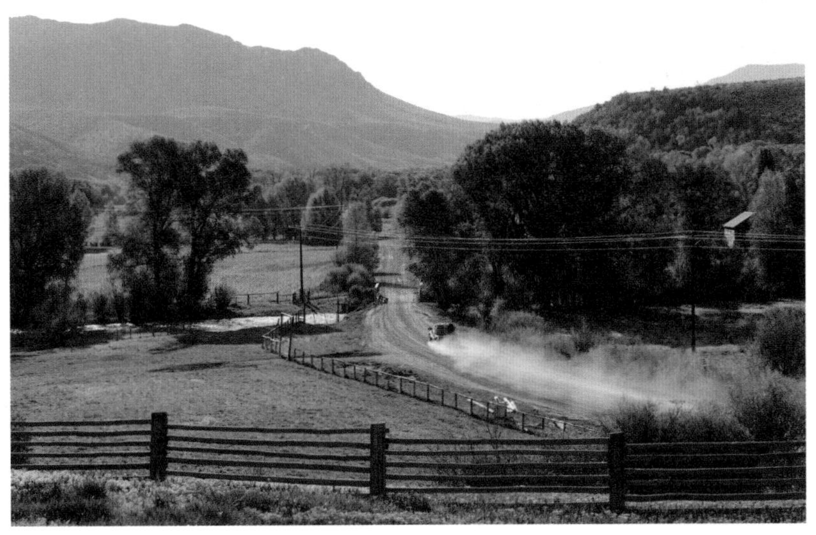

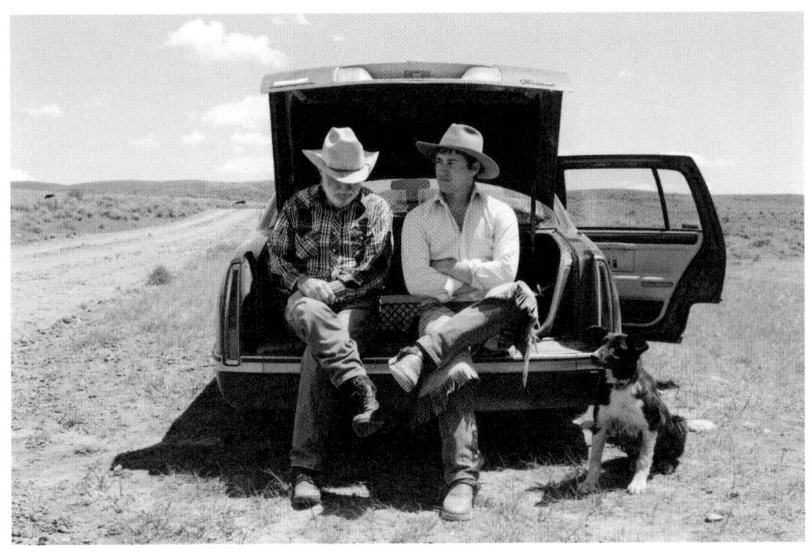

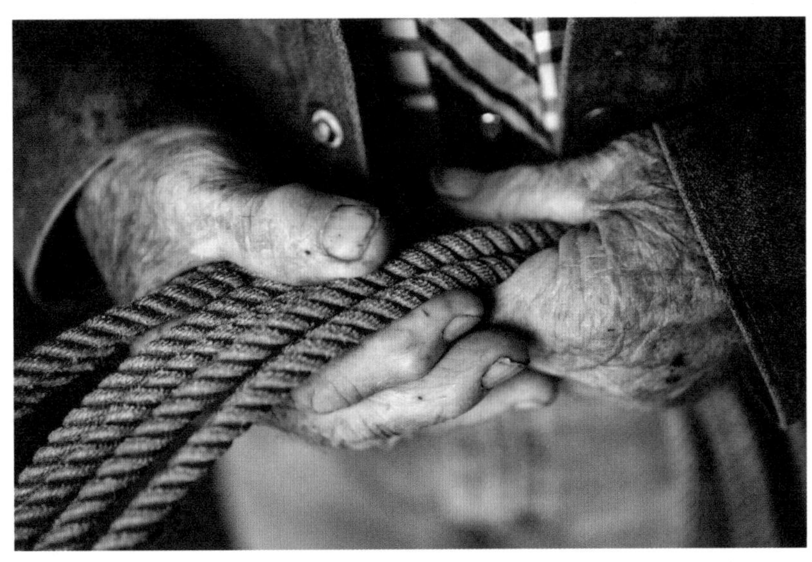

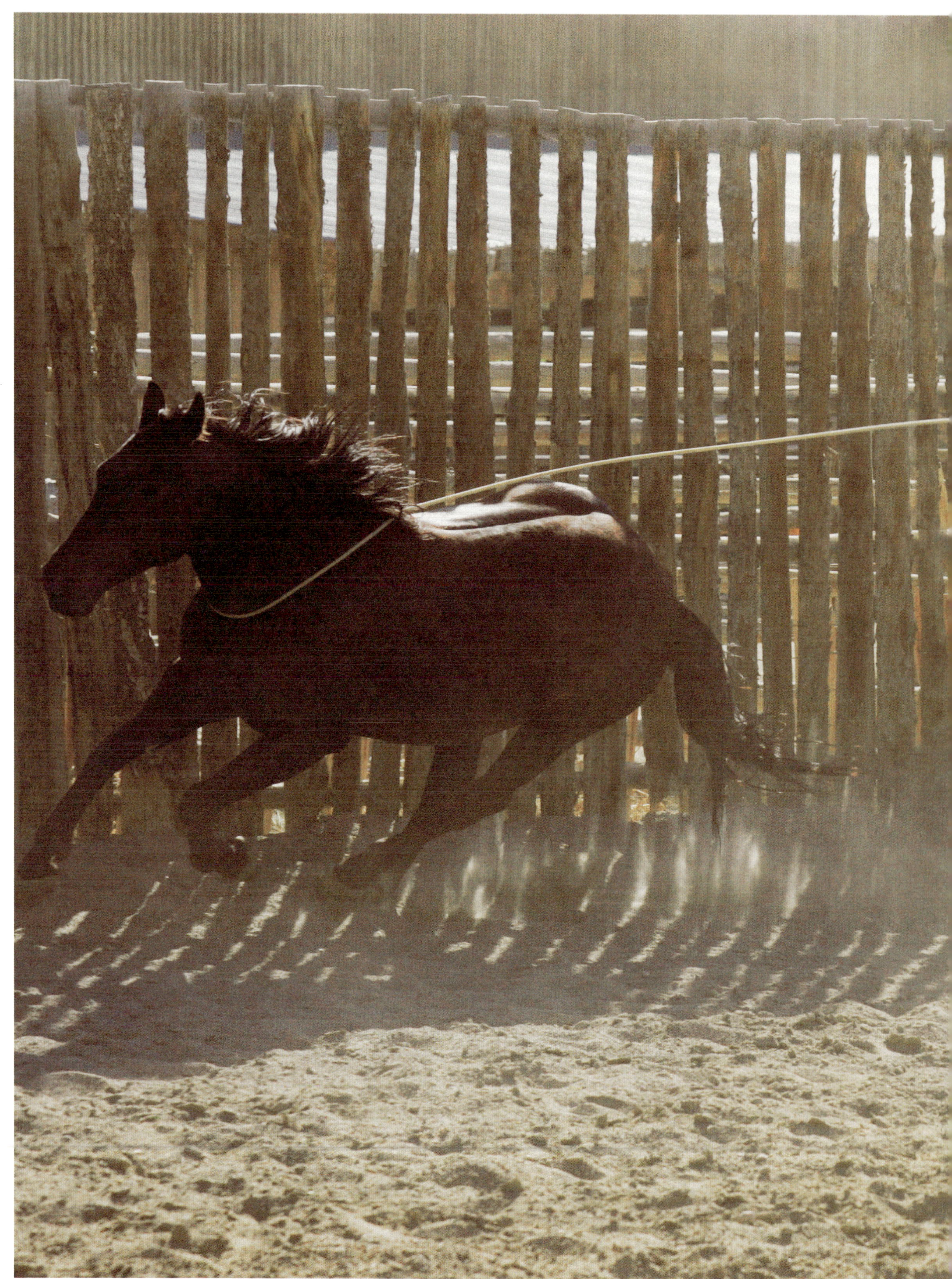

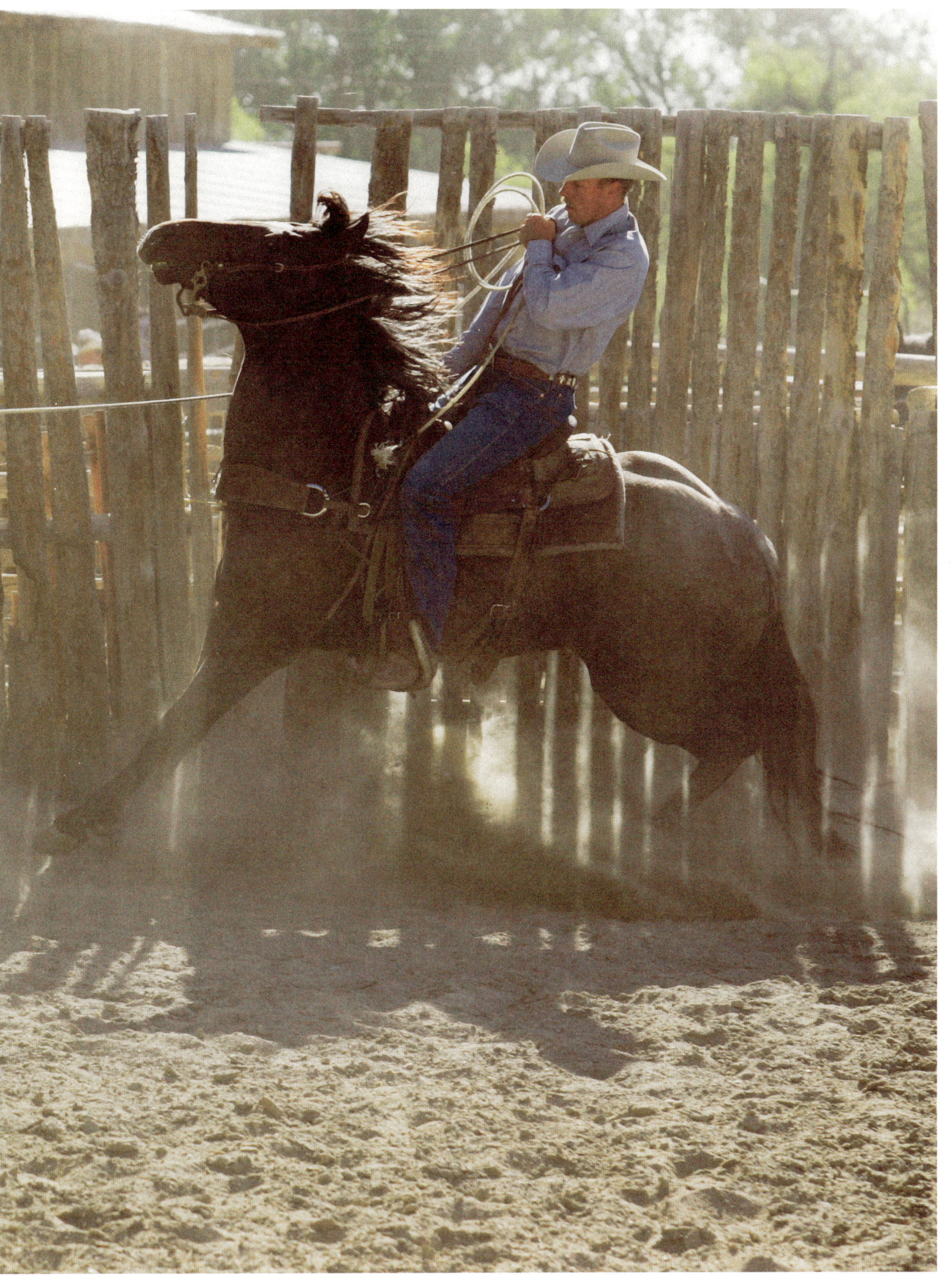

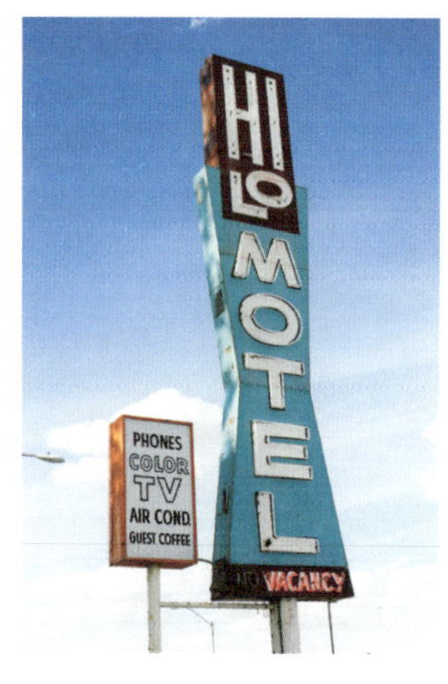
HI LO
MOTEL
VACANCY
PHONES
COLOR
TV
AIR COND
GUEST COFFEE
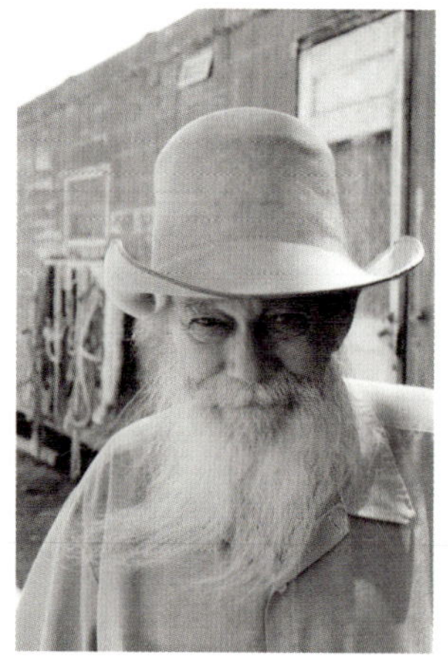
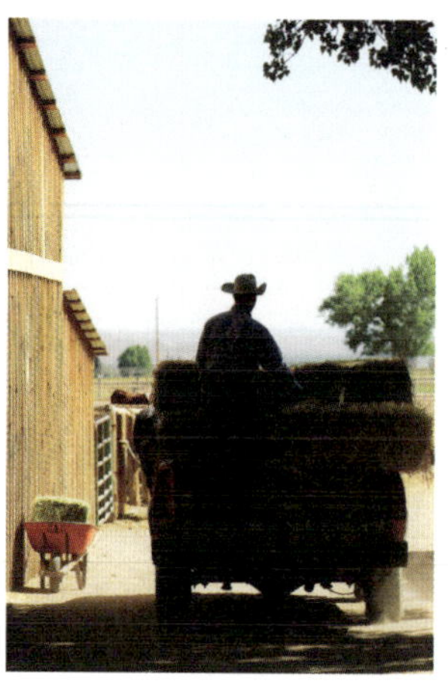
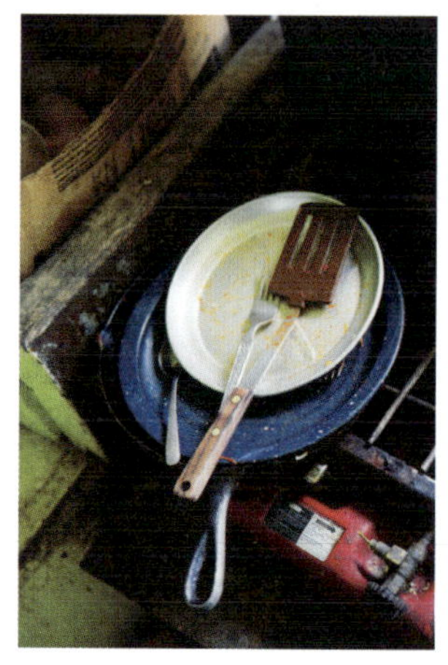
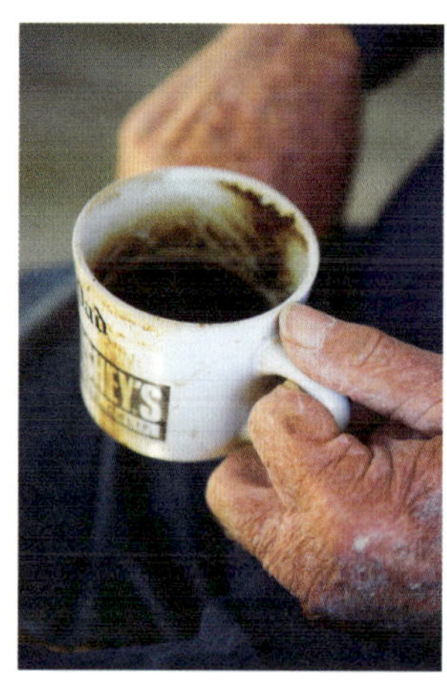
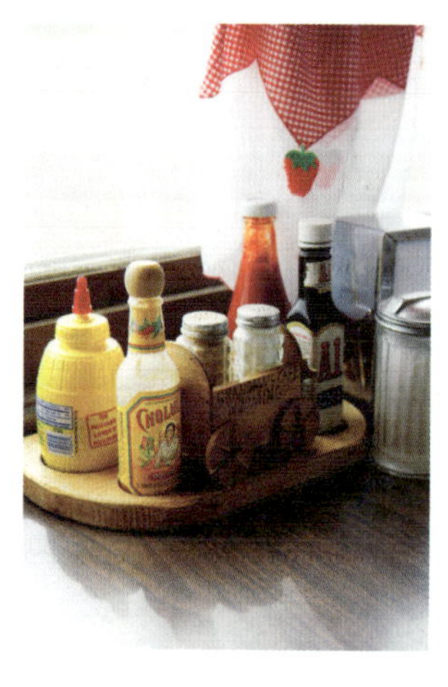
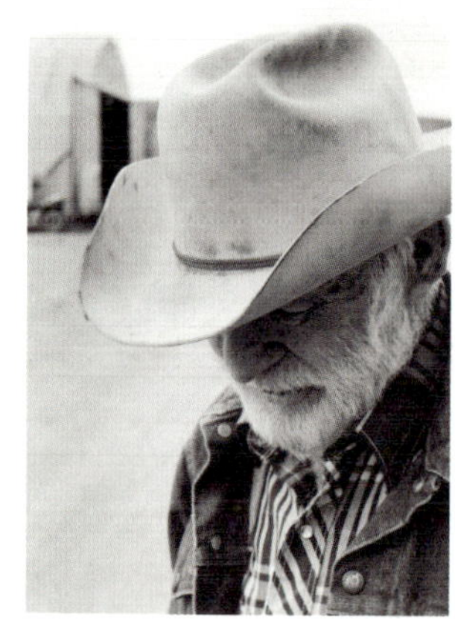
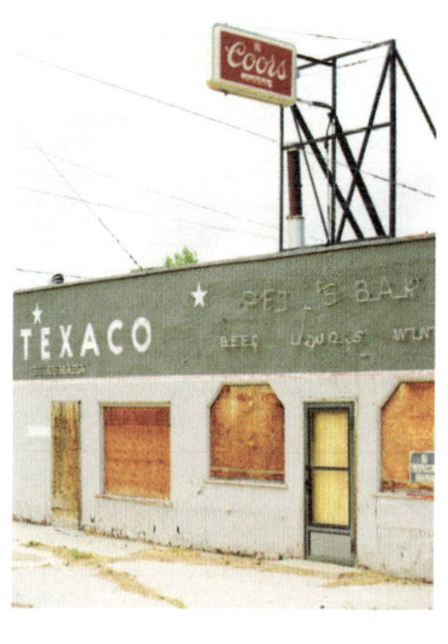
Coors
TEXACO
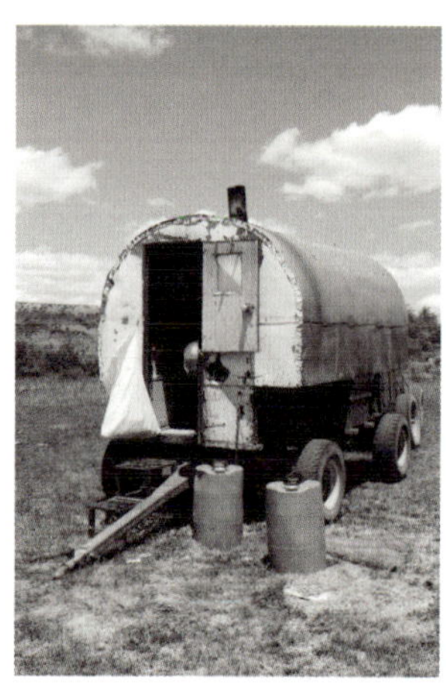
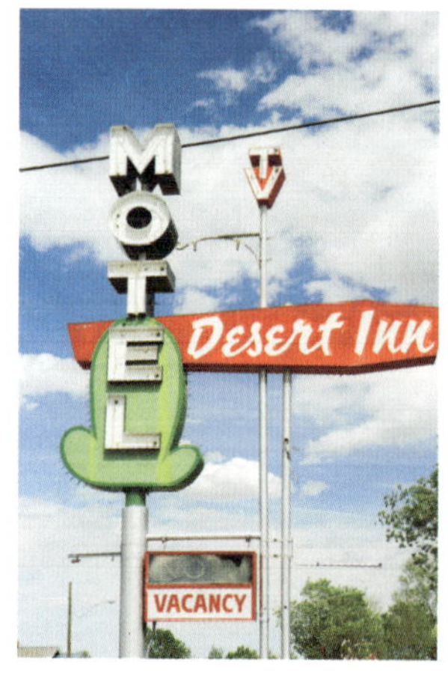
MOTEL
TV
Desert Inn
VACANCY
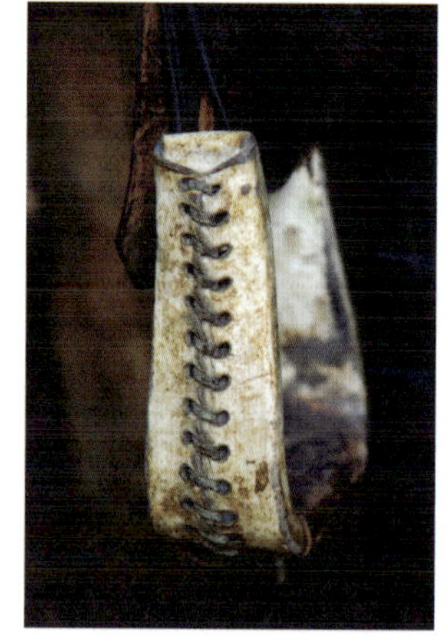
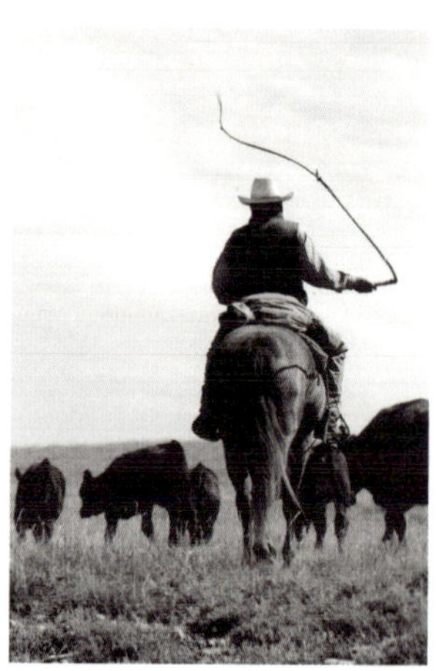
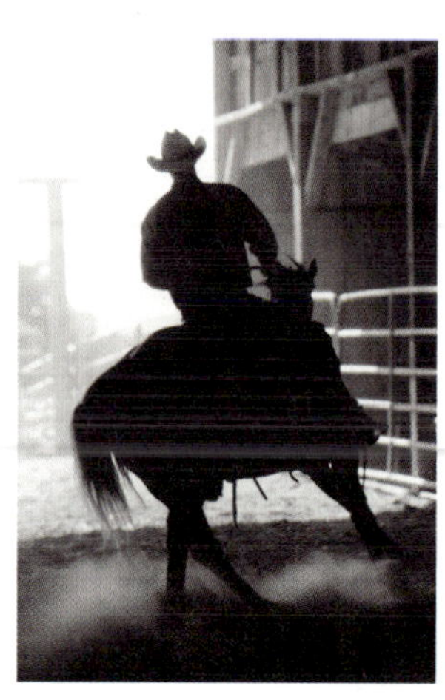
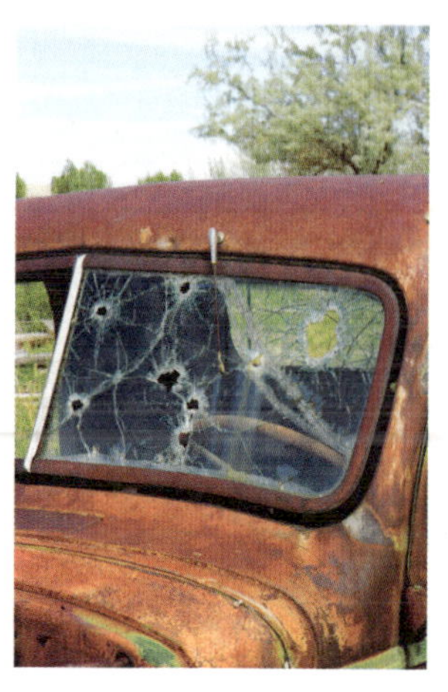
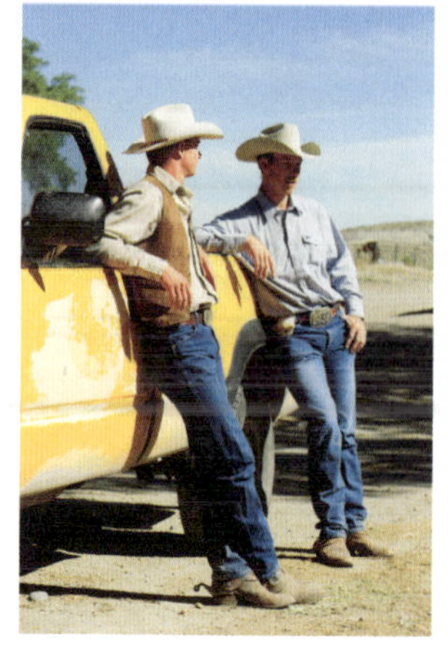
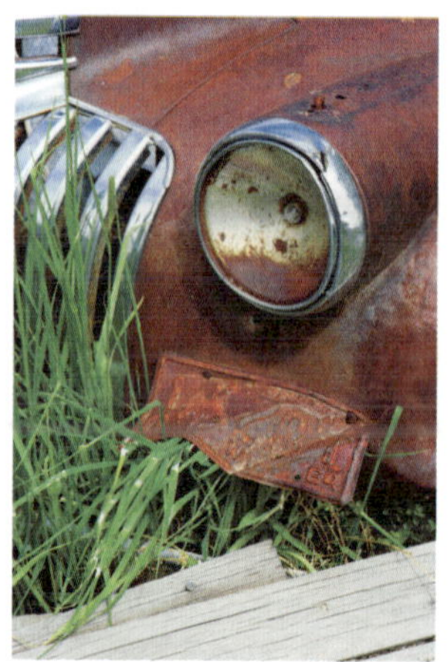

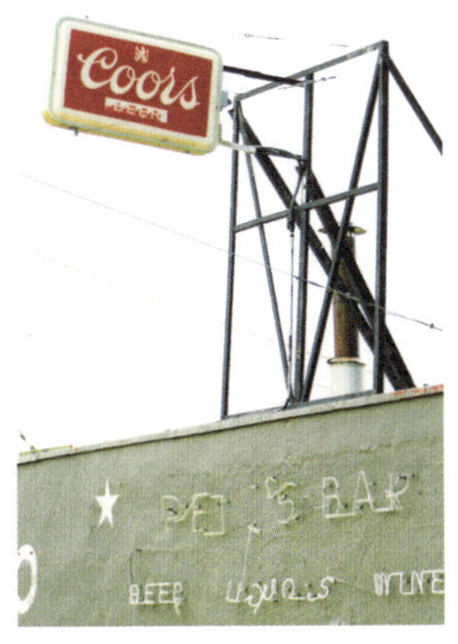
Coors
BEER
BAR
BEER WINE
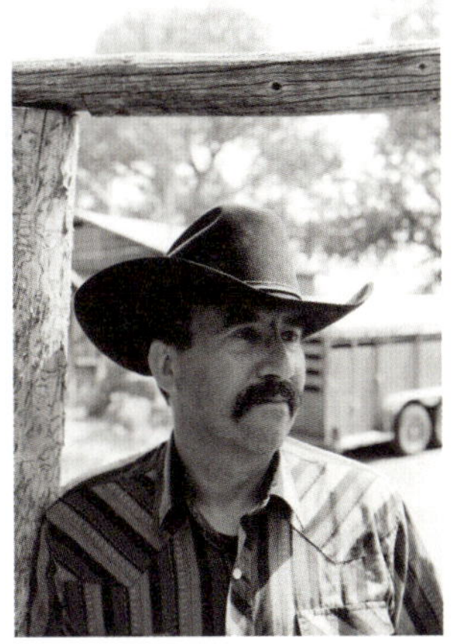
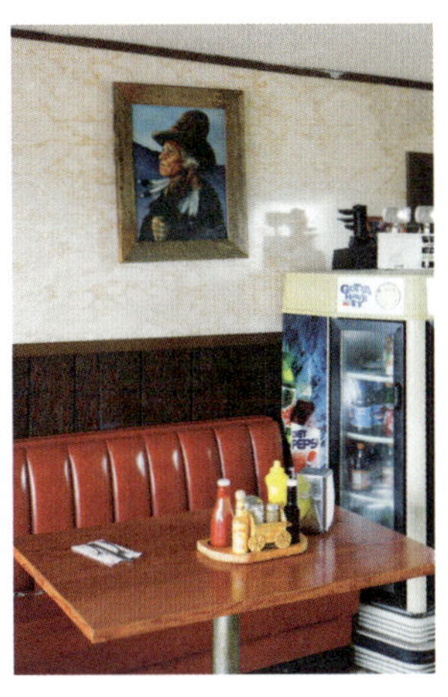
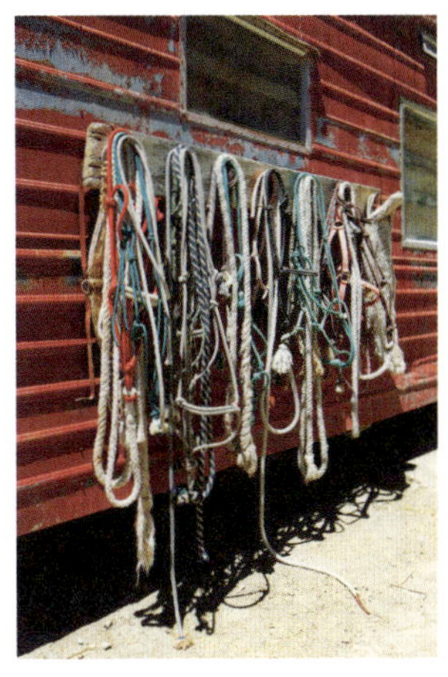
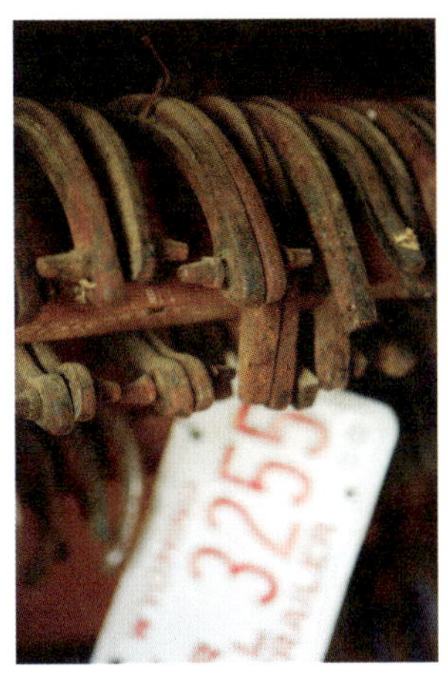
3255
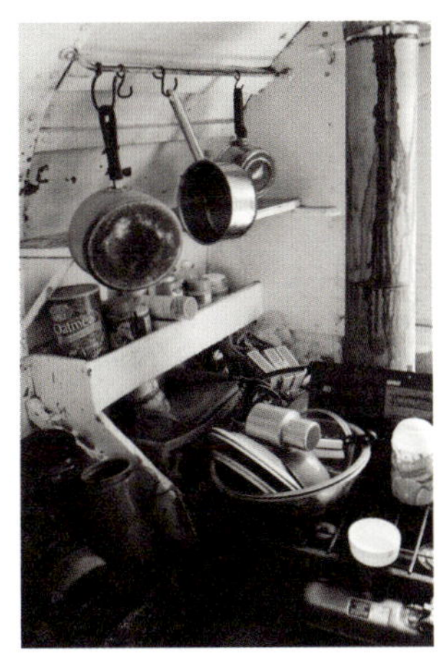
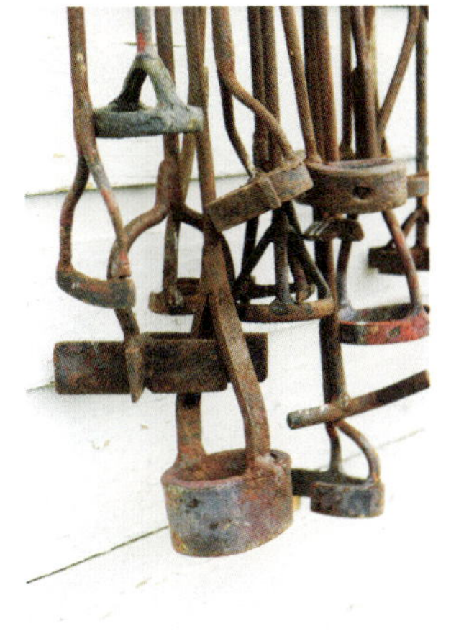
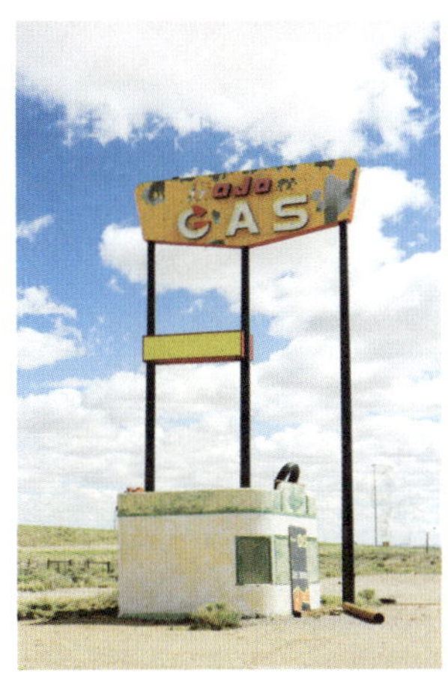
GAS
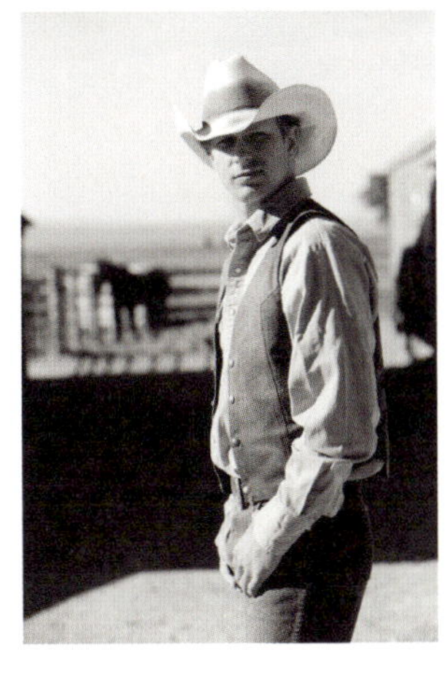
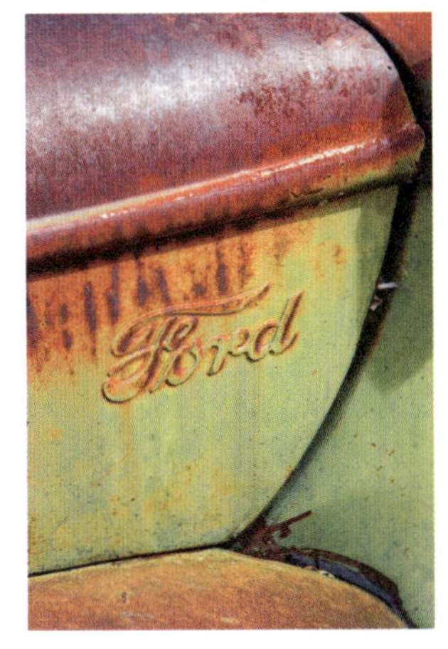
Ford
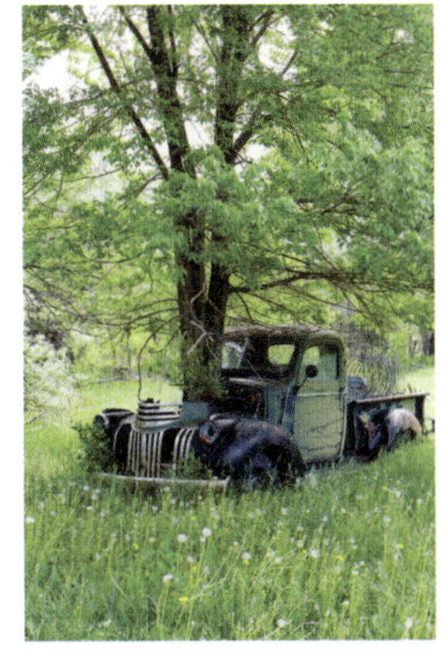
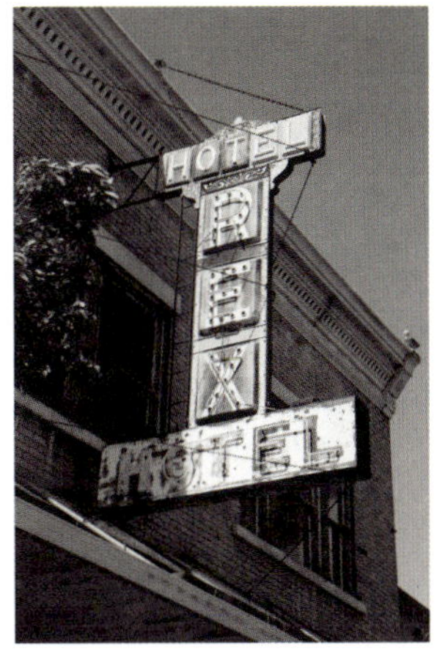
HOTEL
REX
HOTEL
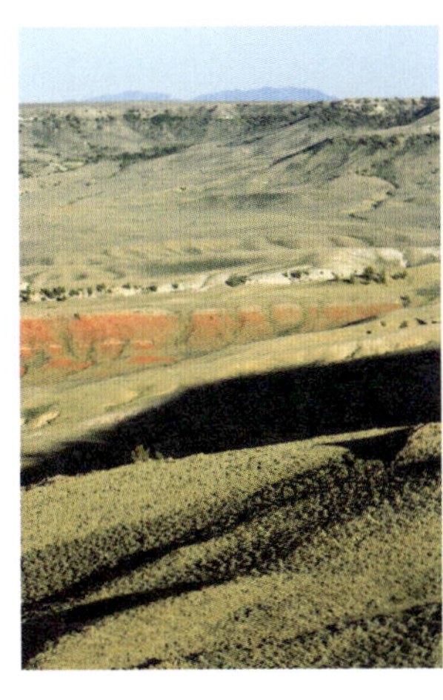
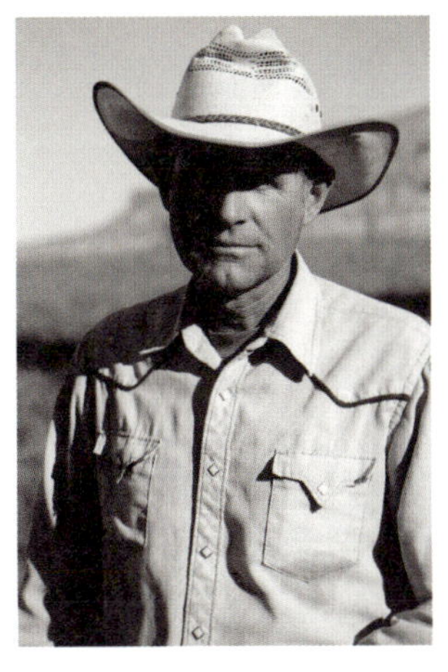
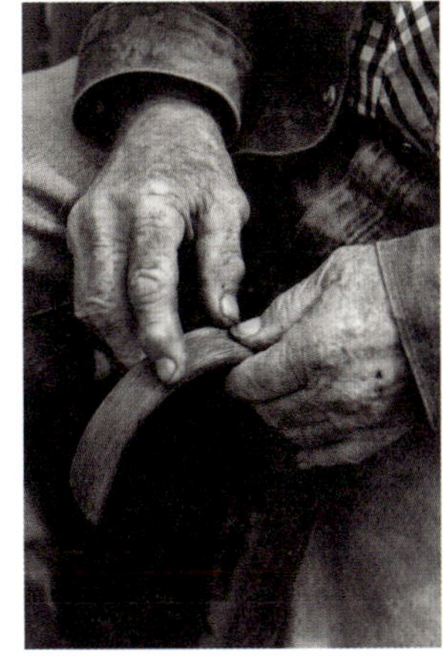
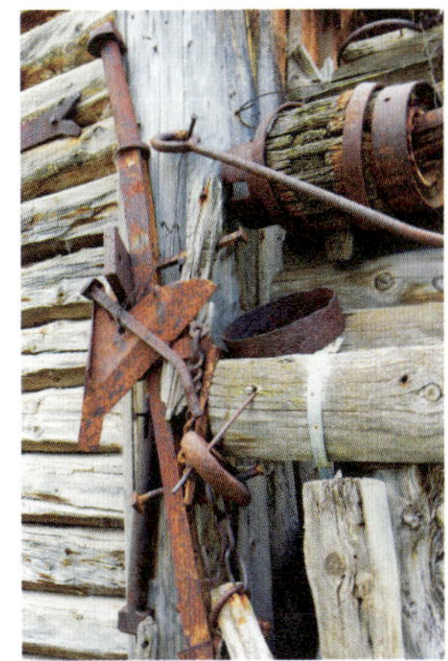

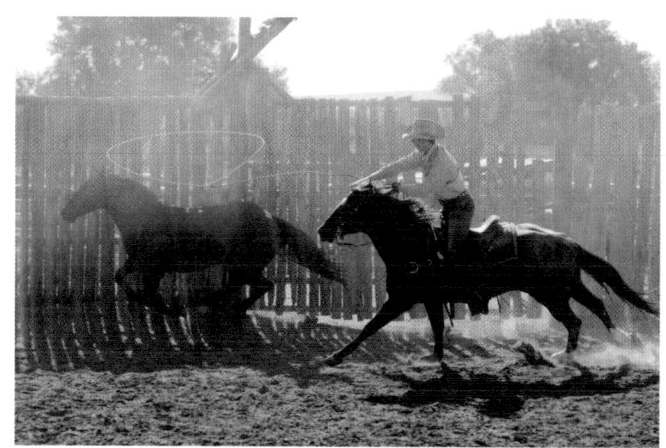

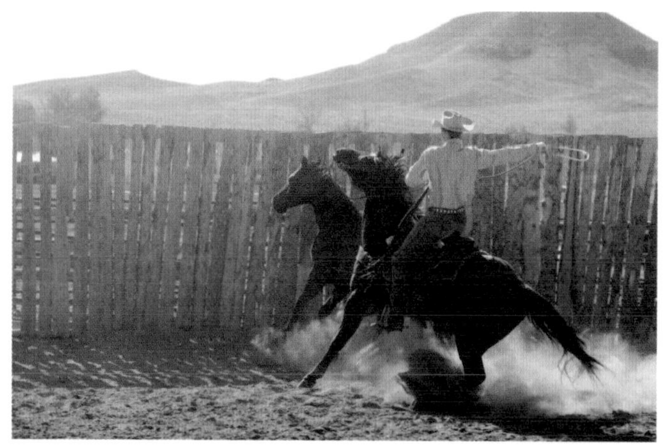

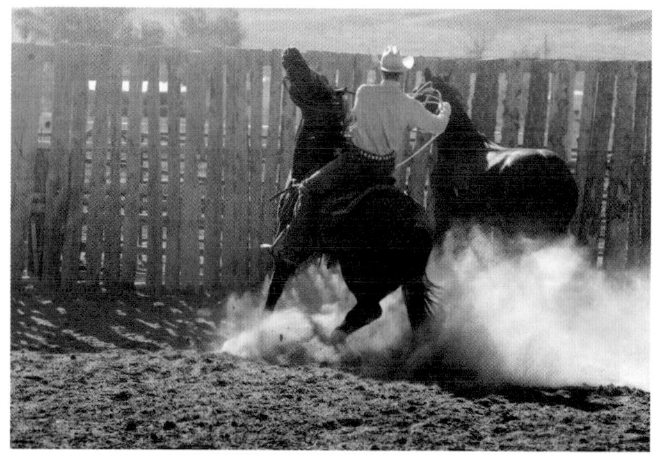

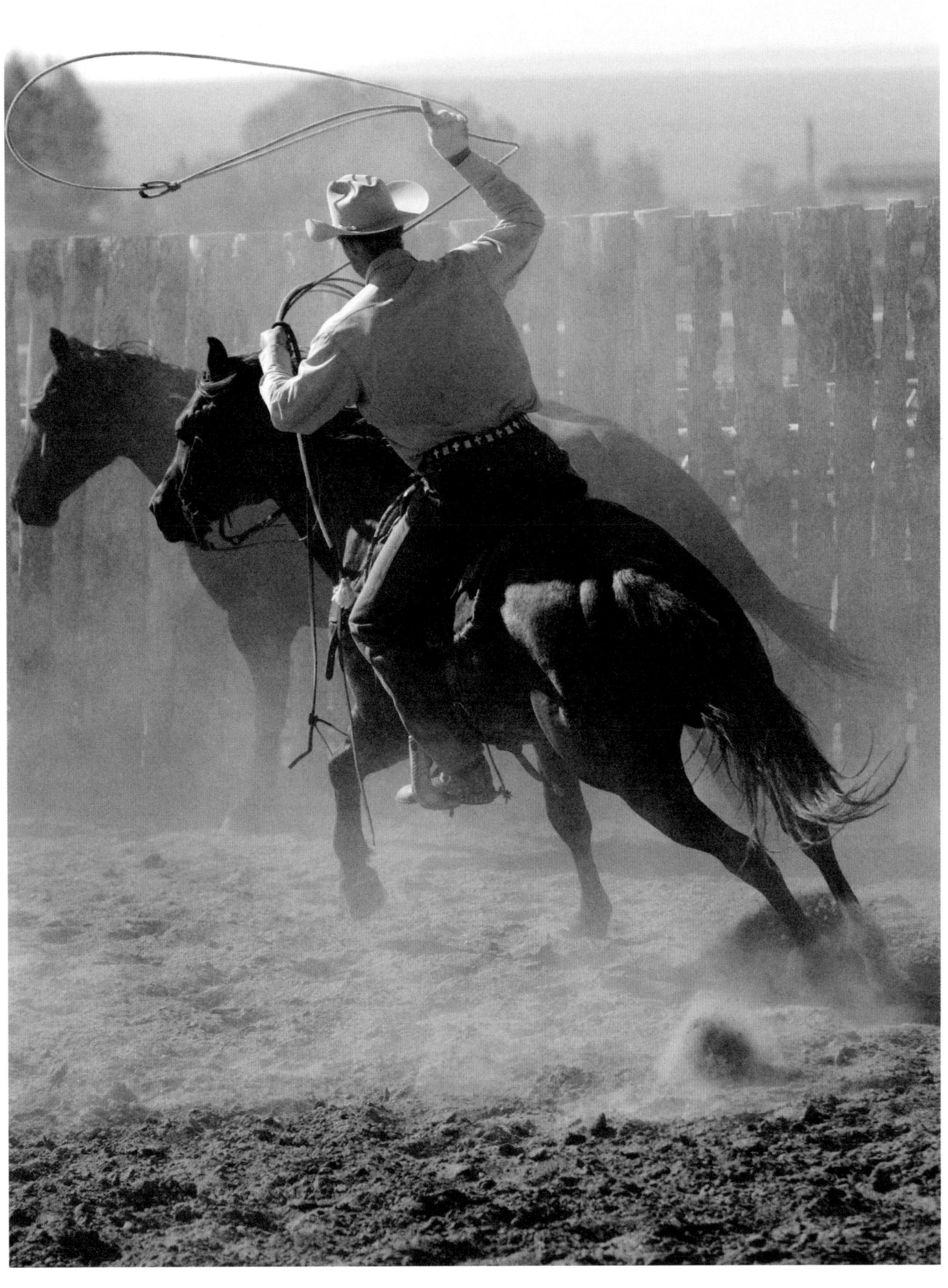

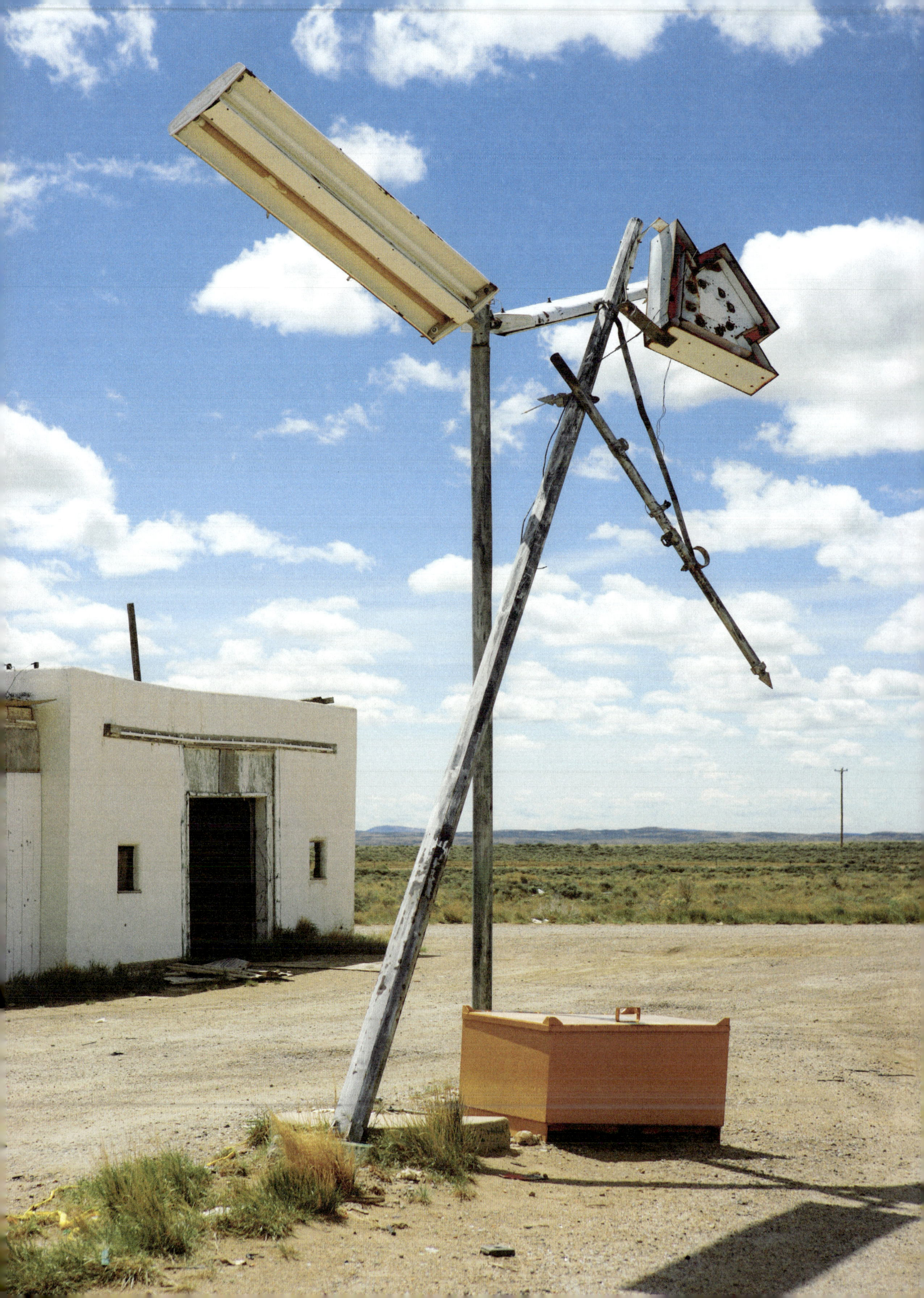

THERE WAS A COOL BREEZE FROM THE EAST LAST NIGHT. LOCAL FOLKS CAME OUT TO SNIFF IT, DECIDING IT WAS NOT FOR THEM.

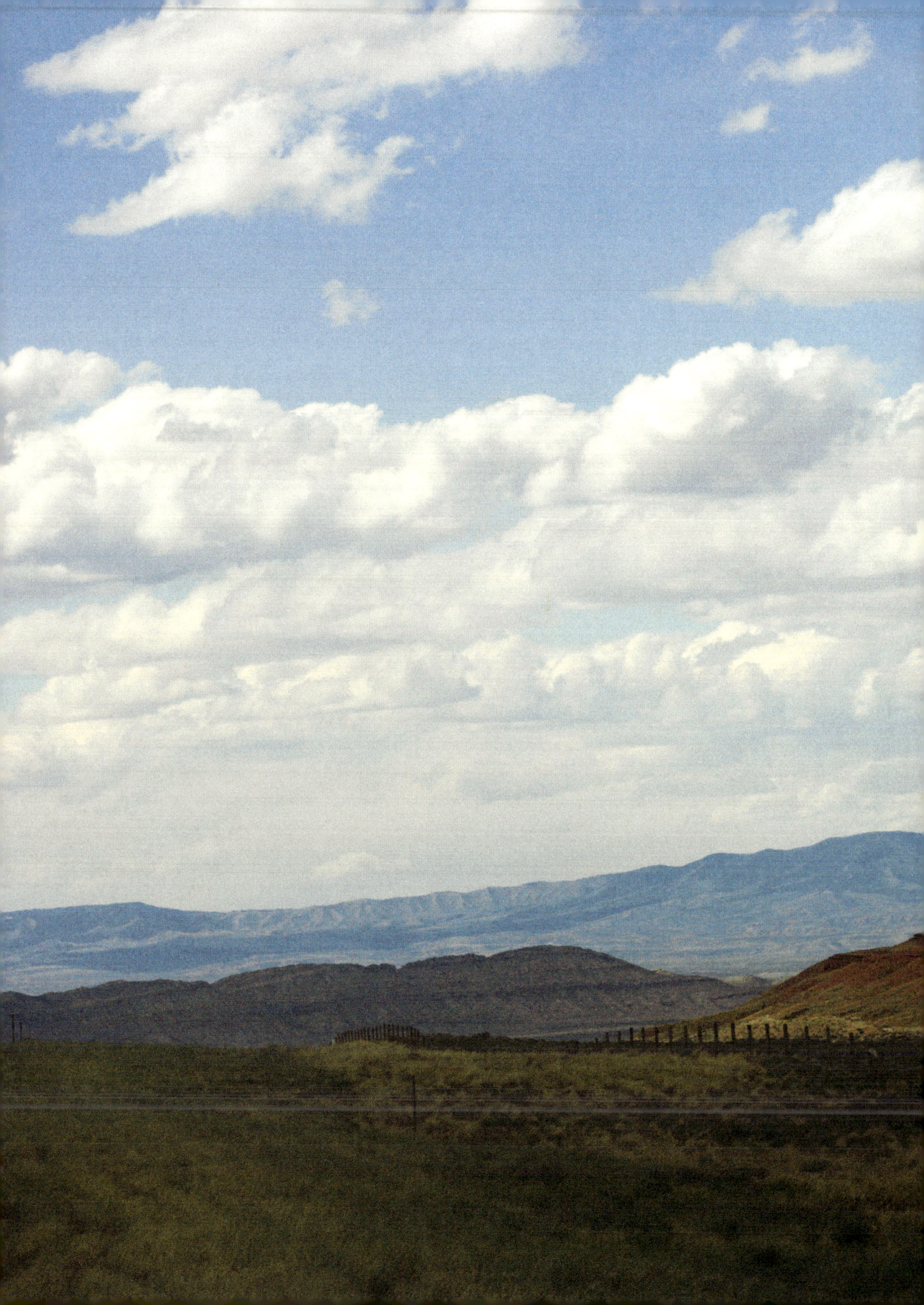

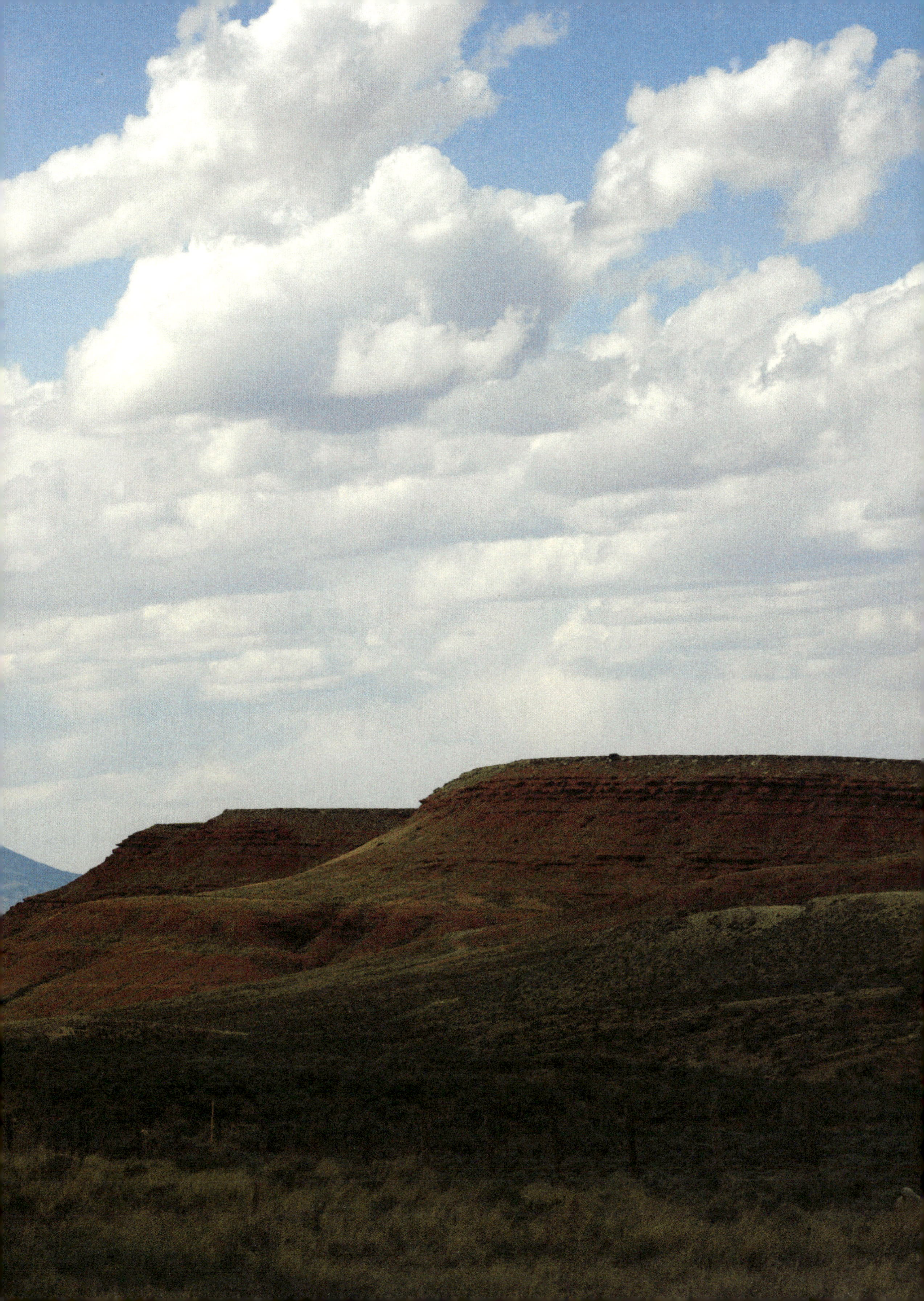

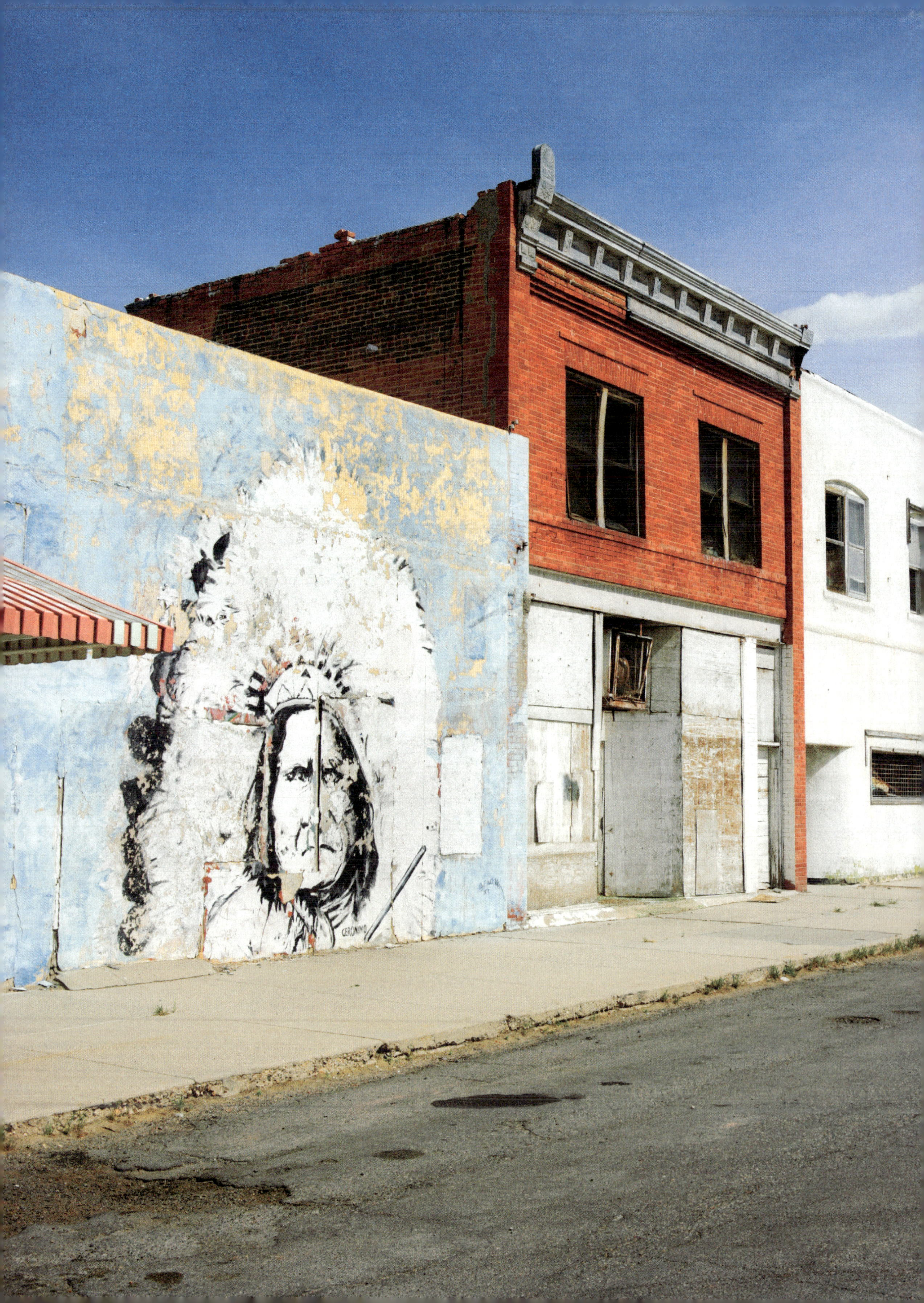
GERONIMO

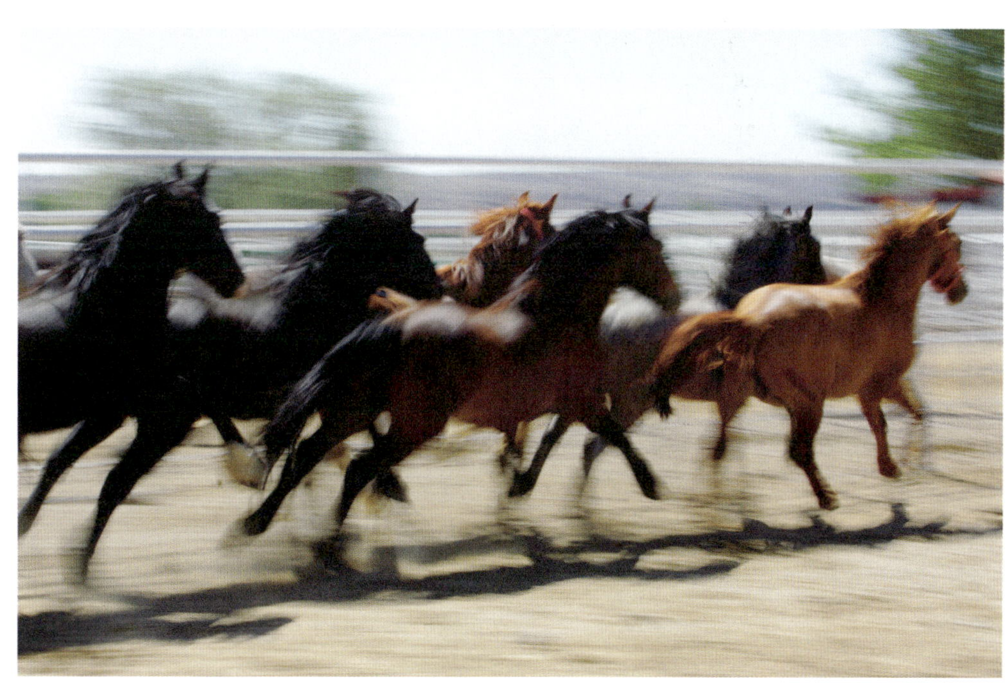

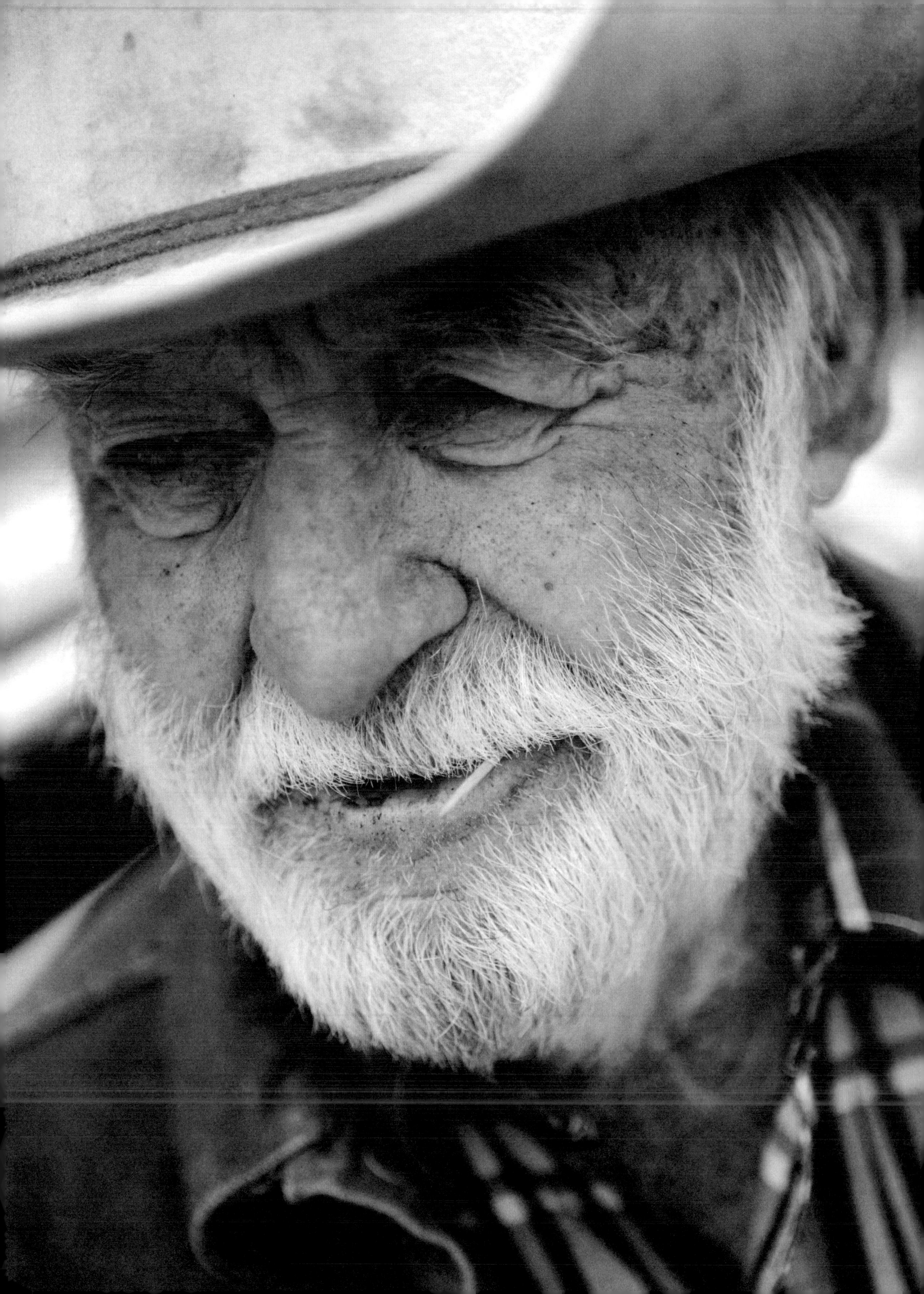

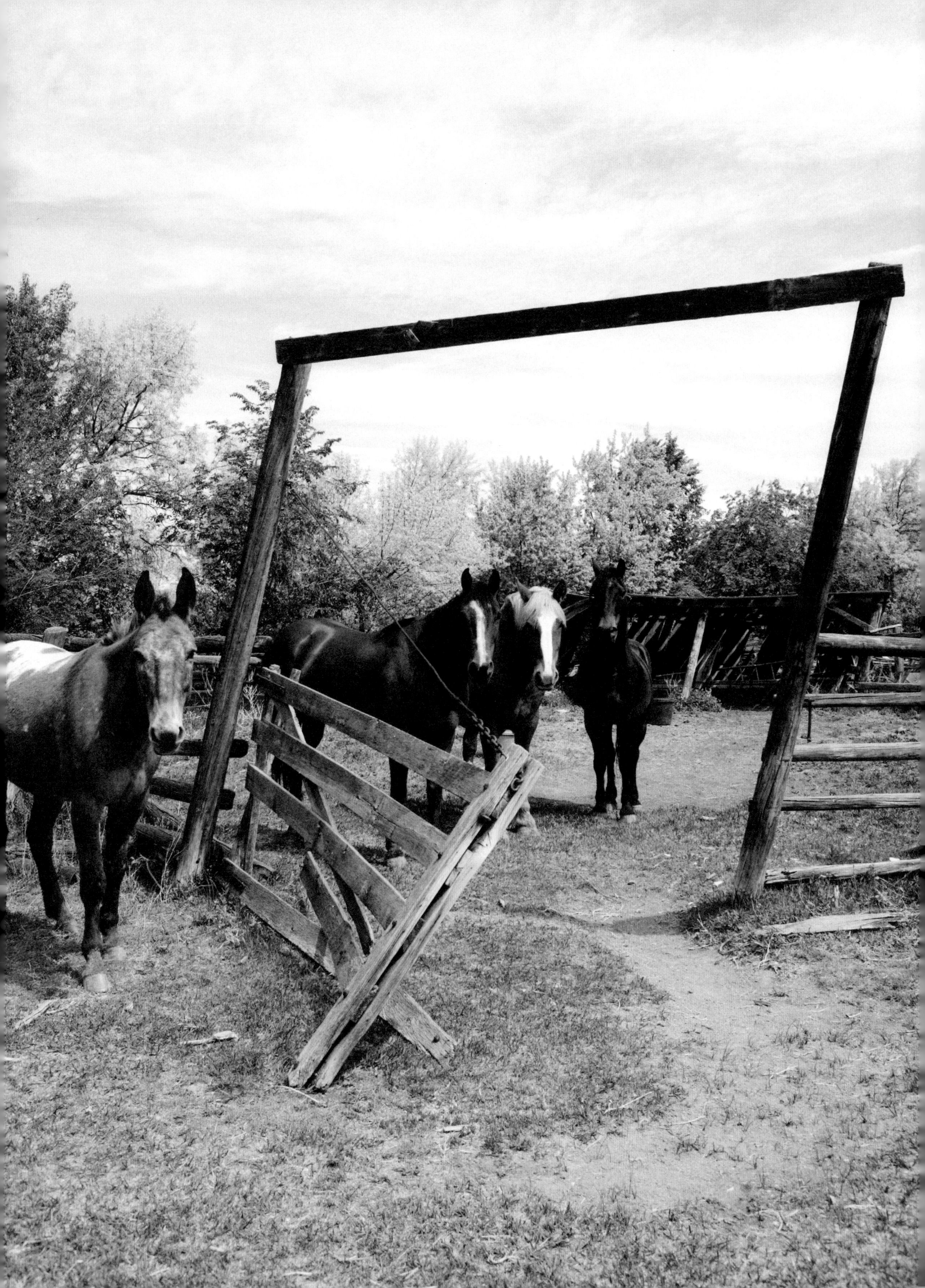

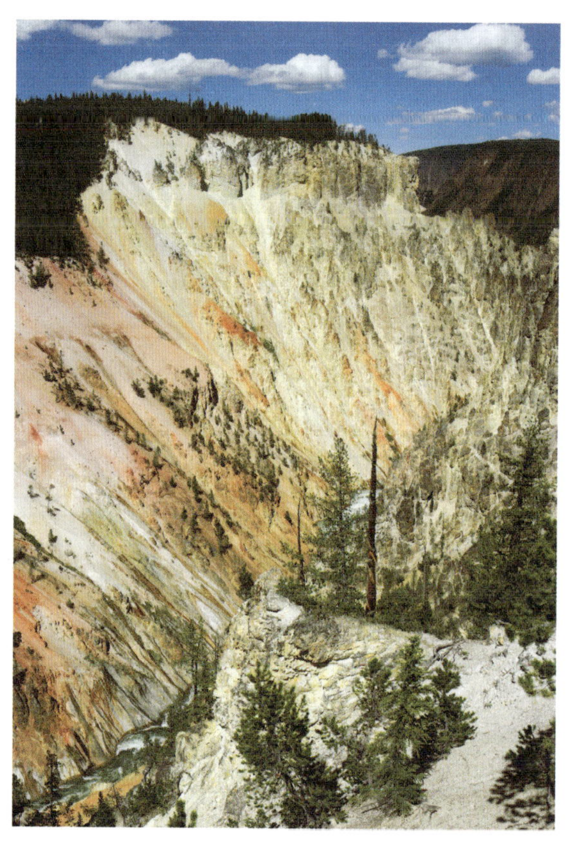

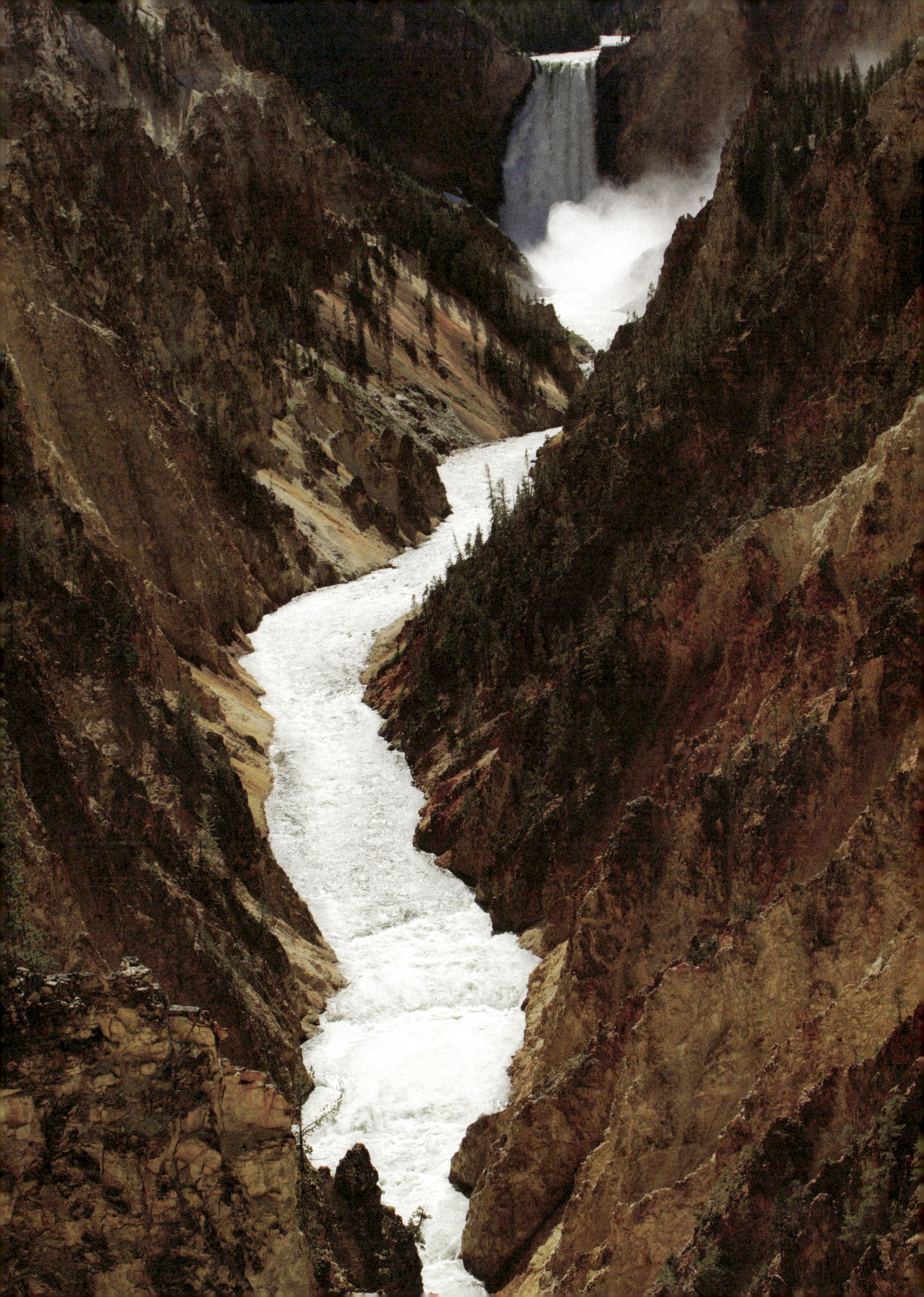

EVERYONE KNOWS THIS IS NOWHERE; THERE ARE WISPS OF DUST DANCING ALL AROUND. OUT HERE, IT'S LIKE WE NEVER EXISTED.

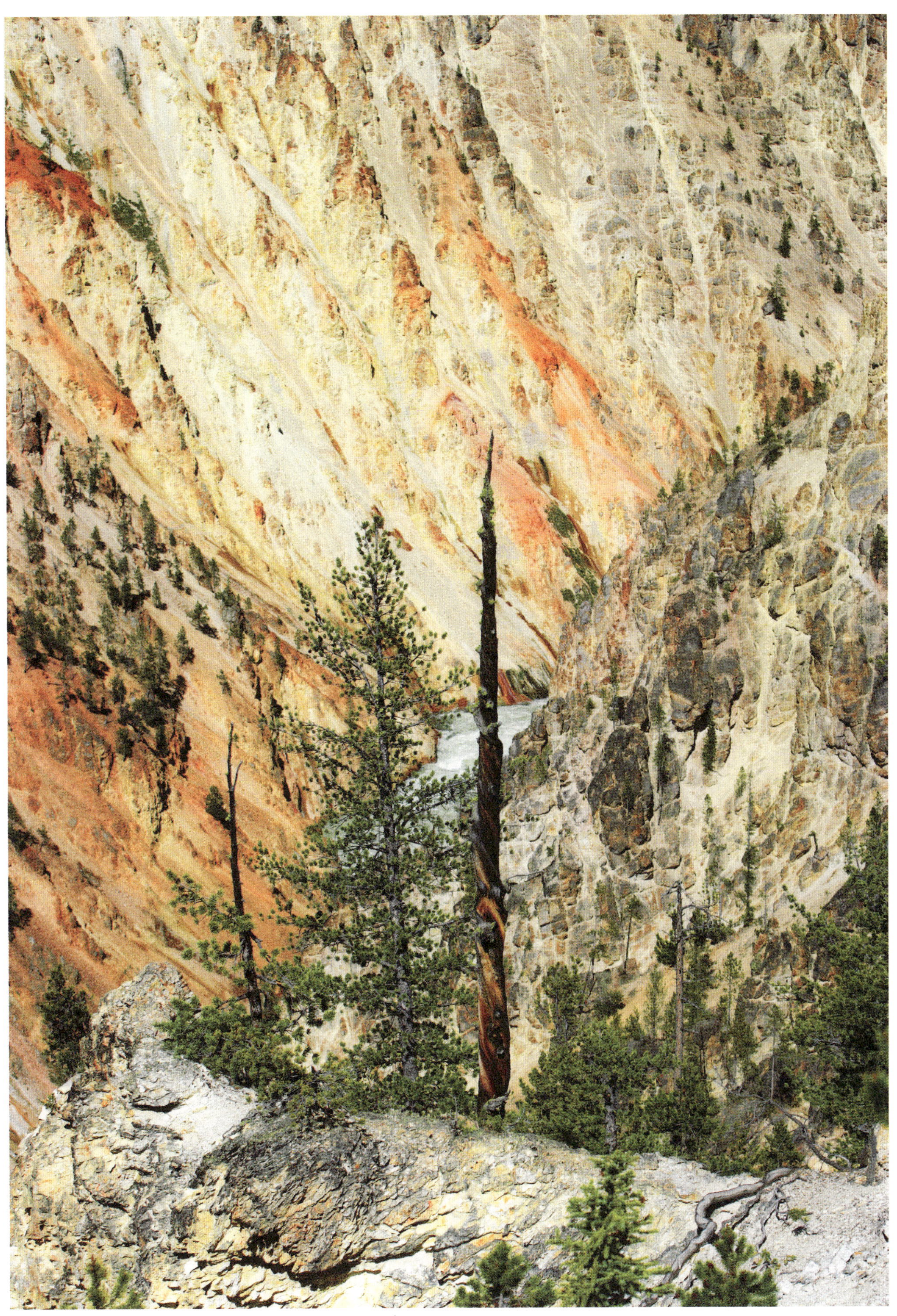

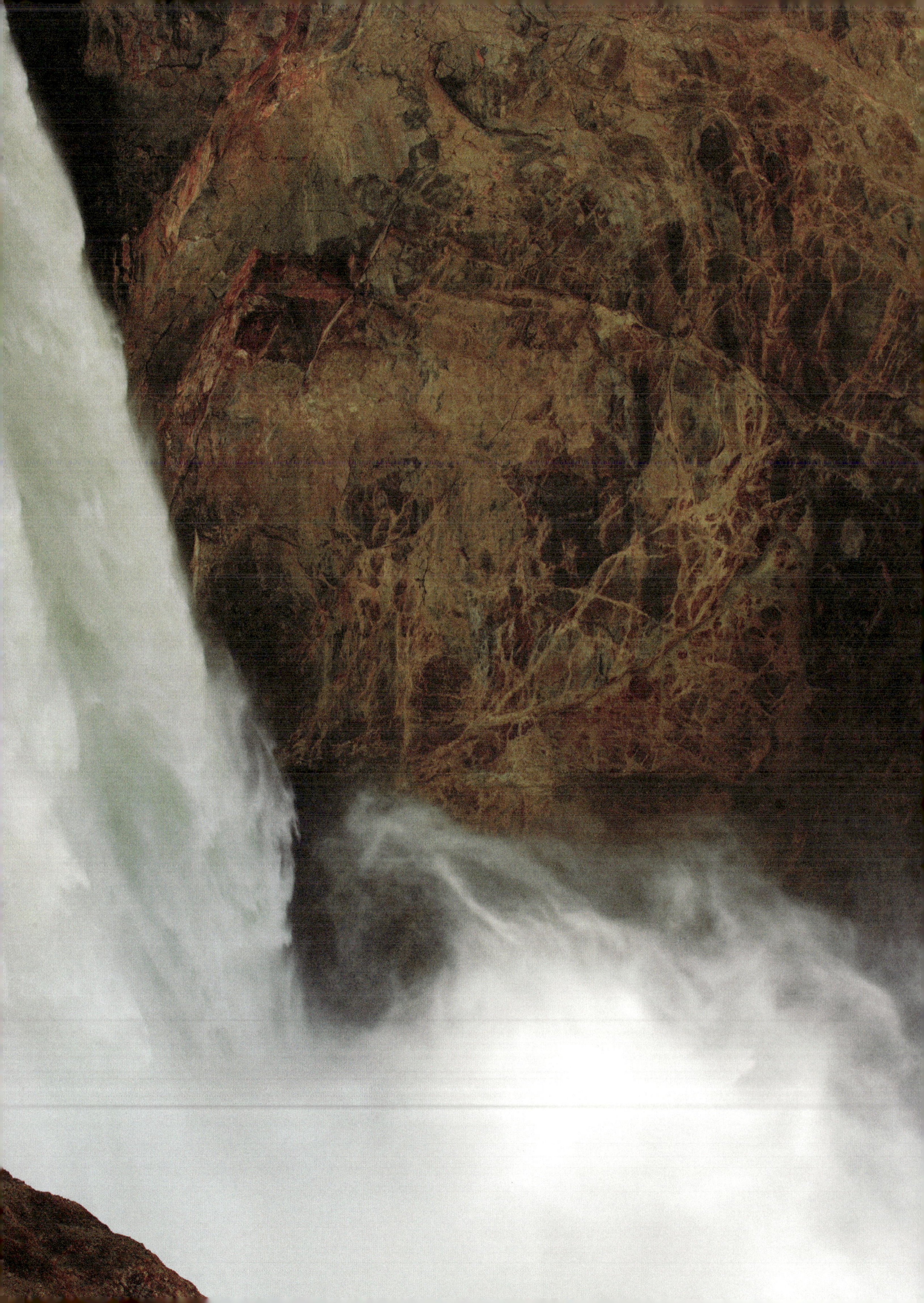

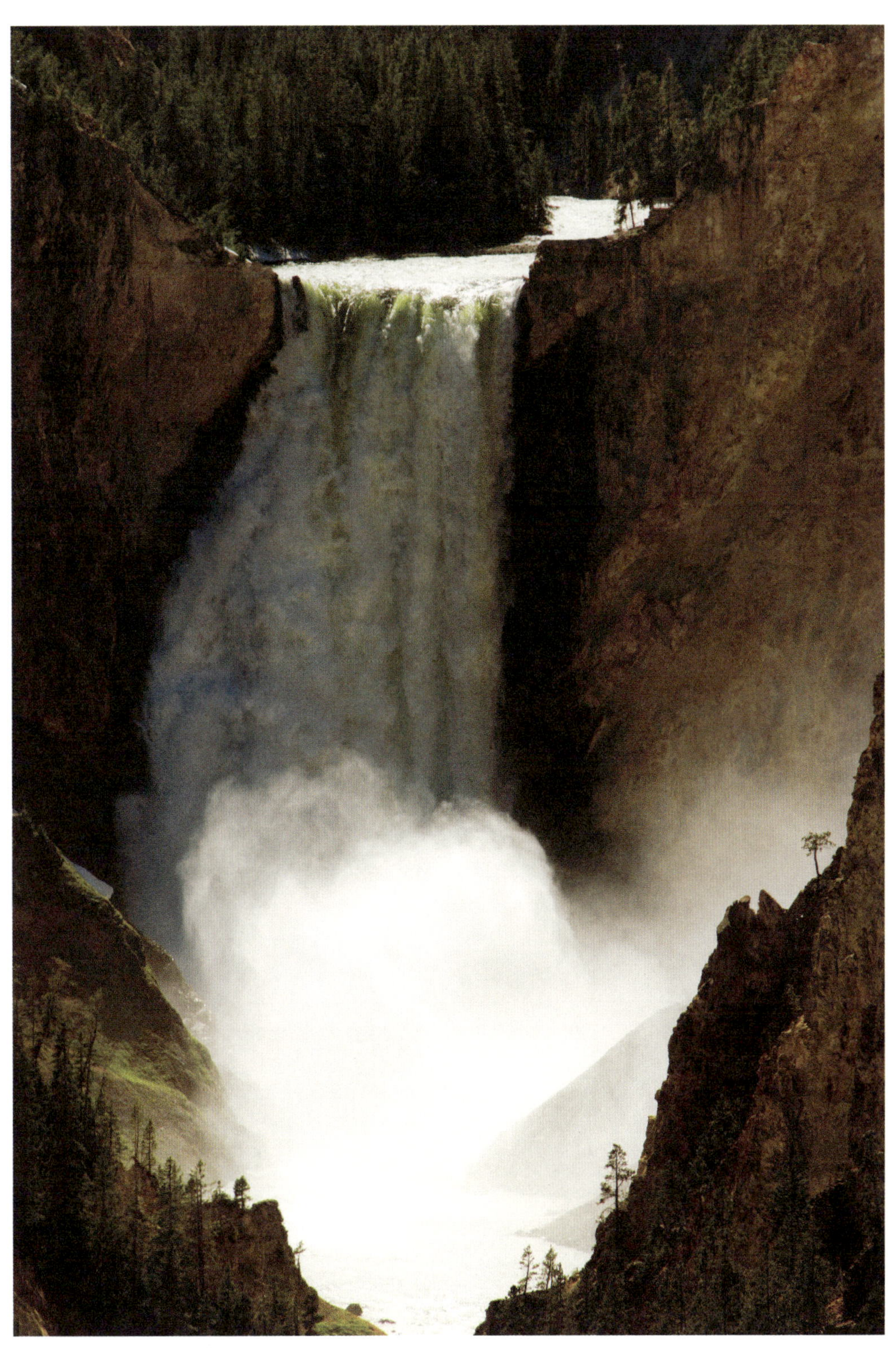

THE EAGLE BY THE ROADSIDE HAS NOT SEEN A LOT OF CARS TODAY. HE LISTLESSLY FLAPS HIS HEAVY, BLACK WINGS AND SAILS OFF EXPOSING A BREAST SHINING VERY MUCH LIKE GOLD.

THE SHADOW STAYS BENEATH THE OPEN SKY FOR A SECOND OR TWO BEFORE IT IS SWALLOWED BY THE GRAVEL ON THE MOUNTAINSIDE.

The expanses out West often seem familiar even to those who have never been here. They are well-known film sets, people carry the soundtracks close to their hearts; every highway cruiser willingly joins in with the chorus, tapping the beat on the dashboard. There is the dry scent of prairie herbs, and the borderless canyon country – the emptiness of a mighty republic.

It's just us and the eagle.

But more will come as industrial gold and silver mining, once again lucrative, increases. Up in tiny Tuscarora, where the eagles soar, quiet, solemn men hunch in the creek panning for elusive flakes. Mining used to be intense here in the old days, but out of the twelve people who officially live here now quite a few are artists. They paint and are potters and create enough of a communal life to sustain a six-day post office, with a miniscule library, and a school farther down the road.

"Listen! There is no white noise." Sidne Peske came here and shooed away the rats from the old white wooden house, which is now her home and opens its front door to an impressive succession of blue mountains.

Out front, dressed in carpenter's jeans and a small-checked shirt she could pass as a farmer's wife from dust bowl country, but she came here recently to paint by her own design. In her studio there are numerous sketches and half-completed paintings of human bodies and of the mountain range. She practices on a guitar. Magazines fill up a cabinet with glass doors and a wooden surface that looks fire-ravaged. In one corner sits a laptop and, hanging from the ceiling, there is an inflatable plastic globe;

proof that this outpost is linked to others. Peske is a member of the artists network Wild Women.

"You're never bored in Tuscarora," she emphasizes. "Lonely and depressed, perhaps, but never bored."

Curious dogs follow us through the quiet streets with historical memories of saloons, masonic lodges, a ballet school, and two newspaper offices. Many roof trusses are broken, the rough winter wind has gnawed at fences and other wooden structures, the sheetings now coated with verdigris with the same color as the amazing local sunset.

We soon end up on Weed Street, panting as we make our way up the rocky hillsides to where Bill Collins sits kneeling with his metal detector. His makeshift home is a teardrop-shaped trailer with a stuffed prairie dog guarding its entrance door. Ears covered by headphones, he spends most of his time crouching in the creek in a faded sleeveless t-shirt. He tells us the coyote howls kept him awake all morning. In the evenings he listens to books on tape underneath the open sky.

"There are 65 people living between that thin stretch of highway down there and the state of Idaho. There's probably more wild horses." When Collins doesn't pan for gold in the streams, he can sit for hours at dusk, his rifle by his side, waiting for the deer to come out of their hiding. And downhill, Sidne Peske will place her easel in the dirt waiting for yet another sundown over the territory.

"It may sound weird," she says, "but to many of us newcomers this is both a dream-life and a life like in a dream."

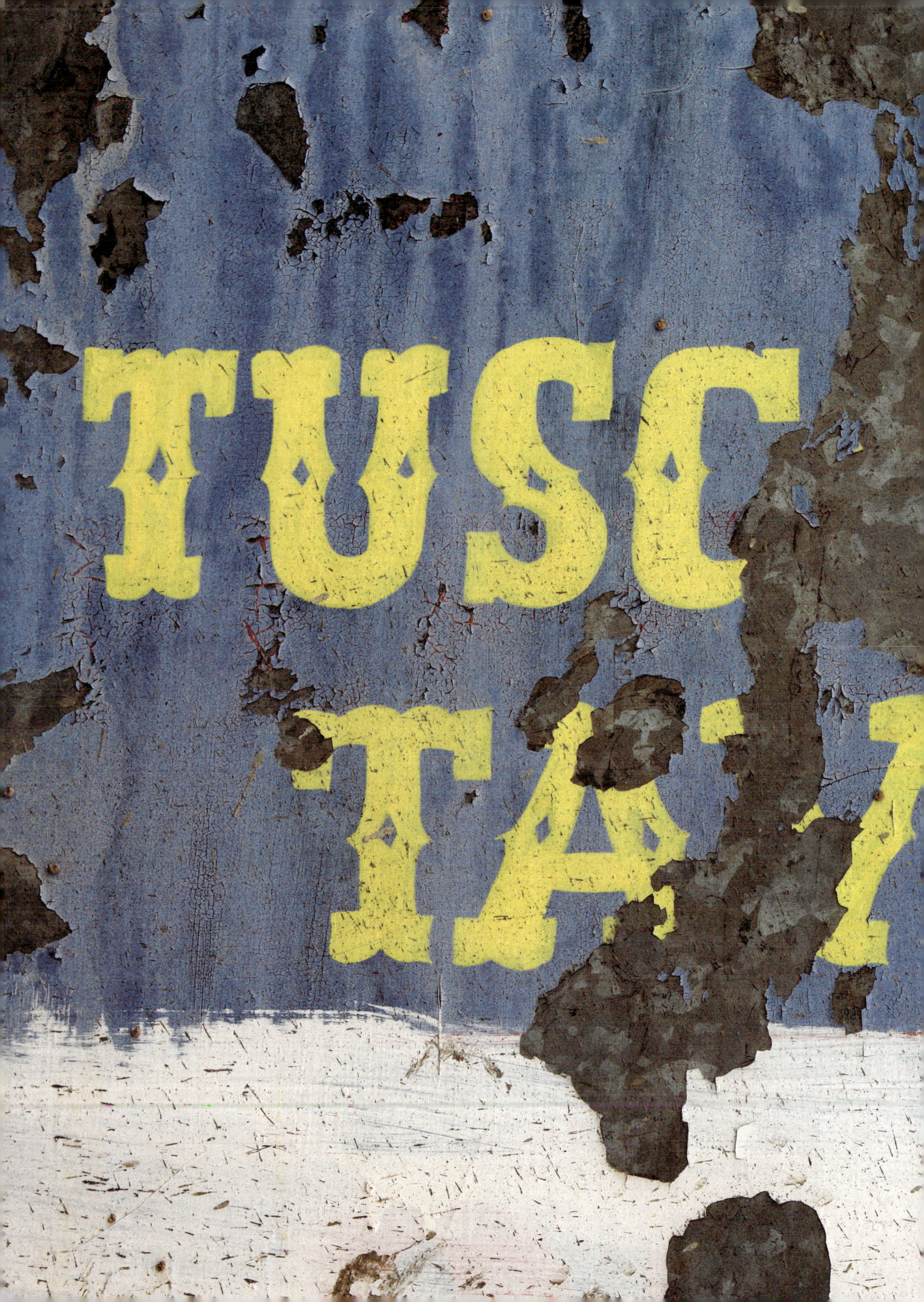
TUSC
TA

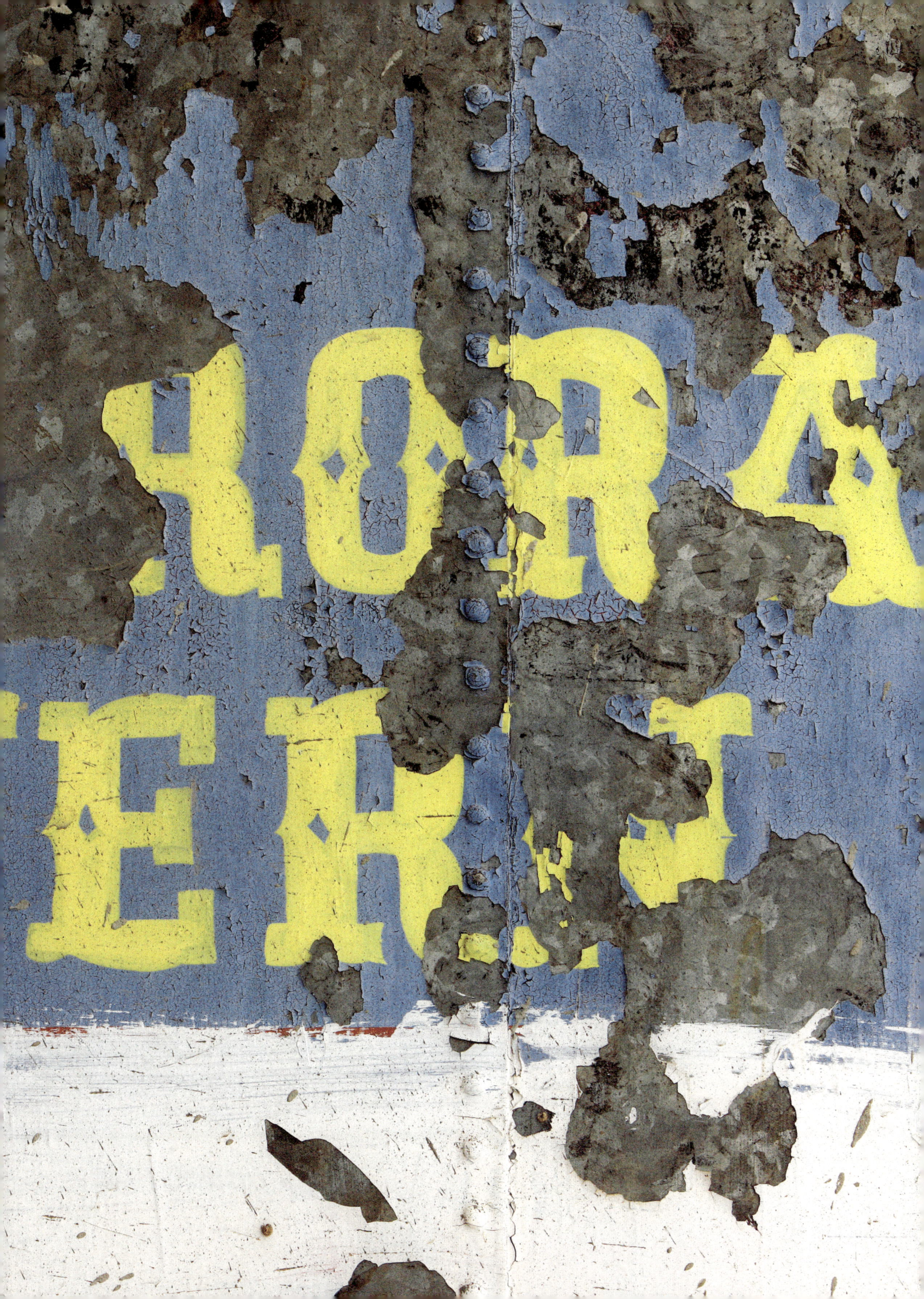

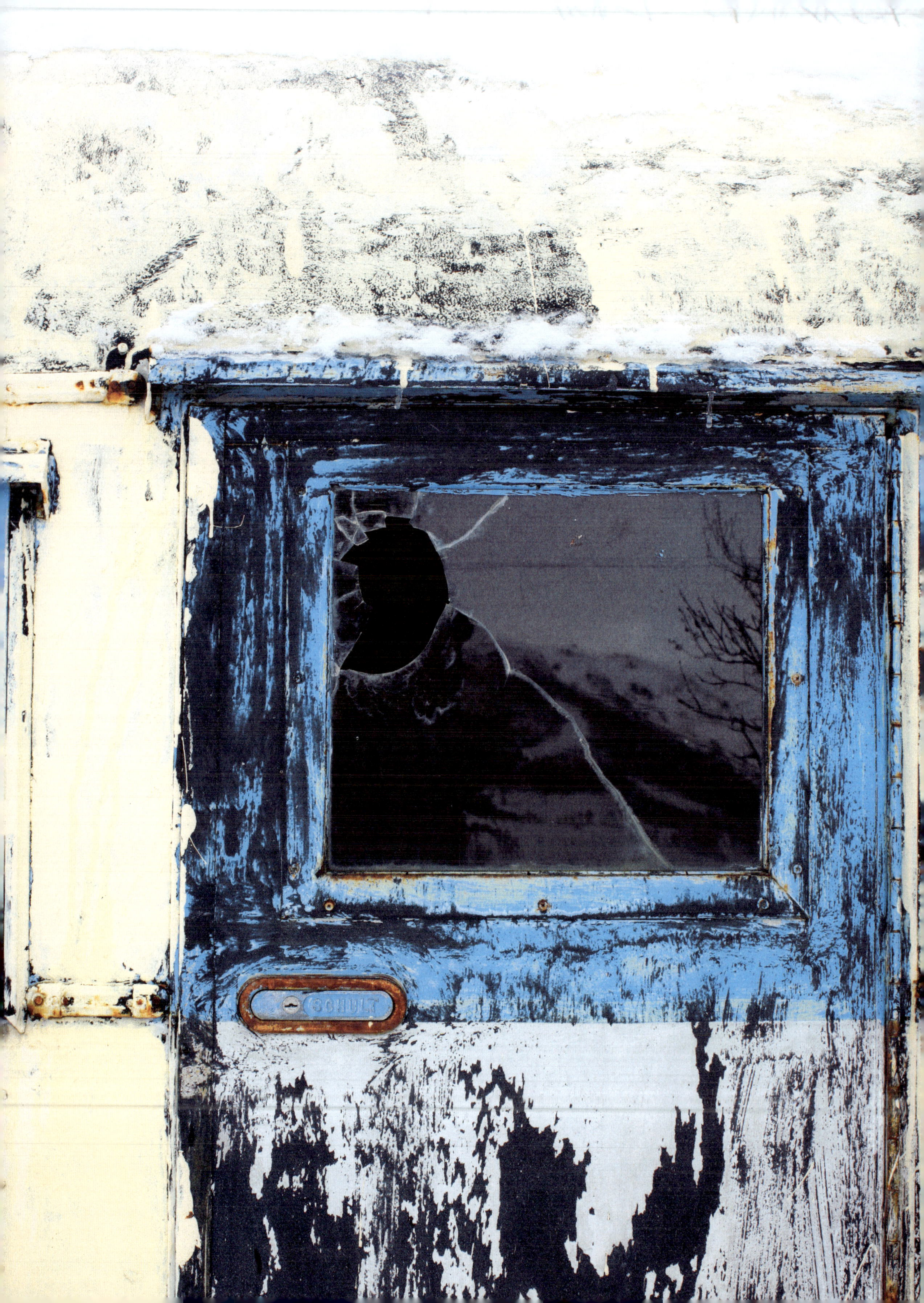
SCHULT

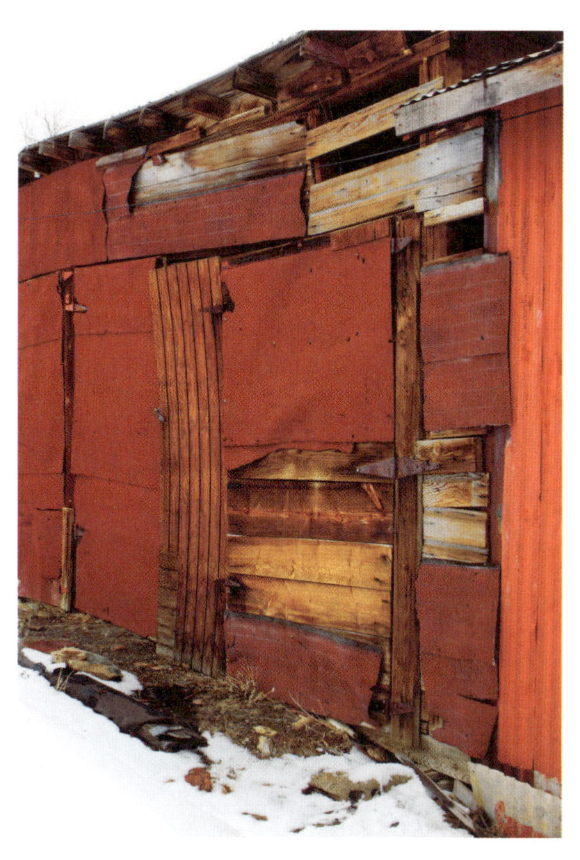

The scenery is so emotionally charged and insistent that it looks almost staged. Memories provide the remaining buildings with a structure to lean on. Nothing out there, that's what people say. Not true, there is a future: it takes five children to demand a school, three to keep it open, and the school up around the bend now has six students. The teacher has moved in next door, like in the days of old when the skies were always open. The thrill is still here. It never wears off. Really, there is no place else to go.

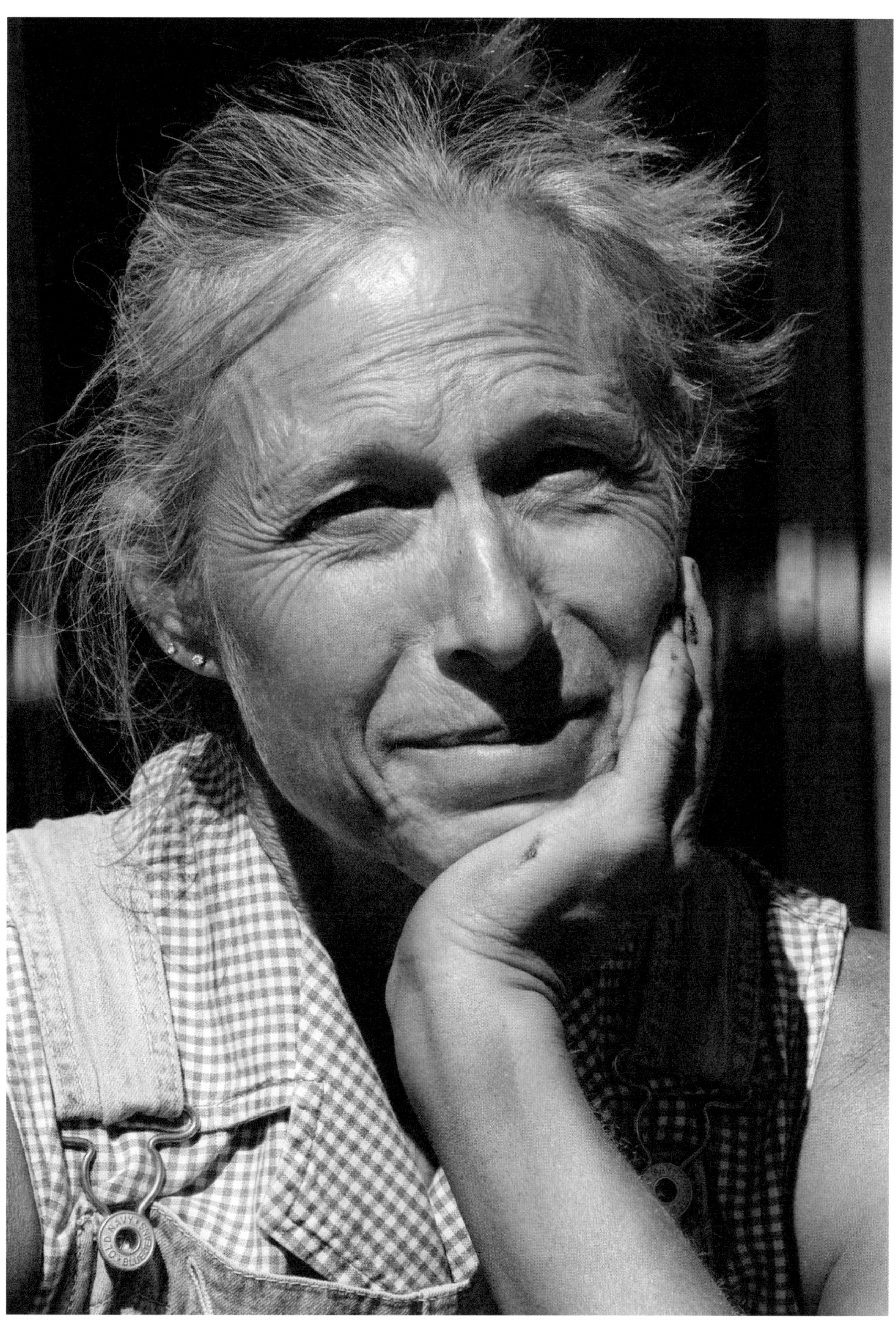

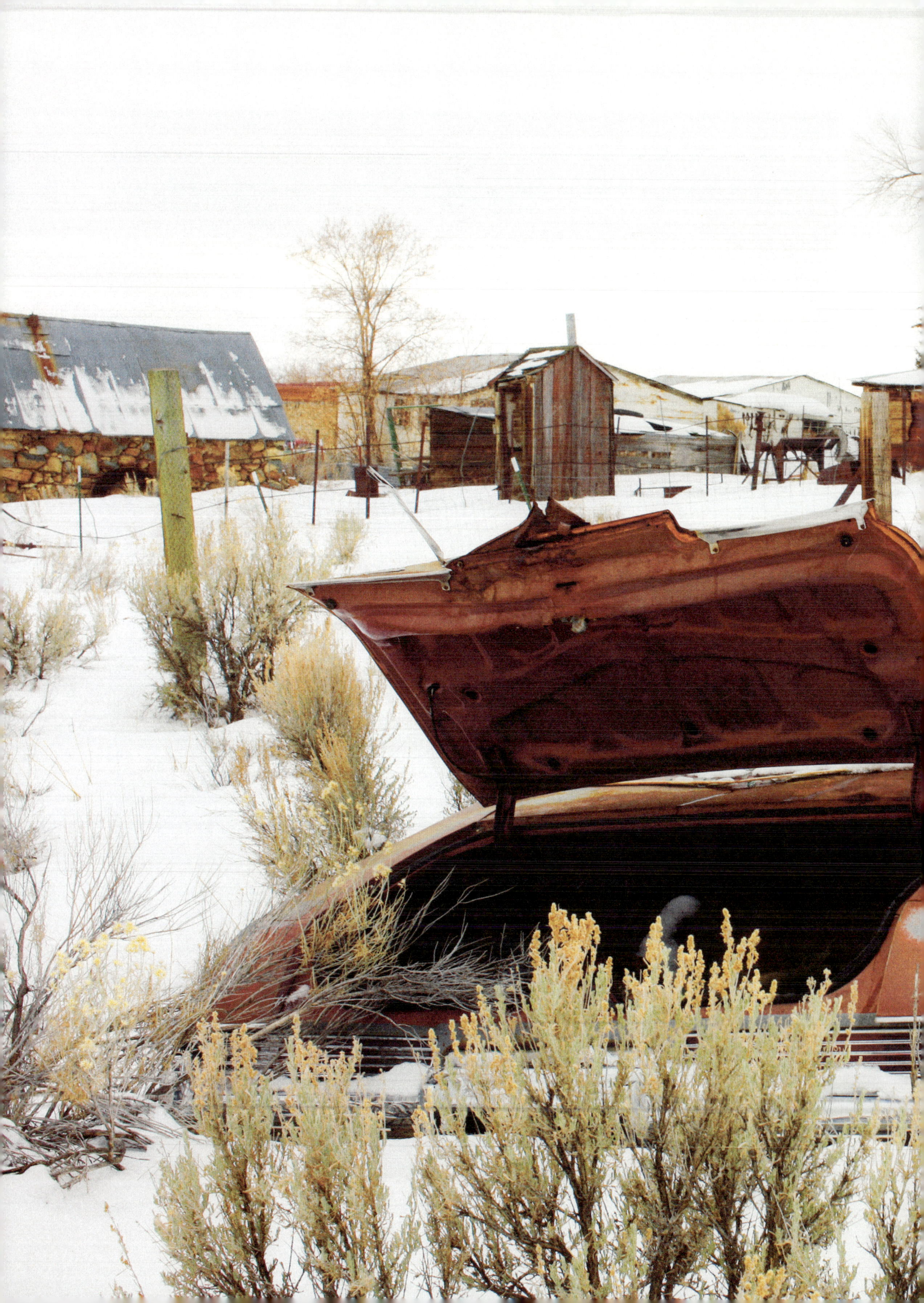

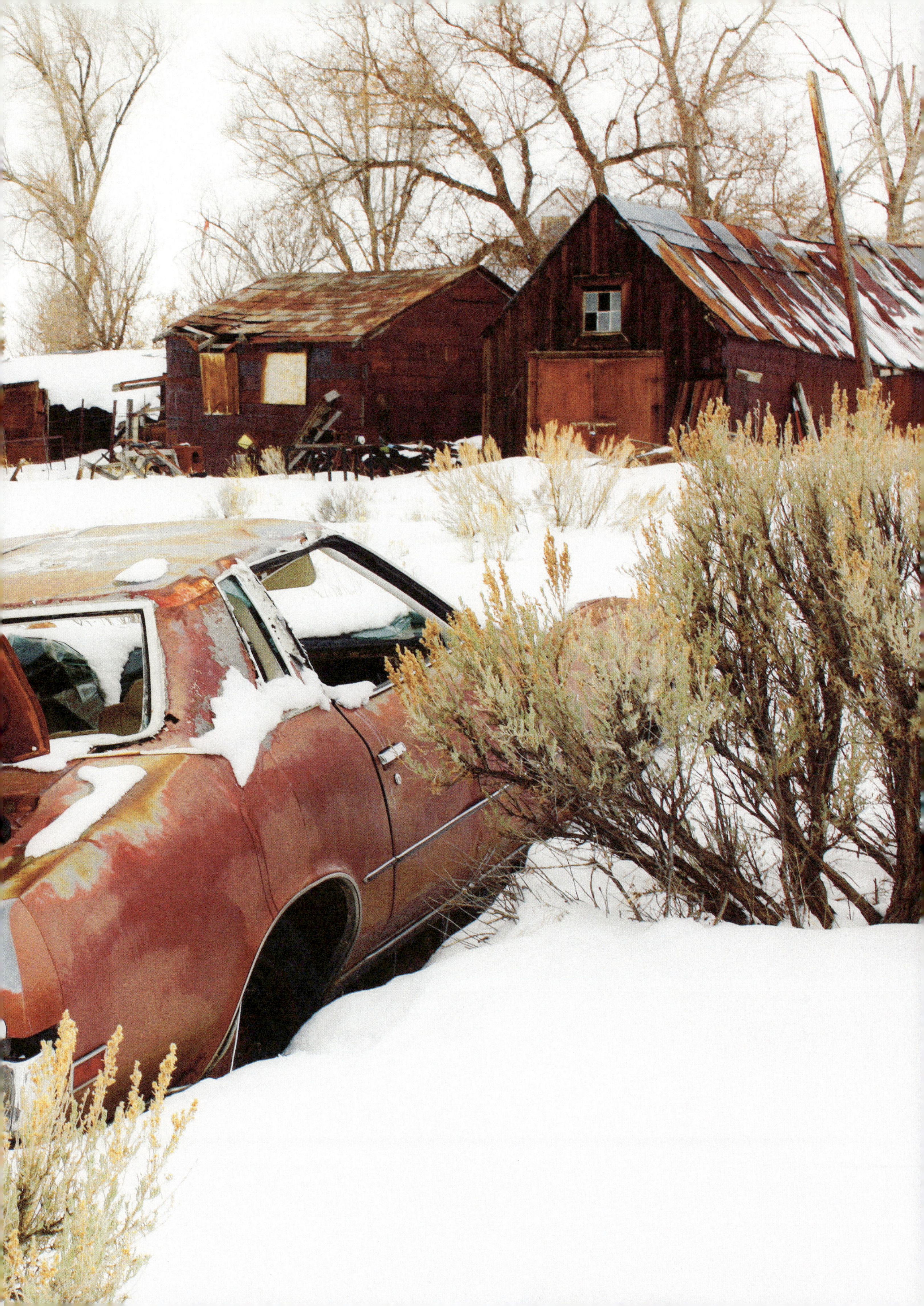

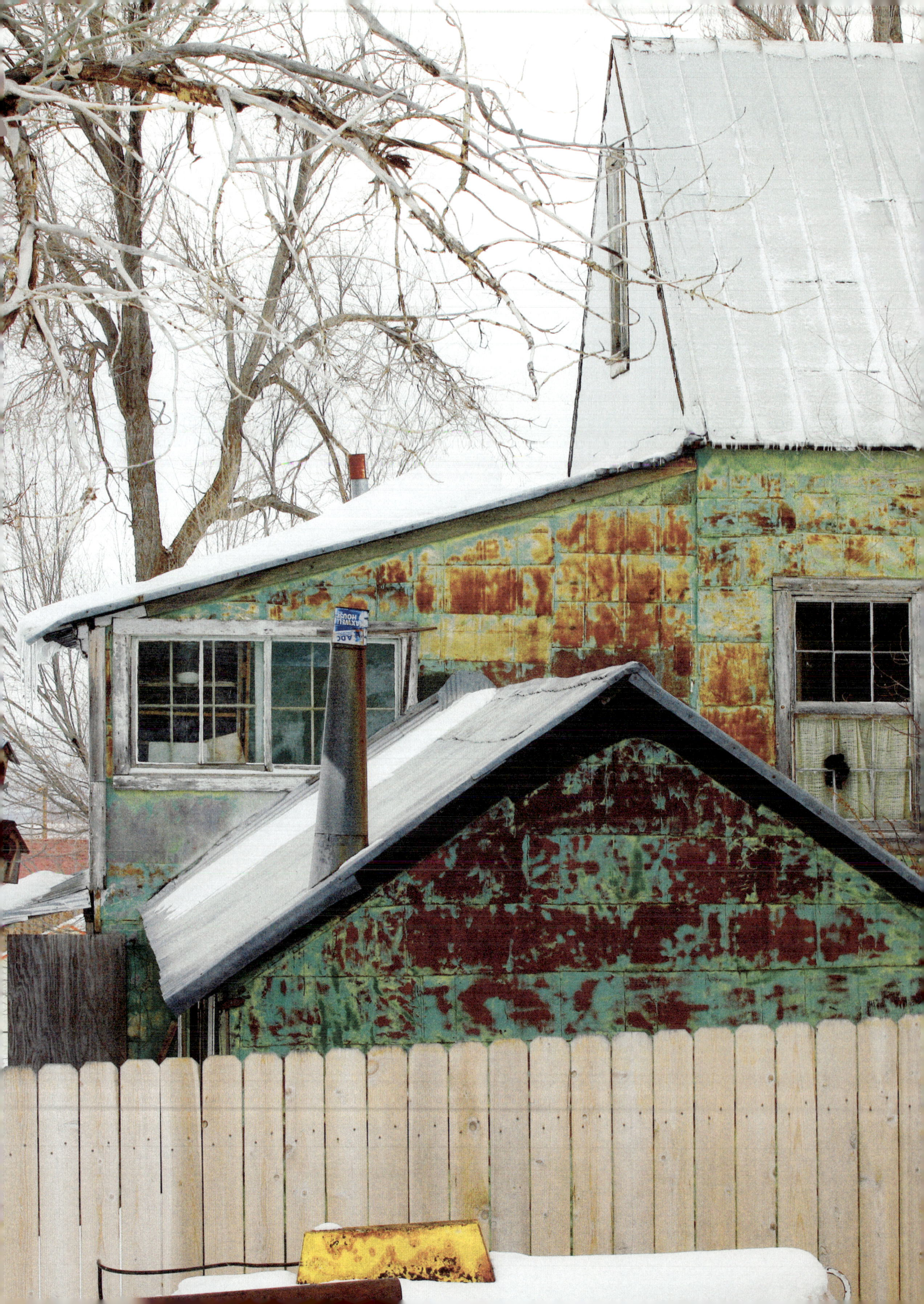
AXWELL
HOUSE
ADC

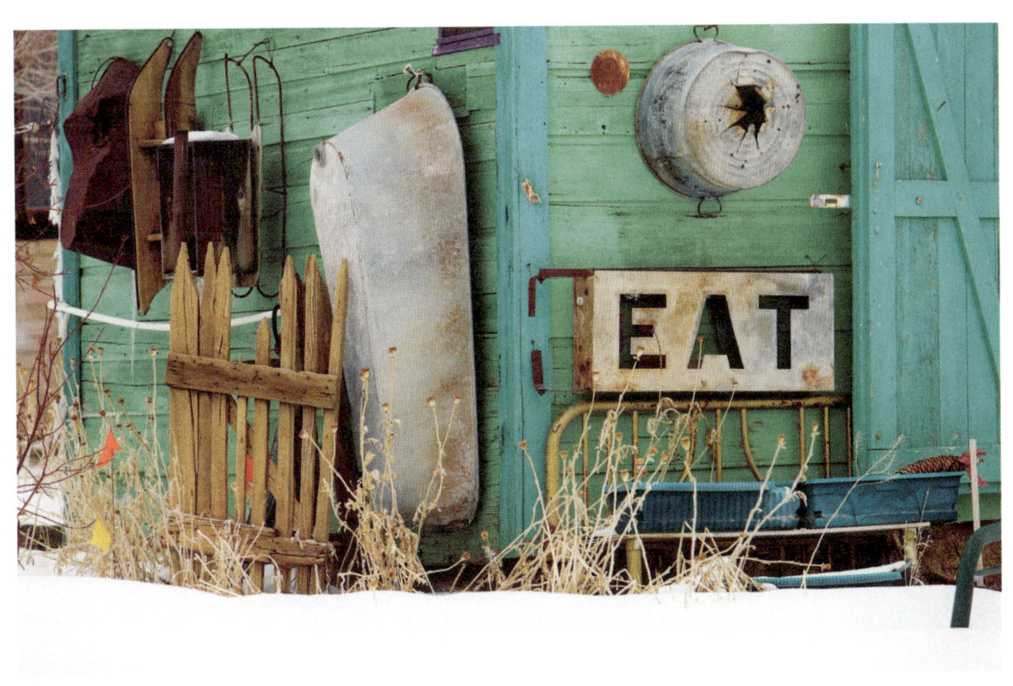
EAT

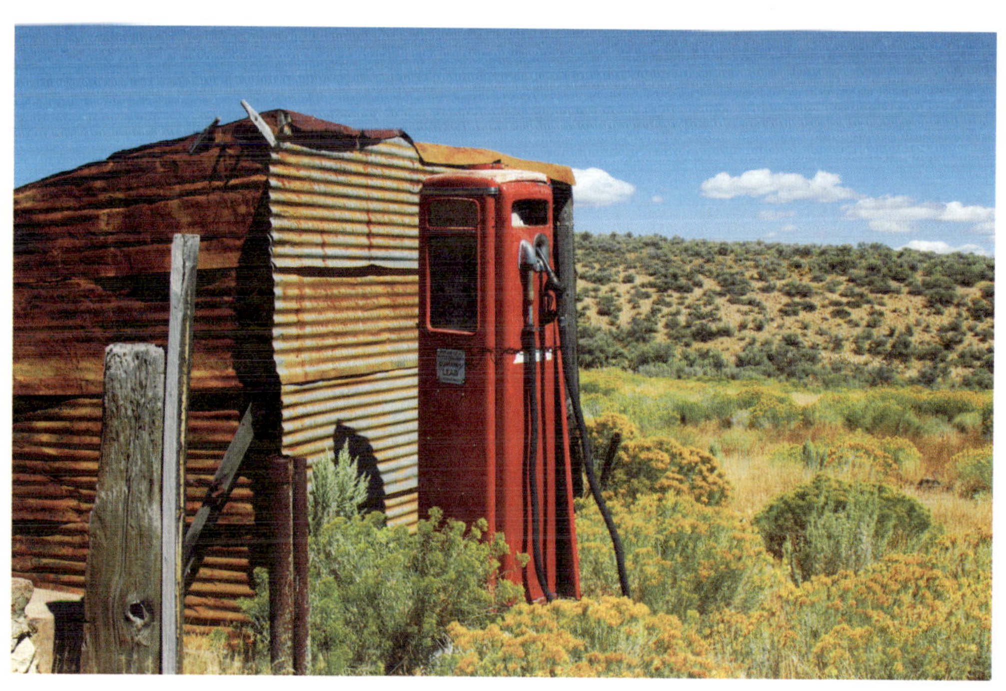

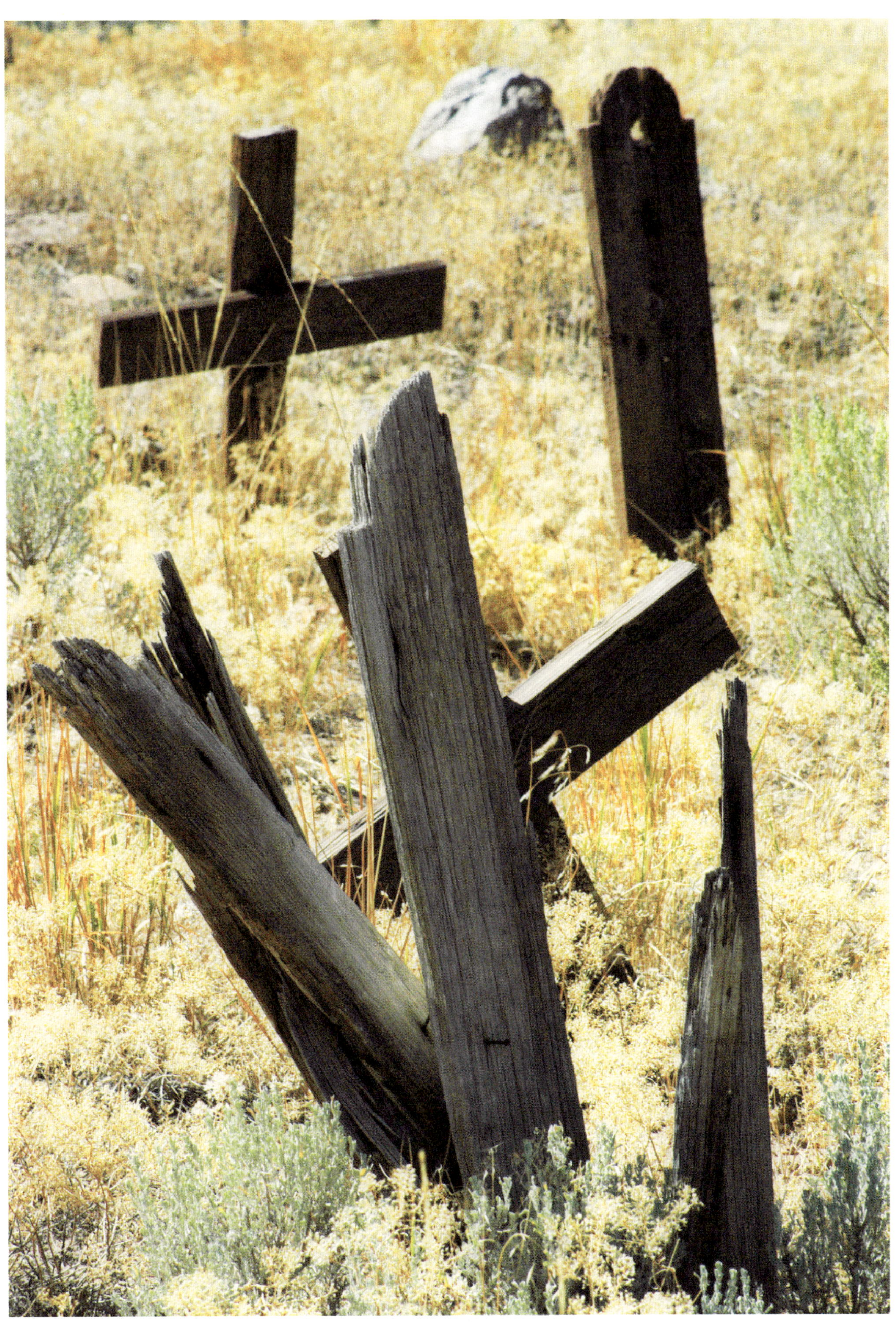

IT'S BEEN CALLED THE LONELIEST ROAD IN THE WHOLE OF AMERICA, THIS STRETCH OF ASPHALT RUNNING STRAIGHT ACROSS NEVADA. OUT HERE, PEOPLE'S INDEX FINGERS ARE GNARLED FROM RATTLESNAKE BITES.

HERE, THE WIND CAN BE HEARD RUSTLING BETWEEN BROKEN BOARDS IN DESERTED CABINS AND PASSING THROUGH THE RICKETY LIVES THAT STILL REMAIN WHEN THE DREAMS OF FREEDOM HAVE FADED.

"Come to America. It's good here." Kanji Patel's two brothers, who had moved to California, wrote letters back to Gujarat in India urging him to join them. Eventually, Kanji and his wife Kusum ended up in Fallon, on Highway 50, where they bought themselves a motel and changed its name from the not completely accurate Uptown Motel. A car seat made for three sits outside our room and on the door there is a loose digit. The swimming pool looks like a photograph.

We have come to Fallon by way of the Sierra Nevada, with its dizzying, meandering roads overlooking salty lakes and ghost towns, and in front of us lies the Big Loneliness. A blacktop string all the way to Utah; you are "a prisoner of the fine white lines on the free, free way," in the words of that old Joni Mitchell song. The call is echoing through the centuries: come to America, it's good here.

And because, deep down inside, you're all alone upon arrival, you cannot hold any expectations of being taken care of. The wolf is howling outside the garden fence; the wilderness is in command.

A huge fire burnt Fallon to the ground in 1910, and in 1954 an earthquake shattered its Main Street. On one side of town the air force offers jobs and exhibits its show pilots, who can dive through thick smoke and swirl around like sparrows in a Caribbean hurricane, and at the other end there are tiny, leaky homes with junk lots and car wrecks and people in undershirts trying to patch up their everyday lives. Hanging electricity lines create cobwebs just like in Mexico.

Where the first humans in the area were sensible enough to seek shelter and game uphill,

European settlers often had an unfortunate urge to establish communities out in the open, in places where nature certainly tried to dissuade them. A few feet into the ground, history will reveal wagon trains gone astray and newcomers who succumbed to the bad decisions of their daring scouts.

Everyone in Nevada hides an inner gambler. That's what local small-time ranchers will tell you when you ask why they chose to live out here. "Farming is our game of chance."

Bullet holes are everywhere in the road signs that warn motorists against loose cattle. Most of the surrounding land is federal, and the government charges the ranchers and farmers a grazing fee. Muttering under their breath, some of them claim that nowadays, because of environmentalist intervention, you can't even cut down a tree if there's an owl living in it. In the new West people sometimes get so annoyed they cannot help but put a bullet through the nearest metal sign.

Henry Dahlstrom used to hunt deer from his backyard before rheumatism got the better of him. Sitting on his stool, he would shoot straight into the twilight. His father had immigrated from Sweden as a teenager, one of many fortune-seekers who had listened to the golden rumors from the faraway country. After the rush, with the glitter gone and floods and fires ravaging the small town, young Henry got stuck in his garage repairing the occasional crippled pick-up truck.

When he finally closed his shop it was because the drive-through people never spent any money, but only stopped to use the toilet. Now he sits there chewing his cigar for breakfast, lunch, and dinner. He has almost disappeared in the back of the dim building; the screw nuts, the oil, the dust, his own skin, the car whose owner never returned to retrieve it; everything is of the same coloring.

This grand landscape can be nasty to its inhabitants. The wind blows and crumbles, what is not solid will molder into memories and wind up in curio stores.

"Sadly enough I only had daughters," says Henry Dahlstrom. "Two of them. But perhaps that was just as well. Had I had a son he would surely have become some damned hippie."

It's common wisdom that every fourth person in the state of Nevada is living in some sort of mobile home, with or without wheels. A great number of them are stuck indefinitely. There is dirt all around, and sage. The breeze will cry any name you sing into it. Every now and then a shadow can be spotted hurrying, or escaping, down the road.

Early mornings in the desert the air is crisp and filled with the smell of herbs; everything is watercolor pale and fresh and desolate, like the landscape had been given an airing, as if someone already cleaned out yesterday's events. You stand there with your stiff hands holding a coffee mug, realizing that it probably is a two-hour drive to the next human being.

It was here, in the Nevada desert, that the government sent out the Light; a rolling fire moving toward the east, across the defenseless lands of the Navajo, and spreading its ashes over isolated Mormon communities with pretty names such as Annabella, Enterprise, and Bountiful, where the faithful would stand at strict attention beneath their flags as radiation was sucked into their genes. The hairdressers in Las Vegas in the 1950s offered their fake-blonde customers atomic hairdos, fluffy clouds with a certain elevation. There was something almost kind of festive about the Cold War, like being at a barbecue.

Then came Darkness. Silenced protests from those whose children were born with faces looking like a cluster of grapes, the Atomic Energy Commission's cover-up and pursuit of compromising witnesses.

Even today, there is no shortage of new weapons being tested among the yucca mountains in the desolate West. In the rudimentary settlements of Nowhere Land rumors abound of supernatural lights in the night and strange tire marks on the trailer roofs. Nuclear waste, the eternal byproduct of civilization, is currently stored at well over hundred different locations in 39 states, and it might one day be deposited here: no smell, no visibility.

Passing between mountain ranges Highway 50 stretches across flat dirt plains, where yellow traffic signs warn of low-flying aircraft and strong gusts of wind. Every now and then white sand is piled up in untouched wave formations. You spot gliding hawks, but never see their prey. One draw of this place is the opportunity to mind your own business. When the new settlers drove off the Western Shoshone Indians they were not just looking for gold and silver, but also for seclusion and absence of binding regulations. They wanted to be on their own, doing their thing, whatever pleased them.

Greg Del Pocco says he doesn't pay any taxes, other than the one on beer. He helps out with practical chores at the Middlegate Station, which was once built as a stable where the Pony Express riders could change to rested horses. Electricity for the bar and the eight trailer rooms is produced by a small generator and a telephone was not installed until 1984.

In this desert, people can withdraw and hide themselves with their own notion of freedom. Crumpled men with suspenders and checkered shirts, their knees curved like they were placers in a golden creek, inform us that they live up in the mountains. Their neighbors are mountain lions and peregrine falcons. How they managed to drag lumber and trailers up those hills, nobody will ever understand.

In her enthralling book about movie pioneer Eadweard Muybridge, "River of Shadows," writer Rebecca Solnit dismisses the kind of cultural theorists who have described the desert landscape in western U.S.A. as the center of postmodernism and the place where the future has already arrived. They should, she writes, have read the region's history instead of staring out car windows. Rogue cops, theme parks, actor politicians and fluidly changing identities are all part of the western heritage; in solitude everything mutated most of the time, with settlers inventing themselves anew just like Muybridge's still pictures that would start moving all of a sudden and become film.

Light and darkness also transform everything in an environment that lies wide open to observation. As the sun slides down behind distant blue heights we experience the barren landscape as more dressed than naked, the supply of short mesquite brush apparently enough to keep the scattered cattle alive. We are driving into a purple, velvety twilight and approach one of the old, lonely mining towns of the desert, Eureka, where the lights at nearly all the saloons have been turned off. The last remaining Chinese laundry, a vague reminder of who did most of the back-breaking underground work a century ago, has now closed its business, too. For breakfast the next day we get week-old muffins.

The abandoned mining tunnels penetrate the whole place, adding the peculiar feeling that it could collapse like a house of cards if someone sneezed. Once upon a time, during harsh winters, the only way to get across Main Street, from Eureka Café to Alpine Saloon, was through a tunnel under the snow.

Why do people today settle along the loneliest road in America?

Gilbert Mair sits reading in front of his trailer:

"I grew up in Utah, where Mormon strictness makes the kids revolt, joining gangs and raising hell. We wanted to get away. My son was bullied because he listened to country music while all the others liked gangsta rappers. We moved here so that our kids can learn some real values."

Such as?

"You can't get everything for free. Gotta work for it."

He says he is applying for jobs at the road and sewer departments and at the Eureka silver mine, which has just reopened. Zoe Ann Wilson is married to Gilbert and looks like she stepped right out of a Lucinda Williams song. She wants them to place a bid on a double trailer that is for sale with three acres of land. They could have horses there. Up in the mountains. Farther away, got to get away.

The front town of Eureka, all side-scenes and set-pieces, is on the brink of falling apart on top of its old windblown watering-holes. There is, of course, another America, one that votes and joins clubs and goes to town meetings and reads international news on the web, but it just seems so very far from here.

Awaiting us are many hours of driving on dirt roads that are even lonelier and more deserted. We test our cell phones. There is, of course, no signal.

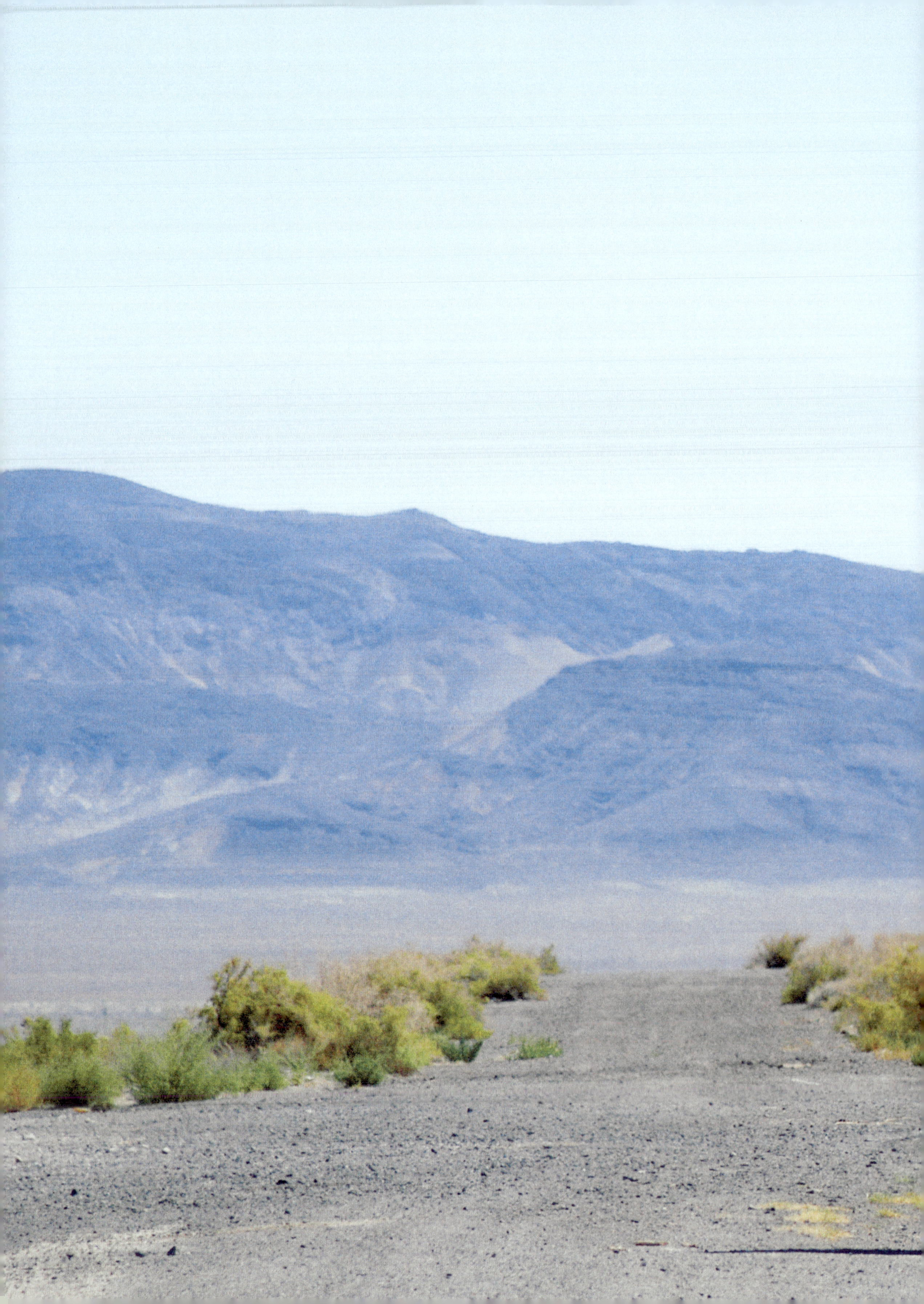

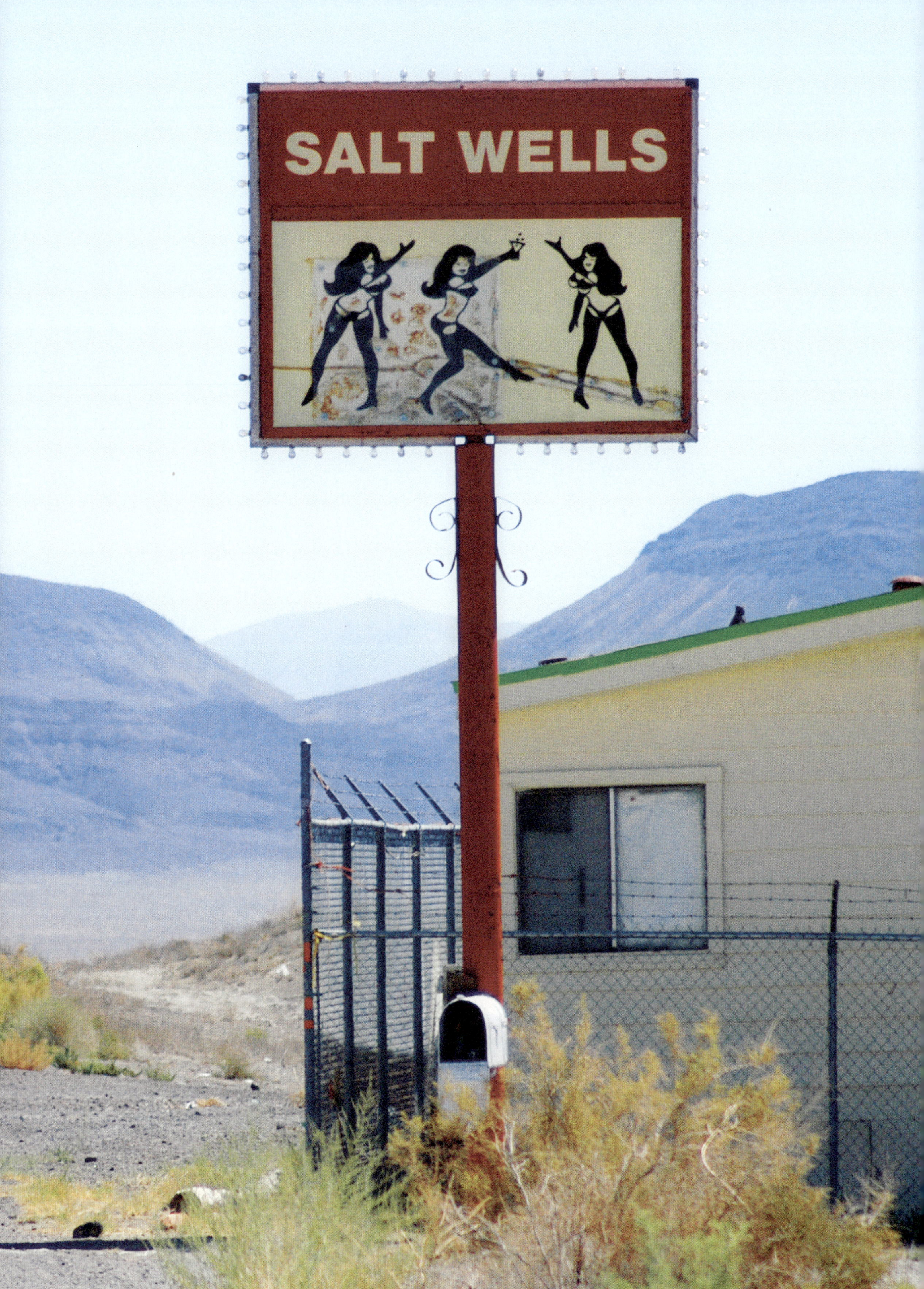
SALT WELLS

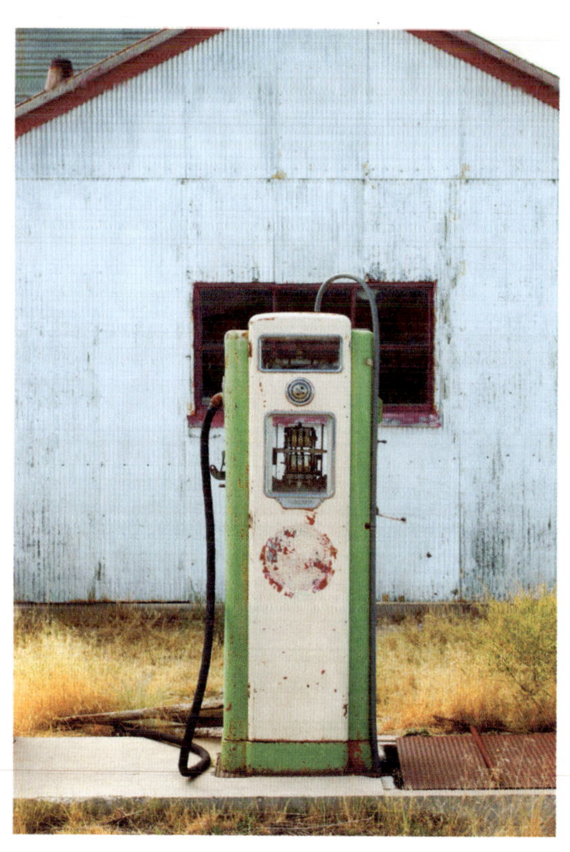

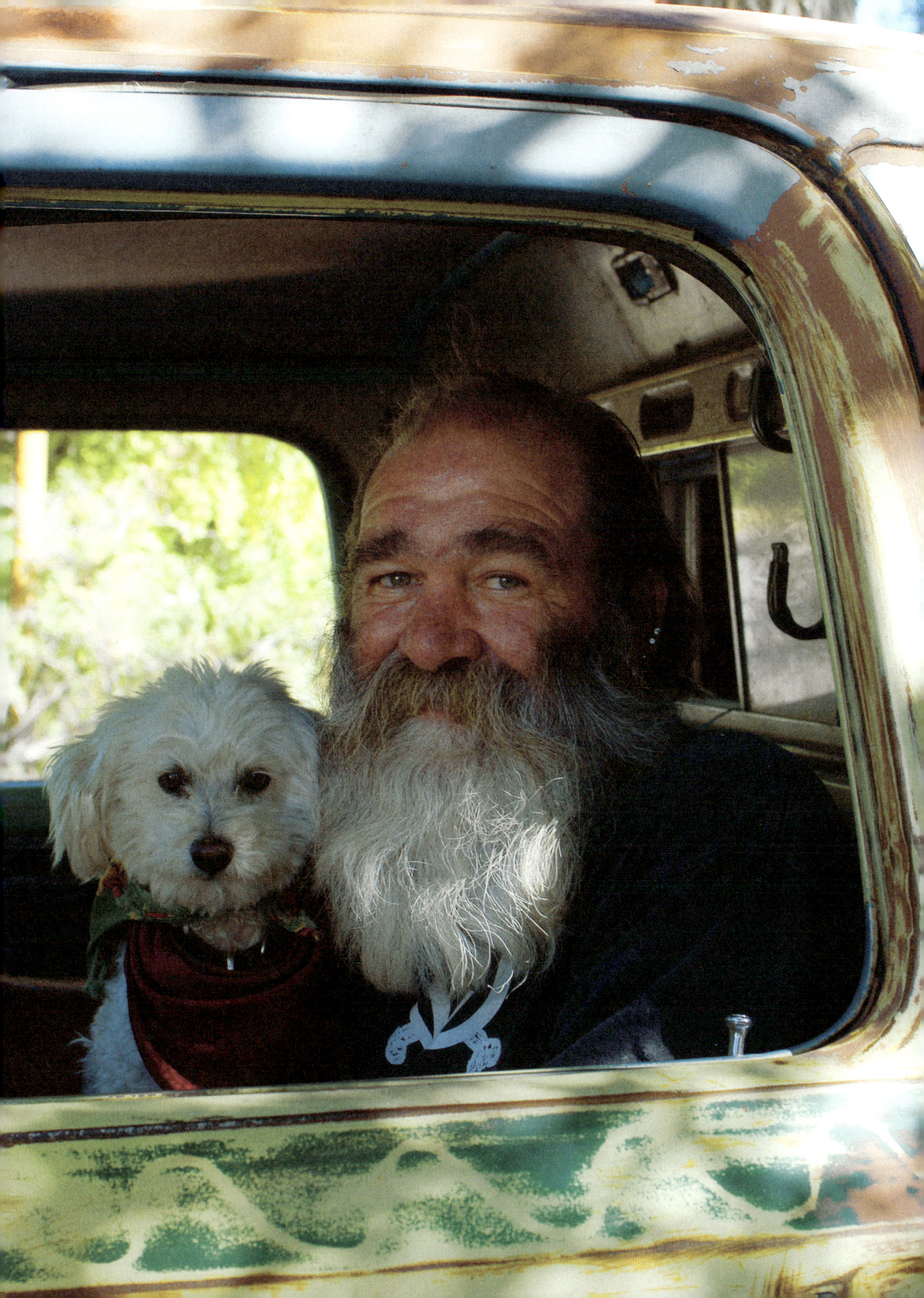

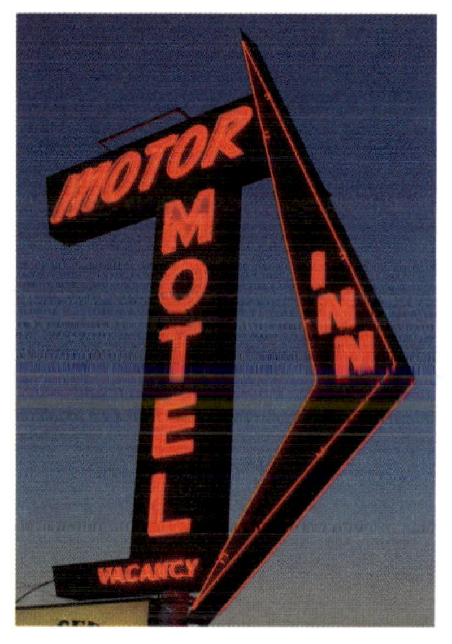
MOTOR
MOTEL
INN
VACANCY

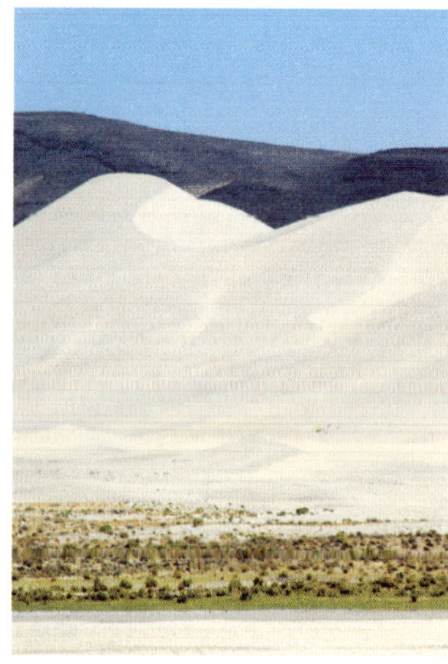

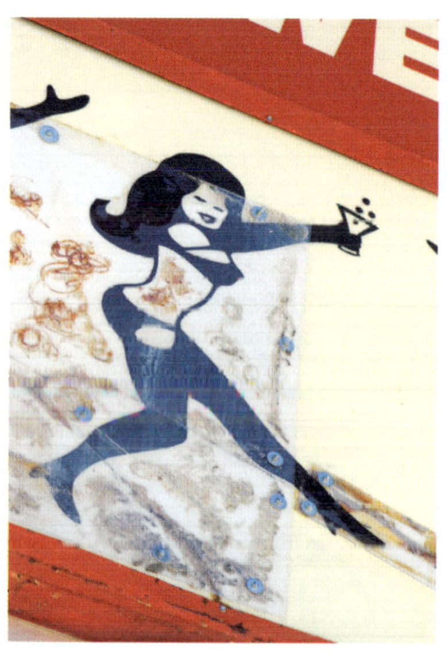

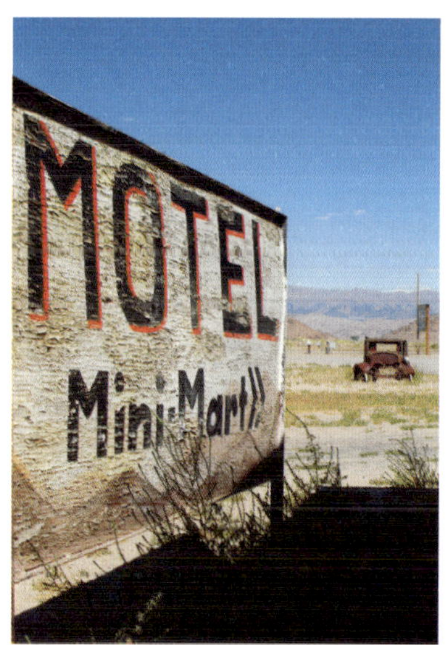
MOTEL
Mini-Mart

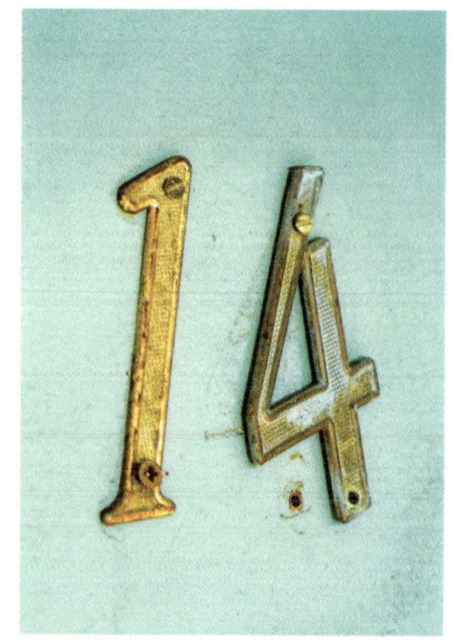
14

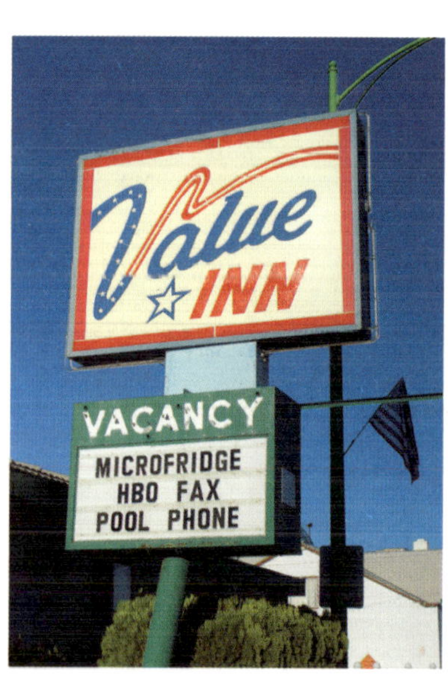
Value
INN
VACANCY
MICROFRIDGE
HBO FAX
POOL PHONE

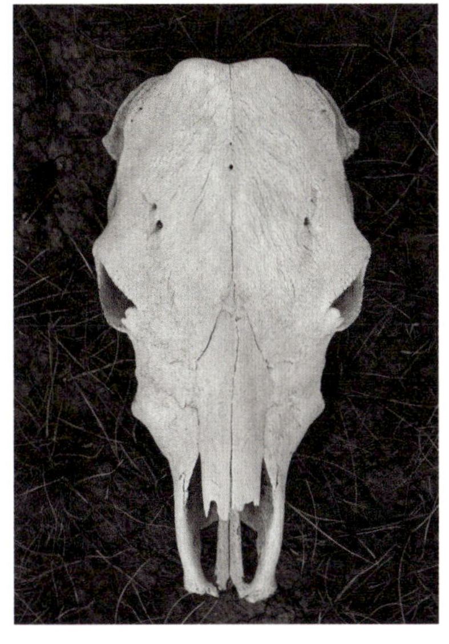

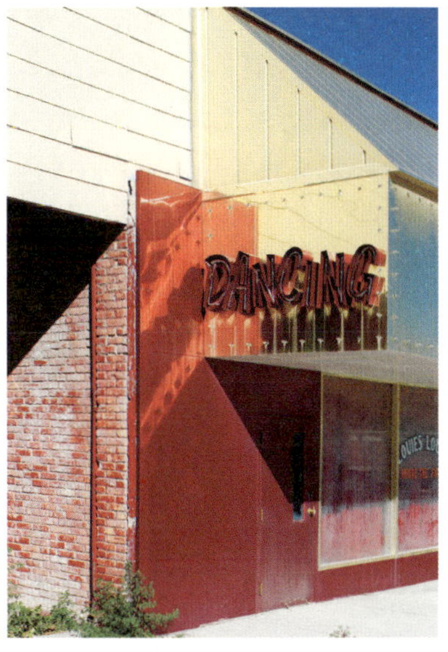
DANCING

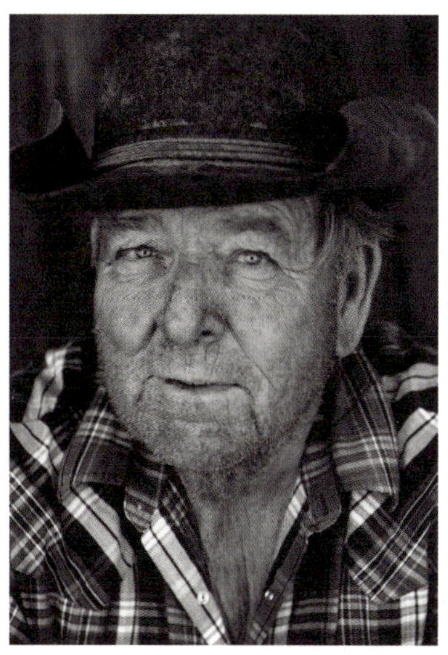

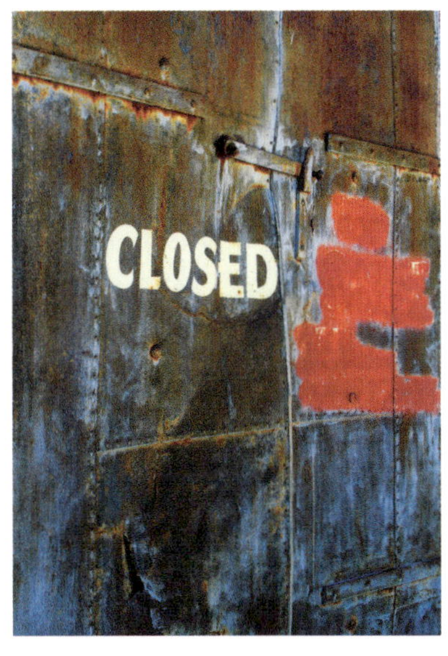
CLOSED

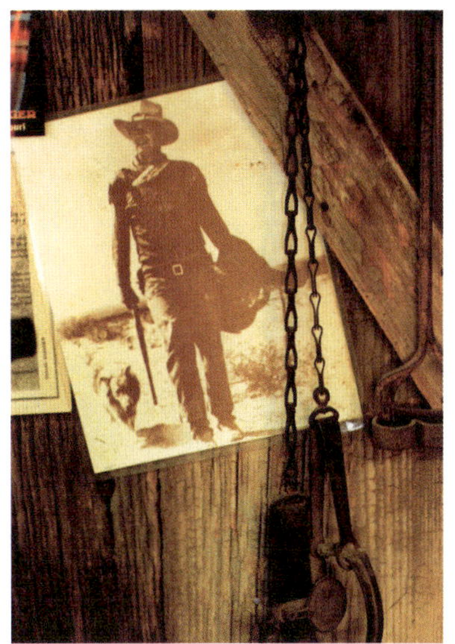

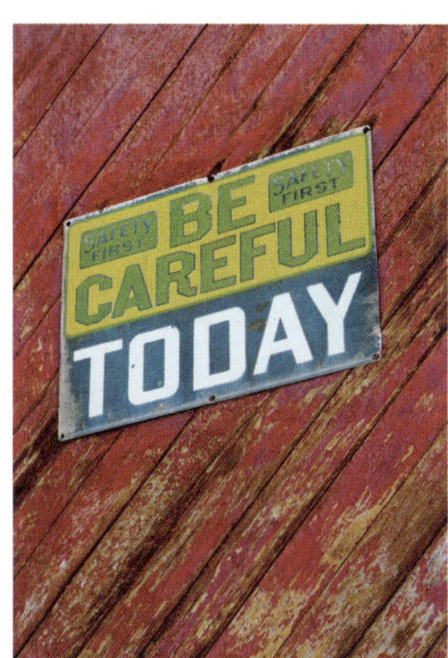
SAFETY FIRST
BE
SAFETY FIRST
CAREFUL
TODAY

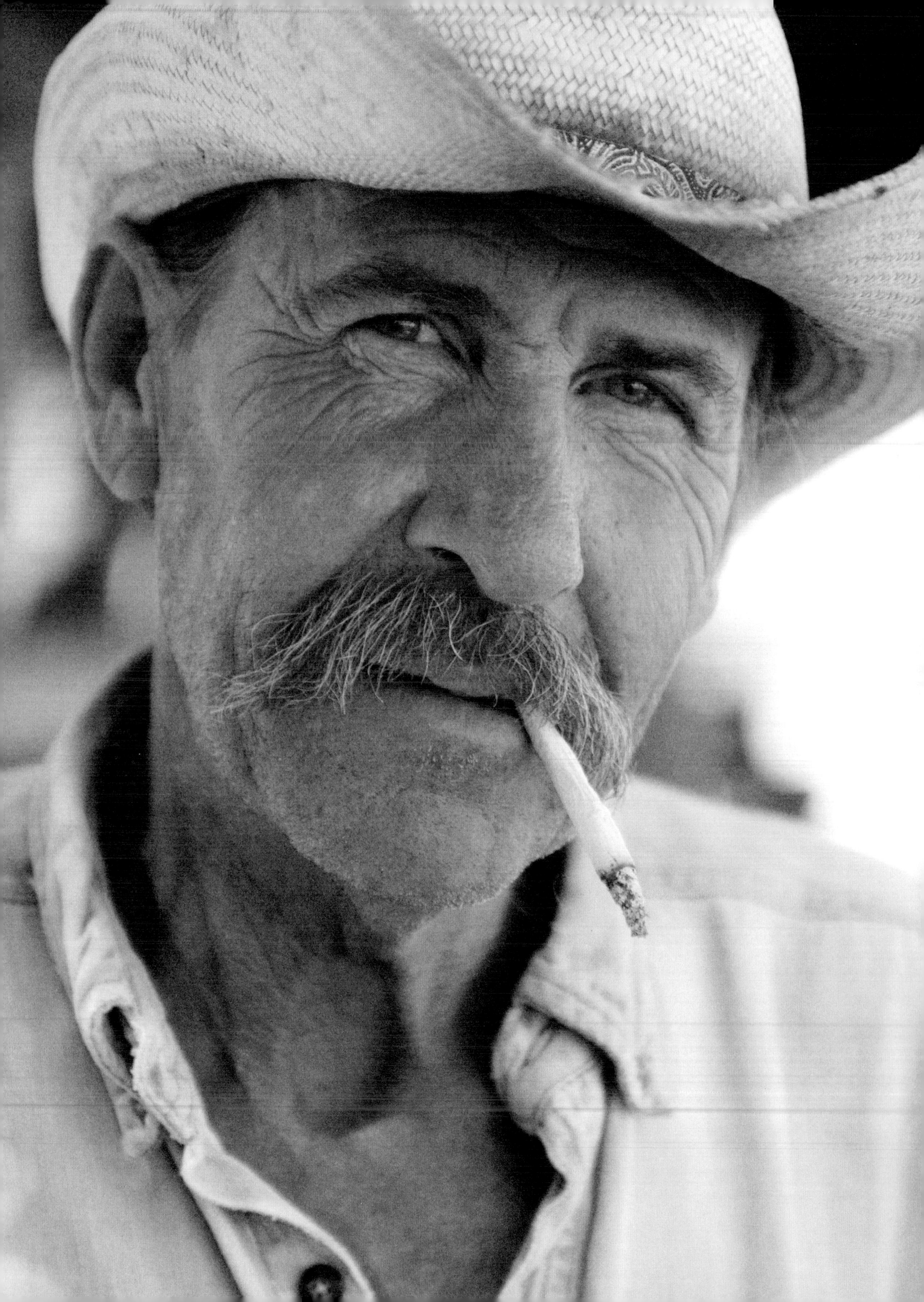

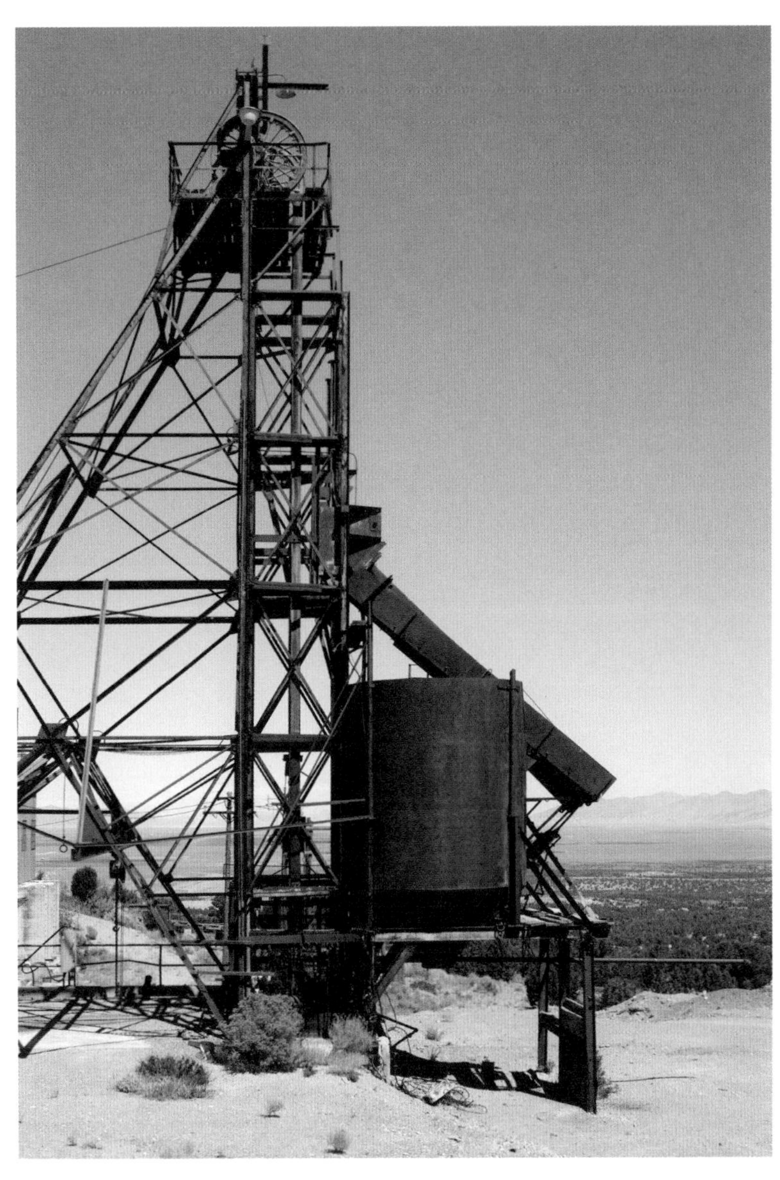

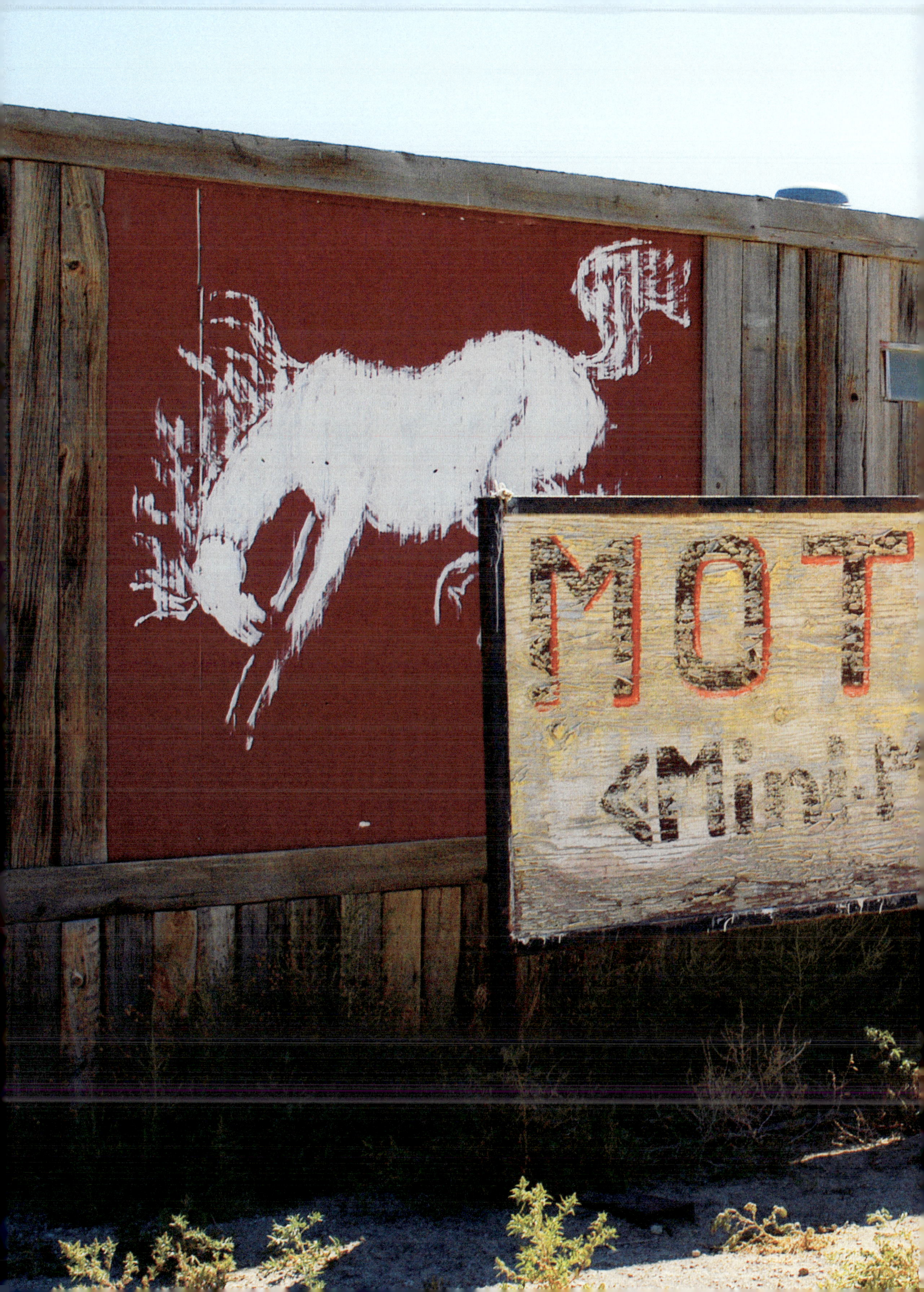
MOT
Mini

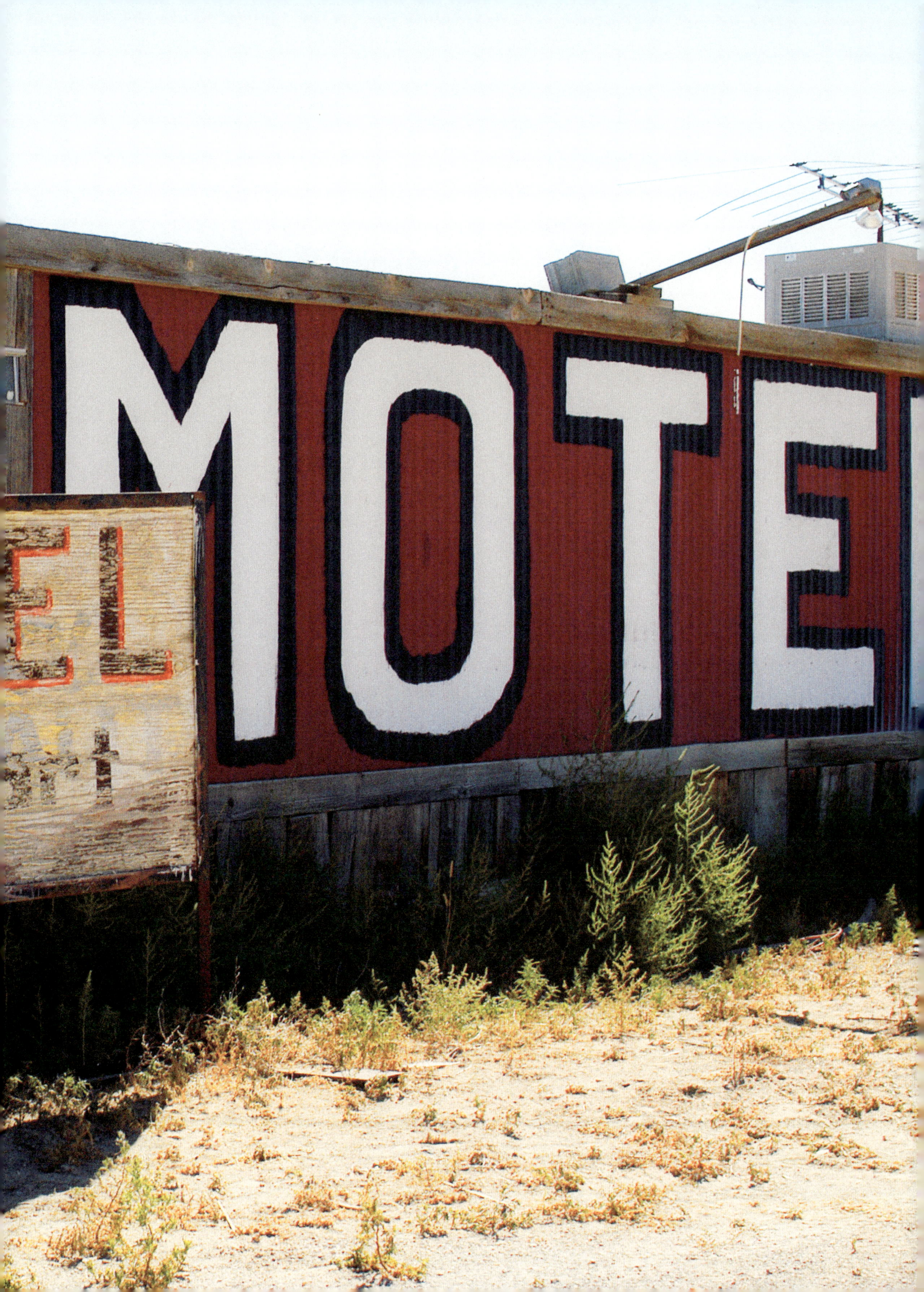
MOTE
EL

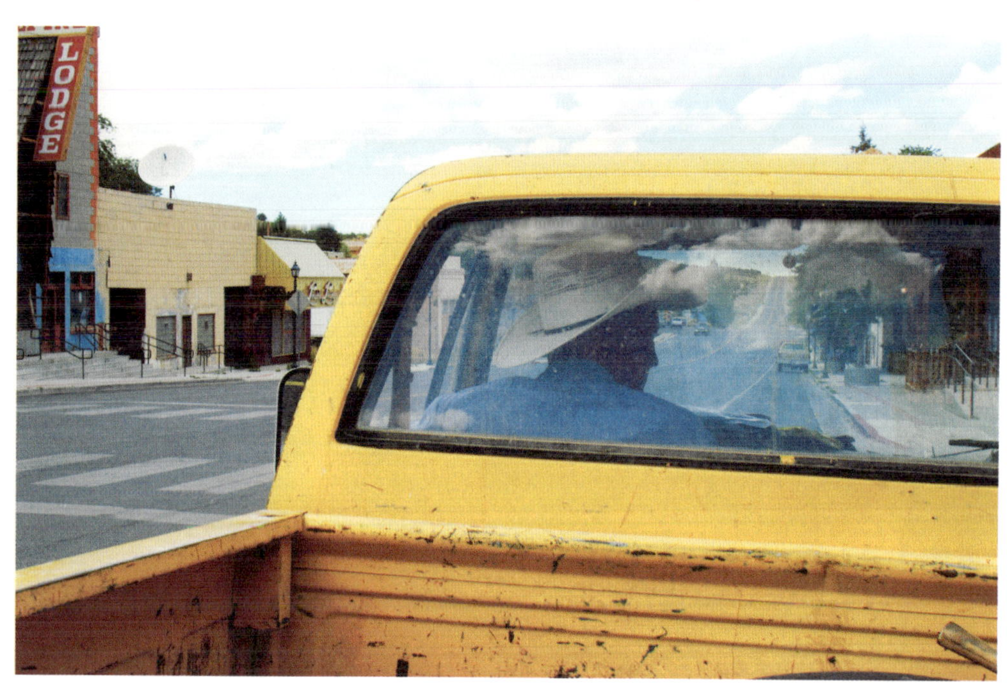
LODGE

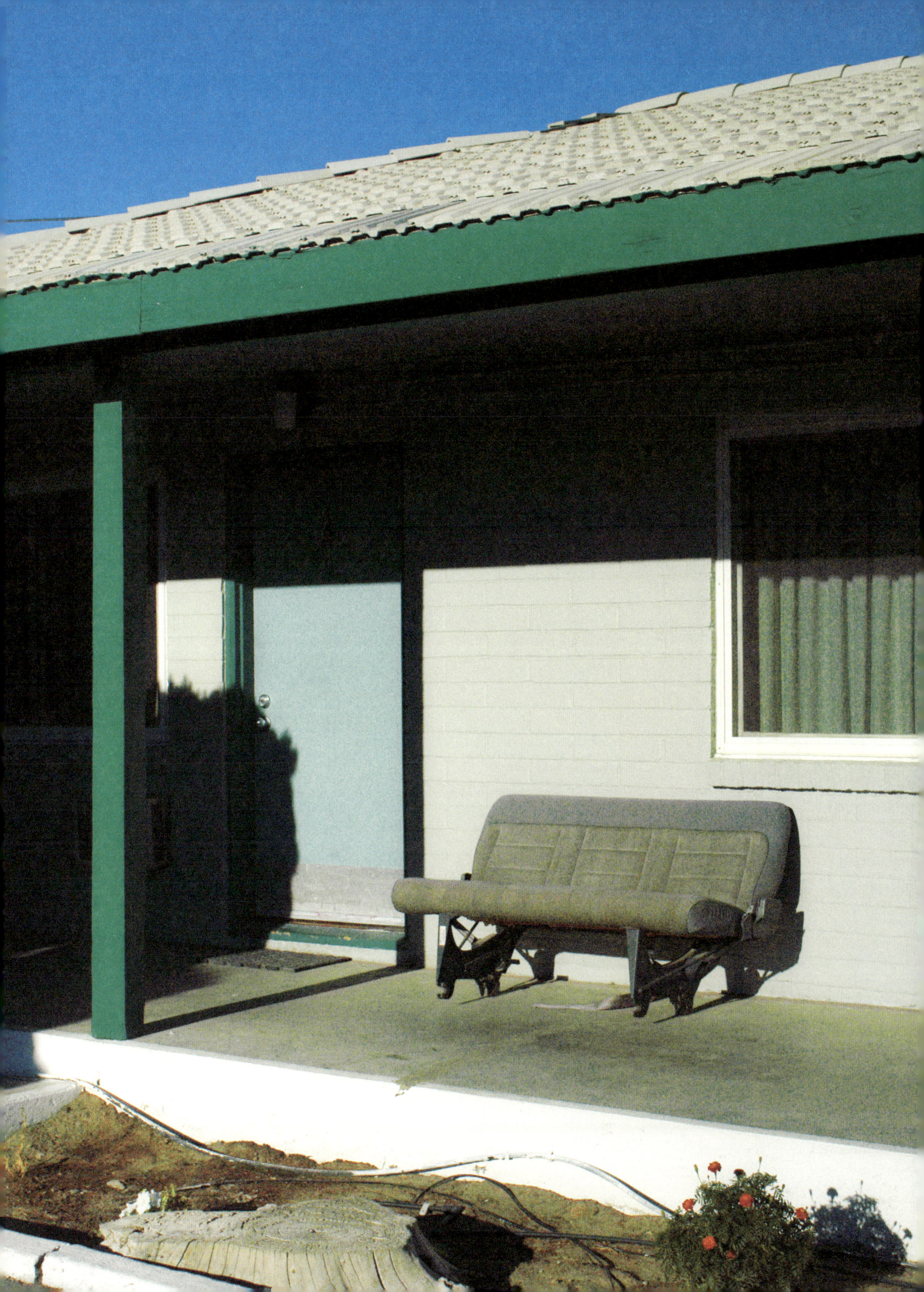

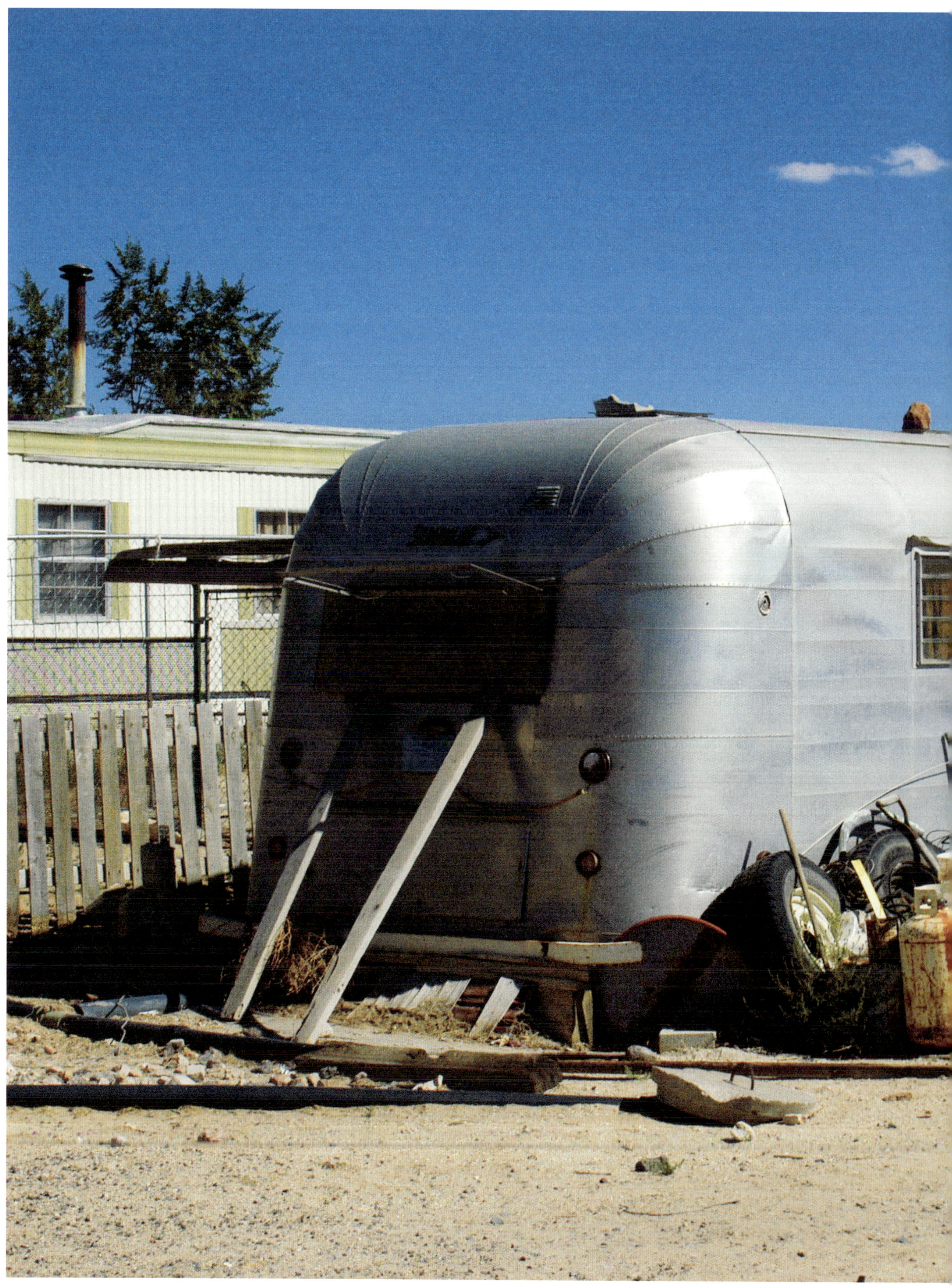

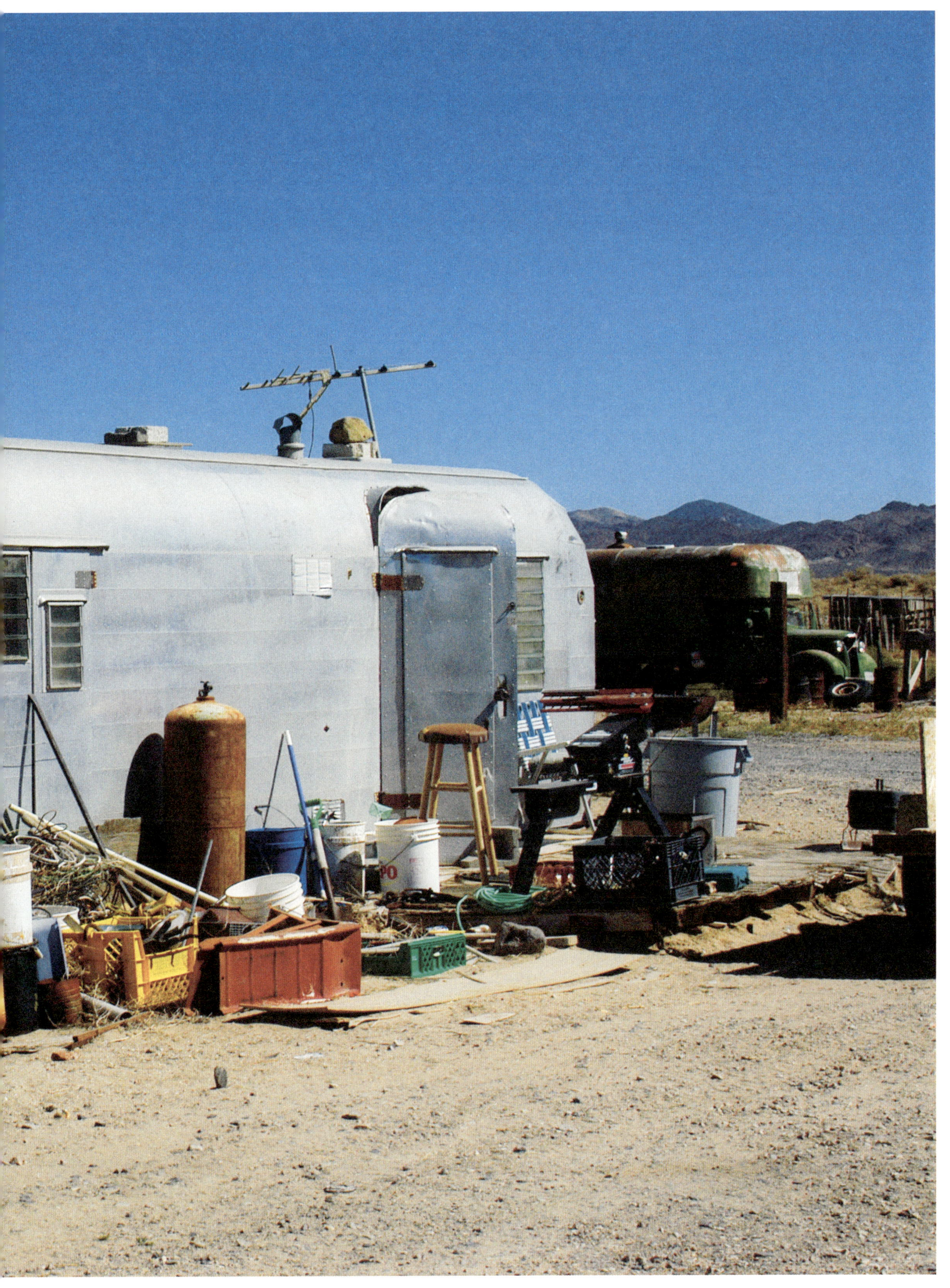

THE DESERT IS NOT REALLY A SEA OF SAND; IT IS A BLOTCHY, SCORCHED AND DRIED-OUT OCEAN BED WITH BUSHY VEGETATION AND

SANDSTONE RAVINES,
THAT LOSES ITS MIND
SOMEWHERE BETWEEN
UTAH AND ARIZONA
BEFORE THROWING ITSELF
INTO THE GRAND CANYON.

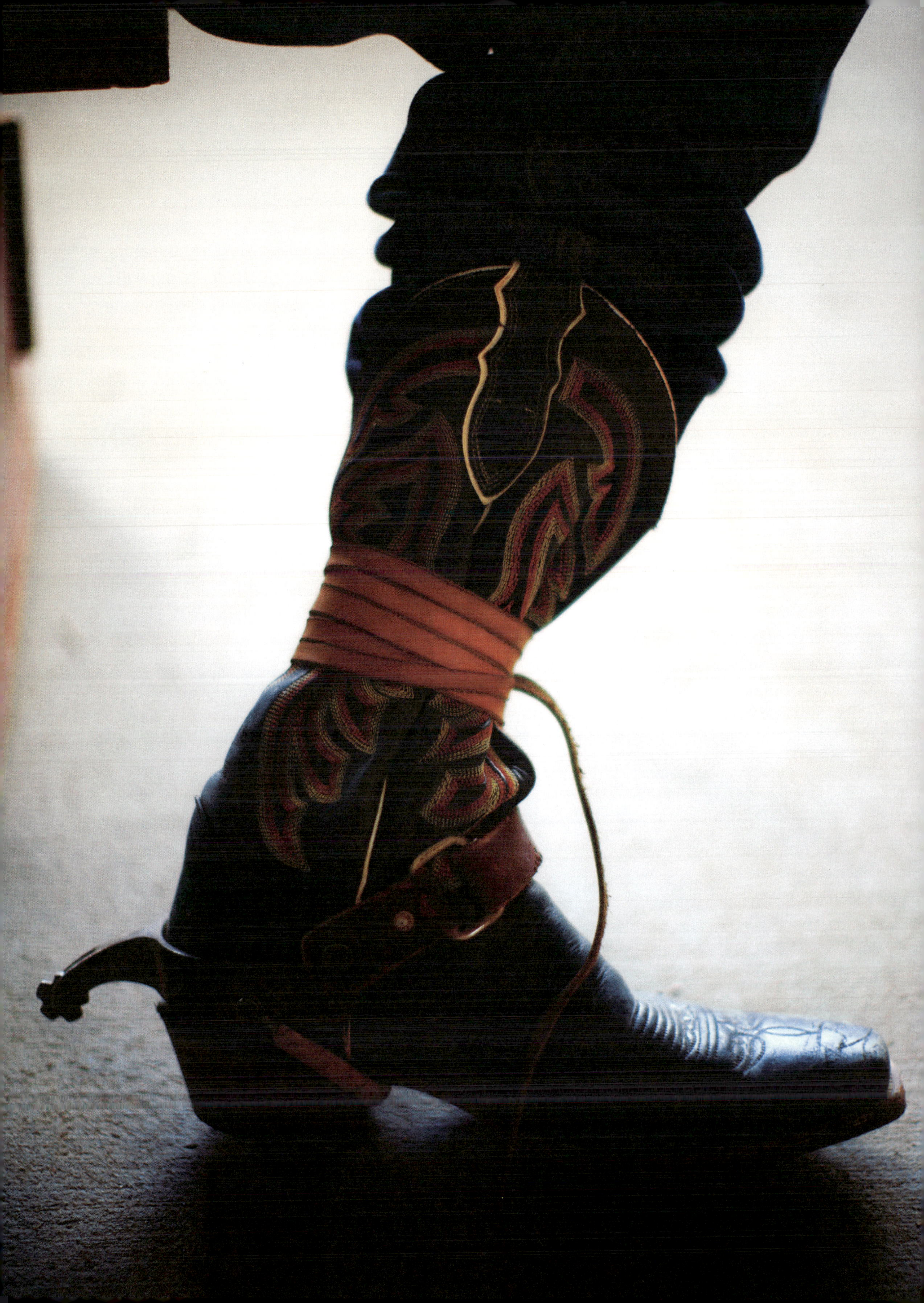

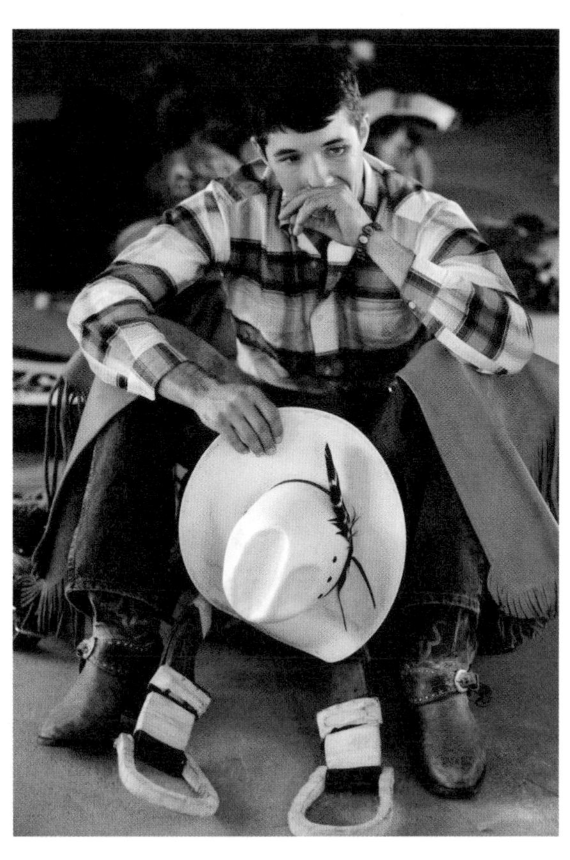

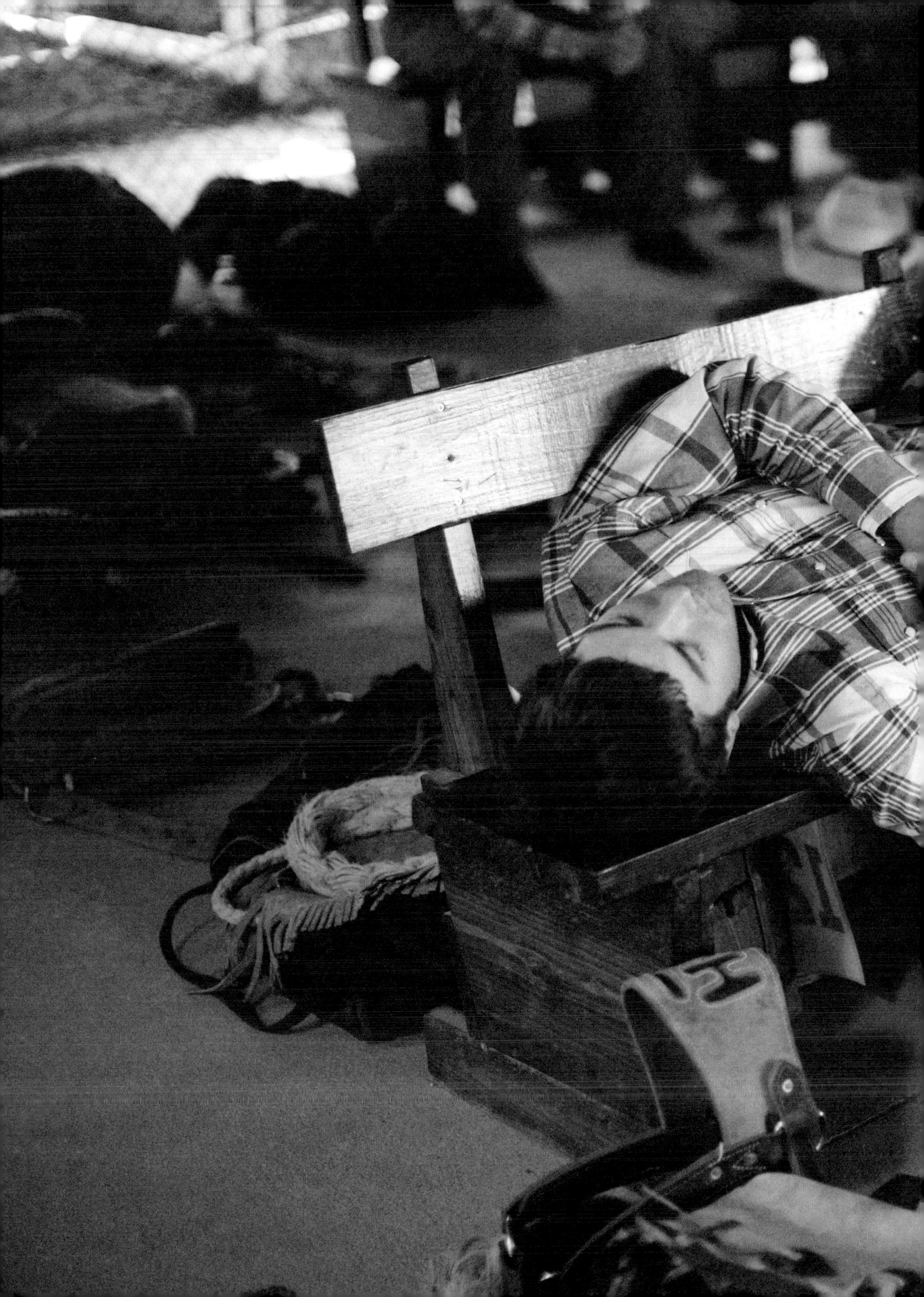

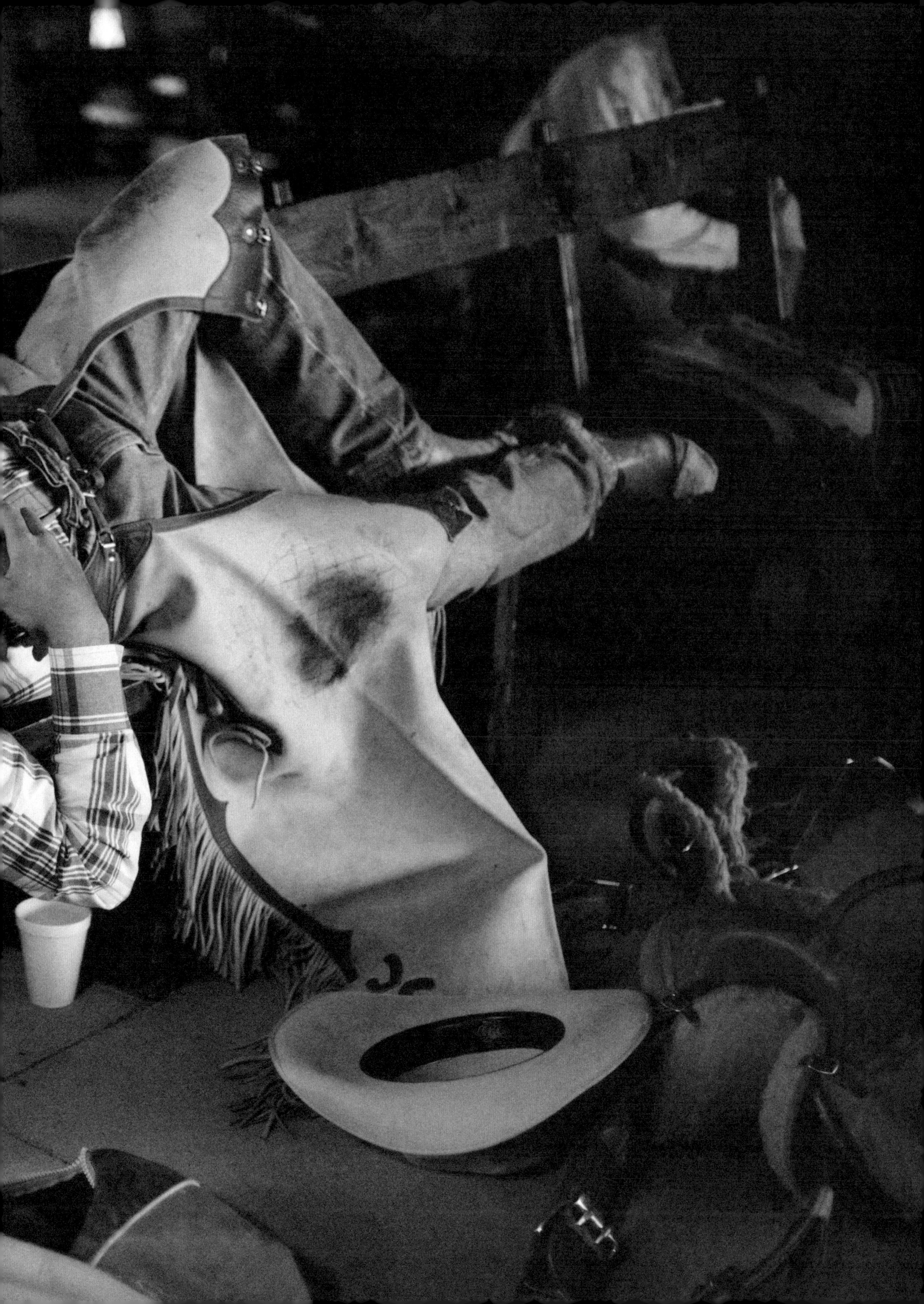

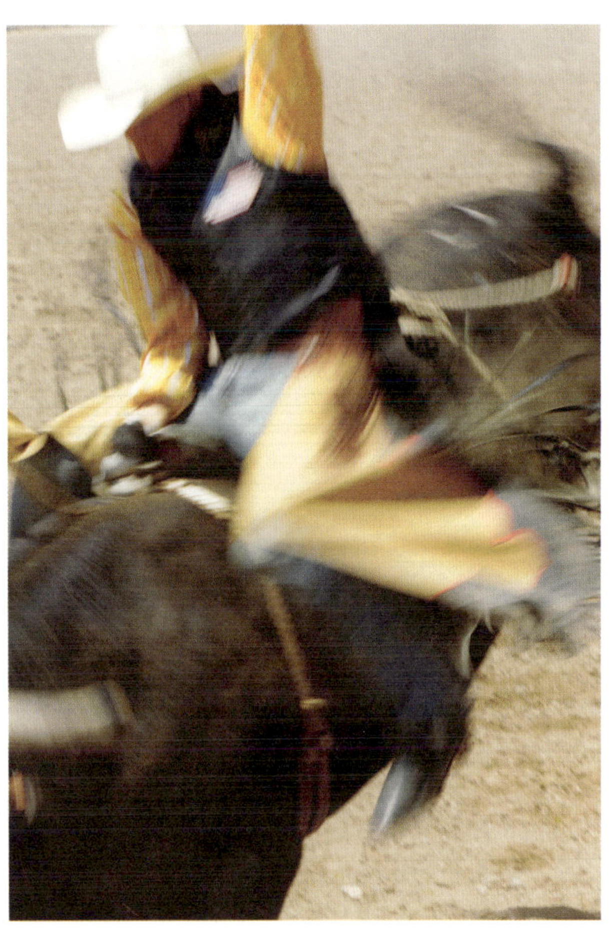

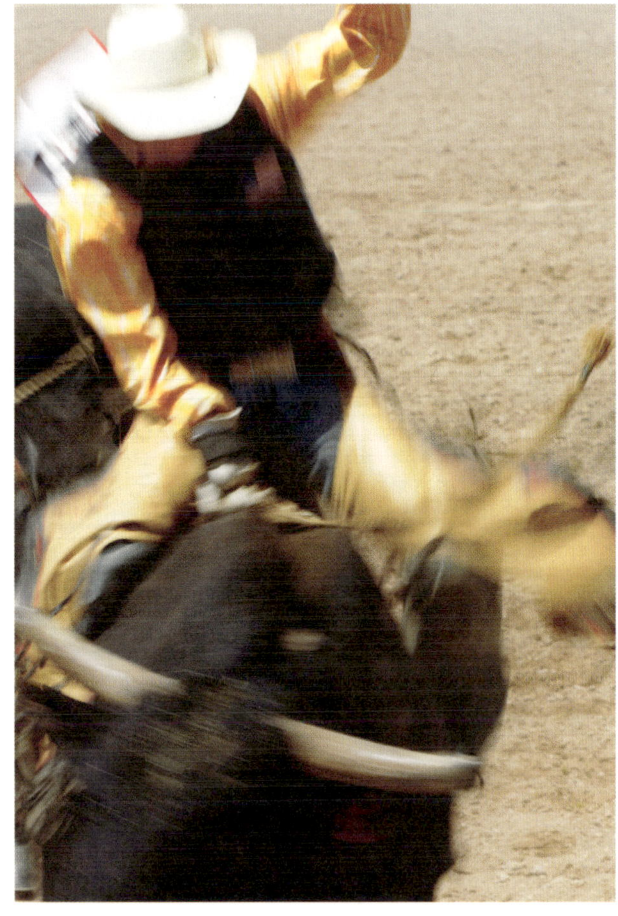

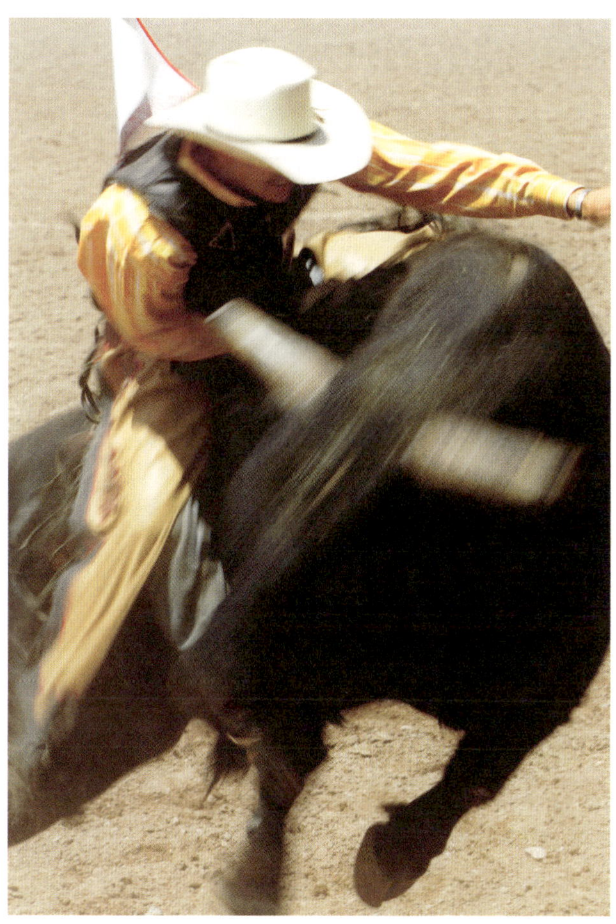

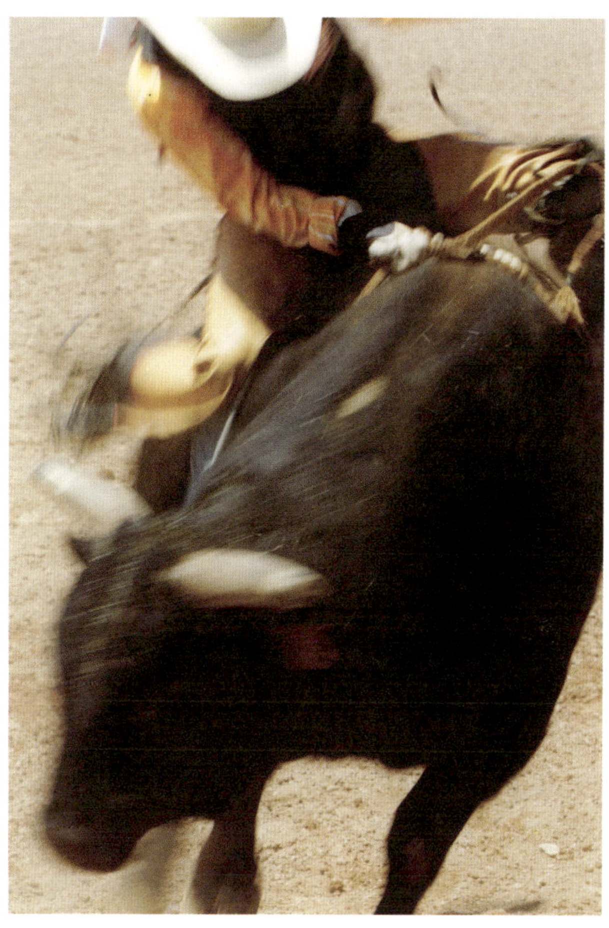

It's a summer's night and we can barely see beyond the length of our own arms. We hear the heavy breathing of the animals, their snorting and uneasy pawing, and in the black rain their dark bodies are jammed together by men in oilskin coats and soaked hats.

The initial plan was to camp out here tonight, but bad weather took us by surprise, flushing out all hopes of sleep. Instead of driving the herd through the valley all day tomorrow, you may just as well load the trailers and use the highway. That's not how it was done when the West was won. Life is in many ways easier today, although without the rambling myths of freedom and the nervous flight of horses everything would feel much more mediocre.

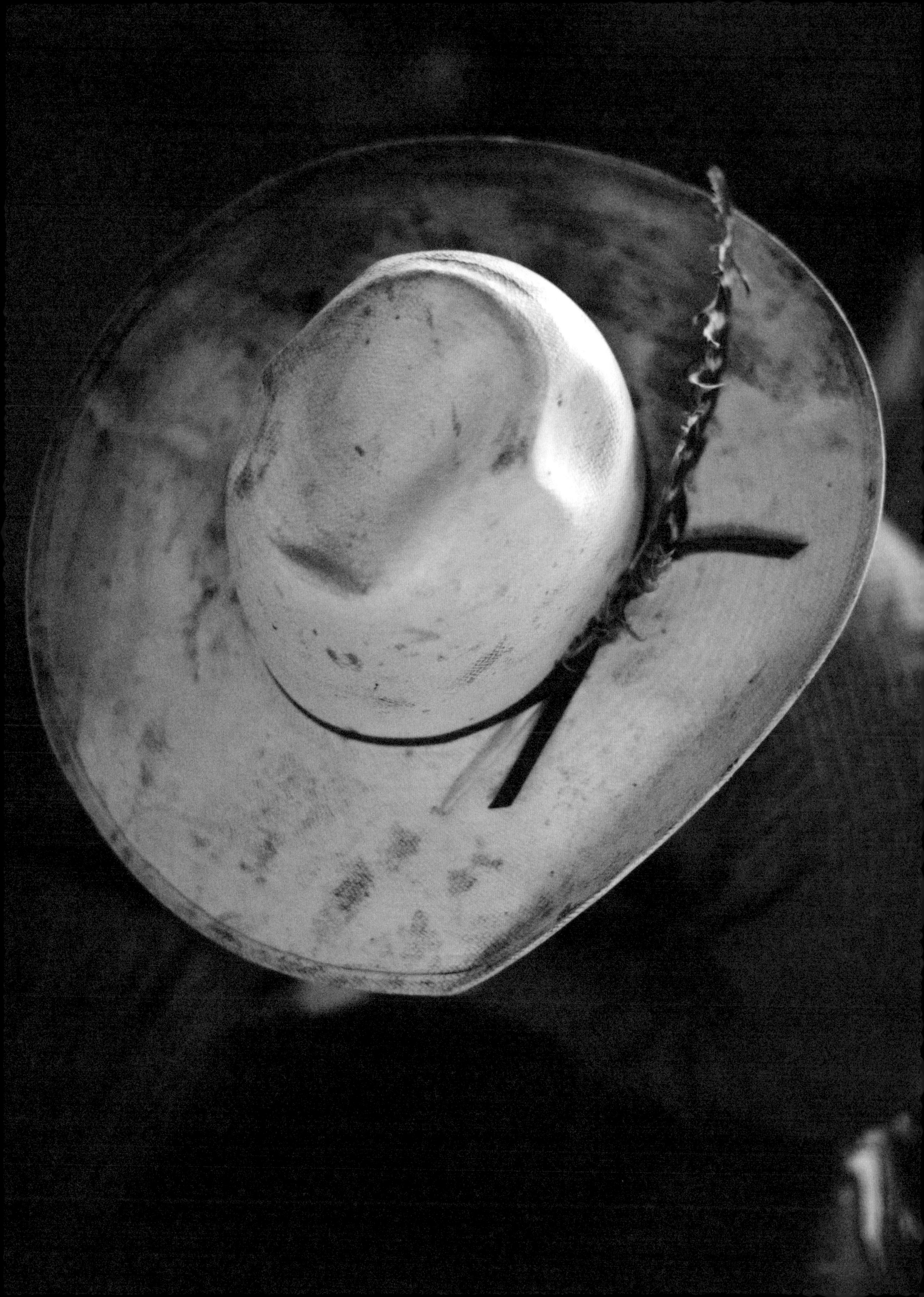

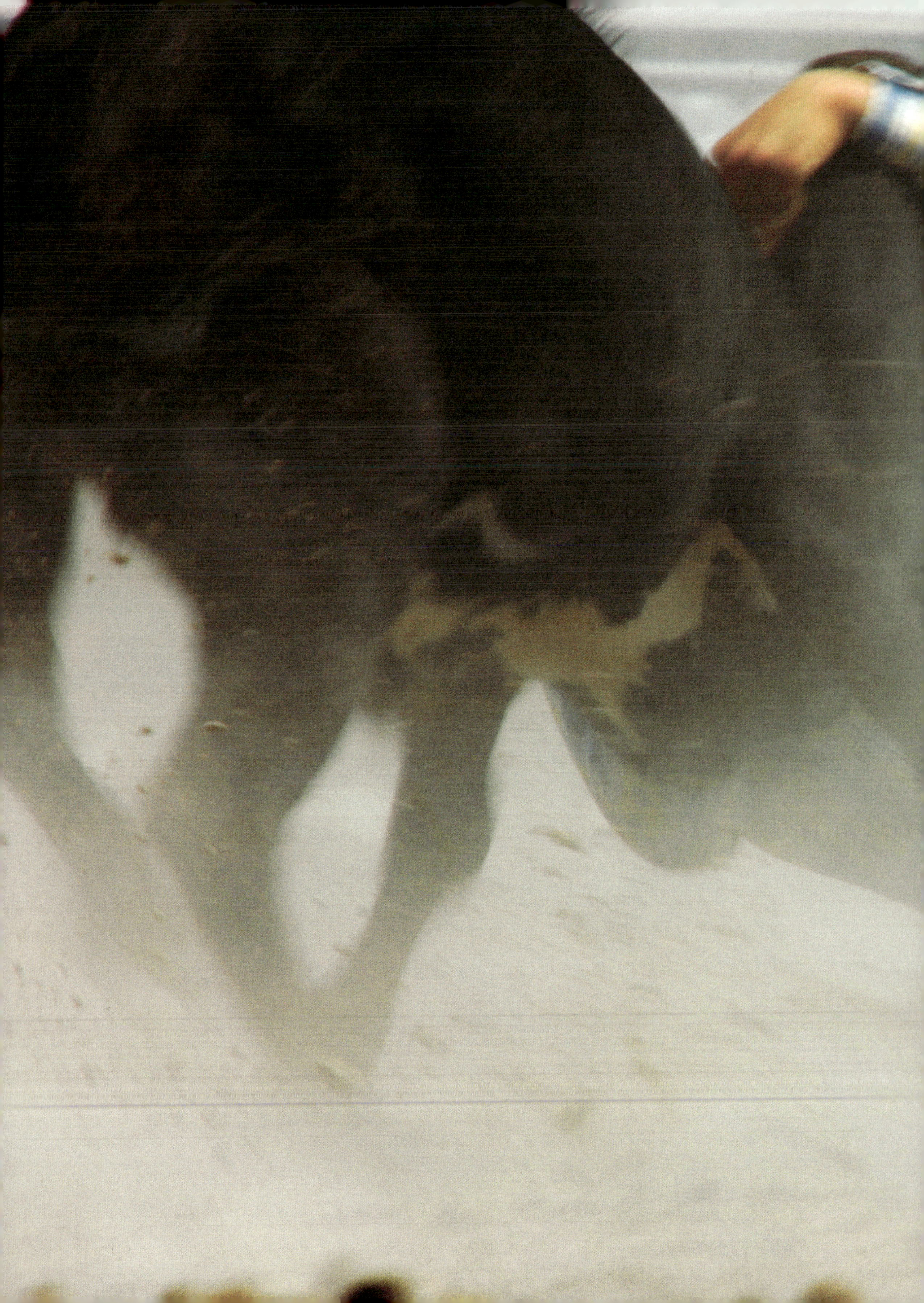

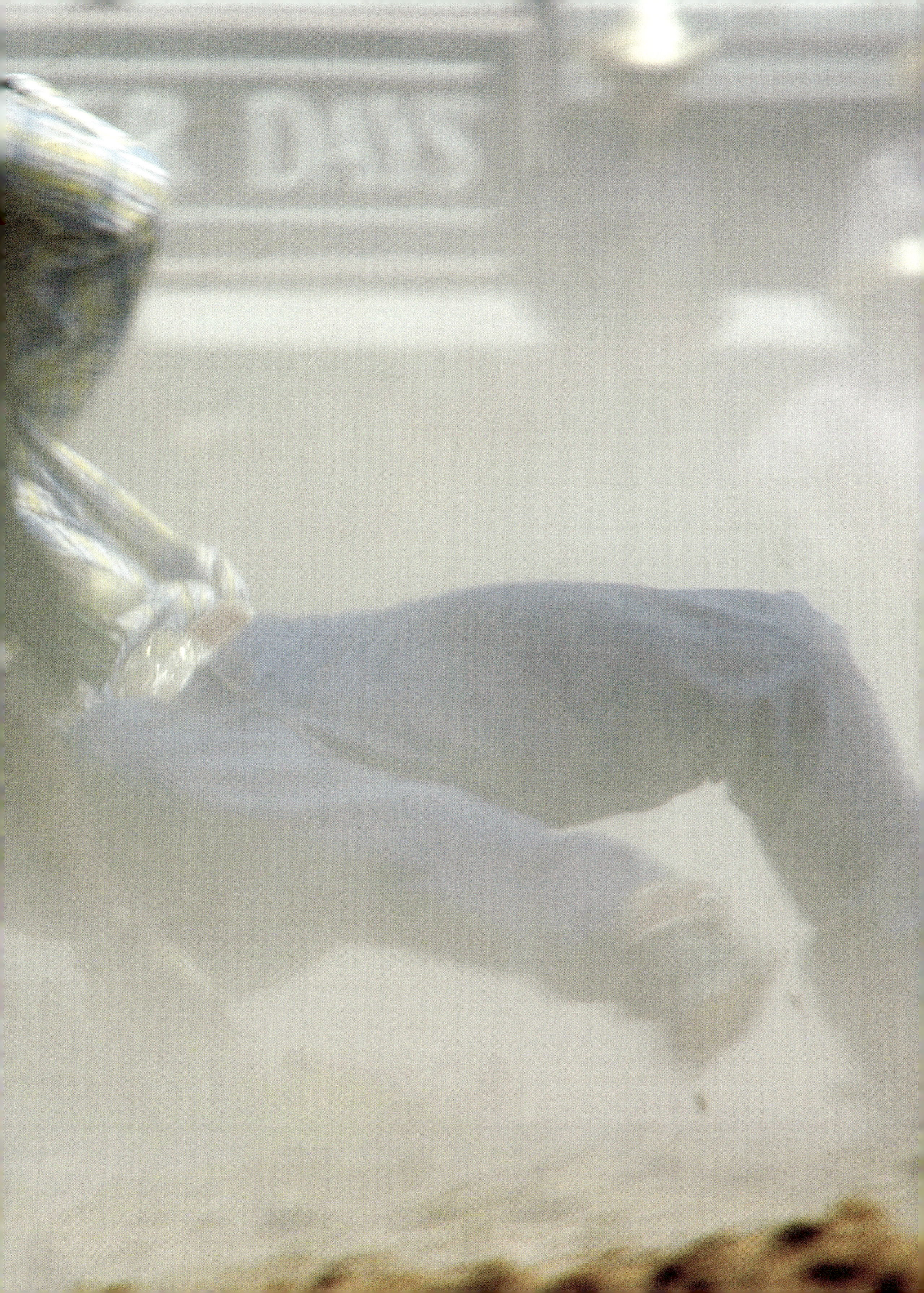
DAYS

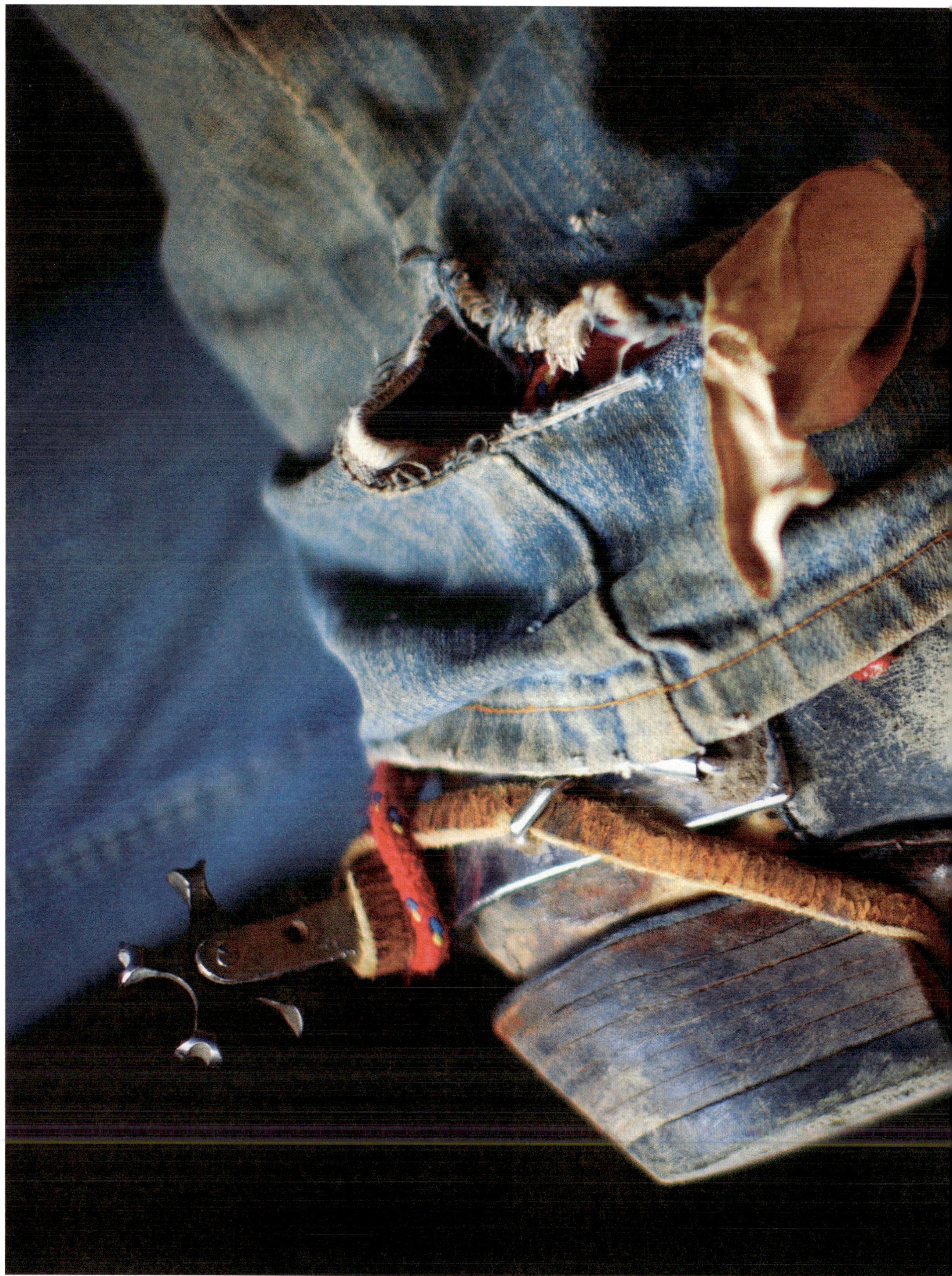

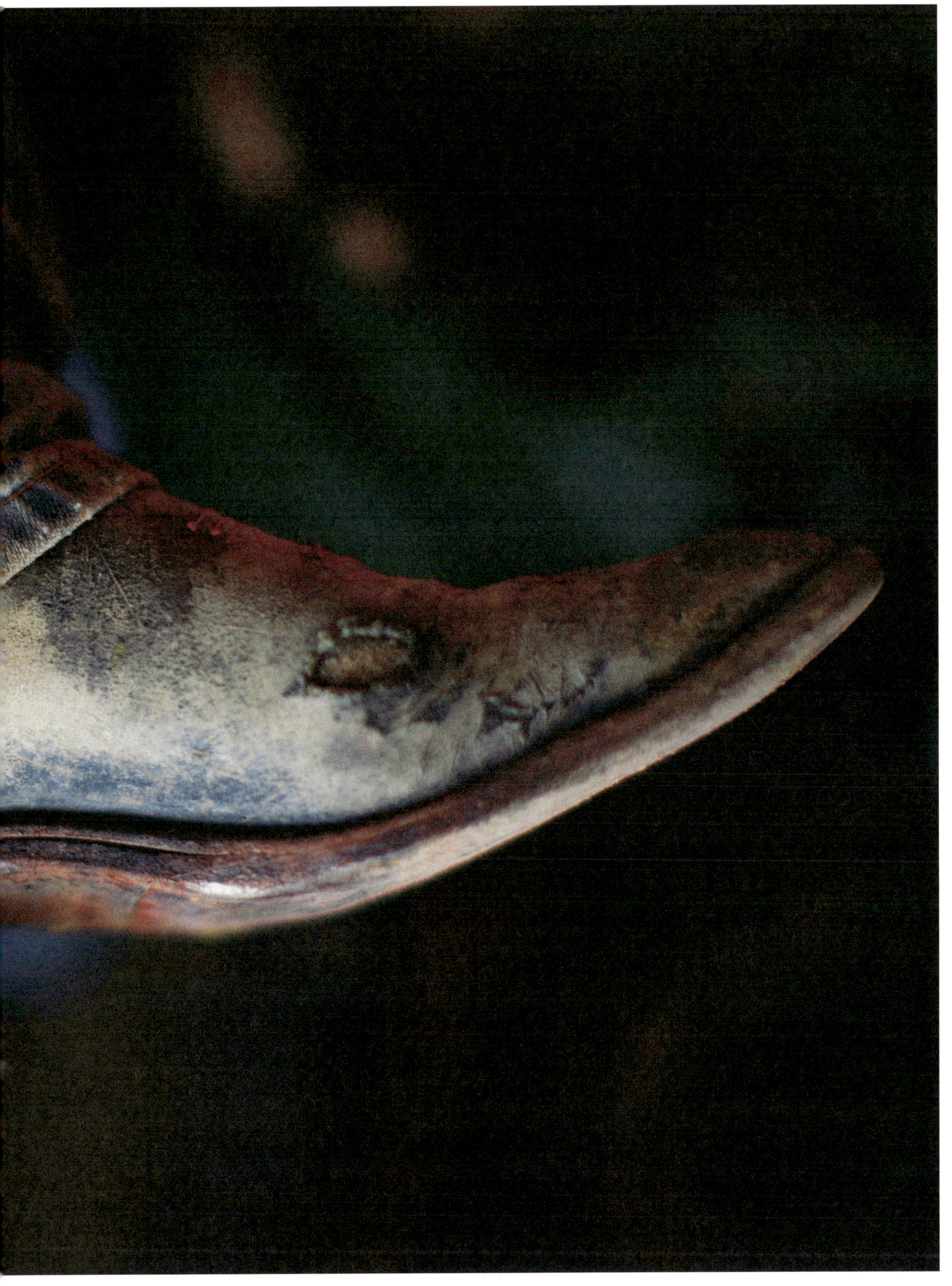

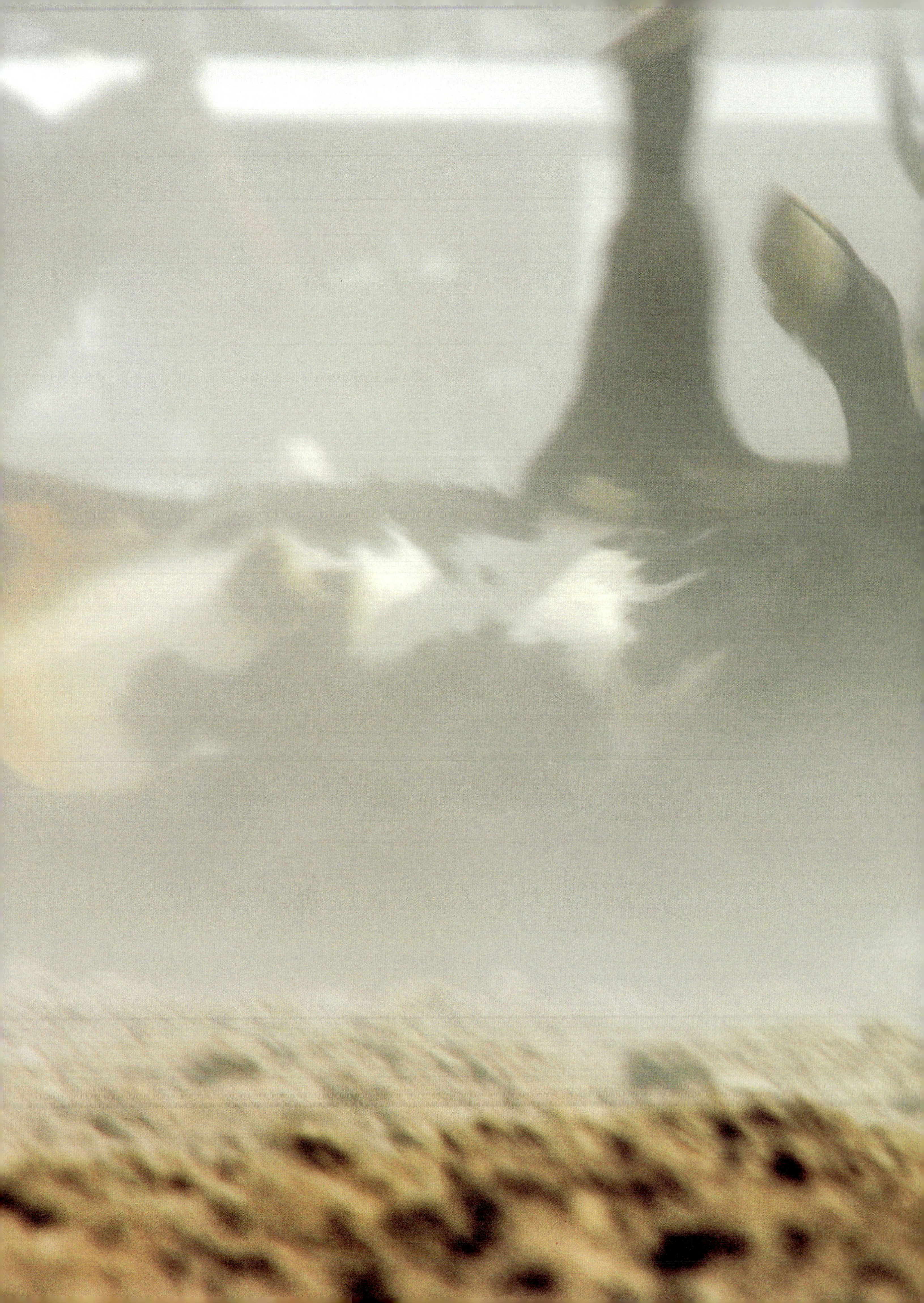

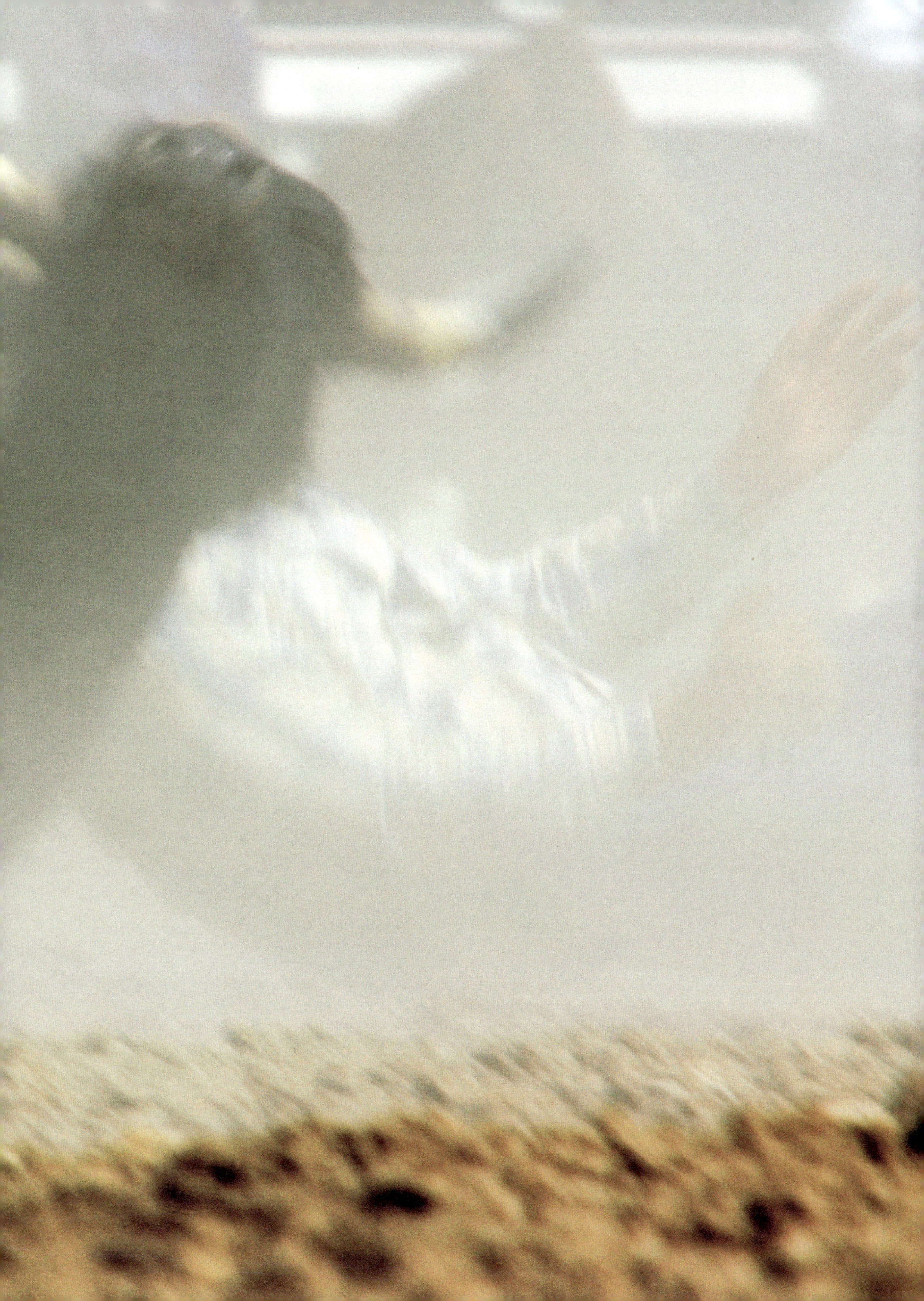

A BUTTE SHOULD STAND TALL ON THE LAND, A SOLITARY STATEMENT MADE BY NATURAL FORCES, AS IF DROPPED FROM THE SKY OR FORCING ITS WAY THROUGH THE SURFACE OF THE EARTH.

THESE ARE A FEW PEOPLE WHO HAVE BEEN ASSOCIATED WITH BUTTE, MONTANA: WRITER DASHIELL HAMMETT ONCE WORKED IN TOWN FOR THE PINKERTON DETECTIVE AGENCY. WYATT EARP'S YOUNGER BROTHER MORGAN WAS A POLICE OFFICER HERE BEFORE HE WAS SHOT AND KILLED IN A SALOON IN TOMBSTONE. THE MOTORCYCLE STUNTMAN EVEL KNIEVEL WAS BORN HERE, AS WAS BOOGIE-WOOGIE PIANO PLAYER MONTANA TAYLOR.

Lucille Ball, of the old TV favorite "The Lucy Show," was actually a New Yorker, but used to insist that she came from Butte because she was so eager to be perceived as a common, regular, average American.

However, few things can be described as ordinary in Butte.

It is a town defined by light and darkness, by steep shadows and razor-sharp lines cutting through black alleys. Phone and power wires, some surely disconnected, crisscross the sky, creating a suggestive pattern above abandoned garages and pawn shops dealing in gold and guns. The blackened iron structures on the highest hilltop look a lot like gnawed bird carcasses.

There is an abundance of brick walls brooding silently, keeping their stories to themselves. The whole town is one giant side-scene; it has either been rigged up for tomorrow's film shooting or was just left behind when last year's crew packed up and hit the road.

So it is the wing-strokes of history that you hear in bed at night, and in your dreams you can pick up the rattle and jingle sounds from the old mines. You can walk down any street at lunch-time or at dusk and feel the presence of the West, pretending that you are in a boom town or a crime story or a commercial for stovepipe jeans. You're so damned cool. This is what Butte does to you: the town makes you cool.

Nearby is a community named Anaconda and another one called Opportunity. You choose whatever you want to expose yourself to.

In the Finlen Hotel on East Broadway the hallway is a mile long in a dull green color and looks well suited for camera trackings. We check into the rooms opposite the one used by Sam Shepard in the Wim Wenders movie "Don't Come Knocking." The neon sign on the outside wall twinkles in a half-broken, yet rhythmic, fashion.

Before its movie house premiere, the film was played to Butte locals. They saw Shepard as an aging cowboy hero on the run from a film shooting in the Utah desert, sniffing at his own tracks, going back in history, looking for his old lover. Filmgoers in other places must have believed that he performed on a theatrical stage. To the folks in Butte every shadow was cast with total authenticity. They sat in the alley watching the very same alley on the screen.

Dressed in ample working man's jeans, the lunch guests in the M & M Bar, frequently featured in the movie, gather around their greasy plates. At the far end of the room, baseball players move across a silent television set and a back door has been left open to face the silence of the town outside.

Butte resembles an Edward Hopper painting without a frame. There is something about this stillness between brick fronts, time arrested in those huge shop windows; every block constitutes a frozen moment.

It used to be the most crowded place between Minneapolis and Seattle, a lively cosmopolitan industrial magnet. In 1878, workers from the copper mine struck for the first time and martial law was introduced after a union hall was blown to pieces. In 1914, Butte elected a socialist mayor. Three years later 160 miners perished in a catastrophic underground fire. Another three years and fifteen striking workers were shot and killed by goons hired by the mining company.

When the last mine closed in the early 1980s, the water pumps were turned off and a crater lake appeared, filled with acid and heavy metals, creating a long-term environmental headache for the entire region. There was a period when you could not drink the town's tap water. Although huge amounts of money have been spent on the cleanup, the crater is still surrounded by loudspeakers designed to scare away the water fowl and keep them off the lake.

The Chinese restaurant downtown, close to a cluster of Irish bars, has a suicidally steep stairway that seems to lead all the way to heaven. A lonesome cab is driving by, perhaps trying to break free from one of these films with lost souls, like "No Country For Old Men," with an internal chaos which could explode any minute now.

Butte is a town in waiting, a stage set to be populated. For a long time, the local rock band in the Silver Dollar Saloon is conspicuous by its absence, letting the instruments stand in neat formation, like a furnishing detail in the grander design.

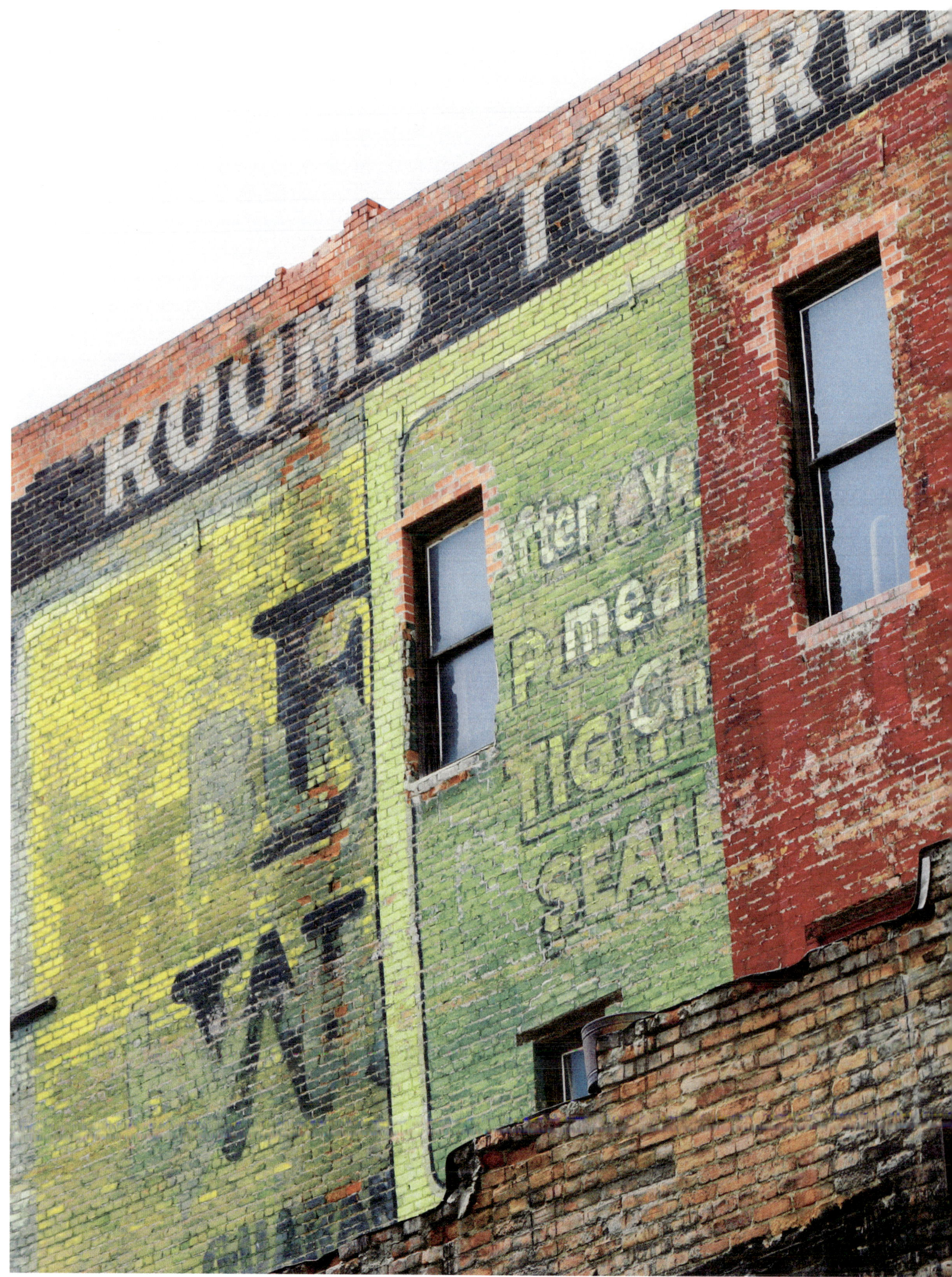
ROOMS TO

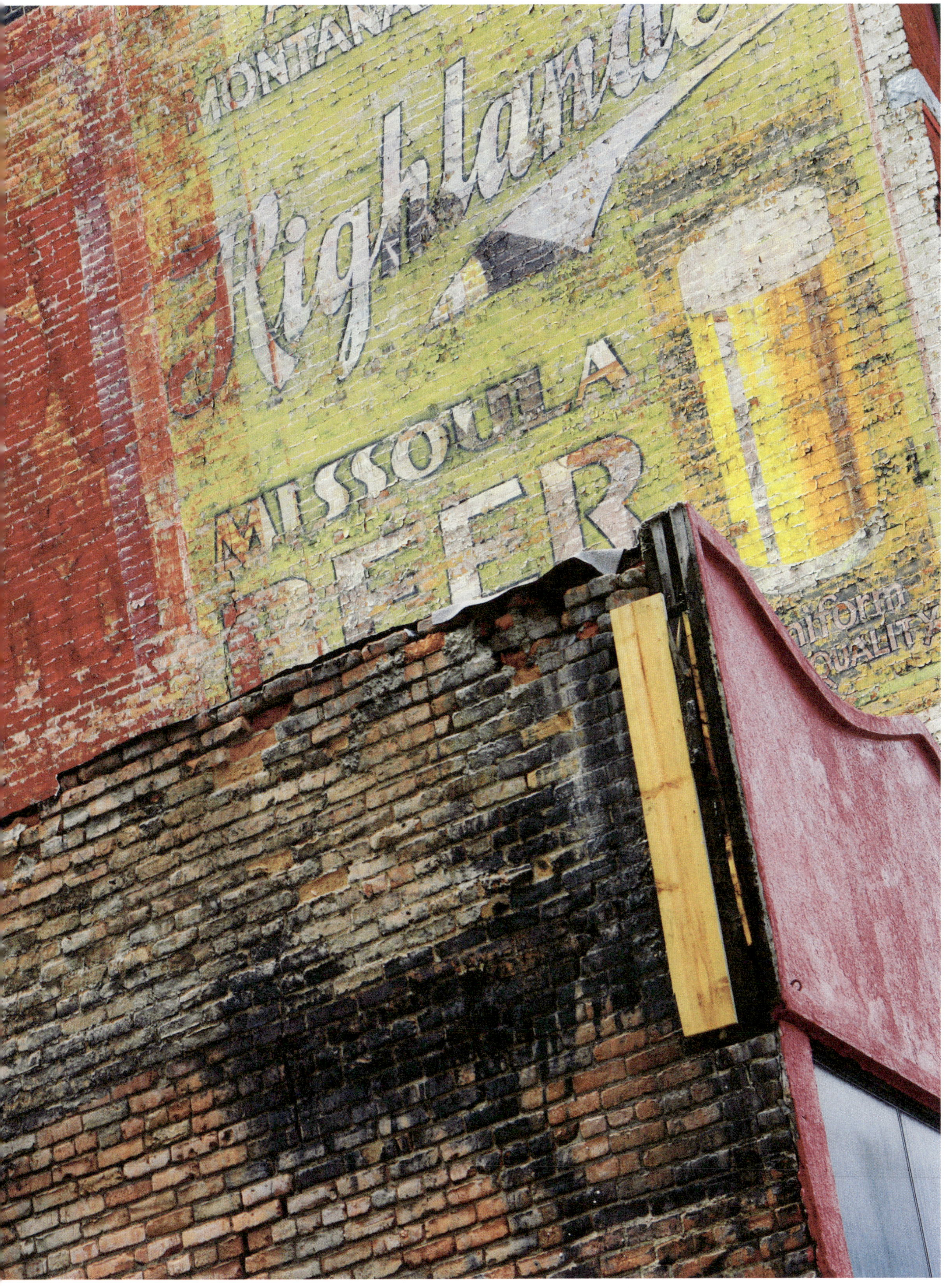
MONTANA
MISSOULA

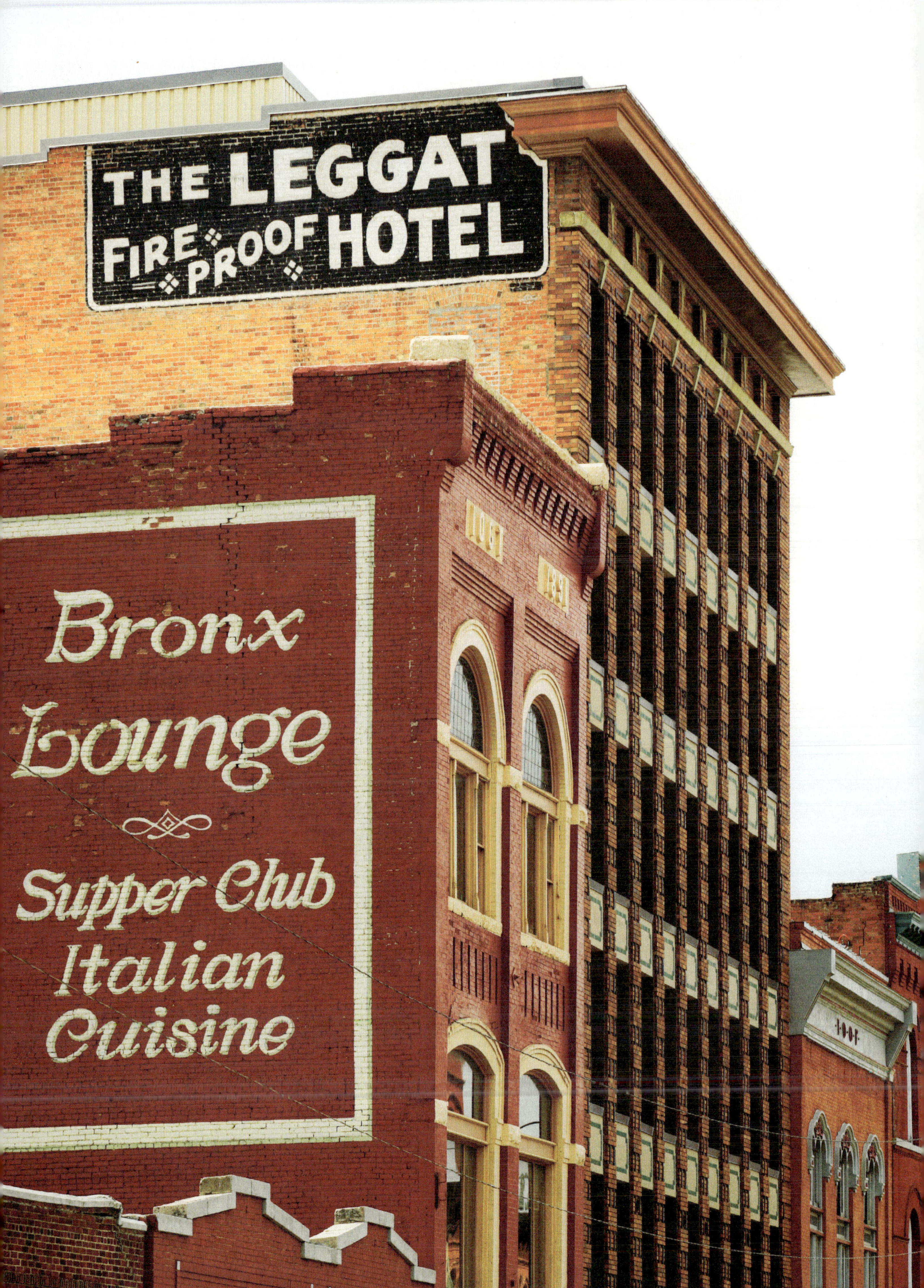
THE LEGGAT
FIRE PROOF HOTEL
Bronx Lounge
Supper Club
Italian Cuisine

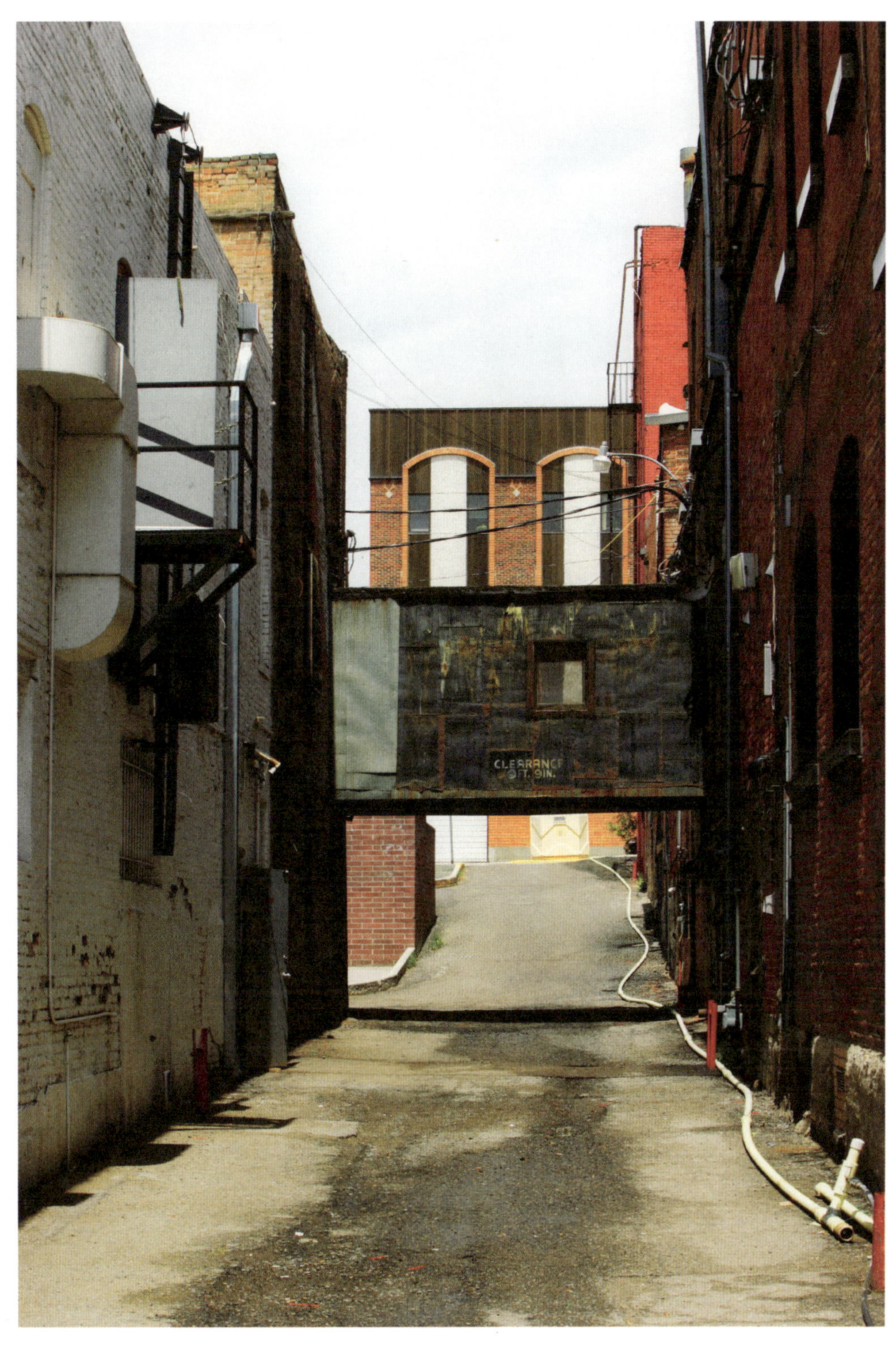
CLEARANCE

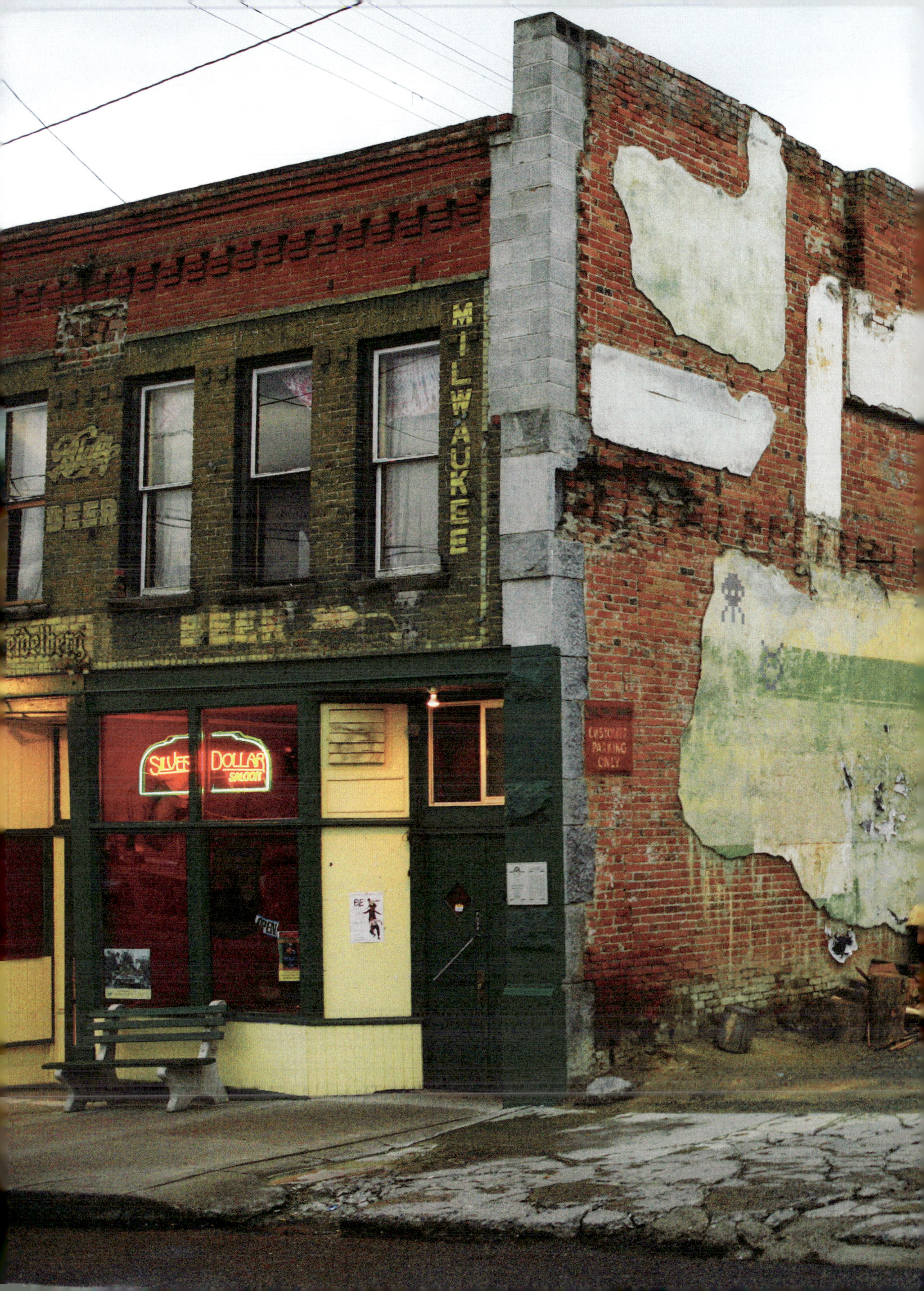
MILWAUKEE
BEER
DOLLAR
SALOON
CUSTOMER
PARKING
ONLY
OPEN

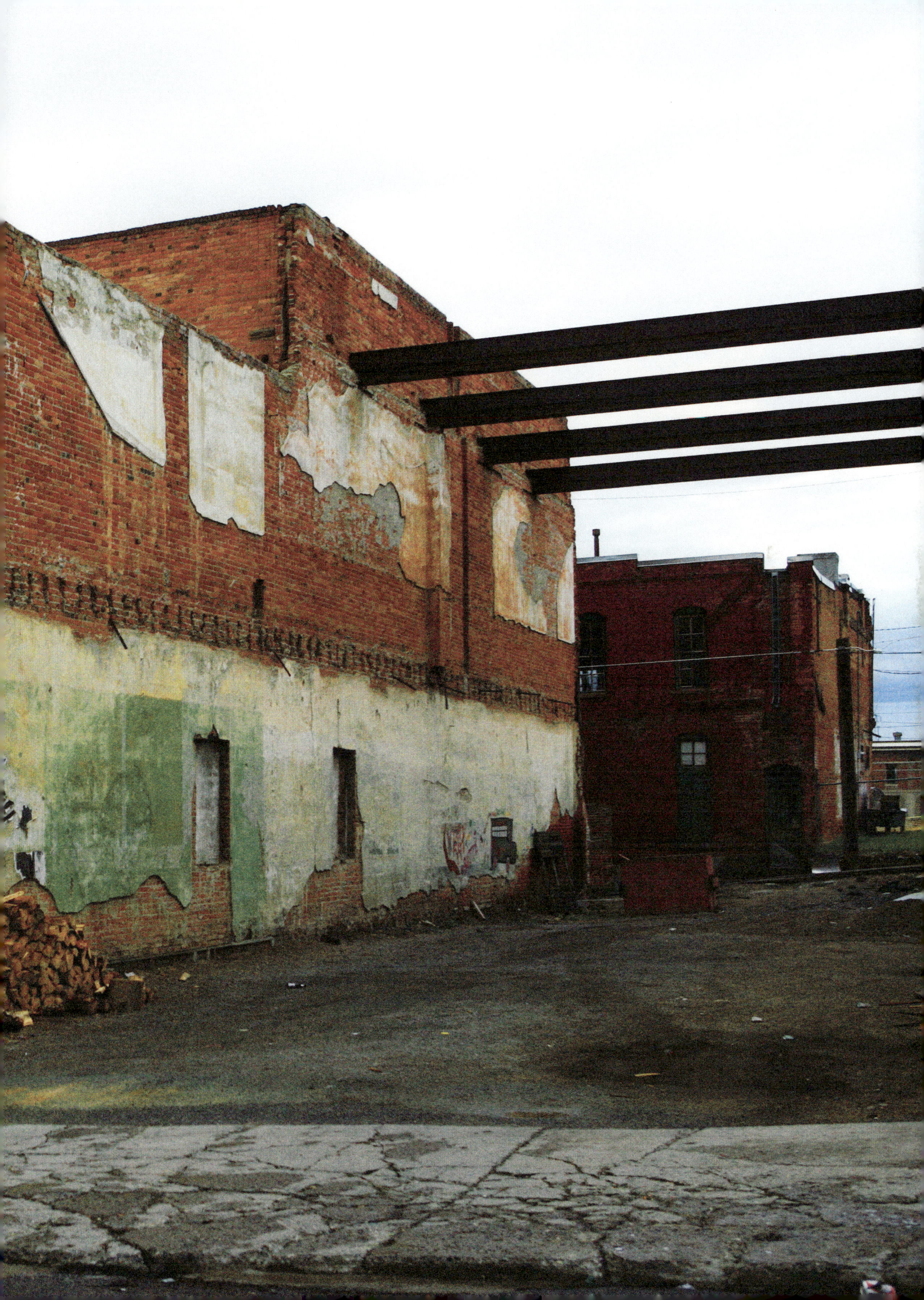

As you check into a certain type of motel you will inherit the diseases from a hundred previous guests, hear loud arguments from a room nearby, and get invited to the Elk's Club by the owner of the premises – who takes an evening off and is eager to show you where the truly important townspeople confer – before being directed to a midnight bar, which will burn to the ground six months later due to bad wiring installed by a local electrician with Elk credentials.

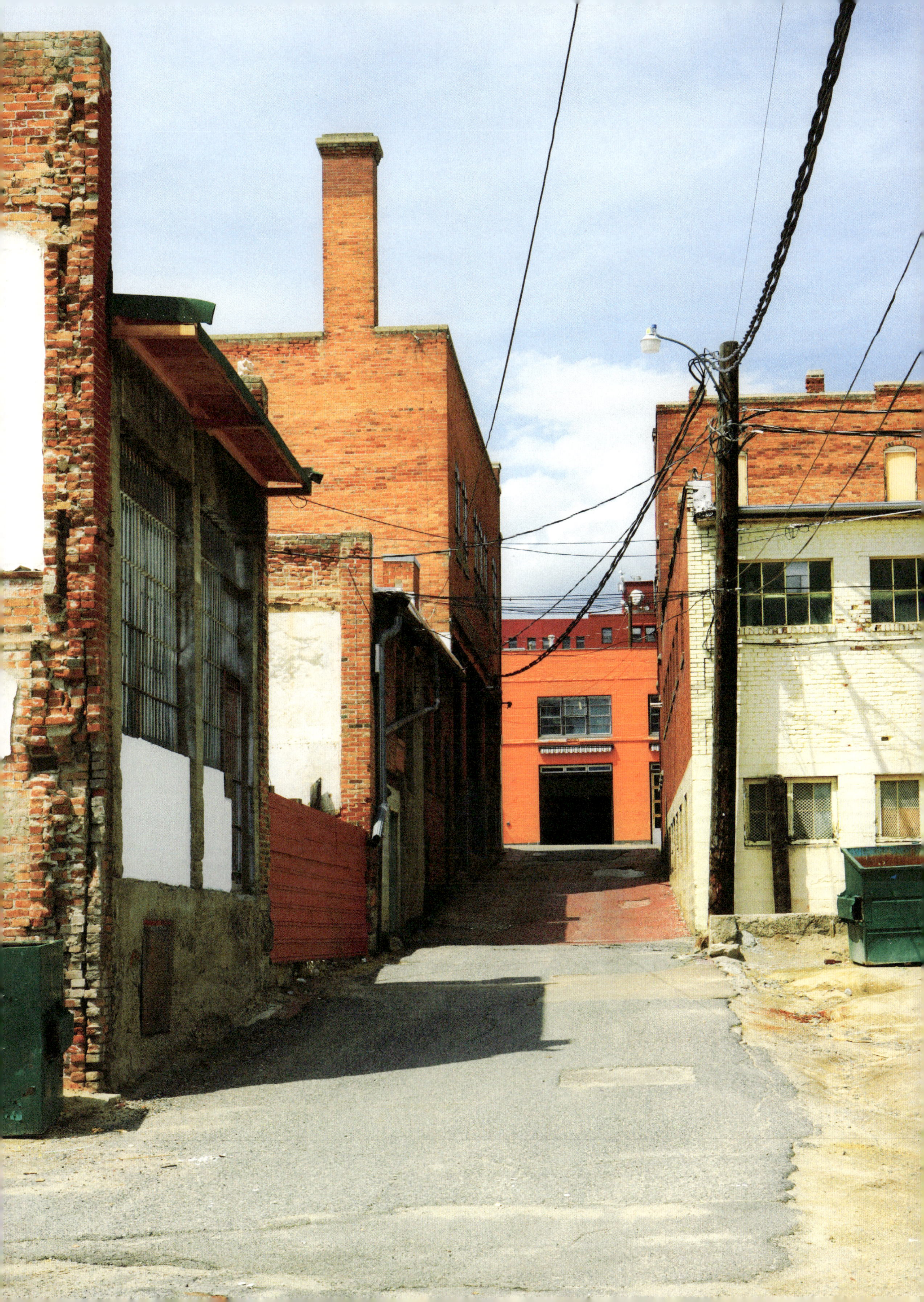

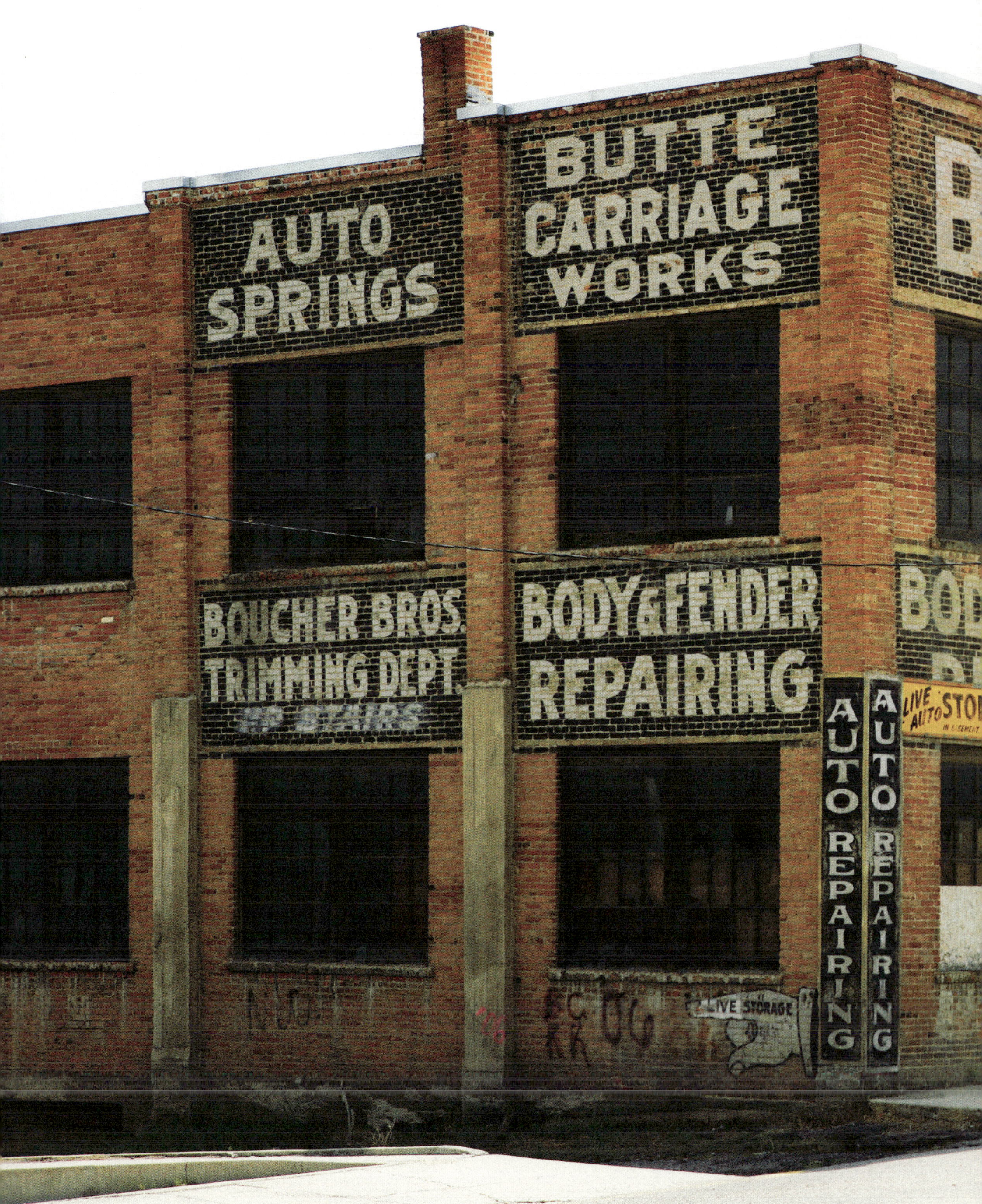
AUTO SPRINGS
BUTTE CARRIAGE WORKS
BOUCHER BROS. TRIMMING DEPT.
BODY&FENDER REPAIRING
AUTO REPAIRING
AUTO REPAIRING
LIVE STORAGE

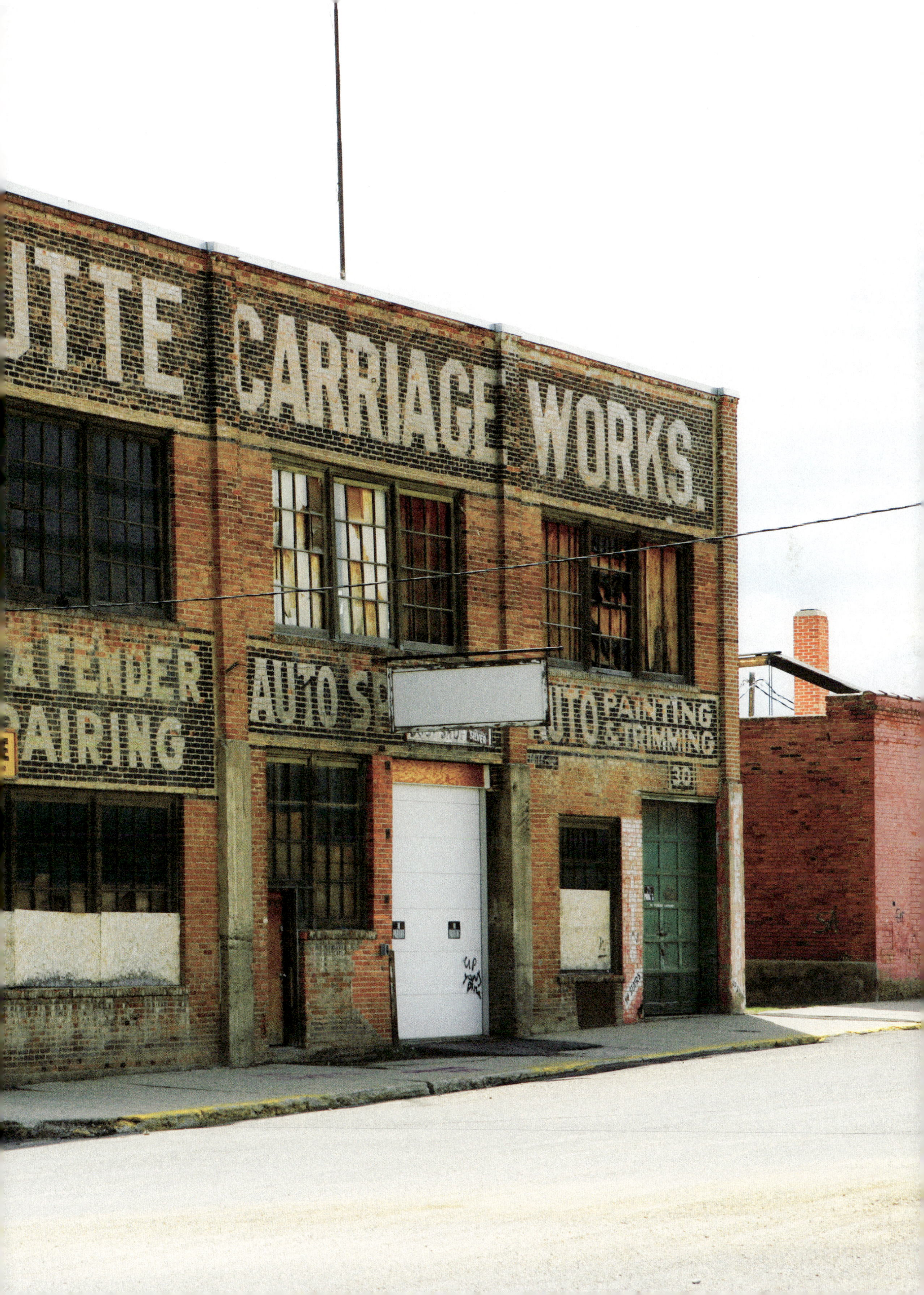
UTTE CARRIAGE WORKS.
&FENDER
PAIRING
AUTO SP
UTO PAINTING & TRIMMING
30

EVERY MORNING AT AROUND SIX, THE GEOLOGISTS DEPART FROM OUR MOTEL IN THEIR HUMMING WHITE PICKUPS WITH TINY ORANGE STREAMERS.

THEY PASS THROUGH THE IDAHO-FIFTH STREET INTERSECTION – POSSIBLY THE MOST TRAFFIC-LIGHT REGULATED IN THE ENTIRE STATE – AND DRIVE PAST THE SLUMBERING SMALL SHOPS WITH ADORNED COWBOY BOOTS, GIRLY PORTRAITS IN RUSTIC WOODEN FRAMES, AND LEFTOVER CHRISTMAS DECORATIONS COVERED WITH GOLD PAINT, ALONG THE SIDEWALKS OUTSIDE THE THUNDERBIRD MOTEL AND THE CASINO WITH FOUR BROKEN NEON LETTERS AND FARTHER OUT INTO THE BUSH-DOTTED SAGE DESERT, THAT COVERS SUCH VAST AREAS IN THE COUNTRY WEST OF THE ROCKIES.

In this part of Nevada, gold fever has risen several degrees over the past decade. Migrating families have bought new prefab homes in the high desert, having been employed by mineral companies that painstakingly flush cyanide through the dirt in order to get to the glitter.

Gold never goes out of fashion. In the summertime, I have seen hopeful diggers with their pans in the creeks a hundred miles north of here. Now, in the midst of winter, it is the season of the geologists.

But more than anything else it's time to let the poets be heard.

One week every year they and an audience of thousands from all over North America convene in the faraway town of Elko to listen to what John Dofflemyer, a rancher and writer from California, describes as

> "the random hum and rhythm
> of certain words on your breath
> that always seemed to help
> get the hard work done."

During this tribal gathering the whole county is transformed; it is put to music, electrified, becoming a buzz of stories, of conversations about drought and fences, about the old West and the new; all of it leading to a flow of sentimental or more penetrating images of a landscape loved by everyone and of a job, that of the cowboy, which a lot of people admire, but fewer would be able to cope with.

This time it is an anniversary, the twenty-fifth National Cowboy Poetry Gathering; the mother of all – and they have become plentiful across the U.S. – meetings for poetic wranglers.

Wylie Gustafson's great grandfather emigrated from Sweden and now this modern rancher is dividing his time between his place in Washington state and the gigs with his band Wylie & The Wild West.

"This Western life that we live is so mystical and real. It's honest," he says. "Maybe it's the connection with the land, with the old ways, a touchstone to the past. All of our ancestors at one time were tenders of lifestock, growers of wheat or whatever. I think it's important to express what's so cool about this lifestyle, and poetry is the easiest way to do it."

When the local Western Folklife Center organized its first gathering in 1985, the core of enthusiasts went around knocking on ranch doors in the district asking if anyone in the family did any writing. Out of this research grew a free two-day festival. Nowadays it is an ultra-professional arrangement covering eight days, from morning till late night in a number of different surroundings, from bars to seminaries, with leather-craft courses, group visits to ranches, and midnight dances to live bands.

One of the pioneer organizers was Hal Cannon, a musician, radio producer, and folklorist with an unbound passion for Western culture.

"Even the reluctant souls will melt with the emotion," he smiles, "because it speaks to the heart. What we see before us is a lifestyle under siege. These are just people being able to raise their voices, to say these words that are so evocative of our feelings. It is sentimental, but it's also just really sweet."

Twenty-five years ago we had no idea that there might be a place for somebody like me, says Waddie Mitchell, an ex-cowboy and poet with a happy moustache:

"Cowboy poetry was almost like an oxymoron, two words that don't fit together. Like 'postal service' or 'military intelligence', the words seem to contradict each other. In my case it's been almost like falling in a big old cowpie and still coming out smelling like a rose. This whole week is about us simple people living simple lives that are complicated as all hell. We had a very small world to grow up in. It was a vast country, but it was all I knew. We didn't even have radio when I grew up. We had no power, no electricity. So we sat around at night and did strange things like talk to each other. That was my TV, those cowboy stories and the stories that my Mum read to us."

When I came to Elko one winter in the mid-90s, Buck Ramsey from Texas entered the main stage in his wheelchair, paralyzed after having been bucked off a horse, and with his battered hat leaning into the spotlight as if it were a prairie wind he recited his most powerful lines, the ones describing the cowboy trade as a fantasy worth taking extremely seriously:

"…And as I ride out on the morning
Before the bird, before the dawn,
I'll be this poem, I'll be this song,
My heart will beat the world a warning
Those horsemen will ride with me,
And we'll be good, and we'll be free"

In less capable hands this might have sounded like a recruiting ad for an army on its way to the next war. Here, in the crowded Elko Convention Center, the words filled the air with clarity and the smell of sage; it expanded the room, made us all realize what the purpose of this gathering really was, what its essence felt like; that particular kind of freedom that is rich on value but does not have a price at the stock exchange, the intoxication and liberation at sunrise, the frozen silhouettes of riders on the range the hour before the yellow light eats the shadows away and modern life sets in.

Perhaps it was the memory of Buck Ramsey, not with us anymore, that made me want to come back to this place.

Was it a wacky and unfashionable notion? Of course not. I knew that the unbeatable sentiment was still here, as was the landscape; so many times I've driven through the rocky deserts and infinite expanses thinking "My God, you don't need those myths, you just pick the right soundtrack and chase from one horizon to the next."

So it is Eko, once again, now that the cowboy poets and bards celebrate their anniversary and the Ruby Mountains south of the small town in northeastern Nevada stand covered with snow instead of the red dust of summer, and thousands of men and women with hats and boots close the stable doors around their daily routines for a drive or flight into the landscape of communal magic.

"As crescent moons come, and go
With each winter of snow
May you walk in beauty"

In a lackluster assembly hall Henry Real Bird, the only Indian poet on stage, is rocking his words into place. Muttering and whistling, he half-sings the phrases in the Crow language that place him, inward-looking with arms swaying, in the long tradition. The mountains, the moons, the horses.

Cowgirl poet Echo Klaproth quickly becomes red-eyed from small tears when talking to me about how the children she meets as a teacher back in Wyoming don't seem to have a history any longer on which to fall back upon.

"If we don't get to hear any stories as we grow up, we become extinct," she says. "I feel that the students that I work with have no sense of belonging to anything and as a result they seem almost like a lost generation. You know that old saying, if you don't believe in something and stand for something, you could fall for anything? If they don't know any value system or a heritage or a history of who they are, it's no wonder that there are so many young lost people in the world."

With the commercialization of Western history there is the obvious risk of cowboy poetry becoming just another label to sell an emotion. But Echo Klaproth also believes that many on the outside are truly envious of the cowboy life.

"These people that for a few days put on their tassels and their hats, they just plain love it, and how can we judge that harshly? In the West still, the cowboy is real. But there's a lot of myths about him and it's because for a little while we can escape our real life and go be something that's ideal to us. Yesterday a gentleman told me he comes here to get refilled for the year. He said it's a spiritual happening for him."

On the latest recording from Wylie & The Wild West, lyricist Paul Zarzyski puts forward what he calls the quintessential western question: "Did you come to ride or did you come to hide?" And, of course, the history of the West also includes giving shelter to people looking to change their wardrobes and identities, sometimes out of necessity, at other times for reasons that have not always been honorable. Crossing the state line. Breathing freely.

As we drive the country roads out of Elko, the wintery bush landscape is a yellowish, pale canvas with white bands cutting into the hillsides and deepening as our car climbs toward the last settlements by the foot of the mountain.

Here, John Sustacha can be found walking around with his seven dogs in tow, in a relaxed low-season mood on his ranch that has modern solar panels in the midst of piles of old, rust-covered machine parts. Here, people drive in 60s pickups with no permits to be on the road. Among the snowy peaks there are deer and mountain lions and black bears.

Several of the road bars smell of cat piss; that's the way it happens when old people take care of every kicked-out creature in the territory. Outside Jiggs Bar sits a small American tin flag with Woody Guthrie's most immortal lines written on it.

In this place, too, we find an old man who has cowboyed his entire life and always lived down in the same ravine. He knows all the secrets about his mountain neighbors and is close with Jack Walther, the 90-year-old rancher who is the dean of cowboy poets in Elko and still resides in his story-telling armchair near Lamoille. "You'll find poetry with people who are more or less solitary," Walther told me when I visited his house back in the 90s. "They have time to think and comprehend what's going on. I tend to think about poetry when I'm alone. To me, the writers who are not inhibited by the rules and regulations of poetry schooling are the true poets."

Before the road was asphalted, Jiggs used to be a hideout for outlaws. Somewhat later someone tried to fit the whole town population into a phone booth, or maybe it was a Volkswagen. Today hardly anyone remains to fit in.

"If you don't believe that a woman like me is up to the job, you're not up to being with a woman like me."

This is the condensed message from Georgie Sicking, 87 years old, who sits chuckling next to me with peering eyes as I drive her to her next performance in Elko. Surrounded only by guys, she started cowboying at the age of 17, a lone girl on the range. She then worked and struggled together with her husband to get a ranch of their own, and when he was killed in a job accident she herself bought another ranch – at the age of 75. Pictures from the old days show her looking just like a movie star. She rides wild-eyed horses at high speed in a rodeo arena.

"I started writing poetry in my teens just as a form of self-entertainment, to pass the time. I was staying by myself forty miles from town with no electricity, no telephone, no car. Just horses and me and taking care of a bunch of cattle."

I tell her that it sounds as if it must have been a rough life for a young girl.

"Well, yeah. It was. But it made me tougher. I was five years old and my sister was nine, we were playing in the sandbush and she said, 'When I grow up, I'm gonna have a nice home and a family', and I said, 'When I grow up, some day I'm gonna have a ranch of my own, and before that I'm gonna hold down a job on one of these big cowboy outfits in spite of being a woman'."

This is how she ends her poem "Housewife":

"I've been a rancher's daughter, I've been a rancher's spouse
But never was I ever married to a house"

Her eyesight is bad these days, and she misses her ranch like crazy, but in the company of poets Georgie Sicking has found a warm, extended family.

According to Wallace McRae, one of the founding traditionalists in this congregation, there is a risk that the authenticity gets lost when the festivals grow and the stages demand showmanship and more polished texts. It's just like ranching itself: everything seems to be moving toward mechanization and increased energy-dependence; profits are expected at every corner.

"Most other occupations have a spokesperson. The cowboy really doesn't," says McRae. "We have cowboy poetry because we don't have a union or a national association that goes to the Congress. So who is going to speak for us? Also, the reason for writing is the boredom you feel sitting on a stupid horse under the moon with nobody else in sight."

And he sincerely believes that there is a future in boredom.

"Yeah, I think there is a place for isolation and being alone, I really do. I want to avoid some of the impressions that keep bombarding us. I may not even answer the phone."

One would be forgiven for thinking that Wylie Gustafson was coming from a different world. Born in 1961, he comes strutting down the alley in his smartest cowboy jacket and a hat that clings to a thin, meticulously shaved skull. When he was younger and rode among the rolling hills of Montana this head was full of Rolling Stones and Johnny Cash; an influx of impulses from faraway metro places that turned him into a songwriter with swaying rock'n'roll knees.

Still he is more western than anyone would expect.

Well, yes, somebody discovered that he was good at yodeling, too, and when he recorded three yodel notes for Yahoo he became the sound trademark of the internet company and financially independent. More cool jackets, an even more stylish hat. But he keeps his old horses waiting for him back home, even though he believes you should be forward-looking.

"A lot of western songwriting and poetry looks backwards. They have blinders. It's very important to me to make our genre and our music contemporary, to not just be a re-enactor, a copy of what was going on fifty years ago."

And so the dancing continues way into the Elko night with Wylie & The Wild West as electric prompters; conscious of history and with an unfailing sense of style, and with a bold curling of the upper lip.

"I hope that what I do will be understood by the hardest working cowboy. I wanna impress those guys more than anything," says Wylie Gustafson.

Lately, he has collaborated with a rodeo poet from Montana, Paul Zarzyski, who seems to ride his poems as if they were wild creatures aiming for the moon. Before his readings he bends and stretches like an athlete warming up for a sports event. Then he exposes a big chin beneath a sad-looking droopy moustache.

"Riding bucking horses in the rodeo, you want to stay on their backs for eight seconds. That's a very long time when the horse is coming apart and boiling over. For me, every line's like an eight-second ride and I want those words to jump and kick hard, to rock and roll off the stirrup bone of the middle ear."

Zarzyski, whose father was a miner who immigrated from Poland and did not have a single book in his home, is cowboy poetry's most charismatic interpreter. It's clear that he is moving further onto untraditional territory, where the 60s music he grew up with gives him a rhythmic backbone and the wide-angled landscape of the West adds space to his fantasy. Still pounding away on a portable typewriter, he is repeatedly thrown into new wilderness adventures, either by a crazy mustang or a motorcycle defying every curve and speed limit.

"We throttled
wide open, torrid on lust, hopped-up
on the 4-stroke's solo
double-tongued through straightpipes
fired on 2 bits worth of fuel. Hell,
we made our own damn breeze,
we kamikazed the heat, our fevers
breaking into youth's oblivion cool"

"The prairie has been fenced in, but that must never happen to cowboy poetry," Zarzyski says. "I am inviting people to step through the fence. My suggestion is to bust through the wire fences, bust them down metaphorically, spiritually, emotionally, philosophically – and let's see what's out there. It's my mission to keep the poetry and the West wild."

What does he think is so special about cowboy culture?

"It's gotta do with the land, it's gotta do with the wide open spaces. I have an experience of my own: it was 80 below one night on a ranch and I went outside to check the horses and wrap my sleeping-bag around the regulator on the propane tank, and the wind was blowing fifty miles an hour through my clothes and filling in my tracks in the snow. I don't think I've ever felt a greater sense of solitude and aloneness on this planet of ours, and I don't think, in the same breath, that I ever felt more connected to this planet."

One morning at our breakfast place in Elko, Paul Zarzyski gets up to go pay for the coffee and Henry Real Bird leaves a self-printed booklet with his poems on our table. When I look at the back page there is a message scribbled with a ball pen: "Lars, may you ride in beauty."

Isn't that what we all hope for?

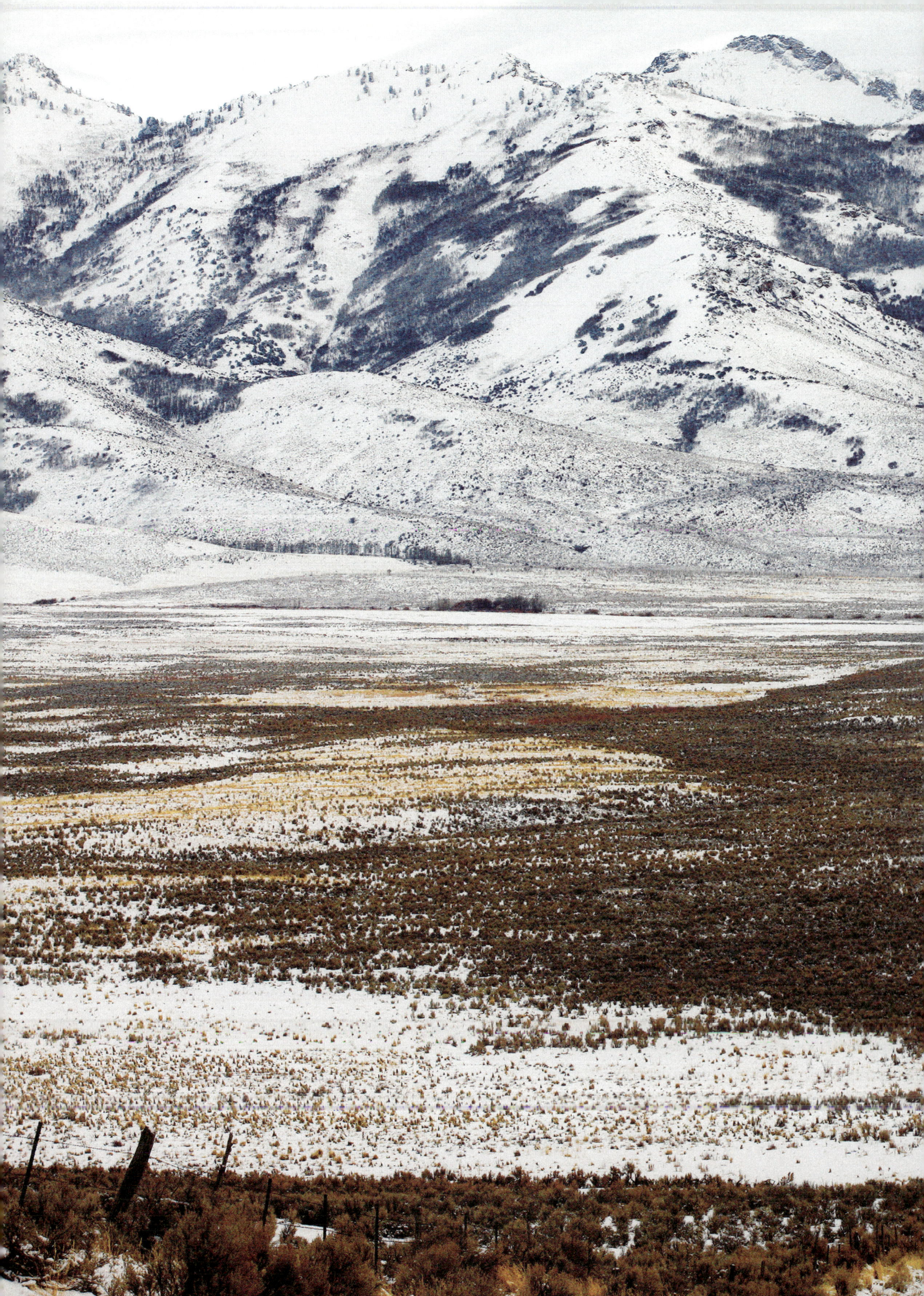

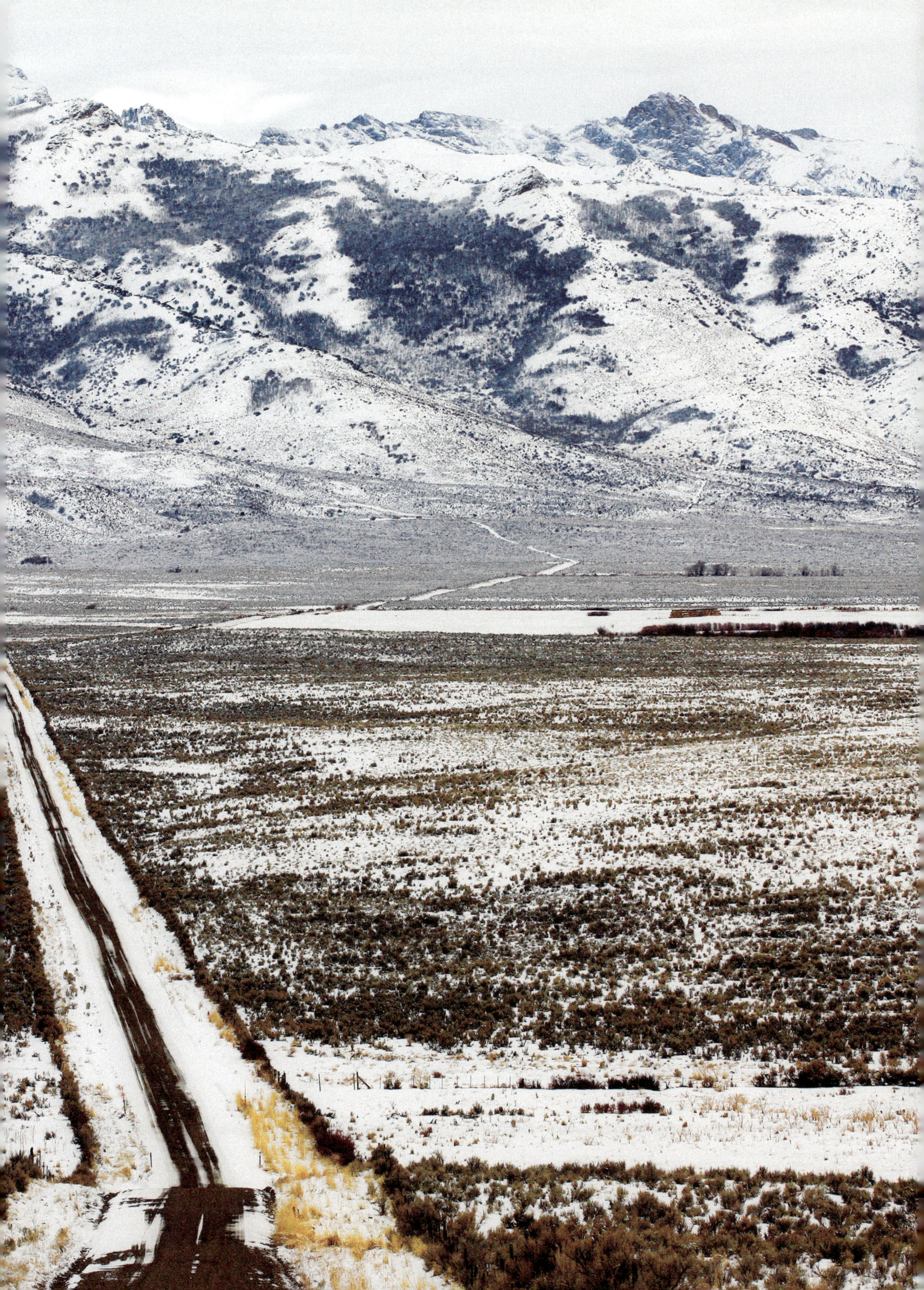

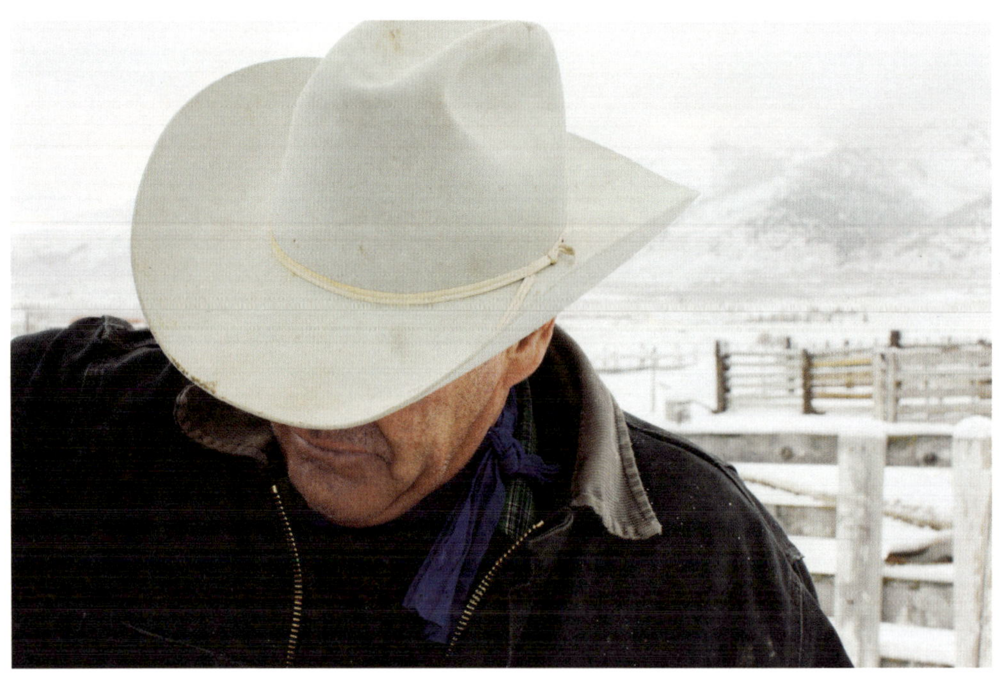

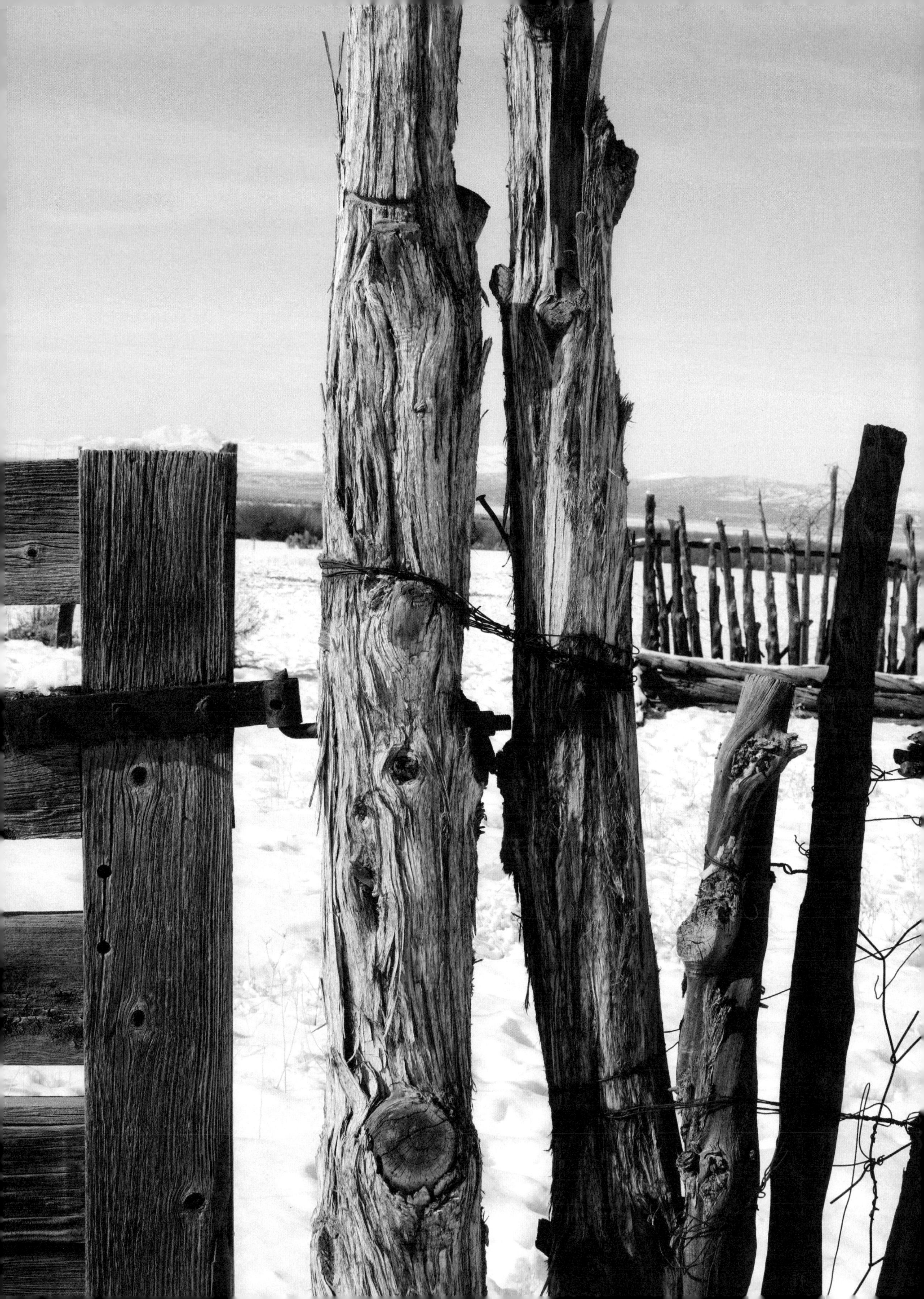

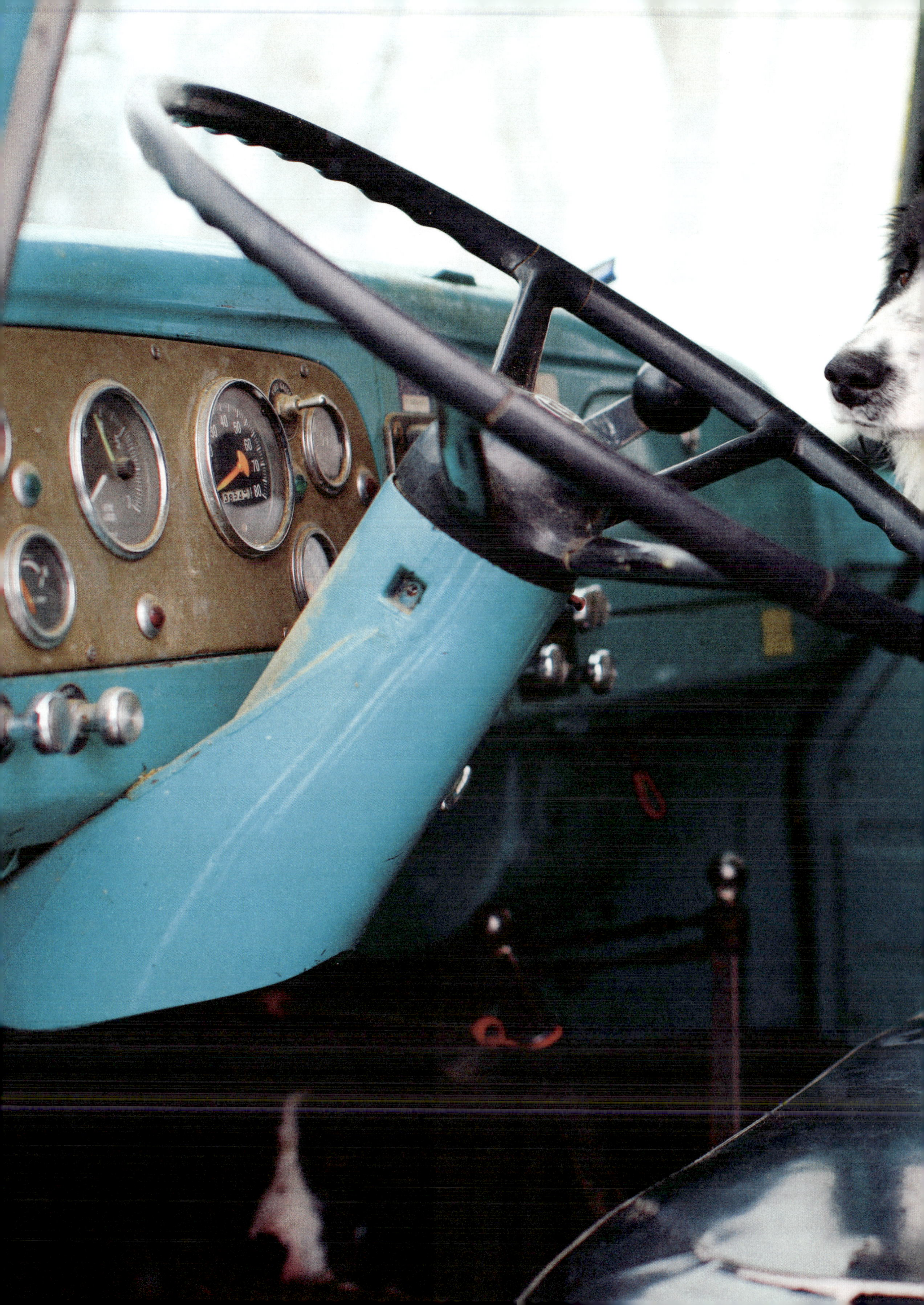

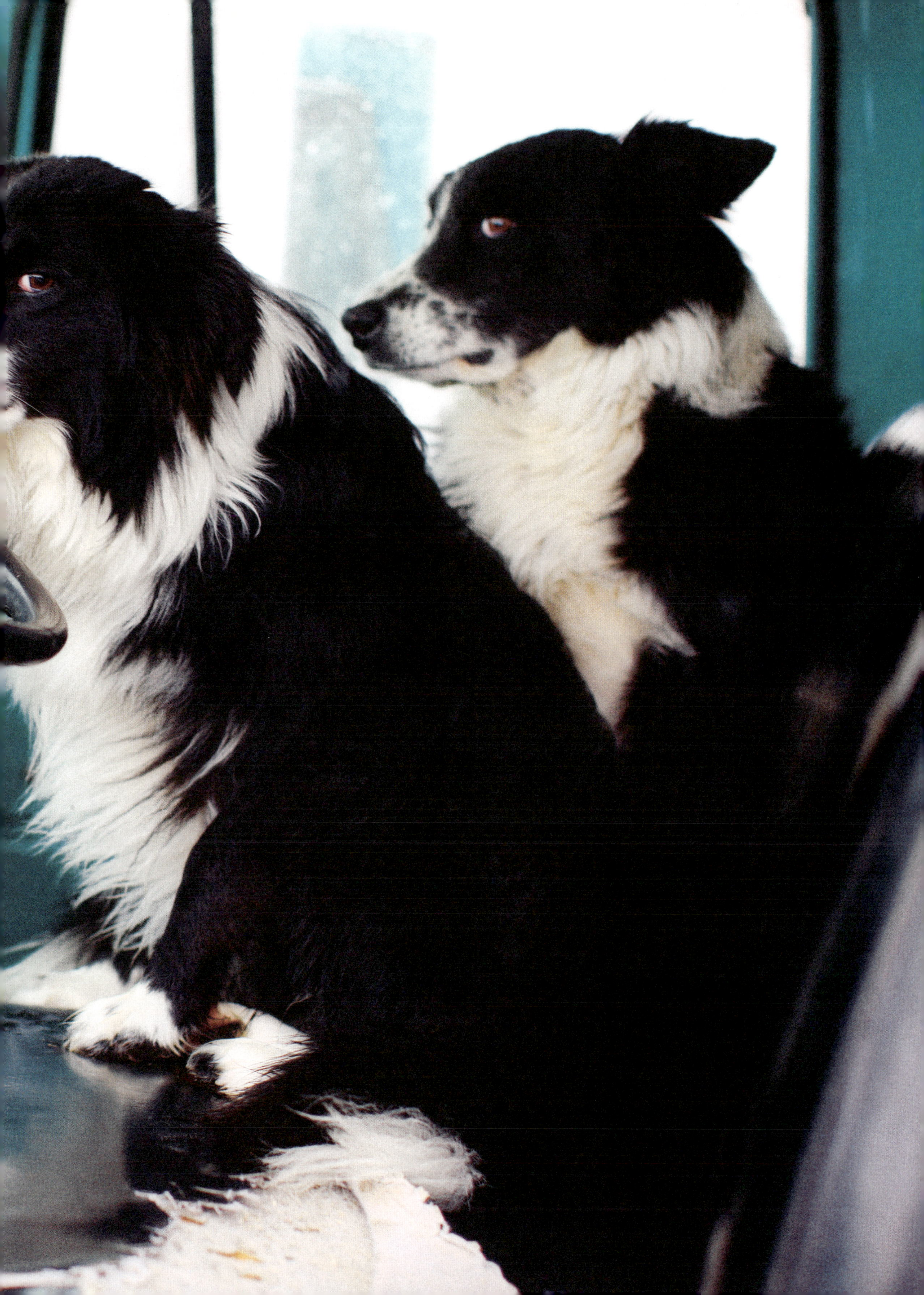

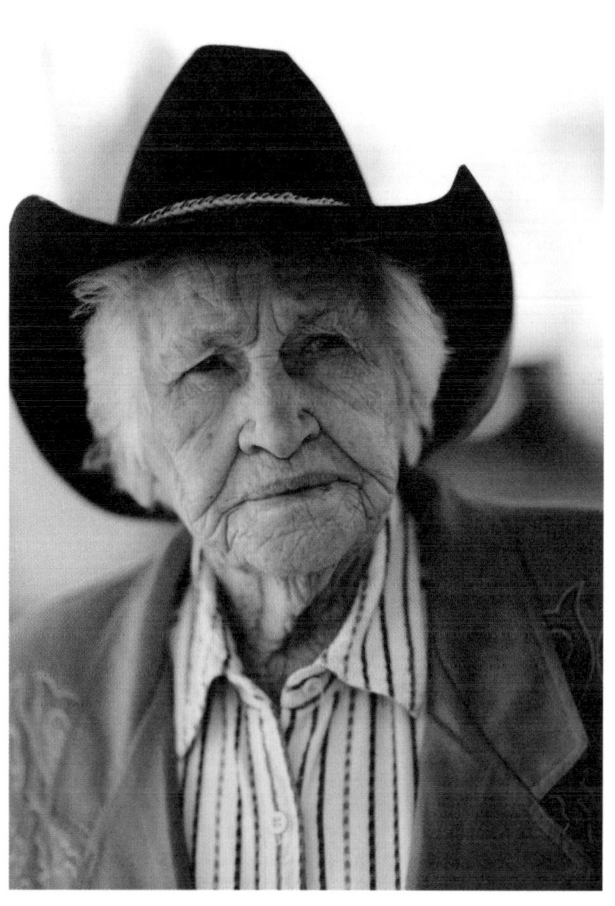

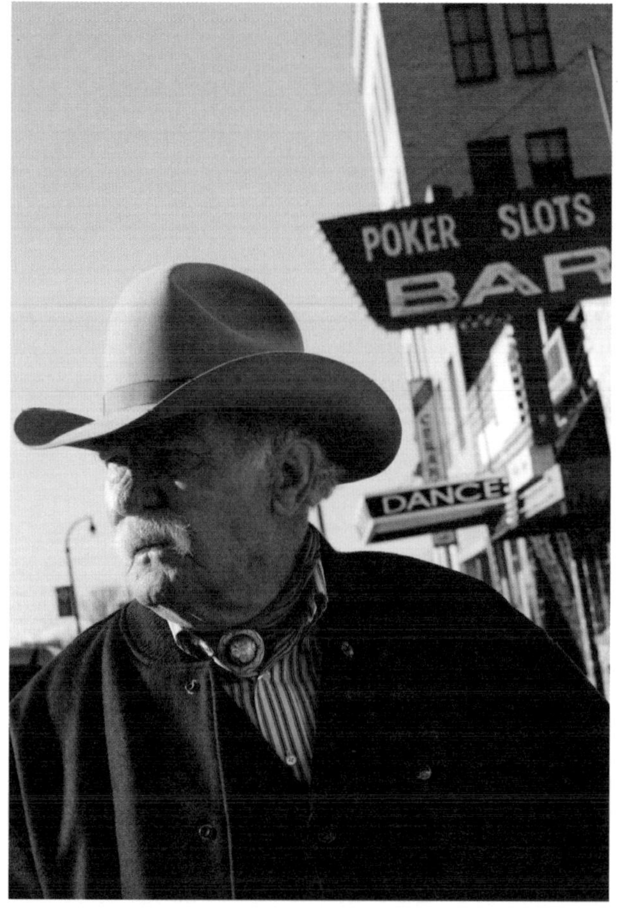
POKER SLOTS
BAR
DANCE

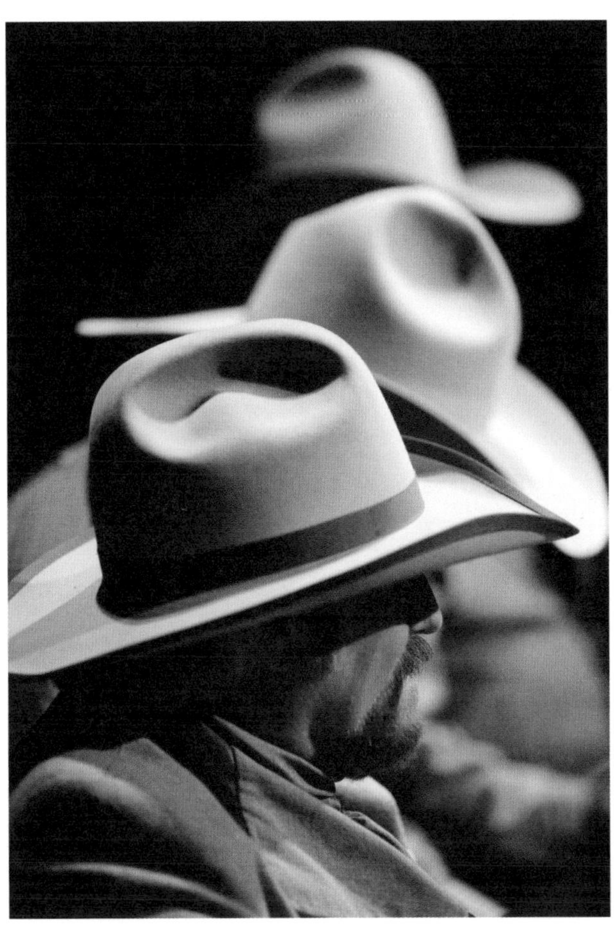

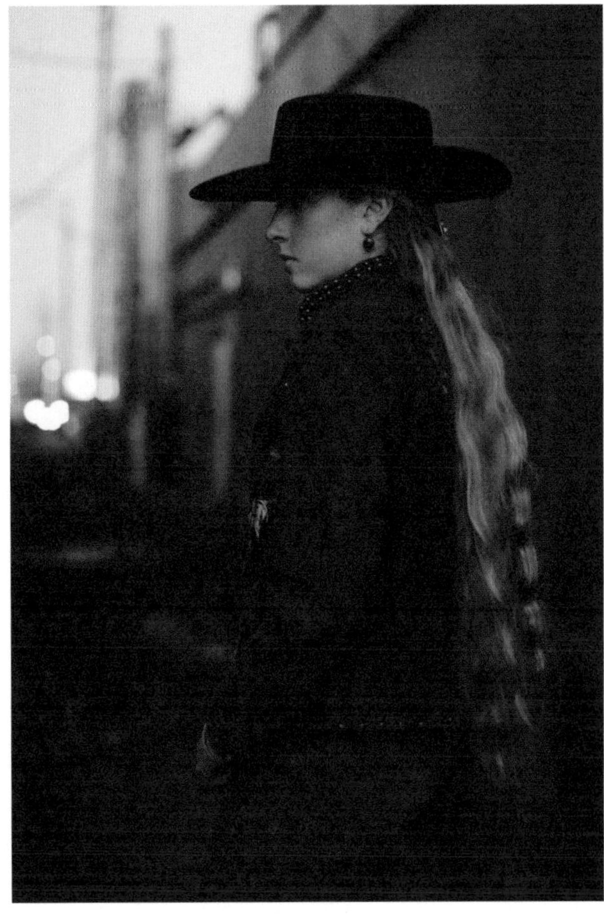

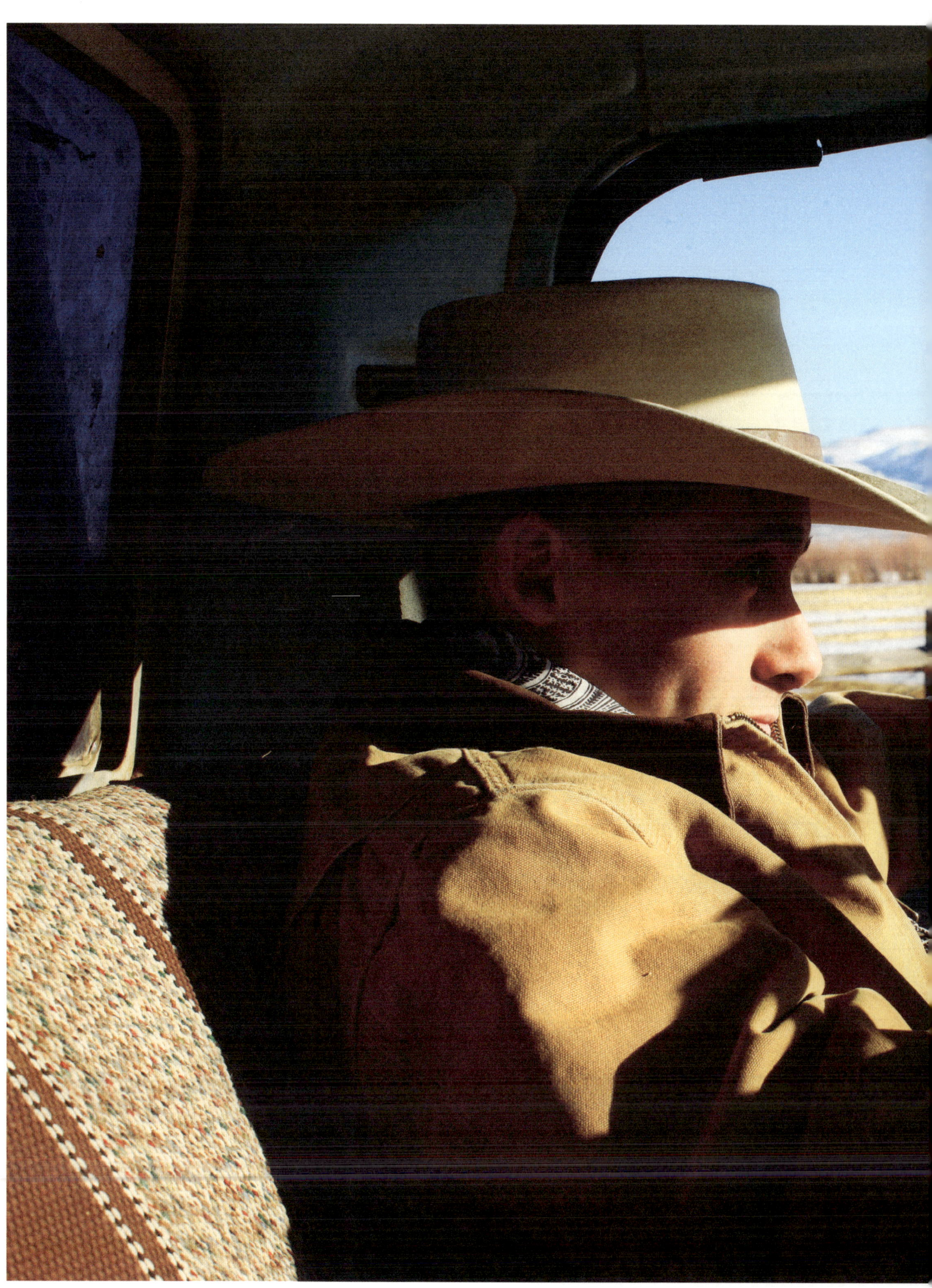

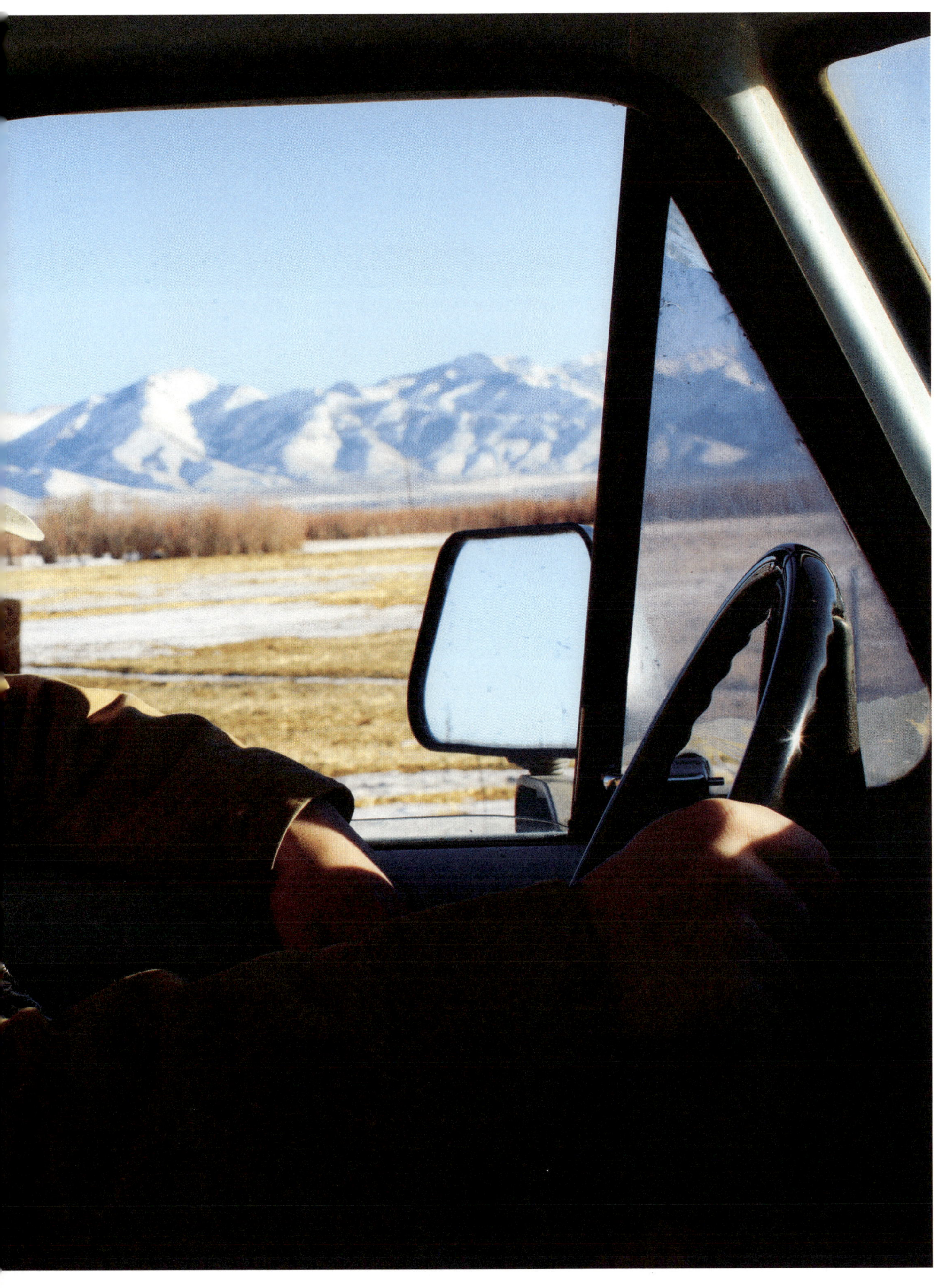

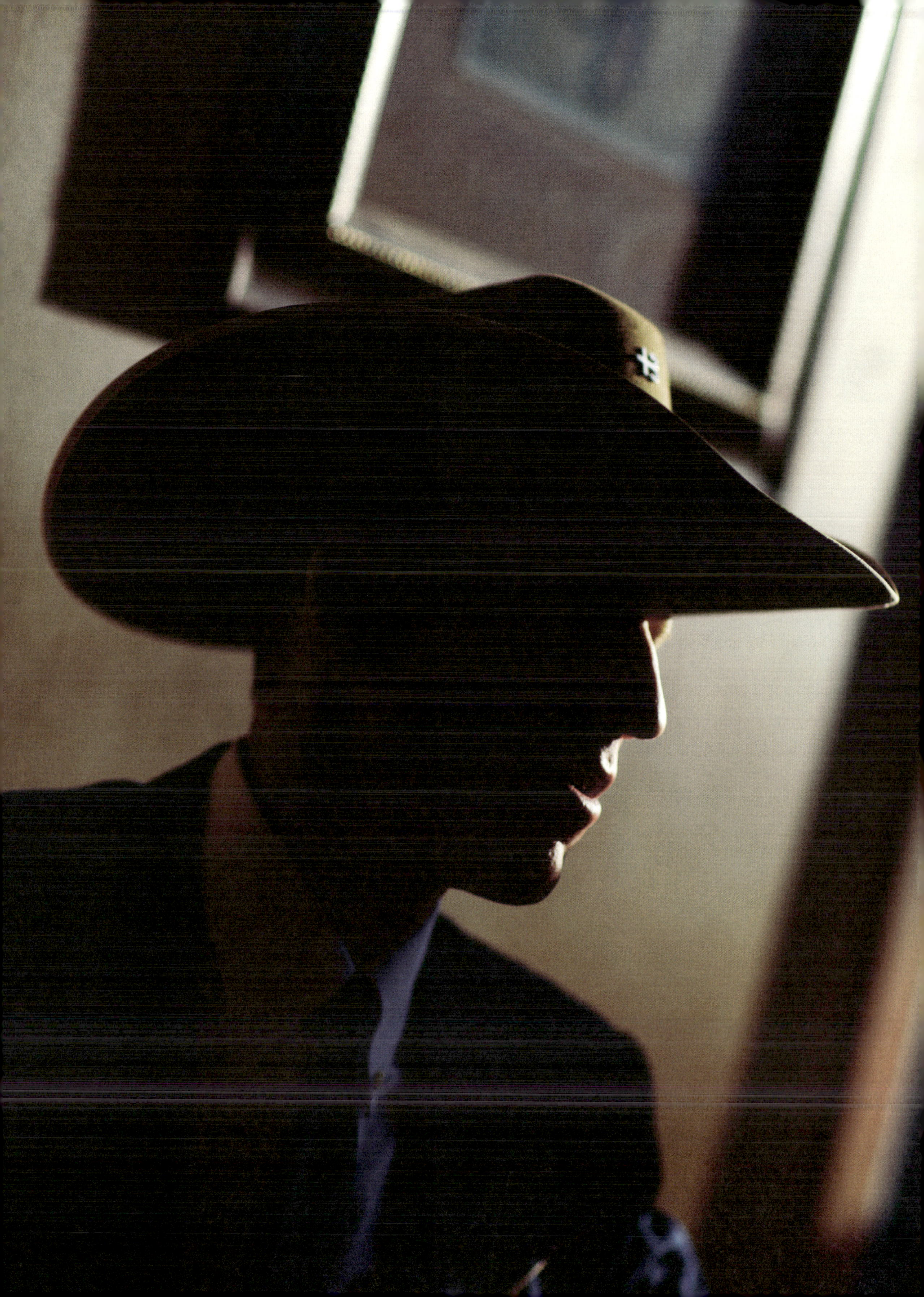

"I'M NOT PART OF THIS FALSE NOTION OF PISTOLS AND SHARP-SHOOTING AND COW-BOYS AND INDIANS. THAT'S NOT ME, YOU KNOW. WHAT BUFFALO BILL DID WAS COOL, BUT I'M COMING FROM A DIFFERENT ANGLE."

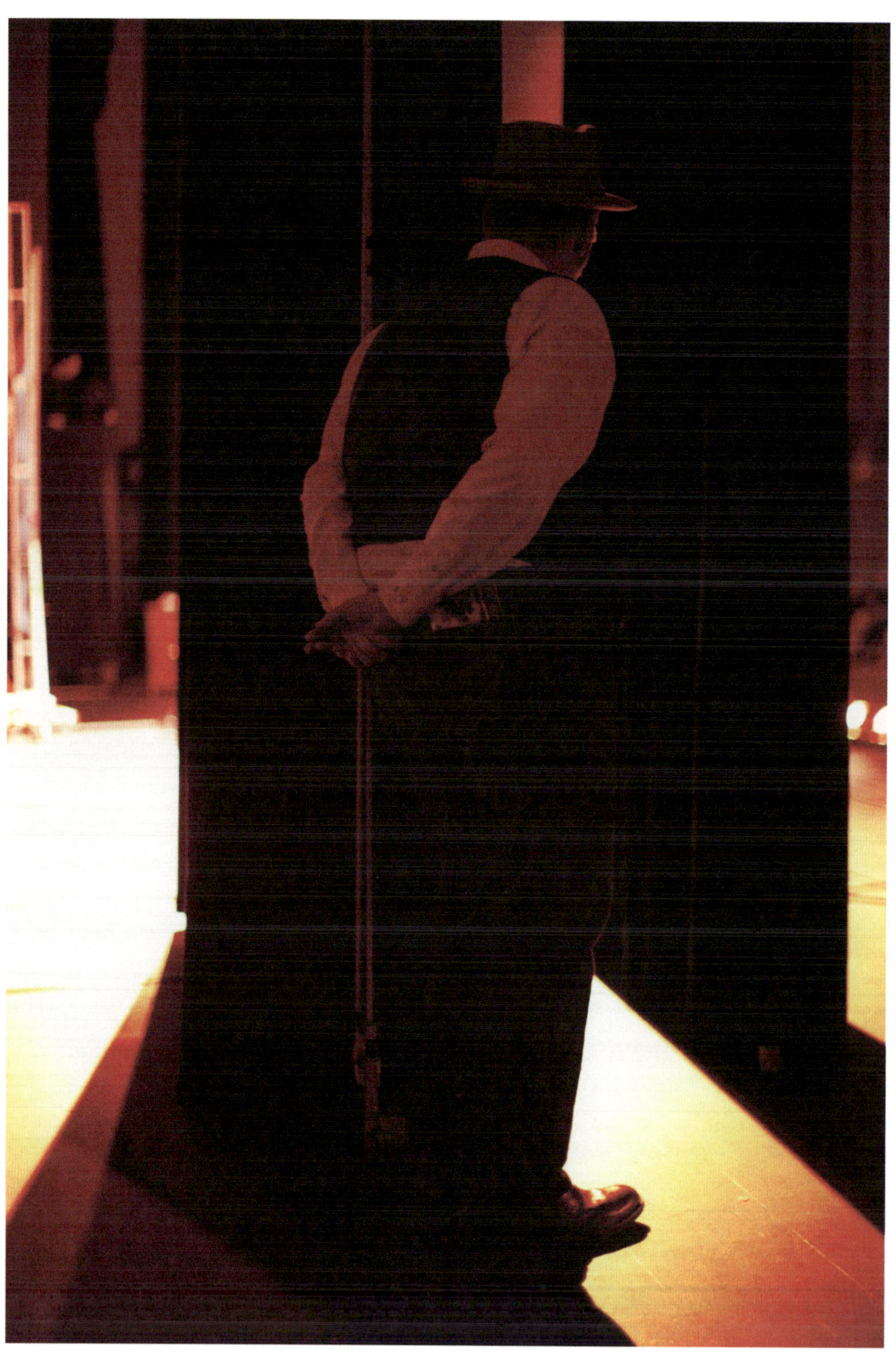

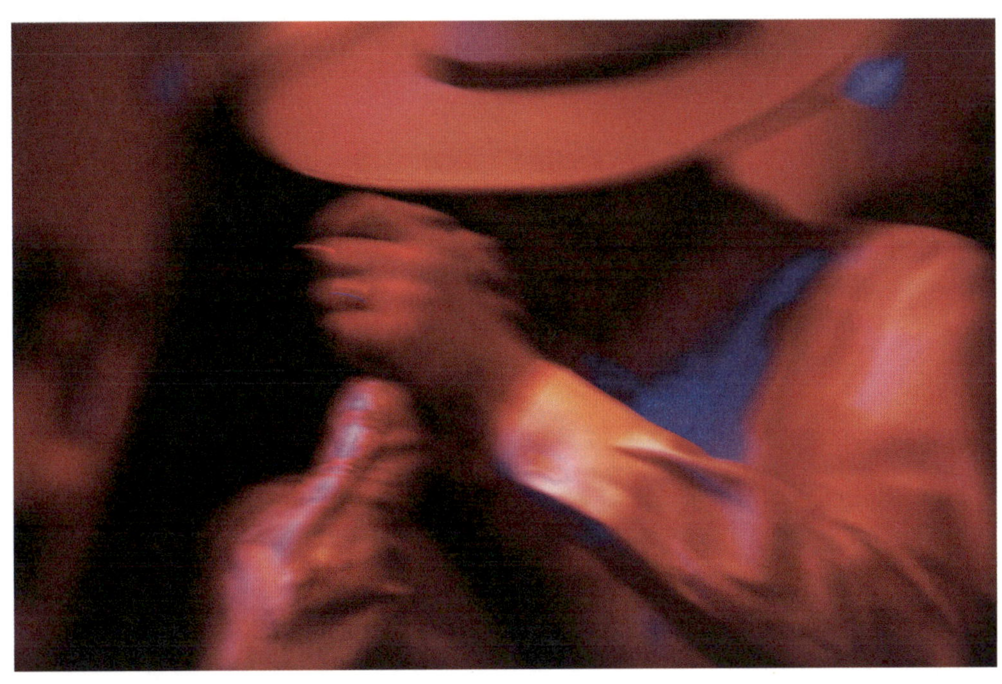

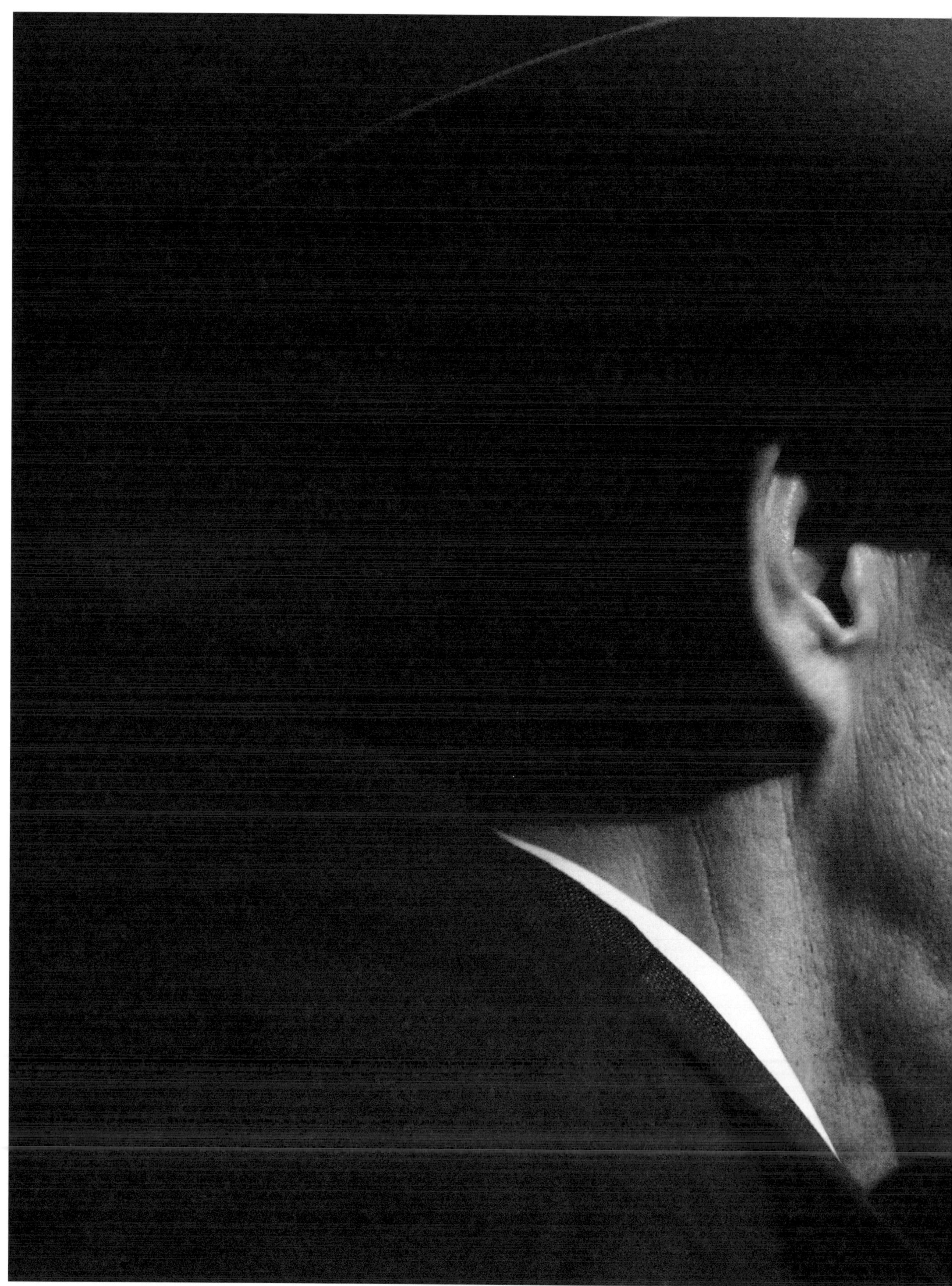

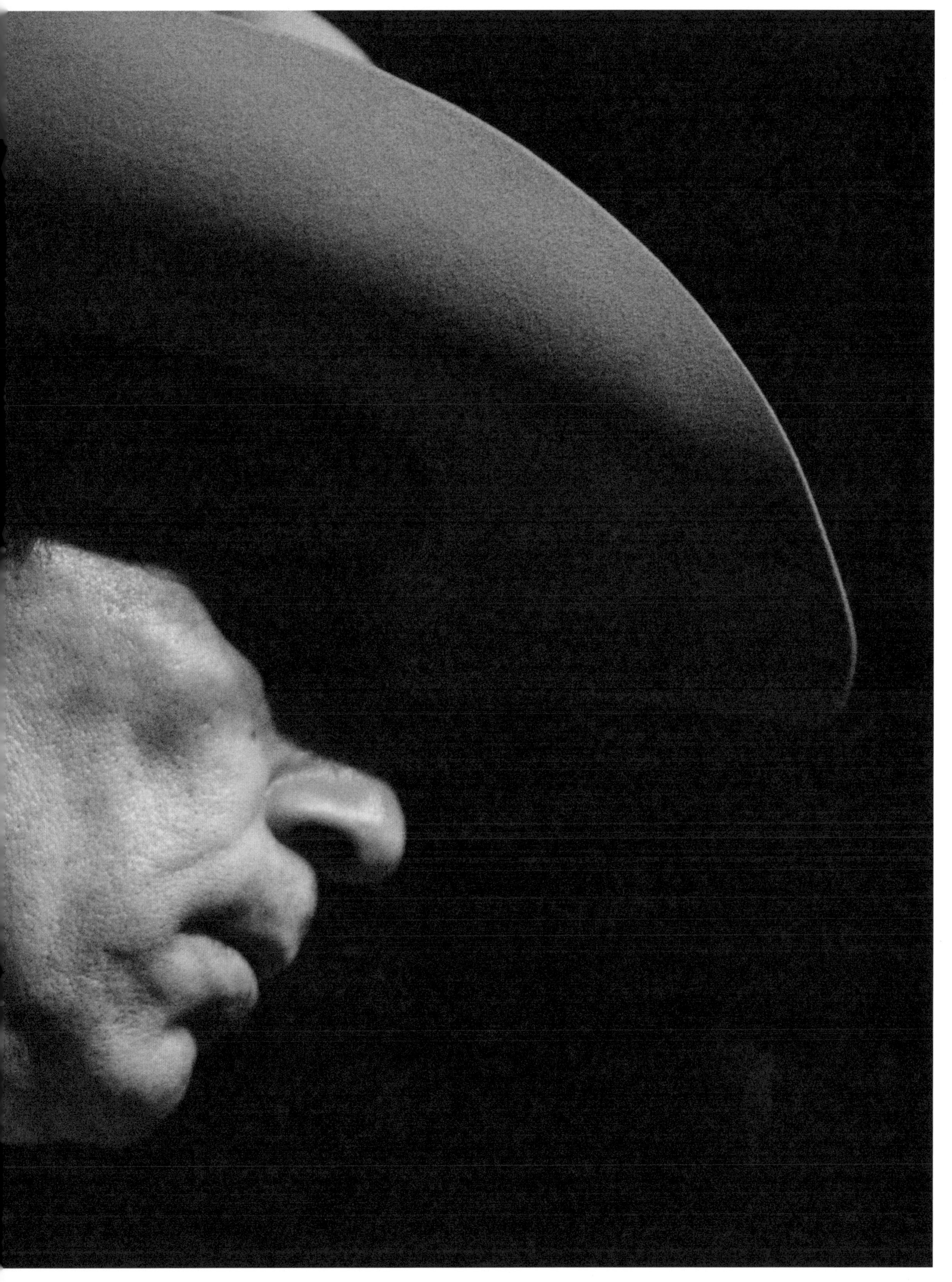

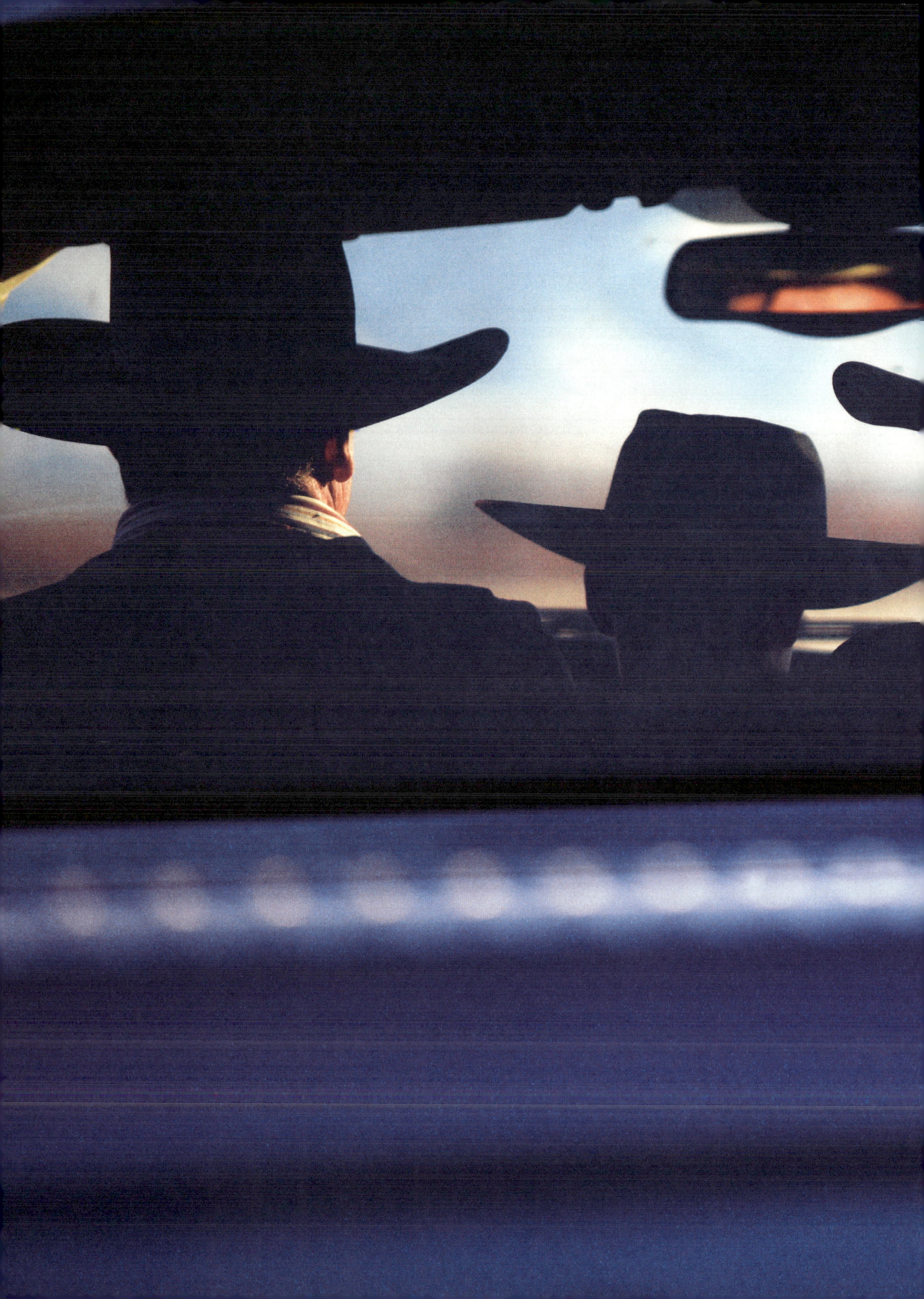

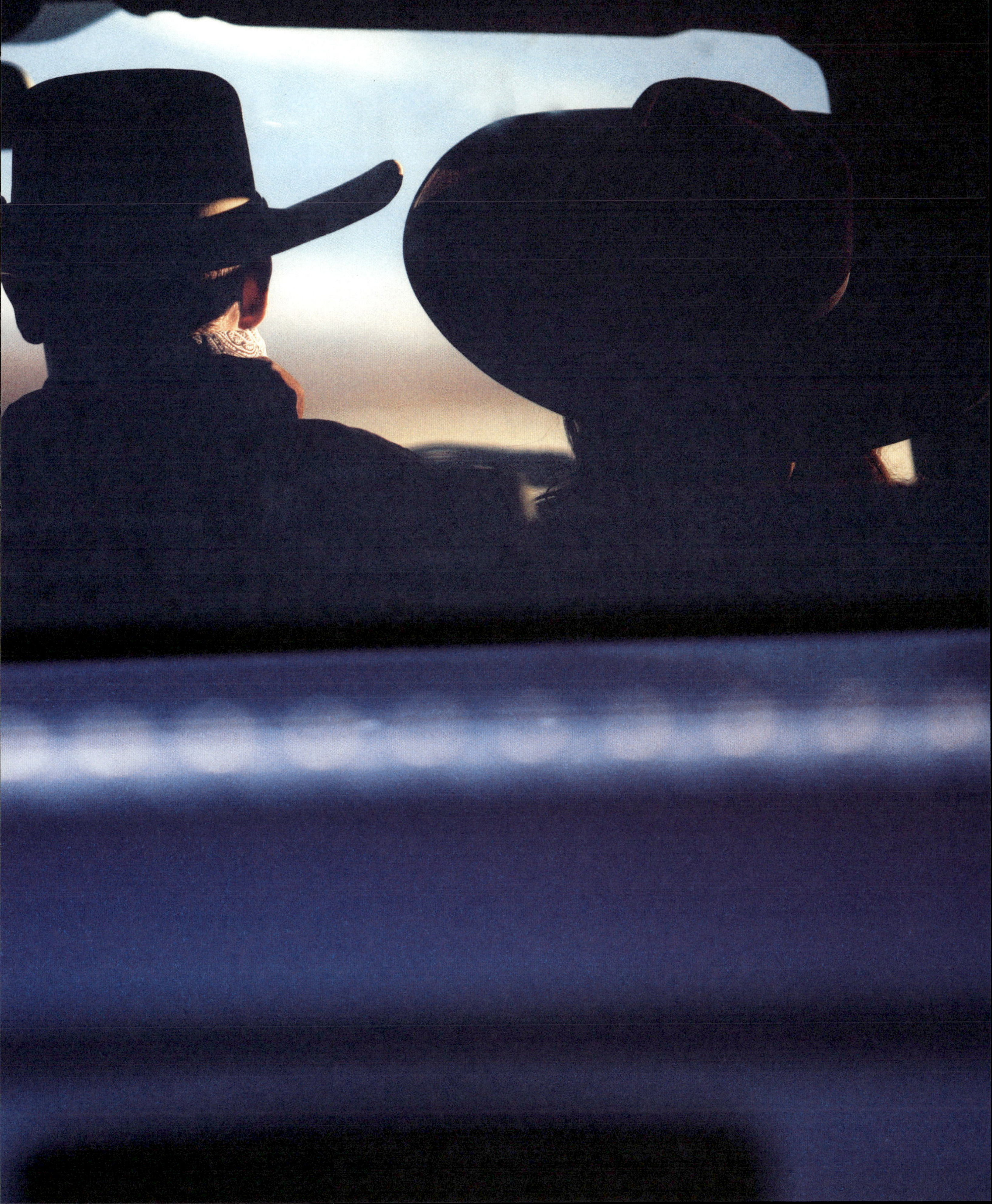

HE NEEDS SURGERY ON HIS BACK AND ONE KNEE WILL SOON BE READY FOR REPLACEMENT. LAST YEAR HE WAS BUCKED OFF AND THE HORSE STOMPED ON HIS RIBCAGE.

"I'M HERE BECAUSE I WANNA BE HERE. IT'S DARN SURE NOT THE INCOME, BUT IT'S A GOOD, CLEAN, HEALTHY WAY OF LIFE. PERSONALLY, I LIKE BEING AROUND HORSES AND CATTLE. IF YOU DON'T ENJOY THAT, THERE'S NO OTHER REASON TO BE HERE."

43-YEAR-OLD CHRIS DAVEY IS IN THE PRIME OF HIS LIFE, BUT HE WALKS A LITTLE STIFFLY, WITH SPURS JANGLING LIKE BELLS IN A RELIGIOUS PROCESSION.

The first rider looms into view at five past six, his head pulled down deep into his collar. Far away the cattle are moving in circles, like dark spots on a vast canvas. Gradually they drift across the pale green sea of grass, heading for the branding pen. Greyish winds have swept in during the night and the dawn rears up, hesitant and frozen.

For two months, ever since their birth, the calves have been roaming the range with the herd. Now the branding irons lie red-hot in the fire. In a couple of minutes their lives, once care-free, will be changed forever.

It was only 3:30 when Chris Davey, the cow boss, stuck his head in under the tent flap. "Heeey, breakfast!" One of the guys had been snoring loudly all night and, dog-tired, I staggered into the cook tent and wrapped my feeble, frozen hands around a steaming cup of coffee. Topher had already lit his first Lucky Strike. Thin and shivering, he sat hunched up under his hat. Breakfast consisted of eggs, meat patties, beans, biscuits, coffee, and a smoke. Chris Davey and his closest hand, John Edwards, kept up a steady patter of conversation – stories about crazy horses and nutty horsemen – while the rest of us yawned and blinked our eyes. Twelve good men lined up along the sides of the tent. Twelve cowboys on a mission.

In the space of 25 days they will brand 4,400 calves at the north end of this seemingly boundless prairie ranch.

Montana is one of the biggest states in the Union, but people are few and far between and Davey approvingly quotes singer Don Edwards: "I like my fellow man the most/When he is scattered some." Meriwether Lewis's and William Clark's famous expedition passed through here in the early 19th century looking for a navigable passage to the Pacific. They were followed by settlers from back east, hard-bitten loners and worn-down pioneer families with next to nothing to lose.

The newcomers built houses on the prairie and tried to plow the soil when the snow had finally melted on the sagebrush. Among the few single women were the occasional schoolteachers, and before the roof of the schoolhouse had even been laid men of few words would hang around panting in the hall, hoping their breath would not scare the females away. It was a colonization with many setbacks. For once, the white man's cavalry suffered defeat at Little Bighorn and many homes were levelled to the ground by harsh winter blizzards. Grey, swaybacked and abandoned, some of the barns and homesteads can still be seen standing against the horizon in this state of eternal space, the often heartbreakingly beautiful Montana, where only those who knew the ways of the wild country or new railroad capitalism survived.

What was once buffalo country is now cattle country. "I'd have to say, this grass is probably some of the best grass in the state of Montana," Davey says. "But it's a country of extremes. We haven't had a lot of moisture and we're kinda headed for a wreck if the weather doesn't change."

And on this early summer morning the wind does indeed carry something damp, first in the form of horizontally driven snow, later as thin curtains of weightless rain. As the riders approach, their hat brims are white and their shoulders wet. By eight o'clock, all the animals are assembled in the pen, more than 200 cows and just as many calves.

The silence has been broken by ceaseless bellowing, and as the ropes sail through the air and the calves are dragged to the iron and branded on their backs and above their muzzles, their agonized cries pierce the air. There is a harsh smell of singed hair and burnt skin. Nimble hands dehorn the heaviest animals and snip off the bull calves' testicles. Held down by a couple of cowboys, the calves roll up their eyes in fear and desperation, showing the bluish whites.

It is heavy, unpleasant, sweaty work, fraught with risk. The horses and riders are tightly penned in among the cattle; the animals are nervous and follow their own logic, able to deal a deadly blow with the kick of a hoof.

The day's branding is over at 11:00. Coffee, a few smokes. The men disperse the animals, and they all swiftly climb to the top of a ridge where they eventually appear like little black slugs against the undulating hills.

We leave behind us a few hundred square yards of trampled prairie, a hundred or so small furry skin pouches, and the kind of stillness that settles over a scene when all is done.

The cowboys earn a meager wage, in addition to meals and the corner of a tent where they can lay out their bedrolls. The first nights, before they hit the trail with their wagon, the youngest stay in a little two-room wooden cottage, where the washing machine has been stuffed full of jeans on which the terrified calves have peed. Empty soft-drink cans, piles of blankets, in the toilet three magazines with color pictures of women baring all. There is also a TV set showing fuzzy images from Fox and PBS.

Tyler Cox is here for the first time. His parents run an unprofitable ranch in Washington state. He sees five years of agriculture business studies in front of him. "I want to make myself hireable and raise a family," he says. "I want to become like Chris. Or else I need to apply for a job in a bank or with an insurance company, but that's not something you do voluntarily if you can work with horses."

"I wouldn't trade this for anything, it's a helluva life," says Michael Tingle, who is a qualified welder and has worked as a roughneck on oil rigs back home in Louisiana. Nick Hix, who recently left high school in South Dakota, adds: "Nothing else compares to the cowboy life. You never stay in one place for long, you pack up and move on. But it's a young man's game. Age catches up with you. When you're good enough to cowboy, you're already too old for it."

Now at around 20, many of these young cowpokes have grown up on smaller ranches where the future looks highly uncertain. Large-scale beef-growing enterprises are swelling, with hormone injections, overproduction, and elimination of small outfits with debts. Something's gotta give; many ranchers take other jobs on the side or resort to tourism. Urban dwellers from the east coast and Europe pay dearly for the chance to live a spartan dude ranch life for a few weeks in the summer, with a hunting rifle and a dappled horse next to the bunk.

When Topher breaks camp, everything is stowed away in its place: his tiny canvas tepee, his boots, bridle, bedroll and a guitar. "This is my life," he says. "This is what I've got." He wears spurs with peace symbols and his real name is Chris Doremus. He's from south Texas, a dusty land of scrub and sand "where you gotta be punchy" and where "cowboying is a ram and jam deal. In the south, you only get one chance to rope a calf, then it gets lost in the brush. Here in Montana they pride themselves on their gear. We go full blast and push the cattle a little harder."

We bring 43 horses with us when we leave the base camp. Topher's hat has a curled-up brim. "That's because Texans want to crowd a lot of people into a pickup," Chris Davey says, teasing. He and some of the others regard themselves as buckaroos; with their straight brims and specially made saddles they are harking back to a Californian vaquero tradition with Spanish roots.

One of the riders, Kevin Gatlin, is also trying to set up business as a silversmith. Before he went West he was a policeman in Atlanta for fifteen years, moving up from patrol officer to lieutenant with twenty investigators under him. "That job kind of wears you down," he says. "You never know what kind of scene you'll enter. There could be diseases and stuff. Most policemen have only a gold watch to look forward to."

In contrast, the scene here is a vast panorama of tranquility and emptiness. The trees are sparsely scattered, as if their effort to create a forest had miserably failed. Robins dart between the thickets. "And then there's the smell in the morning," sighs Clay Jackson.

He's one of the young men, tall and dark, cultivating his cowboy identity, anxious to button his buttons just right. "There's a use for everything we wear," he says. "We wear spurs to make our horses go. We wear our chaps to protect our legs."

"And we look classy," adds Nick Hix, who has a snow-white shirt under his sport jacket.

"Yeah, we look good and that's important, too," Jackson replies. "Nobody's gonna see us out here, but I like to look nice." He claims that ever since he was small he has known that this was the only thing he wanted to do. "People always say they can do it quicker and faster with other stuff, but you can never replace a good horse and a man who knows how to use a rope."

According to Hix, you have to put up with a lot to stand the life out on the range. "You can't just pull somebody out here and think he's gonna be a cowboy; that's just real romantic. The cowboy's been put on a pedestal. You know, this country was born and founded and raised with cattle, but Hollywood has glorified this business so much and made it all wild and woolly and bronc stompin'. I mean, the way they make it out in the movies is just completely different from the way we do it here."

But what about country music, which conveys western sentiments to a large public? "The majority of us listen to rock'n'roll," snorts Hix. "I don't listen to country music at all. That country music line dancin' stuff is just another misconception. Anybody can go to the store and buy them boots and a hat and go out on the dance floor. That's what this country has turned into – they're glorifying the cowboy as a two-stepping dancin' fool."

In this masculine world, beauty is experienced solely in relation to the landscape, animals and items that make up the tack, or work gear. At twilight, after supper, when the sweat has dried and the horses have been unsaddled, the young cowboys stand a little off to the side comparing pommels and stirrups and the hand-tooled patterns that swirl over the curved leather. The tents glow white in the silent sagebrush under a borderless sky.

"What's it all about?" Michael Tingle asks himself, scratching his beard. "A great big love for horses."

That's the obvious answer all over the ranch country in Wyoming and Montana, where, at any time, a herd may come pounding over a rocky plateau and spill out onto the vast grazing lands.

On the surface, there is a conflict over the relations with outsiders who want to tell Montanans how to run their state. "Don't californicate Montana" says one bumper sticker. When a celebrity couple bought a ranch here, they sold all the cattle and released 3,000 head of buffalo on their new land. In Washington, politicians and environmental experts warn against overgrazing and insensitive logging. Quite a number of people in the West are offended by central powers, by federal institutions. They curse them. They may vote for social order while at the same time celebrating the social bandit heritage.

But as always where land rights are involved, it's all about power and money. On the range and in the timberlands out West, an alliance has emerged intent on shrinking public space and limiting federal influence. Wealthy private landowners want to free themselves from political constraints and, at the outer fringes of the populist movement, oppositional extremists refuse to recognize the right of the government to tax them or to make laws that apply to all Americans.

"I think a lot of times people in my line of work tend to be a little apathetic and kinda maybe not give a damn about the rest of the world," says Chris Davey, reflecting on his own relationship with urbanites from the east coast. "It's almost kinda like an ostrich burying his head in the sand. We tend to stick to our own and maybe just concern ourselves with our own surroundings as opposed to more worldly things. But any time a person doesn't take an interest or a part in politics and that sort of thing, it's just kind of a bad deal."

On the other hand, he says, federal legislators don't care too much about what westerners think or feel. "There's a big movement to try to rid public lands of cattle, but a lot of city folks don't understand that grass is an important commodity to us and that, probably, some of the first environmentalists were ranchers. If they were not good stewards of the land, then they would be out of business. If you let grass grow and don't do anything with it, it becomes so bound up that it prohibits growth."

Next day, they're out there again among the bellowing calves and the hissing branding irons. The heat has crept down the hillsides and the dust coats sweaty necks and noses. One of the horses suddenly sprints away with Clay Jackson, who swears and swats the animal's neck with his black hat. Soon, everything is under control. Later, he walks off to the side to whisper secrets into the horse's ear.

As usual, Denise Davey, Chris's wife, is waiting with food at the chuck wagon. Tortillas, beans, minced beef. She grew up with the ranch life and has a warm, easy smile which deepens as she talks about Montana where she has always lived. "I seriously believe I couldn't live in town," she says. "I'd have a hard time seeing a neighbor as soon as I open the door."

She is, strangely enough, a night person, totally out of sync with the rituals and duties connected with camp life. "It's tough getting up at 1:30 in the morning to cook breakfast, but I like being around cowboys." This means she's had to shoulder a traditional female role, something no one around has ever questioned. "It's my responsibility to take care of the kids while Chris brings home the money. Chris never changed diapers on our kids. My place is in the house. I take pride in that; that's how I was brought up. Nothing upsets me more than people asking me what my job is."

For Chris Davey, this life is about a choice of values. On the ranch, the children are not confronted with gangs and drugs. If he hadn't been a cowboy, he might have considered a life as a seaman; at sea there is the same close camaraderie, the same liberating sense of solitude.

But he doesn't think that the cowboy lifestyle will survive very far into the 21st century. "It's pretty much done. This is one of the few ranches with straight riding jobs, where a man doesn't have to get on a tractor. My son is 17 and I've really tried to dissuade him from going into this line of work."

With his sore back and bum knee, he has paid a heavy price for the freedom of having his office on the back of a horse. "It's a tough way to live and, really, a man doesn't have much to show for it. If I was to lose my job tomorrow I'd have nothing. I don't have a house of my own; it's owned by the ranch. It's just one of those things where a man can put in his whole life doing this and at the end he can kinda look back and wonder if it was all worth it."

What does Davey think of the young cowboys who come here to work with the branding crew? "A little romance is probably what's brought them out here. They're attracted by that and by the fact that we're still doing things the old-time way. That's kinda neat, but a lot of them will wash out. I can guarantee a lot of the younger guys won't be in the business five or ten years from now. I imagine it being a bit like joining the French Foreign Legion or being a mercenary or something."

After coffee, the men gather in the corral to saddle twelve of the horses. The paling sun has wandered far westward when the riders pass the cook tent and climb the slope to prepare for tomorrow's work.

"More coffee?" asks Denise.

"No thanks, I´m coffeed up," I reply.

We watch the horses and the bobbing hats until they're out of view. "That's the neatest sight," she says. "I've seen it a hundred times, but I never get tired of it. Every time they leave or come back I just have to get out and watch it."

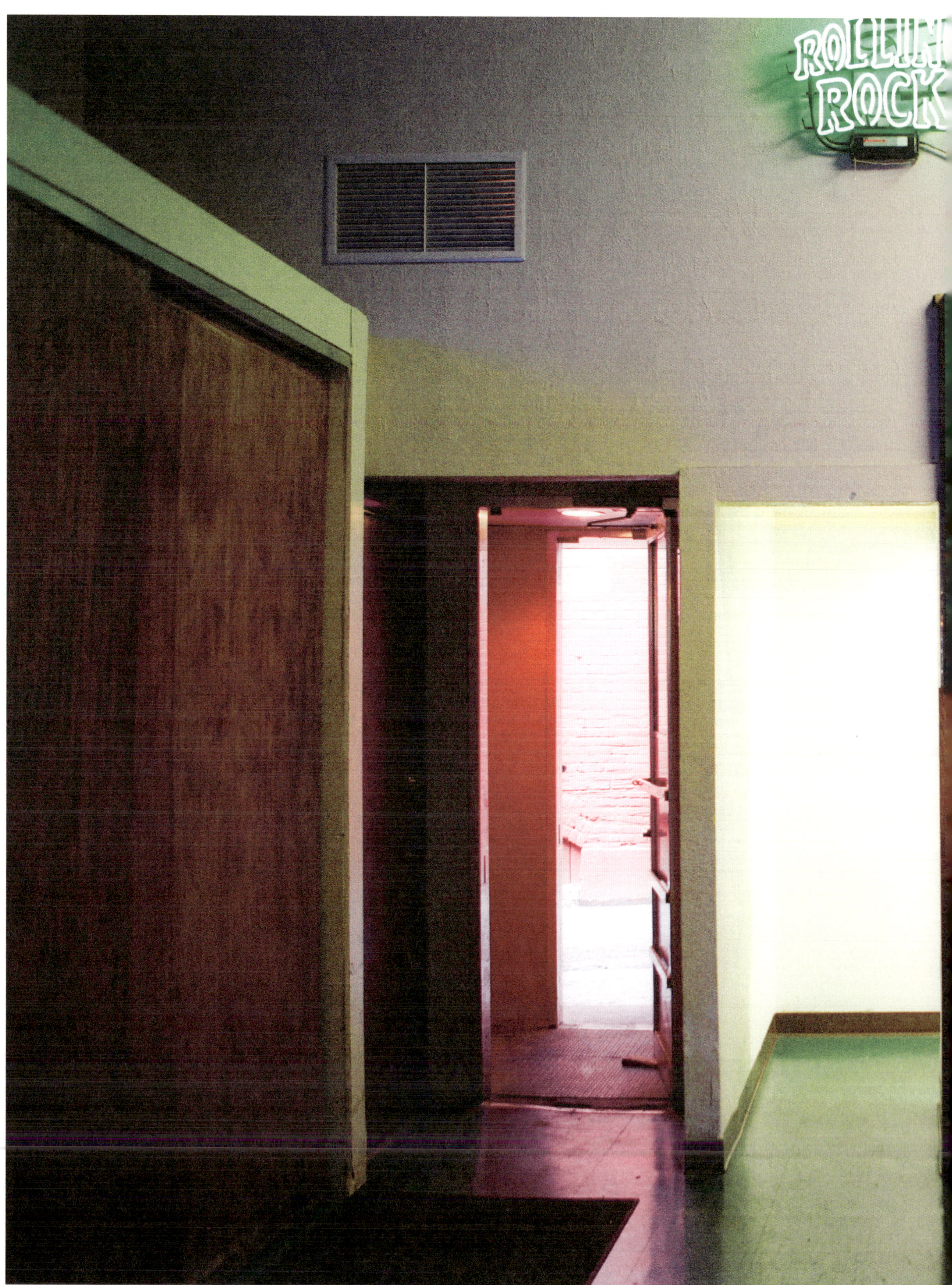
ROLLIN
ROCK

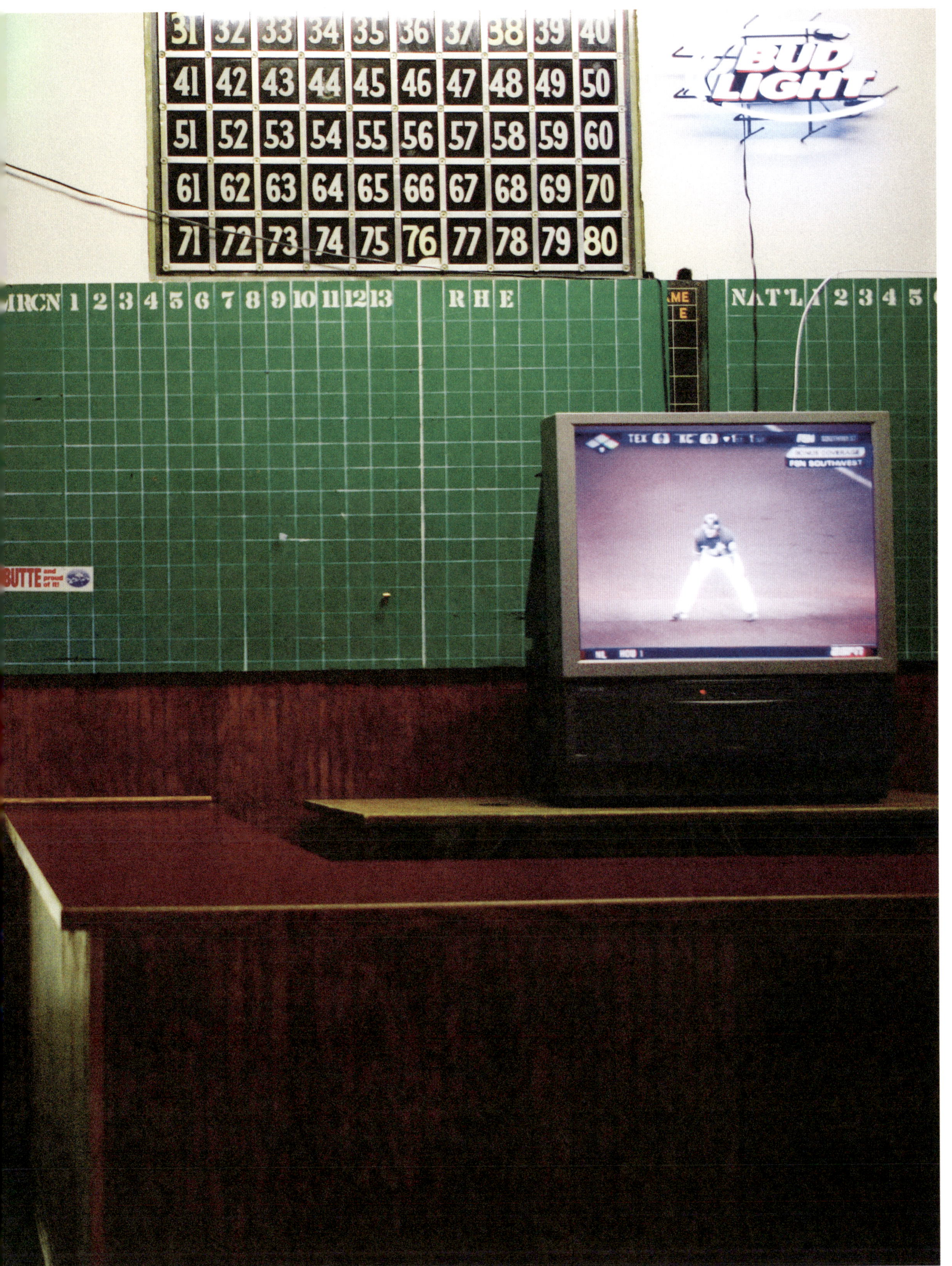
31 32 33 34 35 36 37 38 39 40
41 42 43 44 45 46 47 48 49 50
51 52 53 54 55 56 57 58 59 60
61 62 63 64 65 66 67 68 69 70
71 72 73 74 75 76 77 78 79 80
BUD LIGHT
RCN 1 2 3 4 5 6 7 8 9 10 11 12 13 R H E
NAT'L 1 2 3 4 5
BUTTE
TEX KC
FSN SOUTHWEST

AFTER MIDNIGHT THE ROACHES LET IT ALL HANG OUT; PILED IN DROVES AT OUR FEET THEY GLOW BENEATH THE STREET LIGHTS, WINGS SHINING, FLUTTERING. ALL OF A SUDDEN THEY ALL BEGIN TO FLY, LIKE A SIDEWALK TURNING INTO A MAGIC CARPET RIDE. FOLLOWING THESE WINGED CREATURES, WE SLIP THROUGH THE SQUEAKING TURNSTILES AND PAY OUR WAY INTO THE FIRST BORDER TOWN ON THE RIO GRANDE.

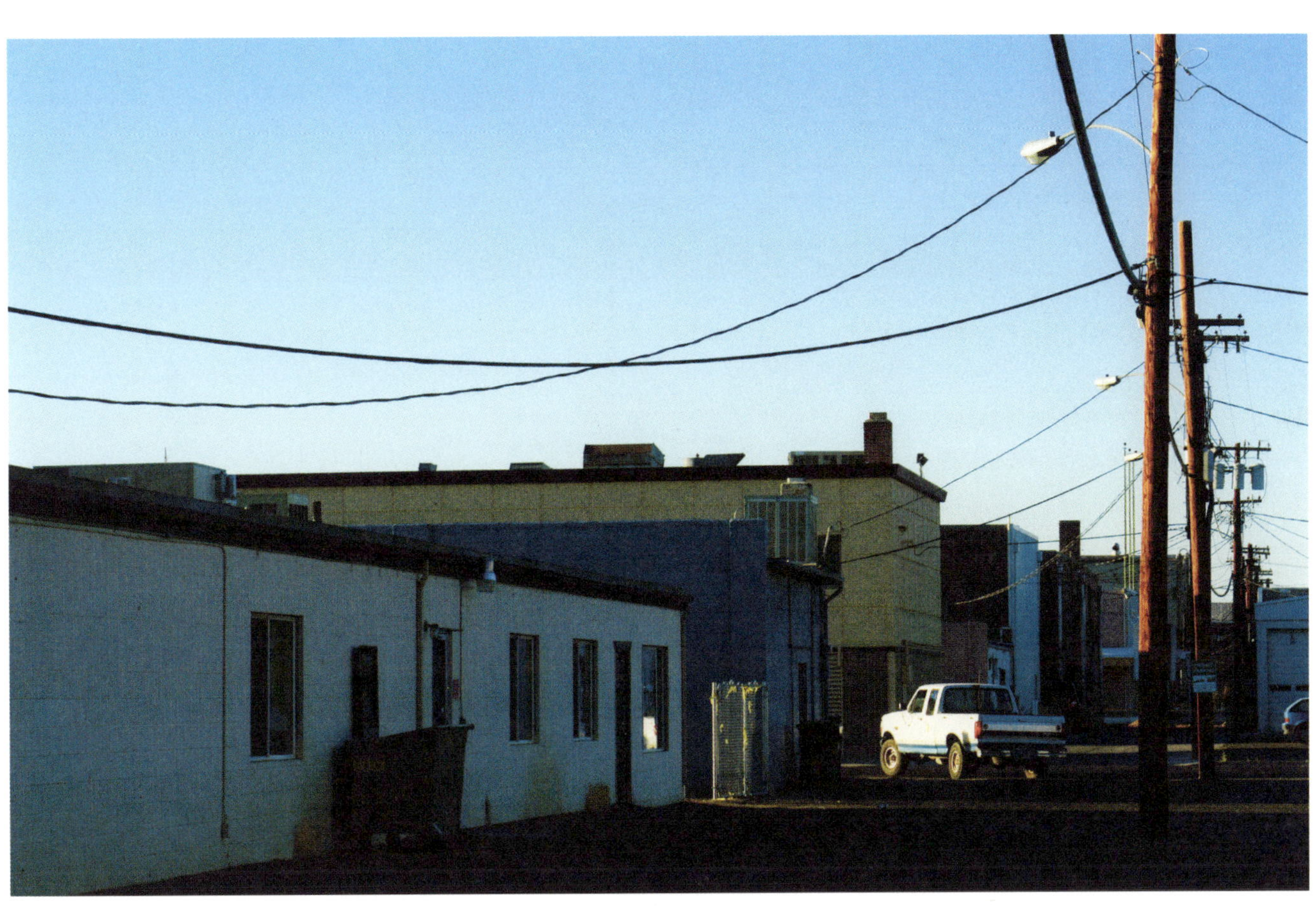

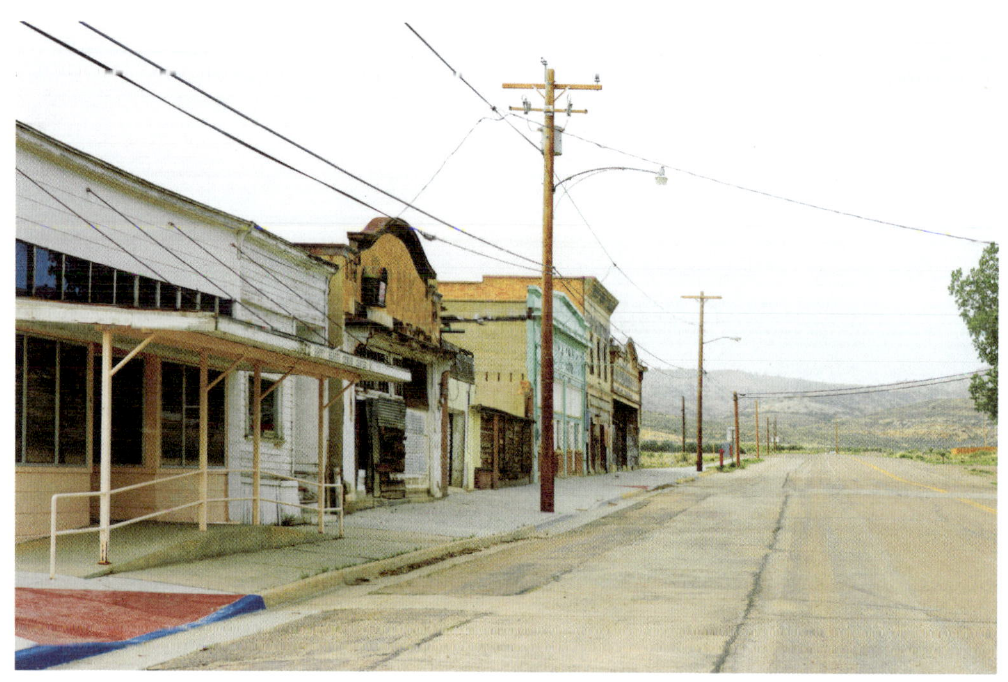

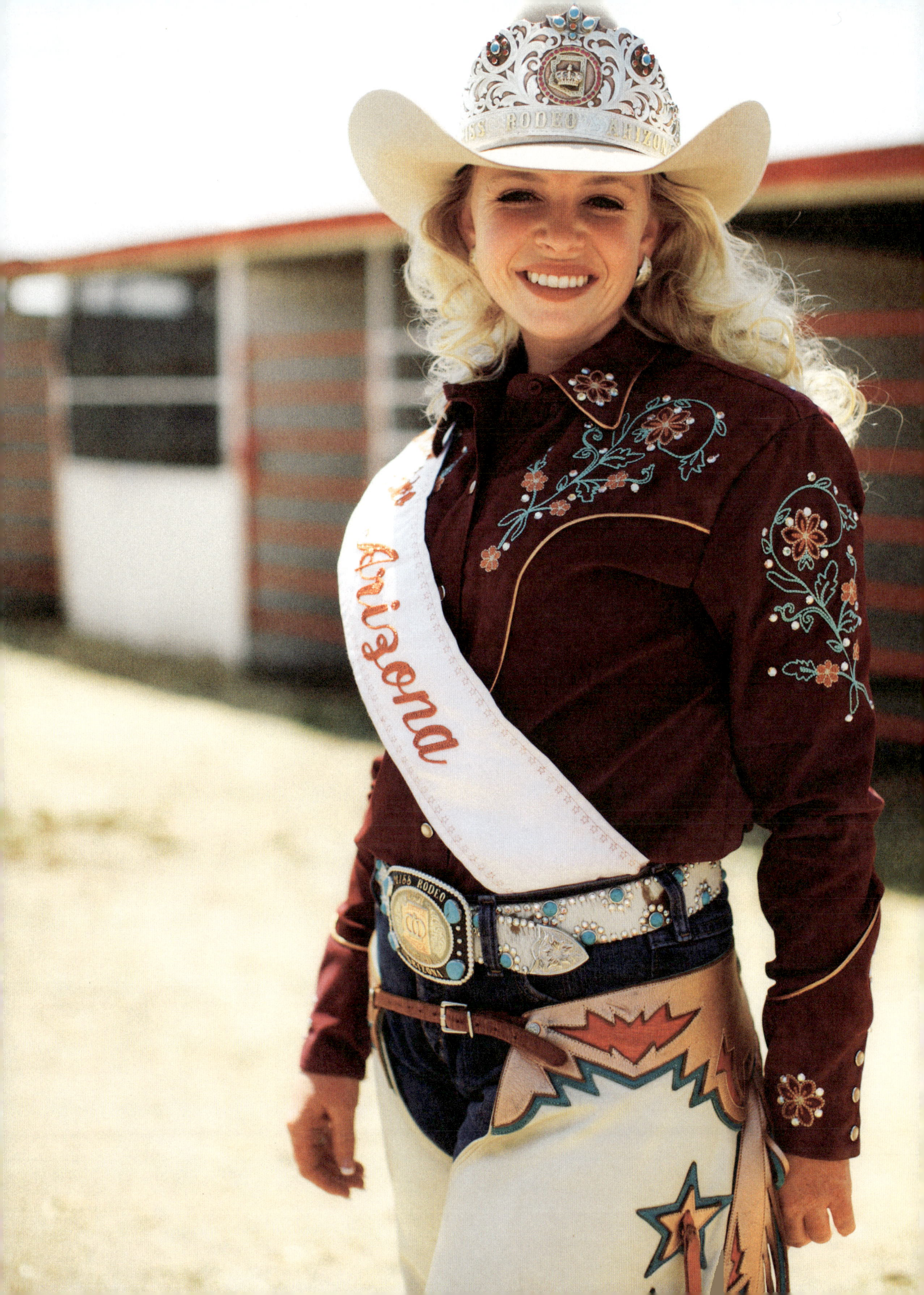
RODEO
Arizona

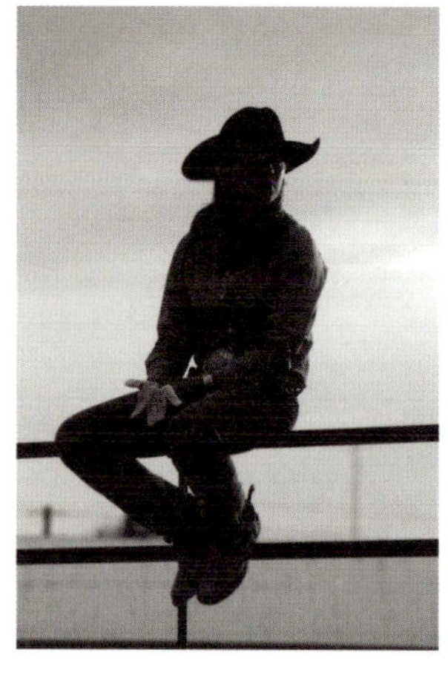
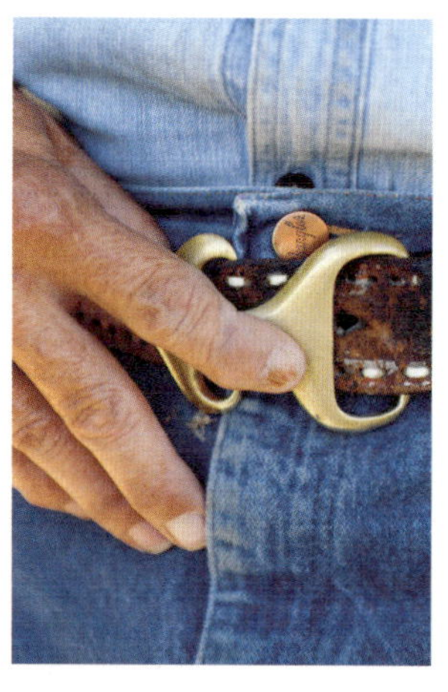
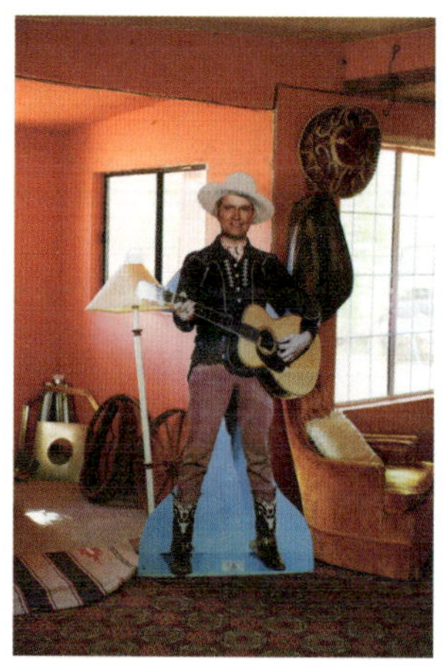
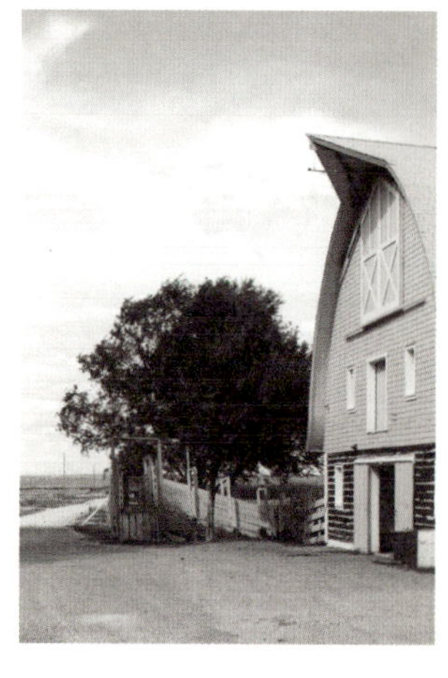
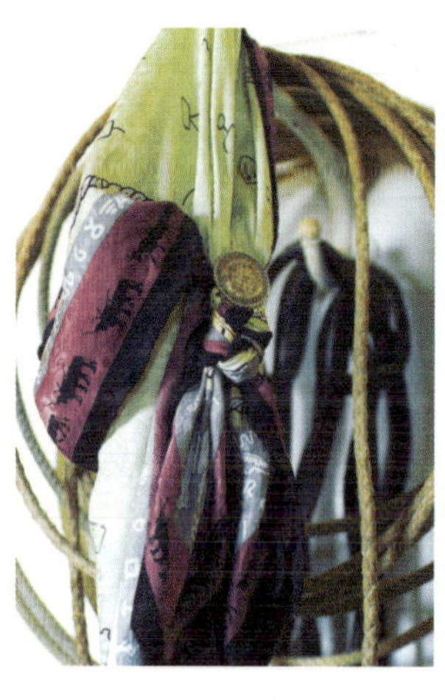
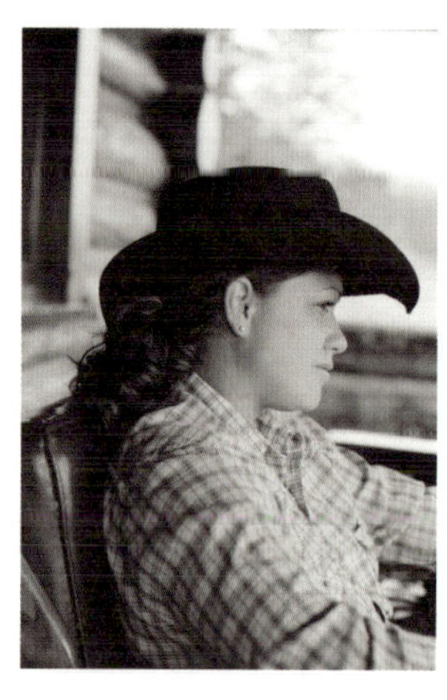
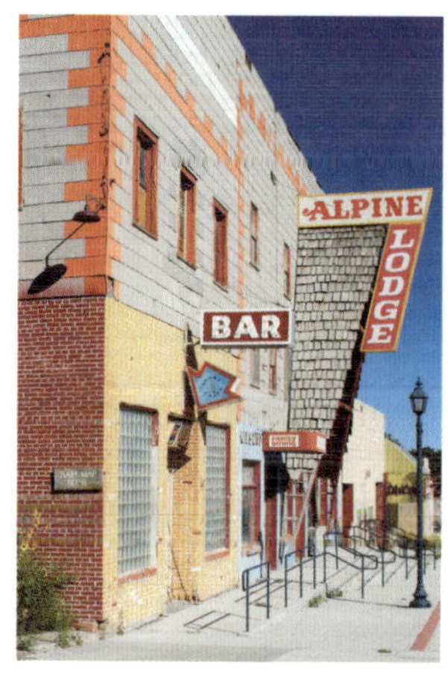
ALPINE
LODGE
BAR
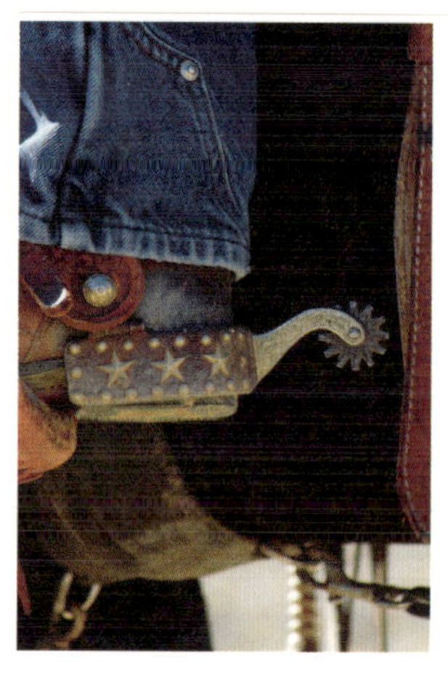
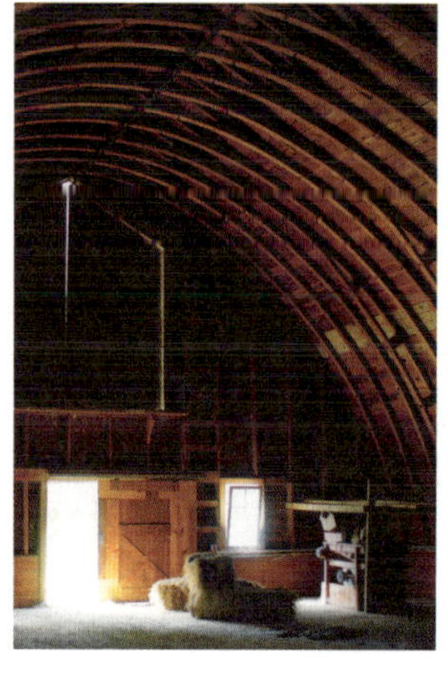
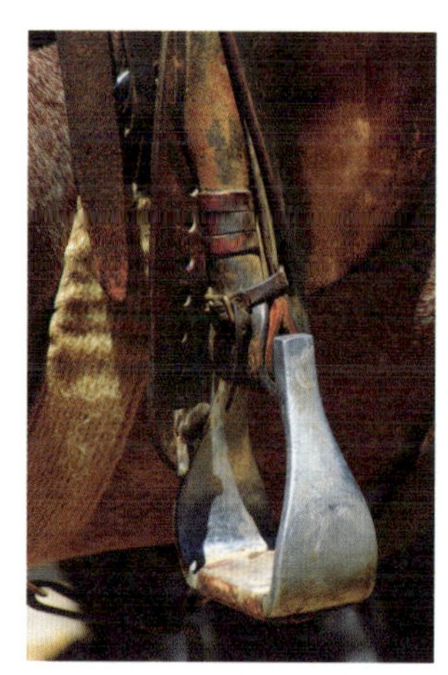
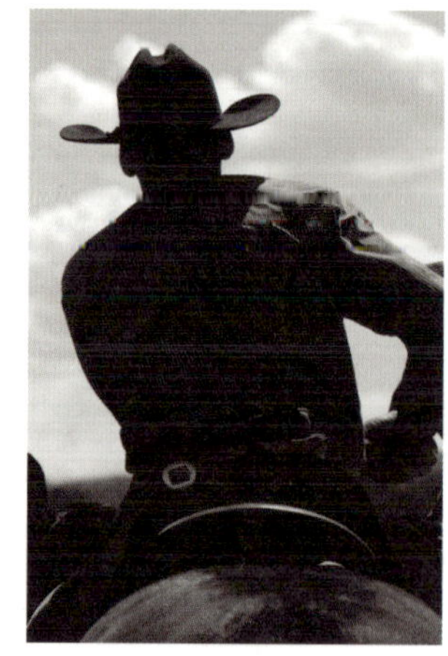
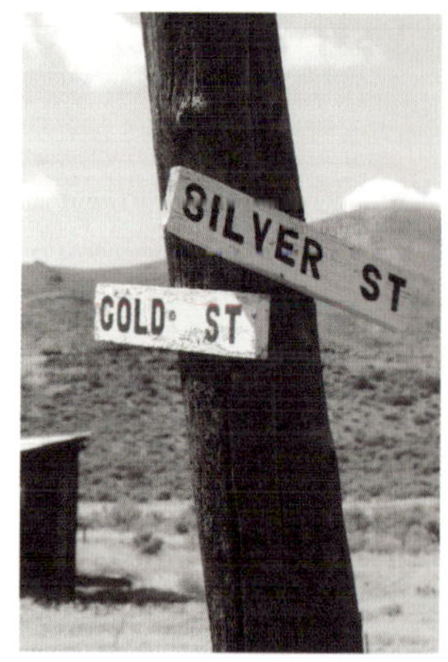
SILVER ST
GOLD ST
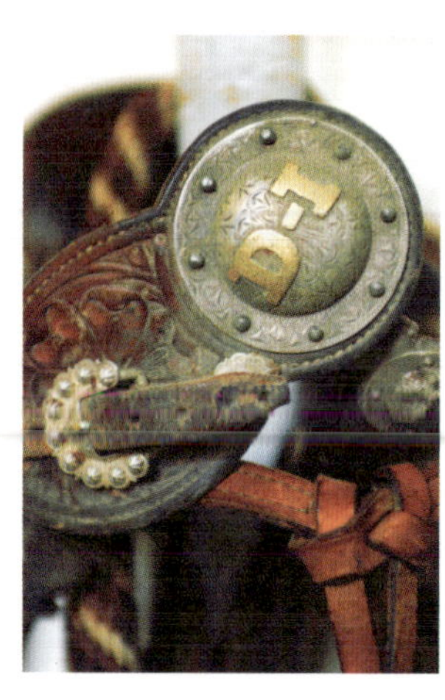
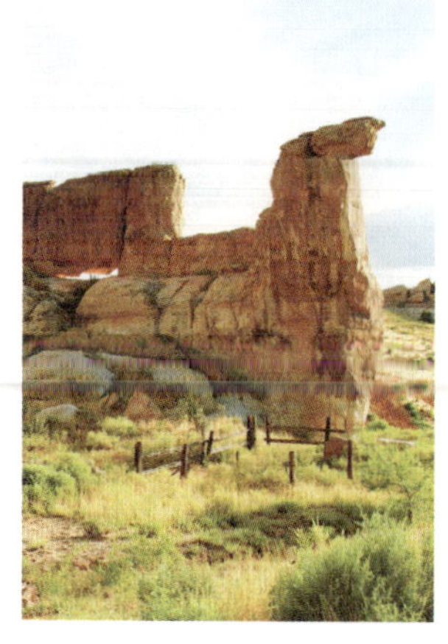
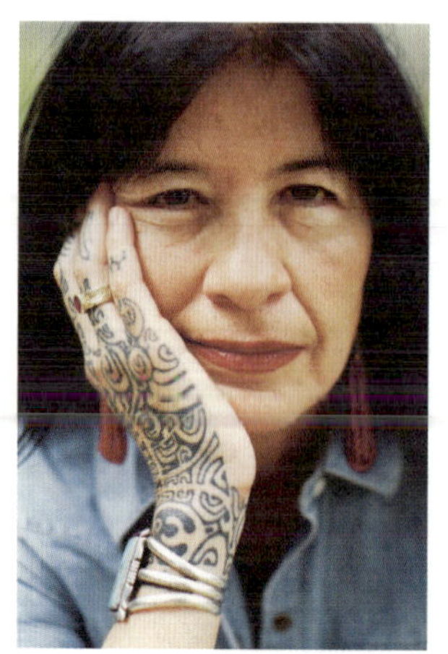
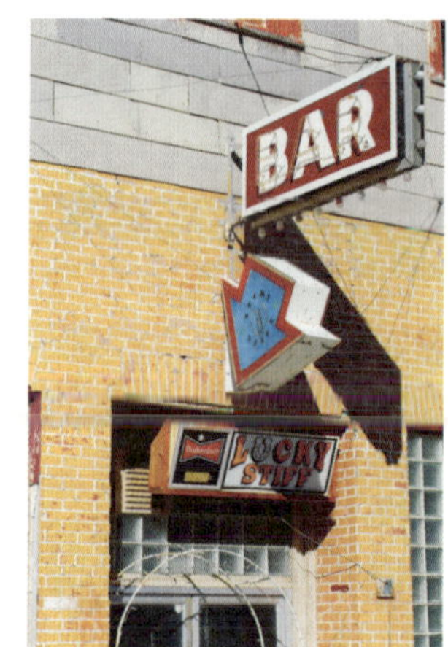
BAR
LUCKY
STIFF

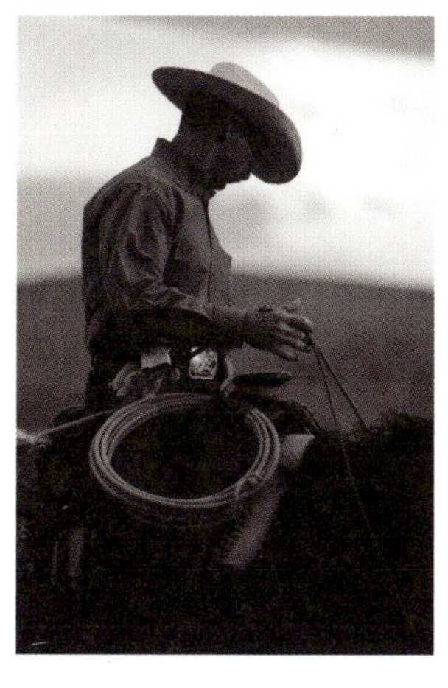
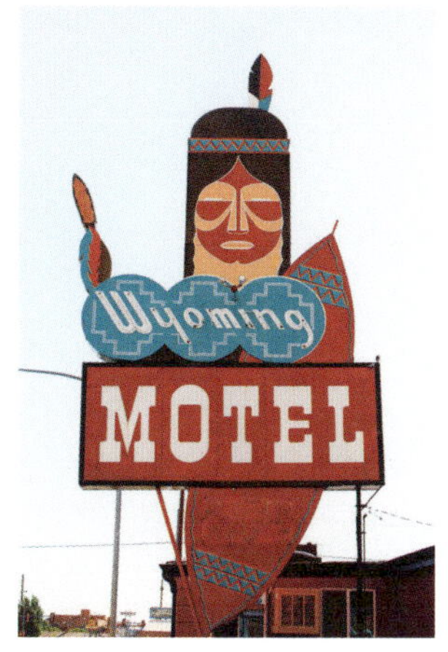
Wyoming
MOTEL
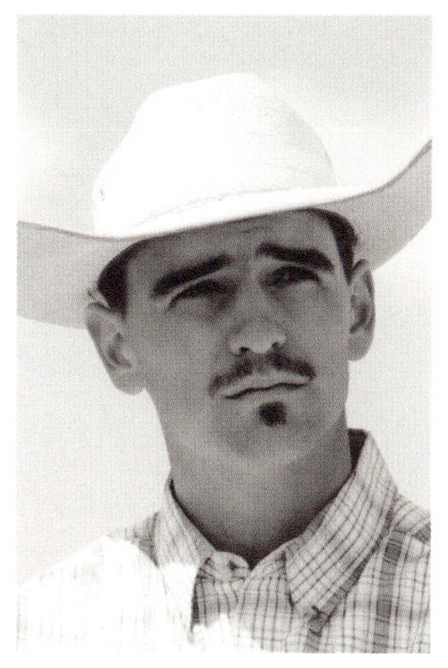
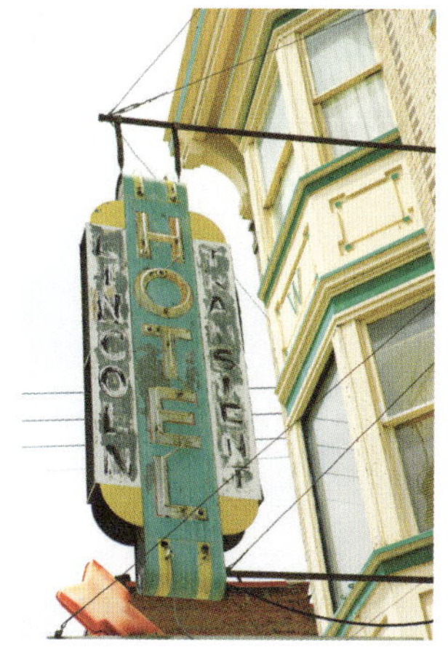
HOTEL
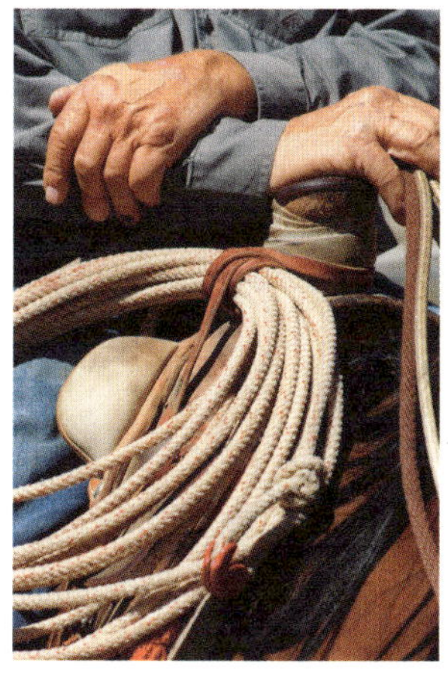
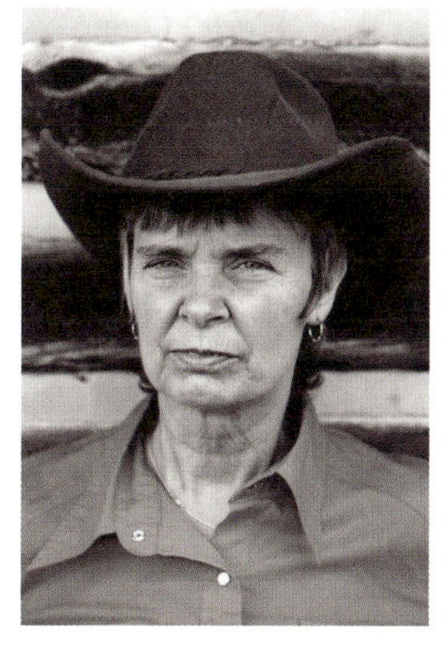
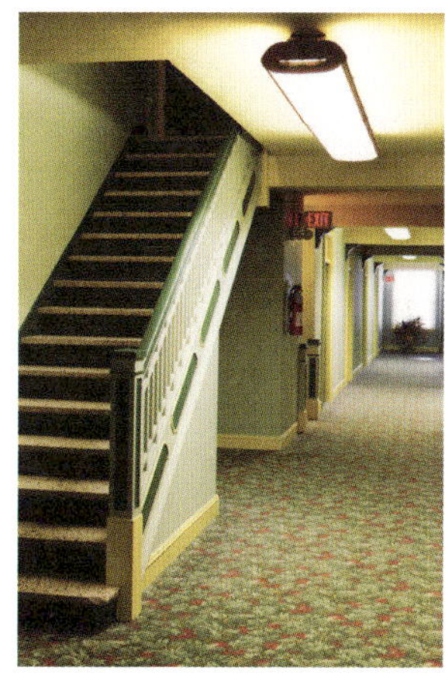
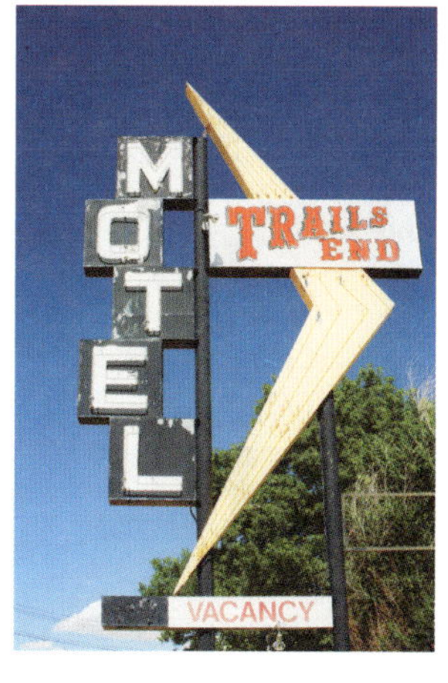
MOTEL
TRAILS END
VACANCY
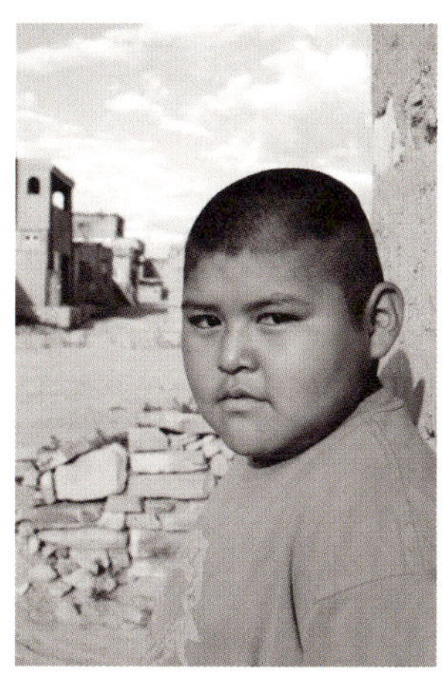
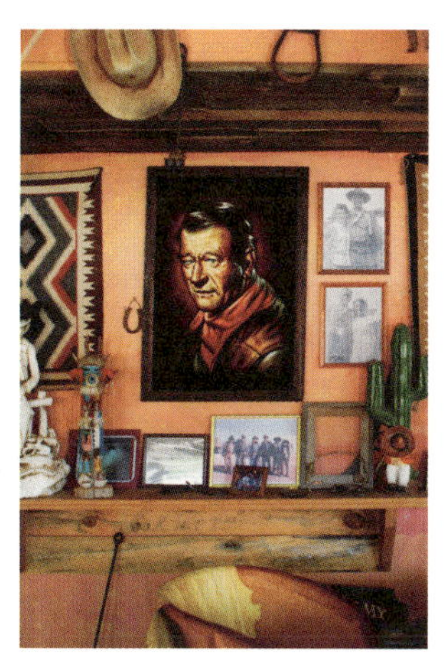
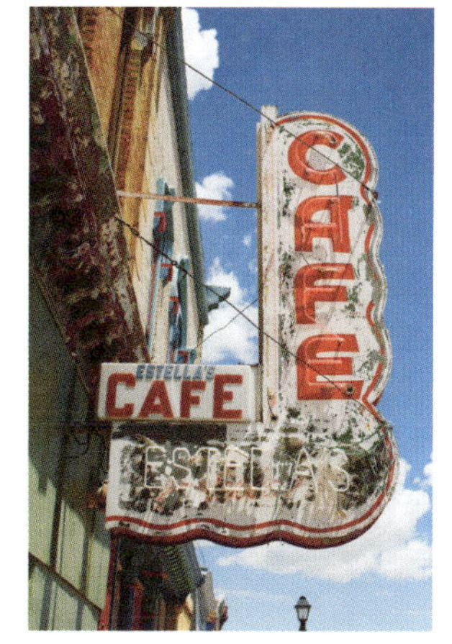
CAFE
ESTELLA'S
CAFE
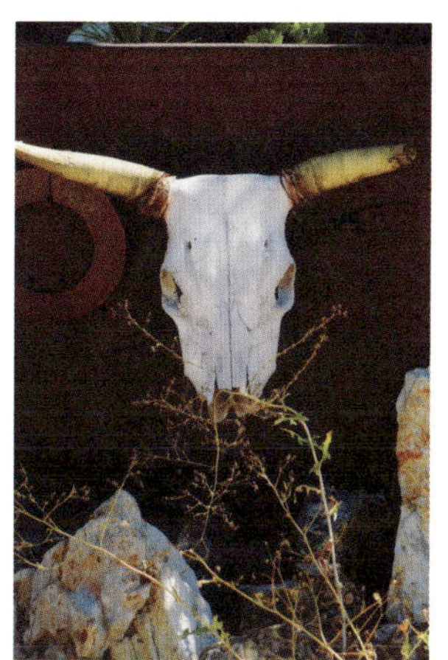
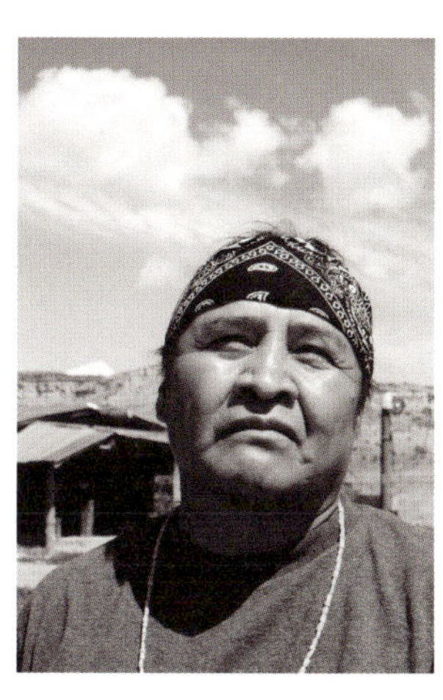
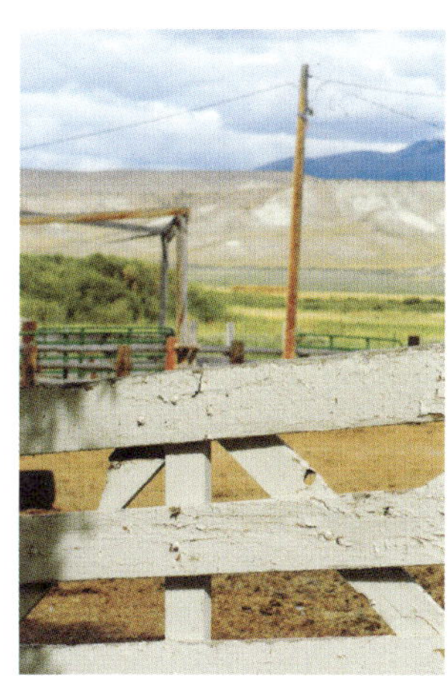
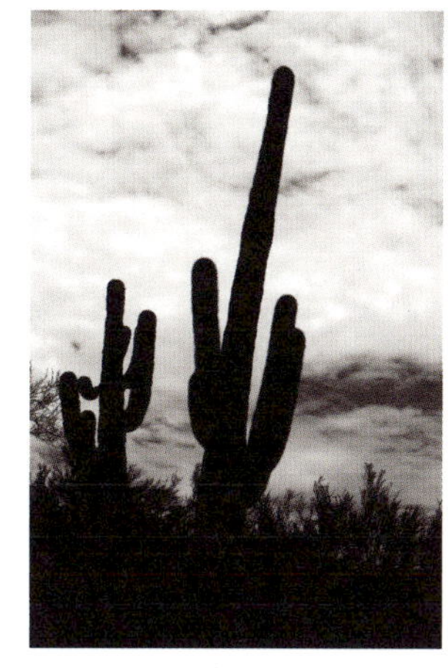
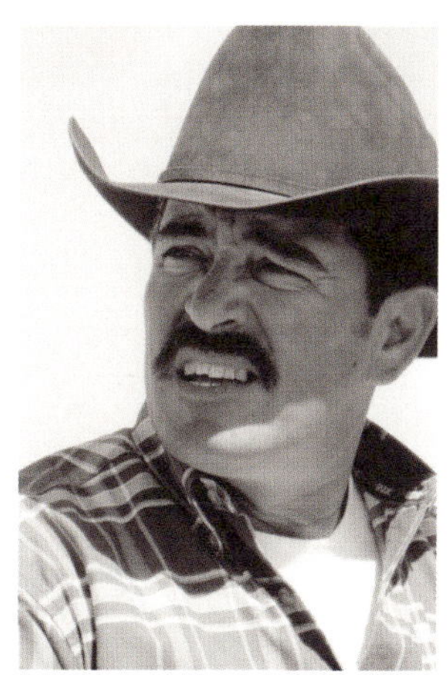

WHEN THE ENTIRE WEST HAS BEEN POPULATED THERE CAN BE NO MORE INNOCENCE, IF THERE EVER WAS ANY. SPRAWLING ACROSS THE INHABITABLE WILDERNESS, THE NEW TOWNS WITHOUT CENTER, SOUL, OR CONTENT BECOME FANTASIES OF INDEPENDENCE, DEVOID OF HISTORY. EACH YEAR AMERICANS BUY ENOUGH PLASTIC WRAP TO COVER THE STATE OF TEXAS.

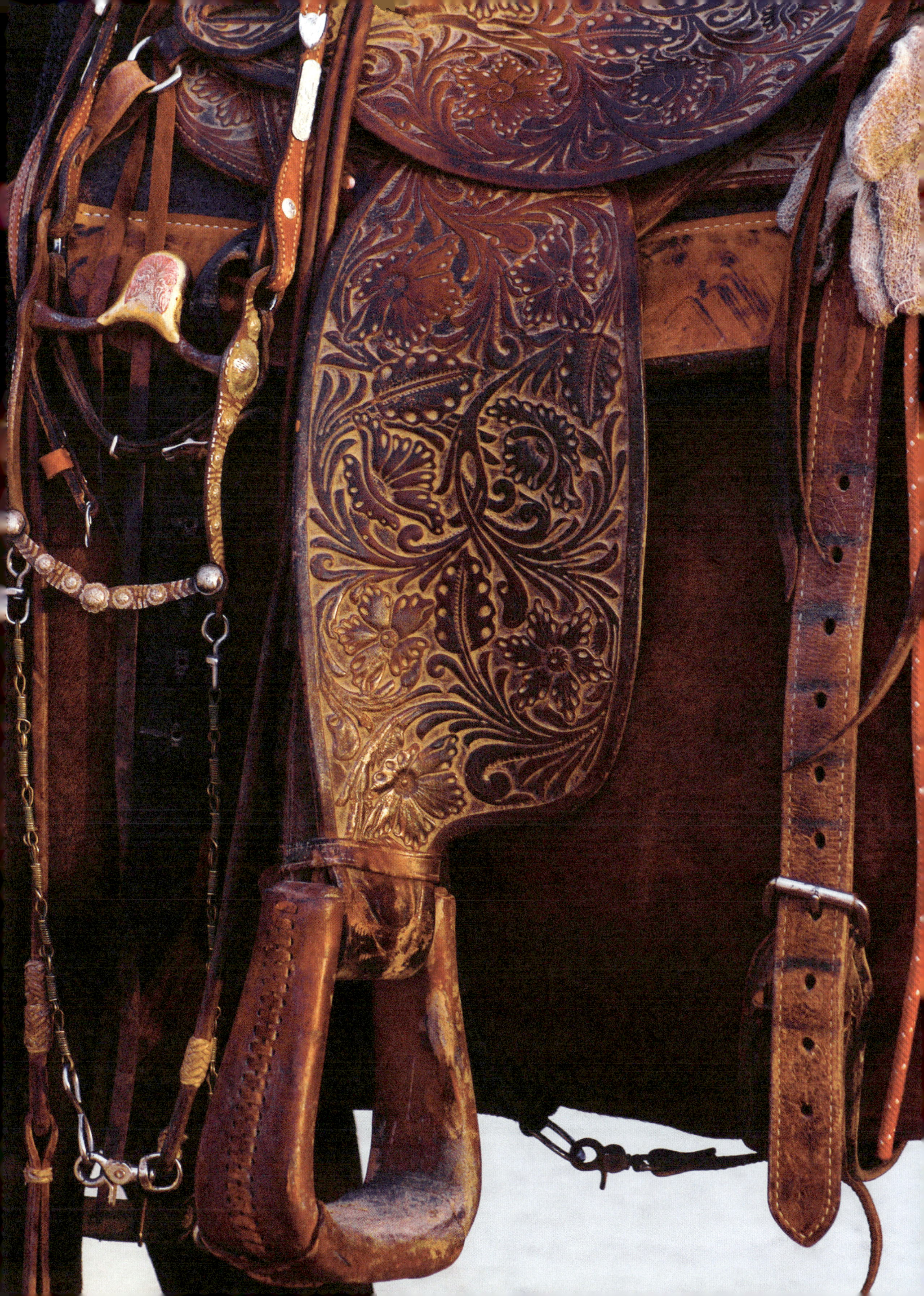

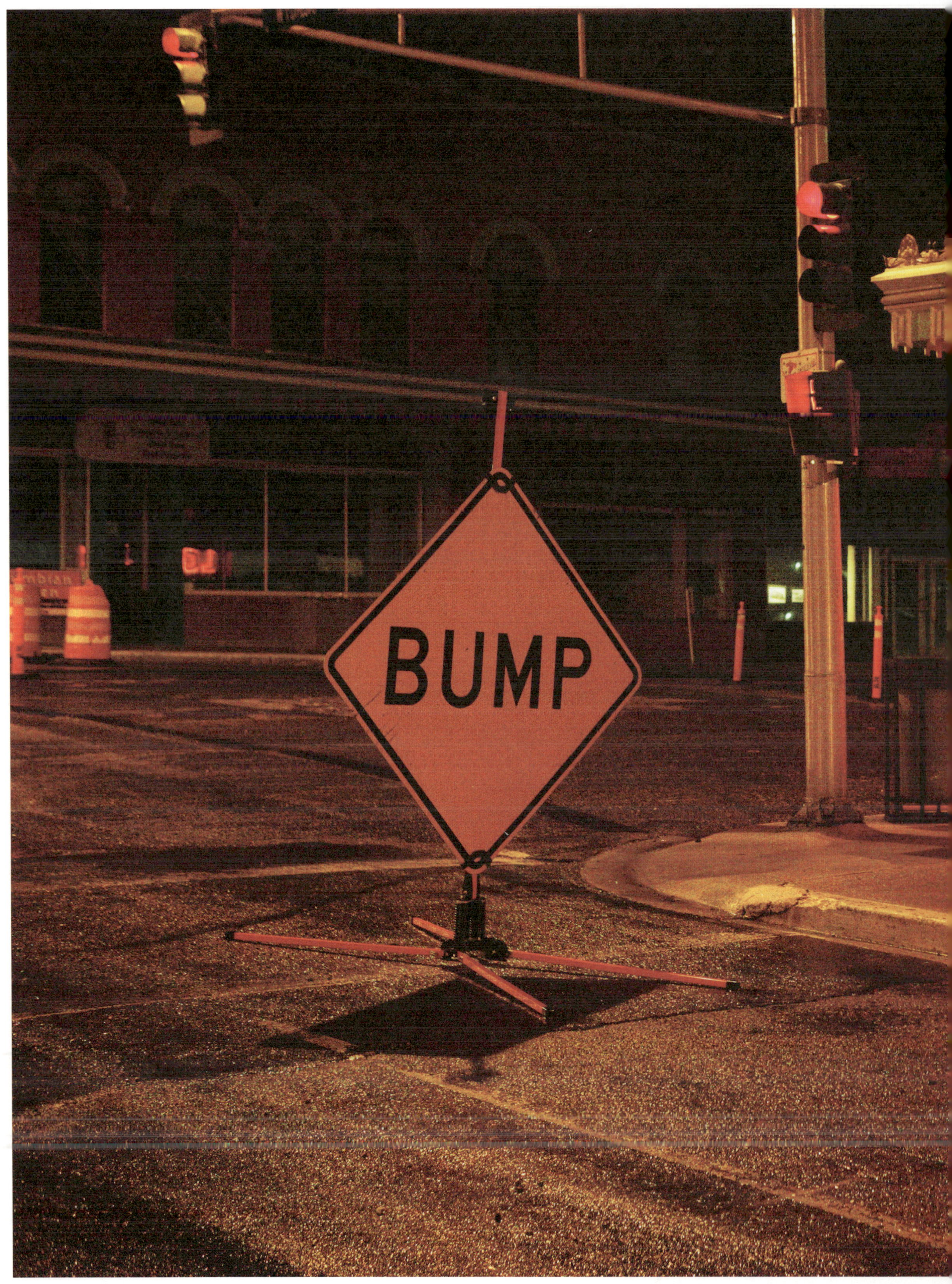
BUMP

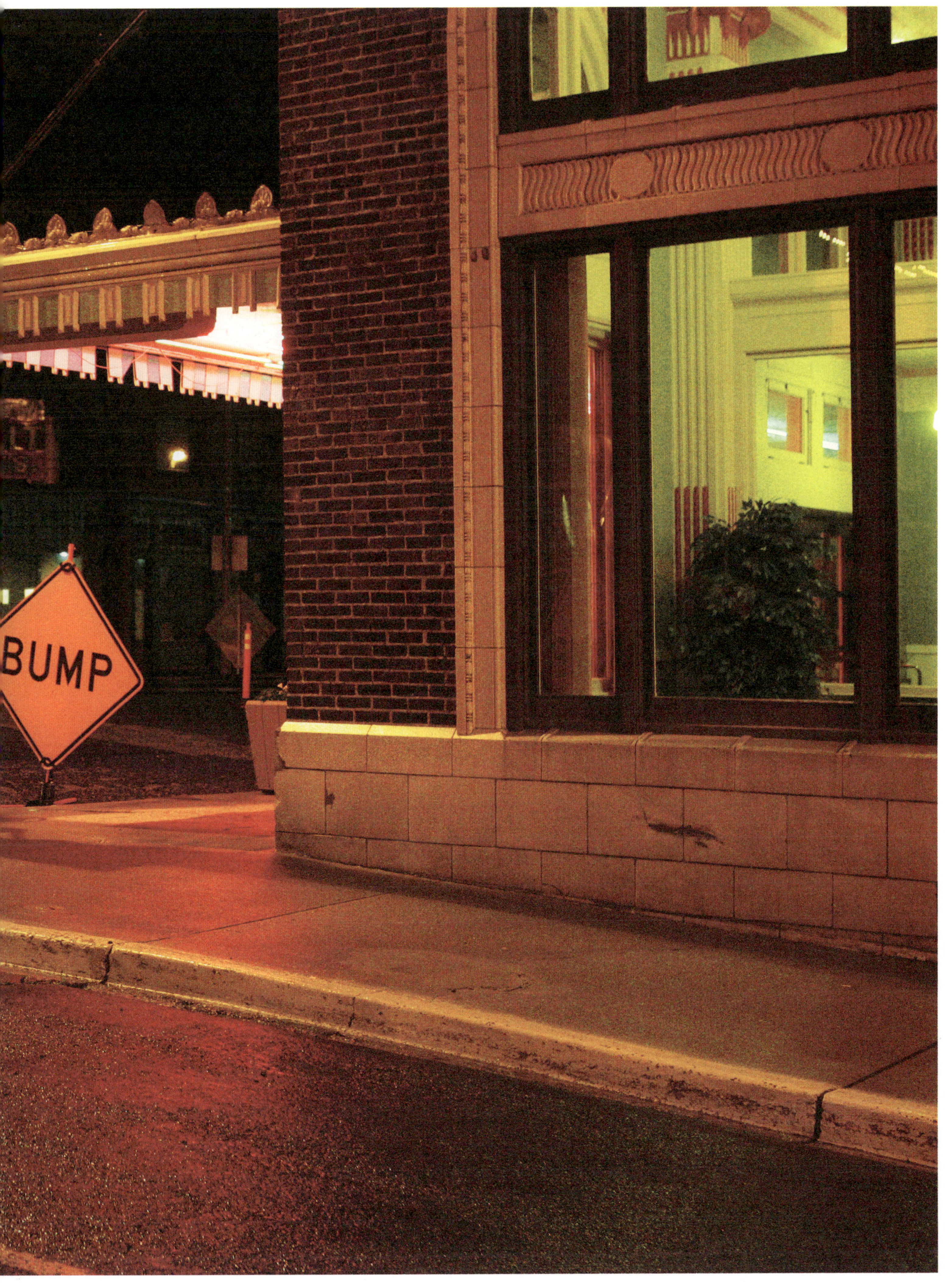
BUMP

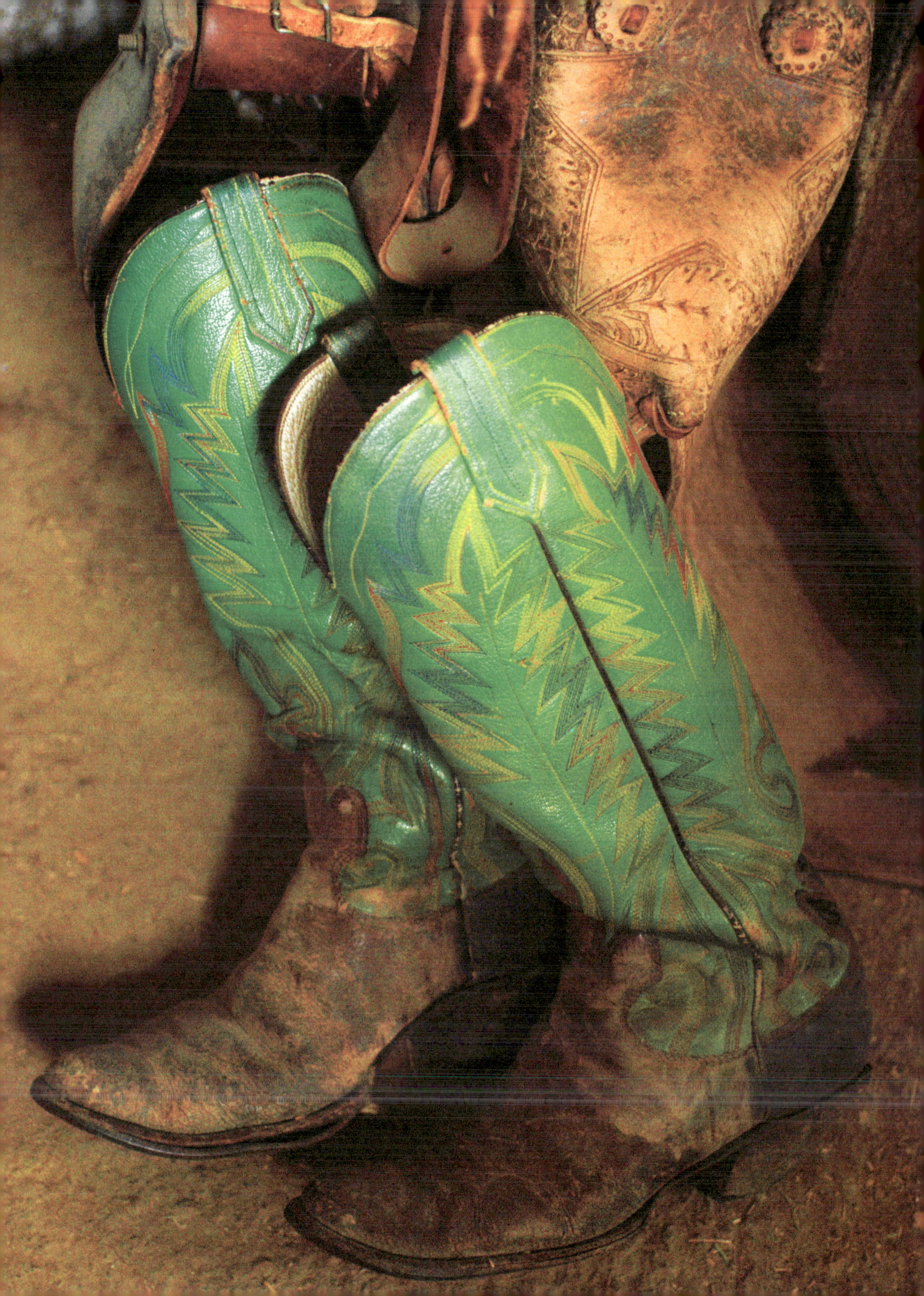

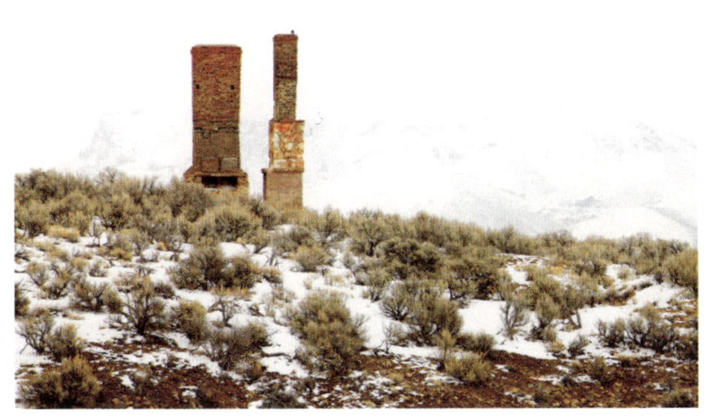

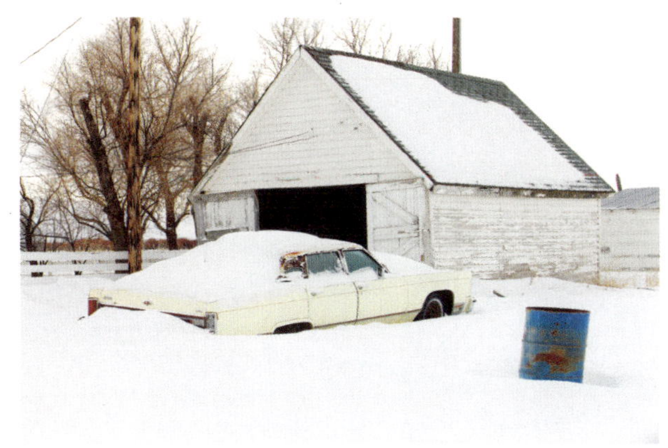

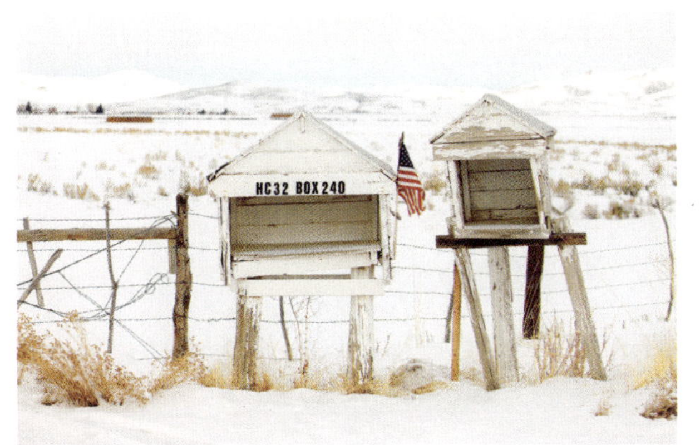
HC32 BOX240

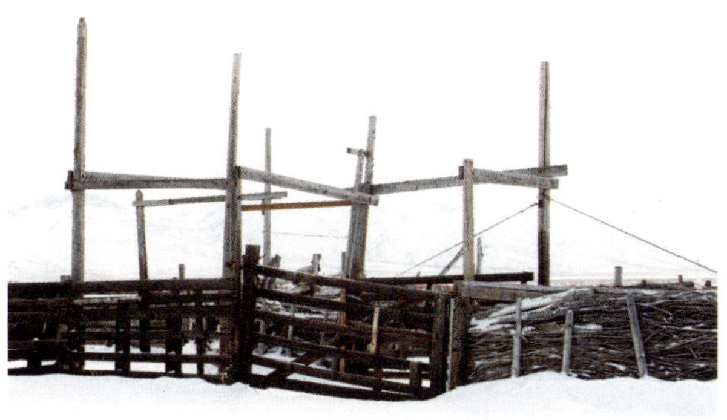

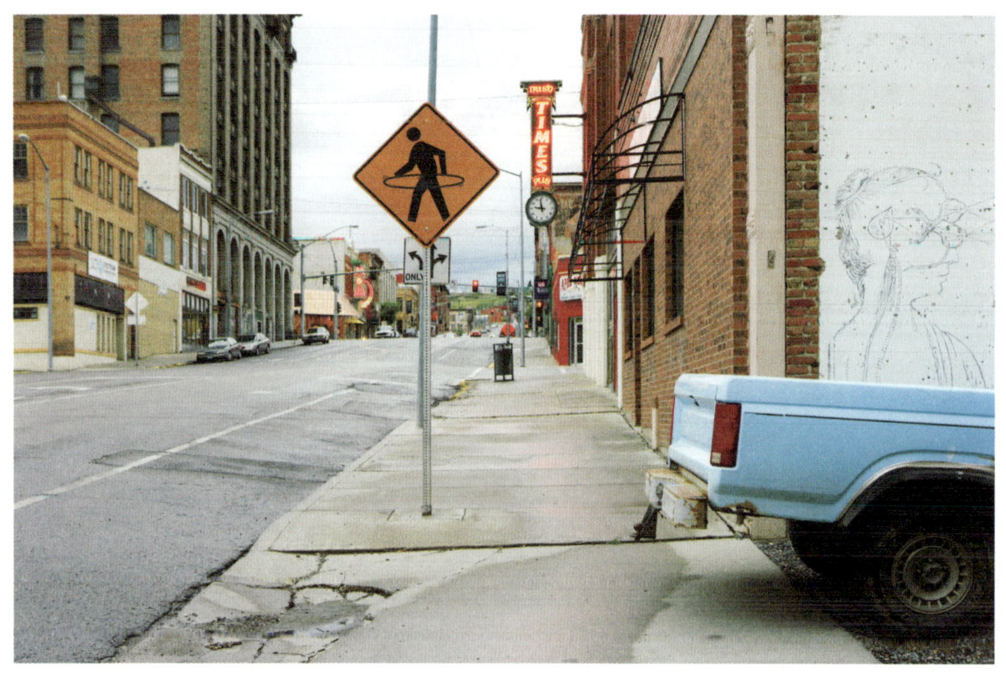
TIMES
ONLY

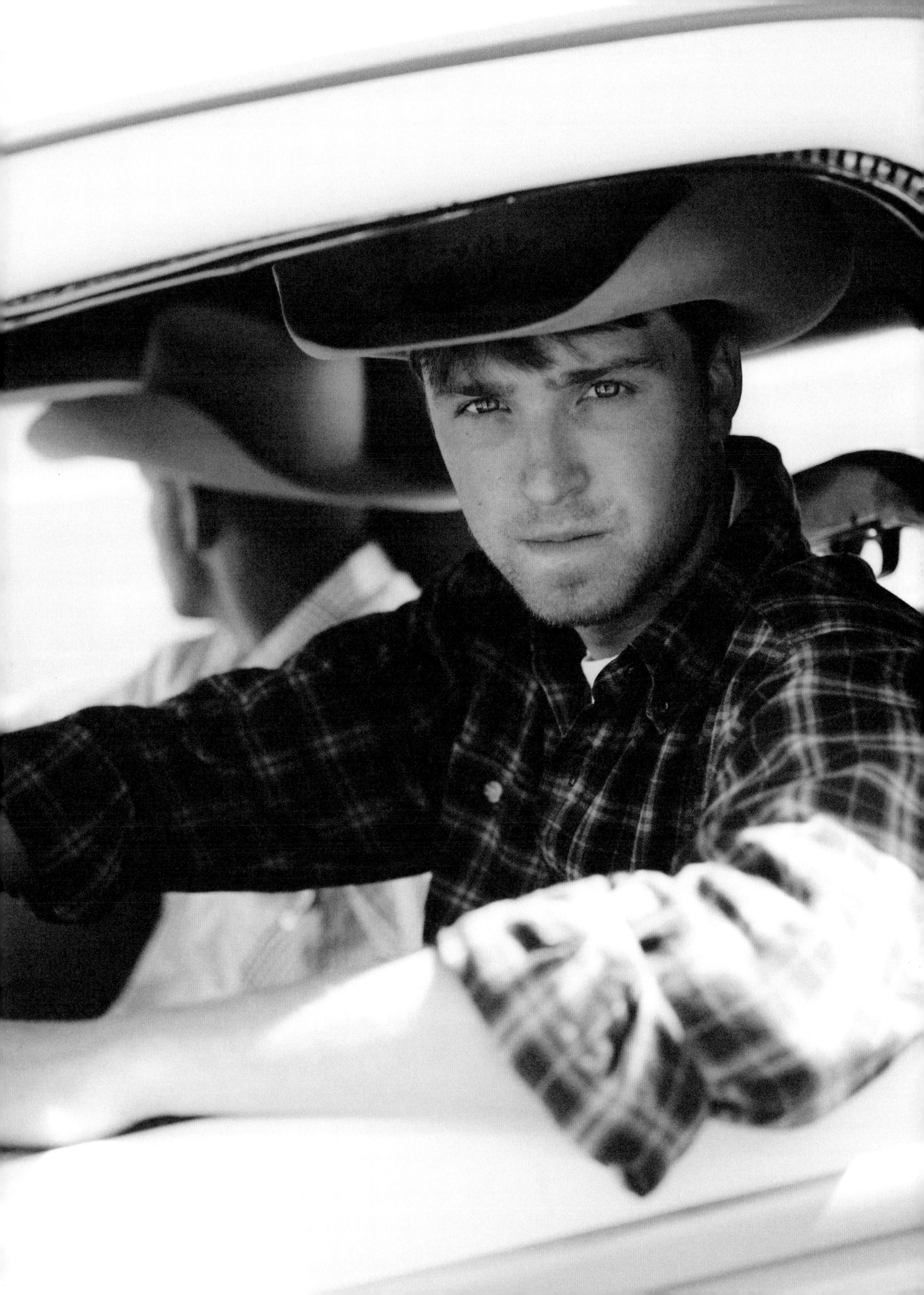

GENUINE FOLK SONGS TRADE THEIR SINGERS AND SURVIVE THEM WITH TIMELESS OBSERVATIONS. THEY DEAL NOT ONLY WITH LOVE AND LOSS, BUT DIG INTO SMALL TOWNS AND FEIGNED ATTITUDES AND HIDEOUS CRIMES. IT IS THE MUMBLE OF THE ORDINARY. THIS LAND IS NOT A GEOGRAPHIC PLACE GIVEN TO ANYONE BY SOME HIGHER AUTHORITY; IT'S GLUED TOGETHER BY A CONSTITUTION, A COLLECTION OF PROMISES, AND AN EVERLASTING SENSE OF DISSATISFACTION. AS LONG AS SOCIETY REMAINS A MATTER OF DISCUSSION EVERYTHING IS POSSIBLE.

COUNTRY MUSIC HAS BEEN MANUFACTURED AS COMPLACENT TUNES FOR PEOPLE WHO WANT TO PLAY AMERICA. BUT THE UNDERCURRENT IS THE FOLK ELEMENT. ITS CENTRAL ELEMENT IS STORY-TELLING, AND WHEN CONCENTRATED, HARSH, AND SENTIMENTAL IT CAN SUMMARIZE THE WISDOM OF A LIFETIME IN THREE MINUTES. THE BEST COUNTRY SONGS TRANSCEND THEIR OWN LIMITATIONS, LEAVING BAD CROPS AND HOSTILE WEATHER BEHIND AND CHARGING THE SIMPLE LYRICS WITH UNIVERSAL FEELINGS OF PARTICIPATION AND COMPASSION. YOU MAY CRY JUST THINKING ABOUT IT.

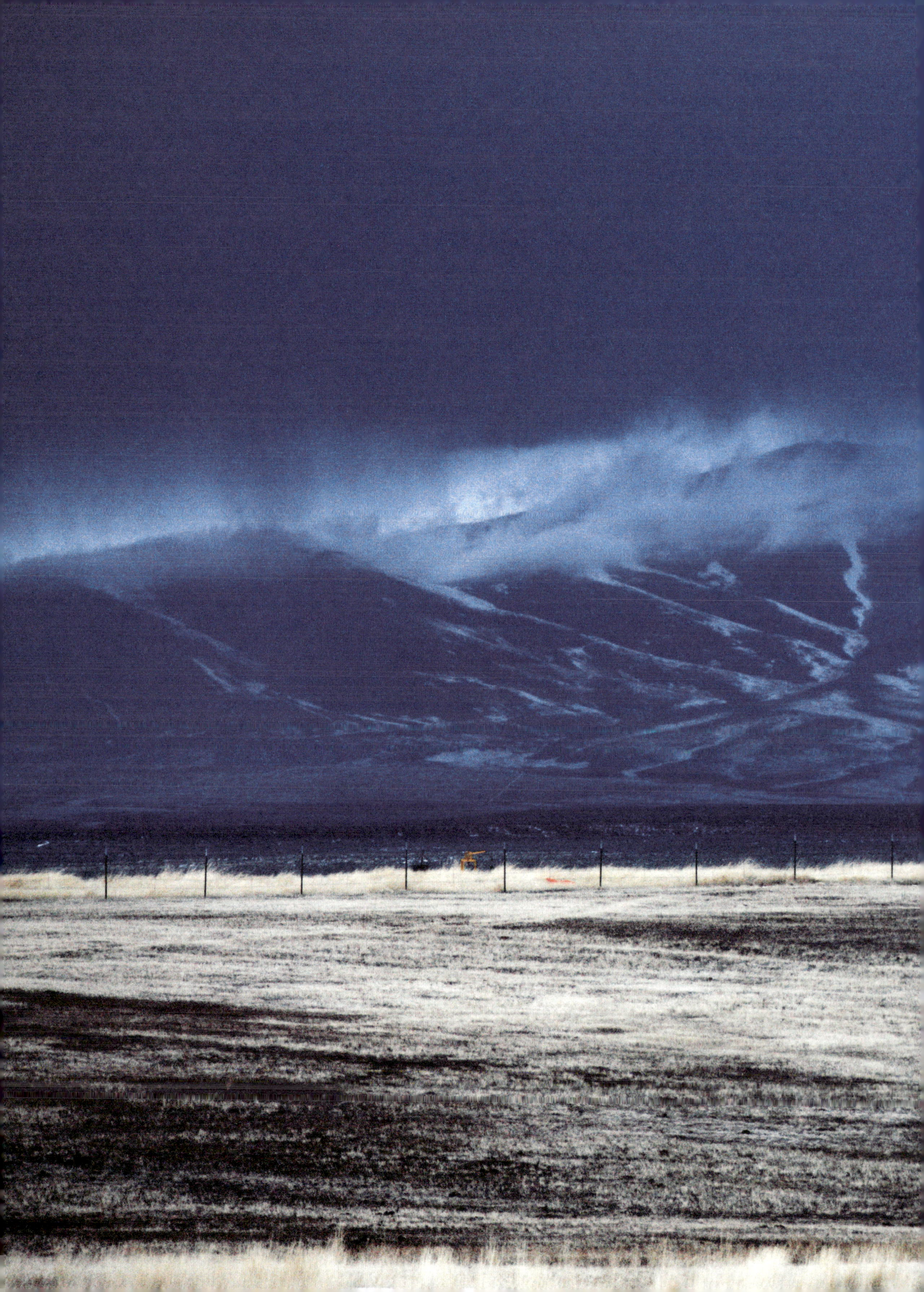

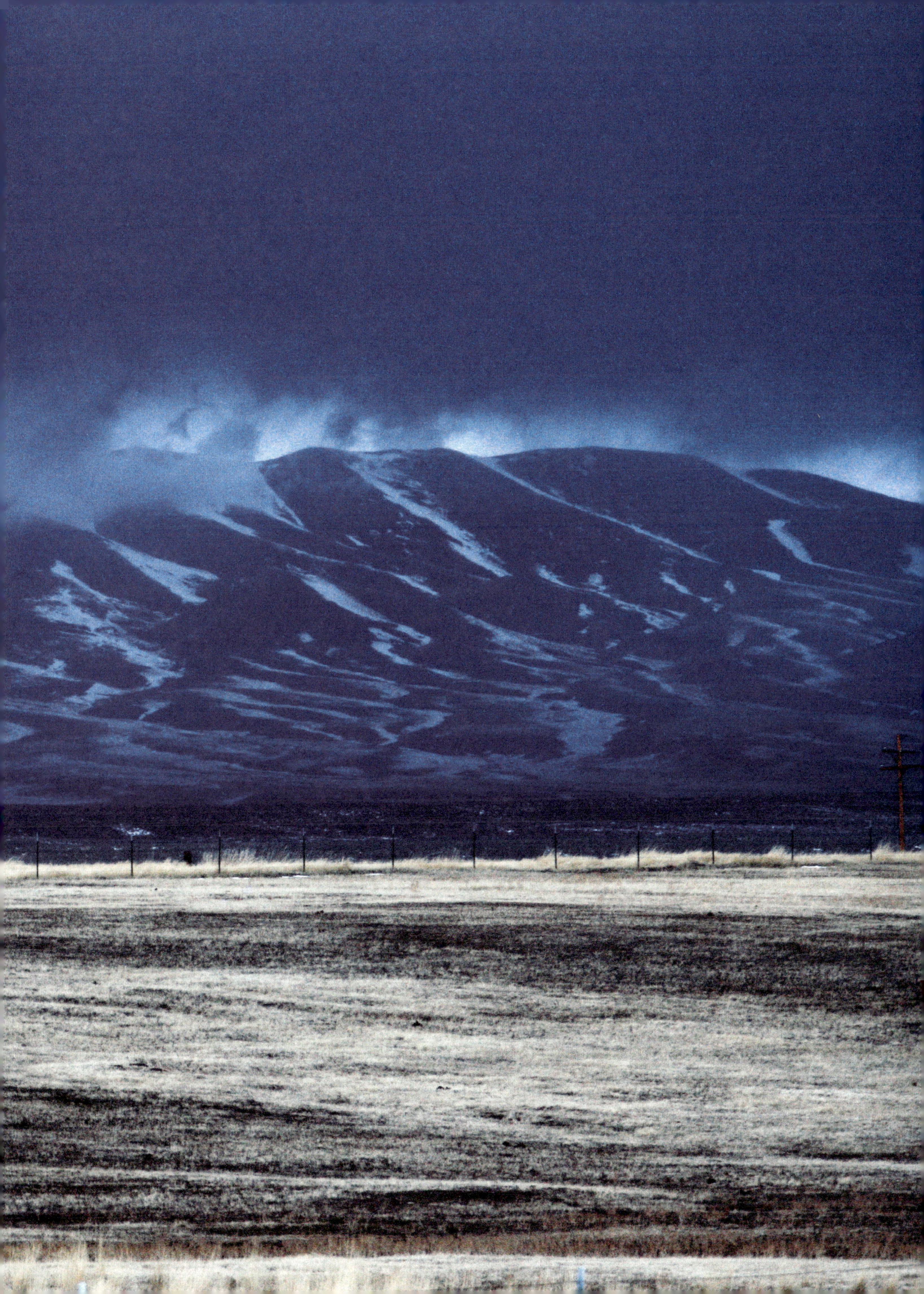

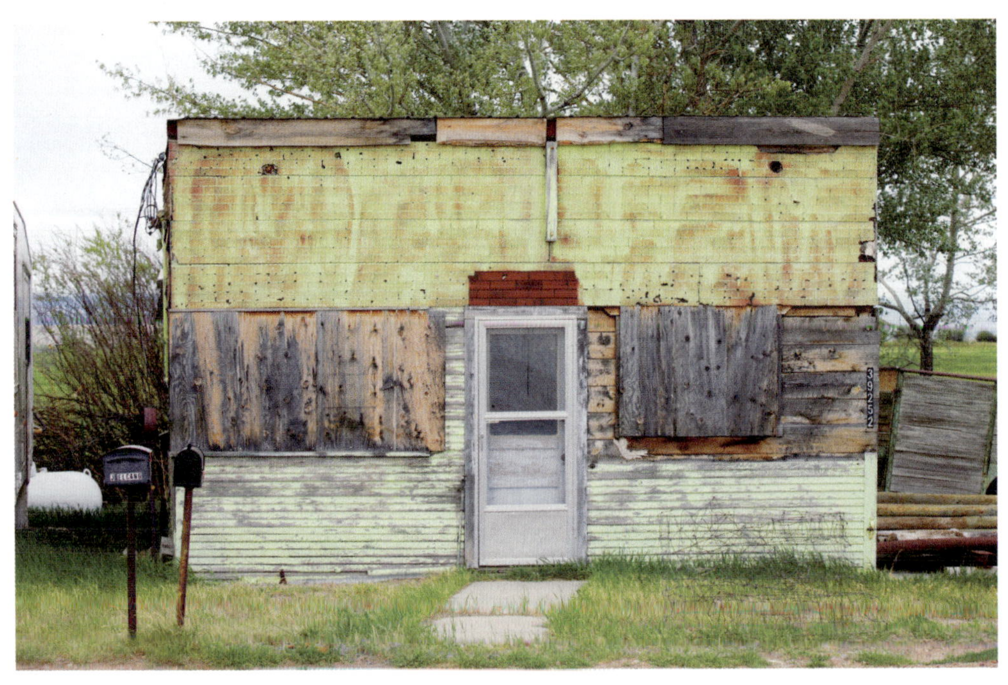

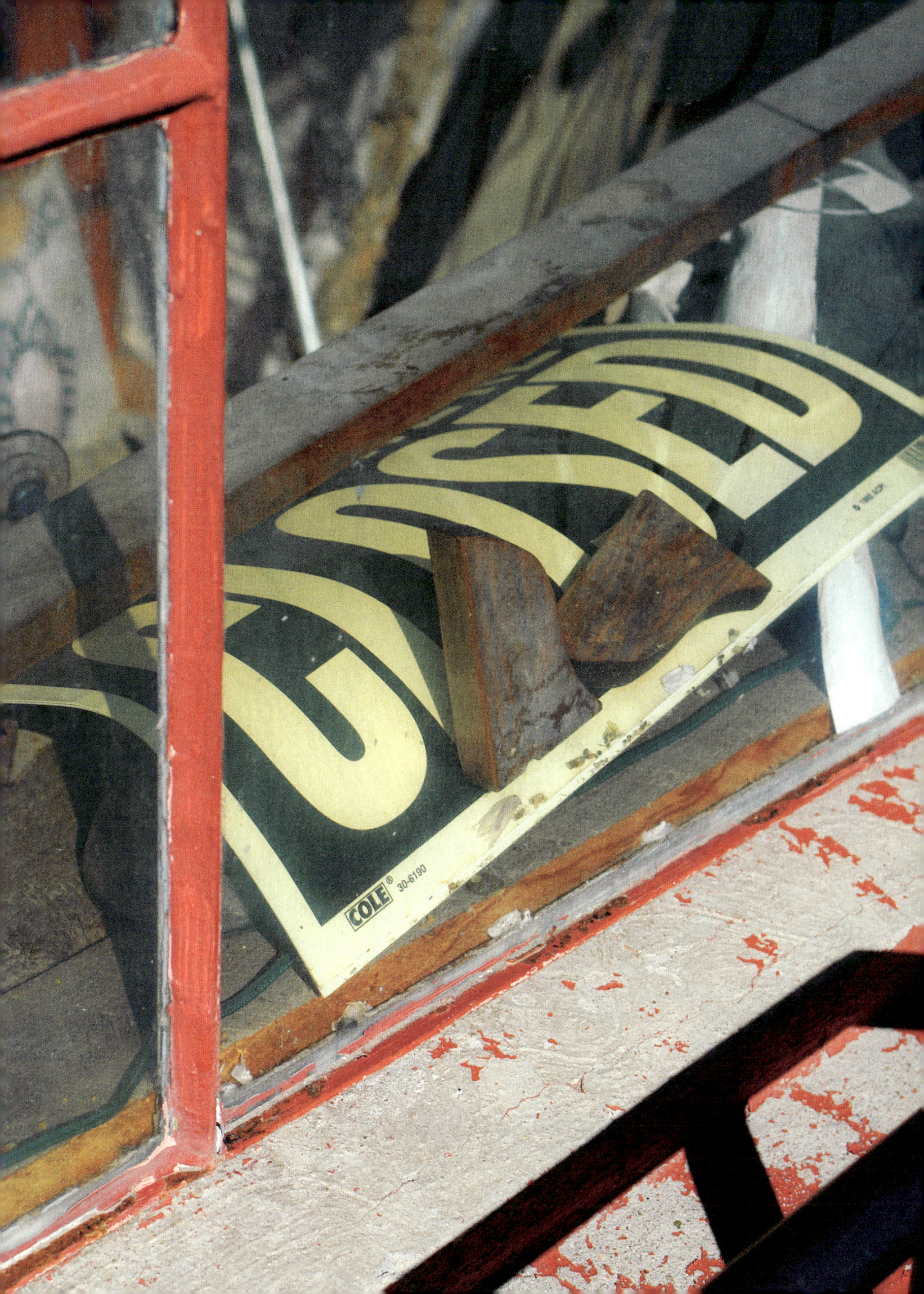
COLE®
30-6190

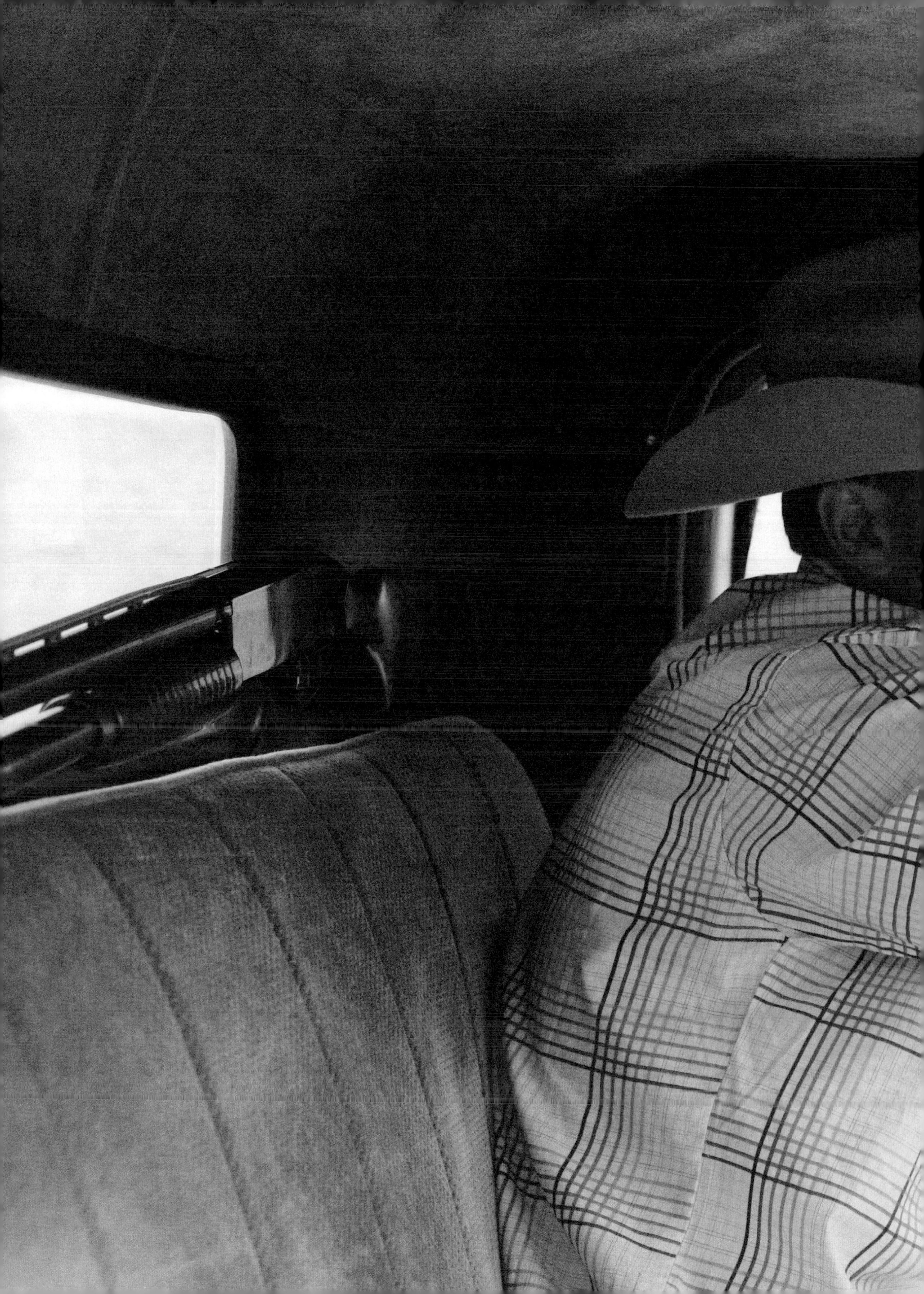

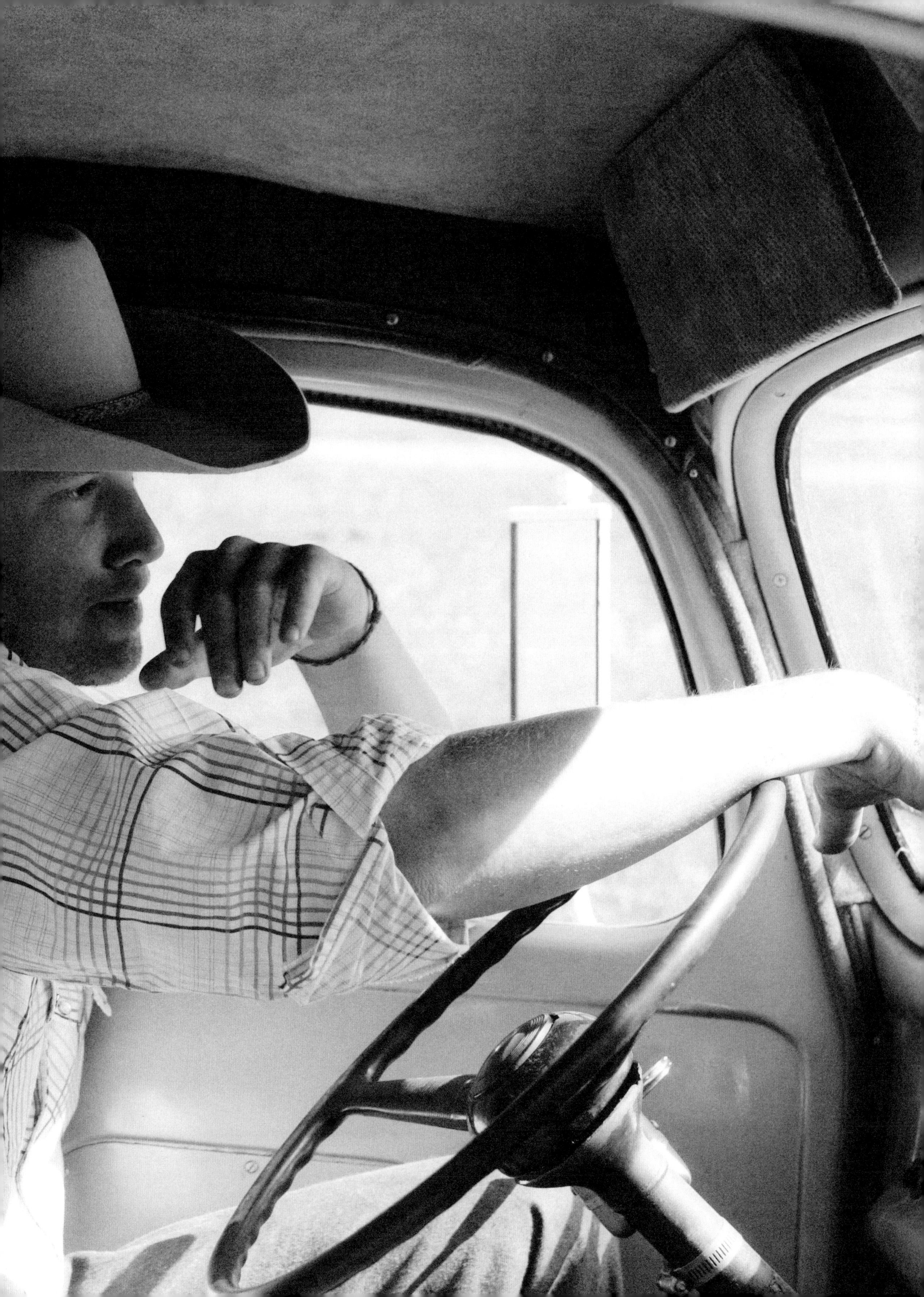

CERTAIN THINGS ARE NOT VISIBLE BECAUSE THEY DON'T COME AROUND.

BUT OUTSIDE IS A HIGHWAY AND OUT THERE IS THE WEST. GO FIGURE IT OUT.

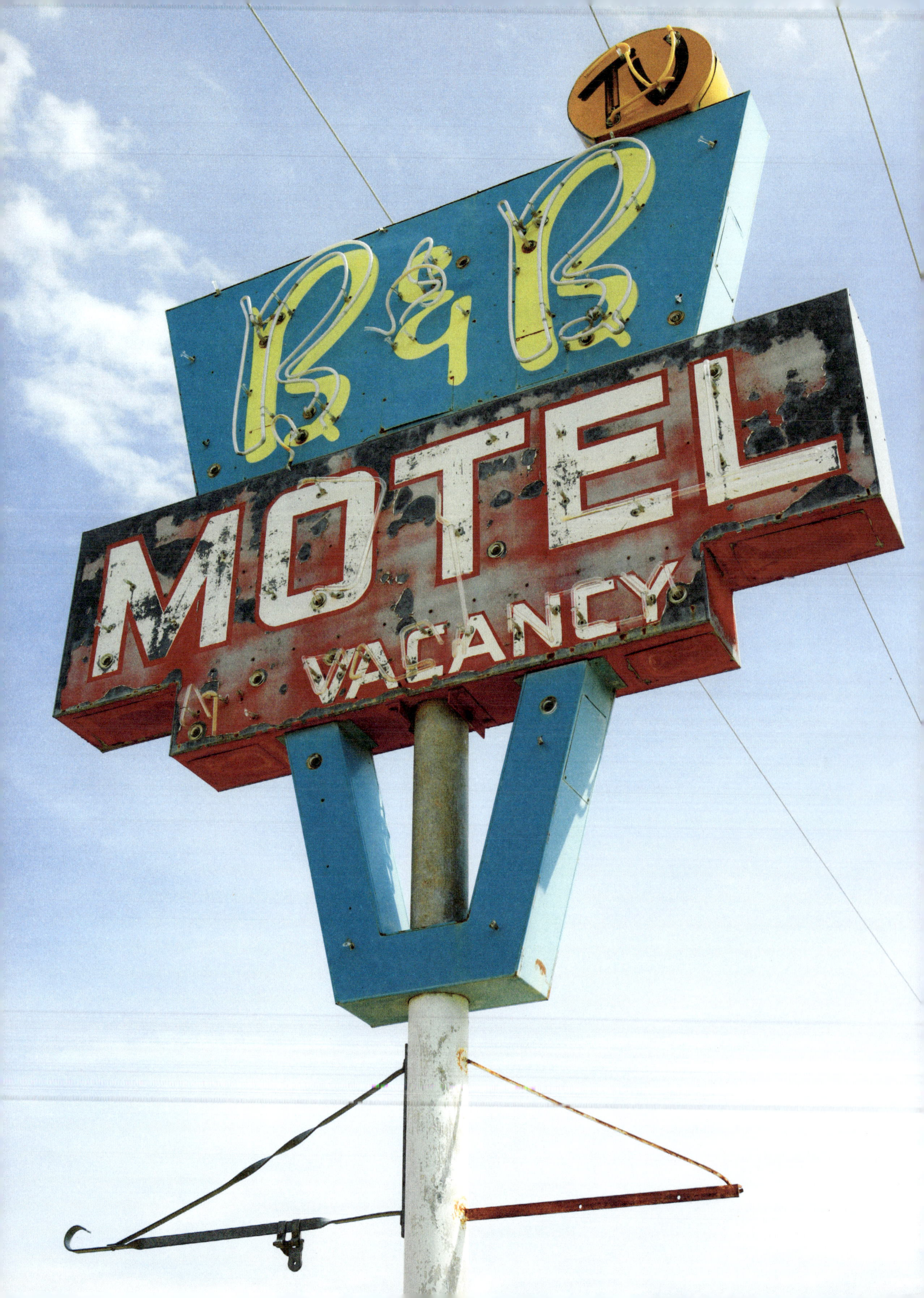
TV
B&B
MOTEL
VACANCY

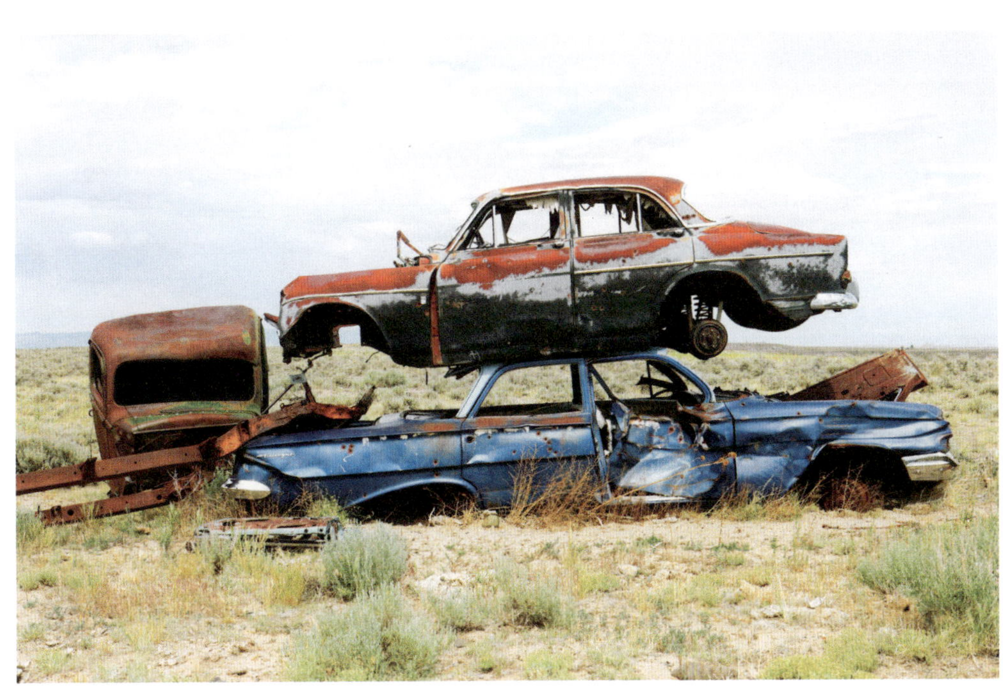

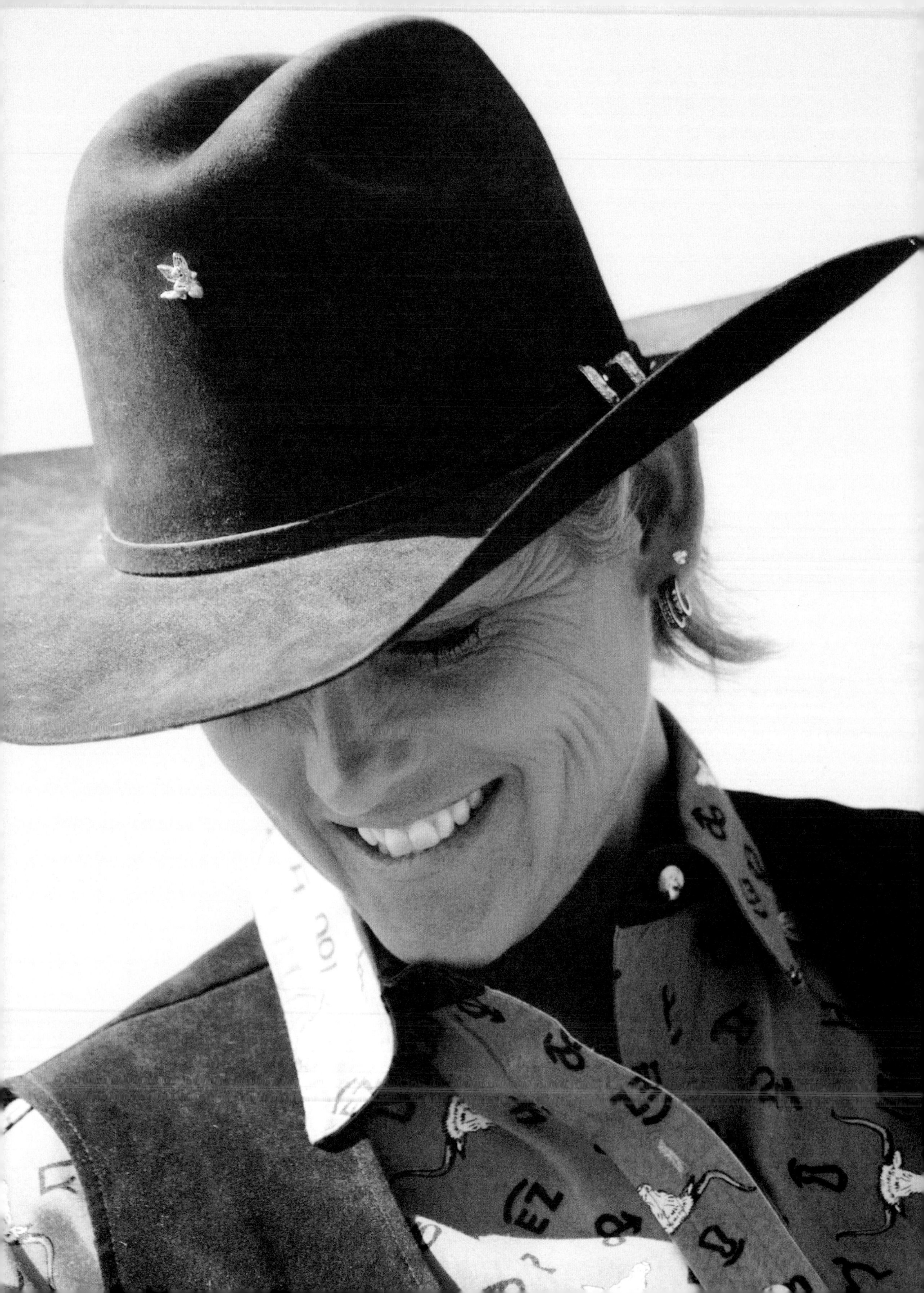

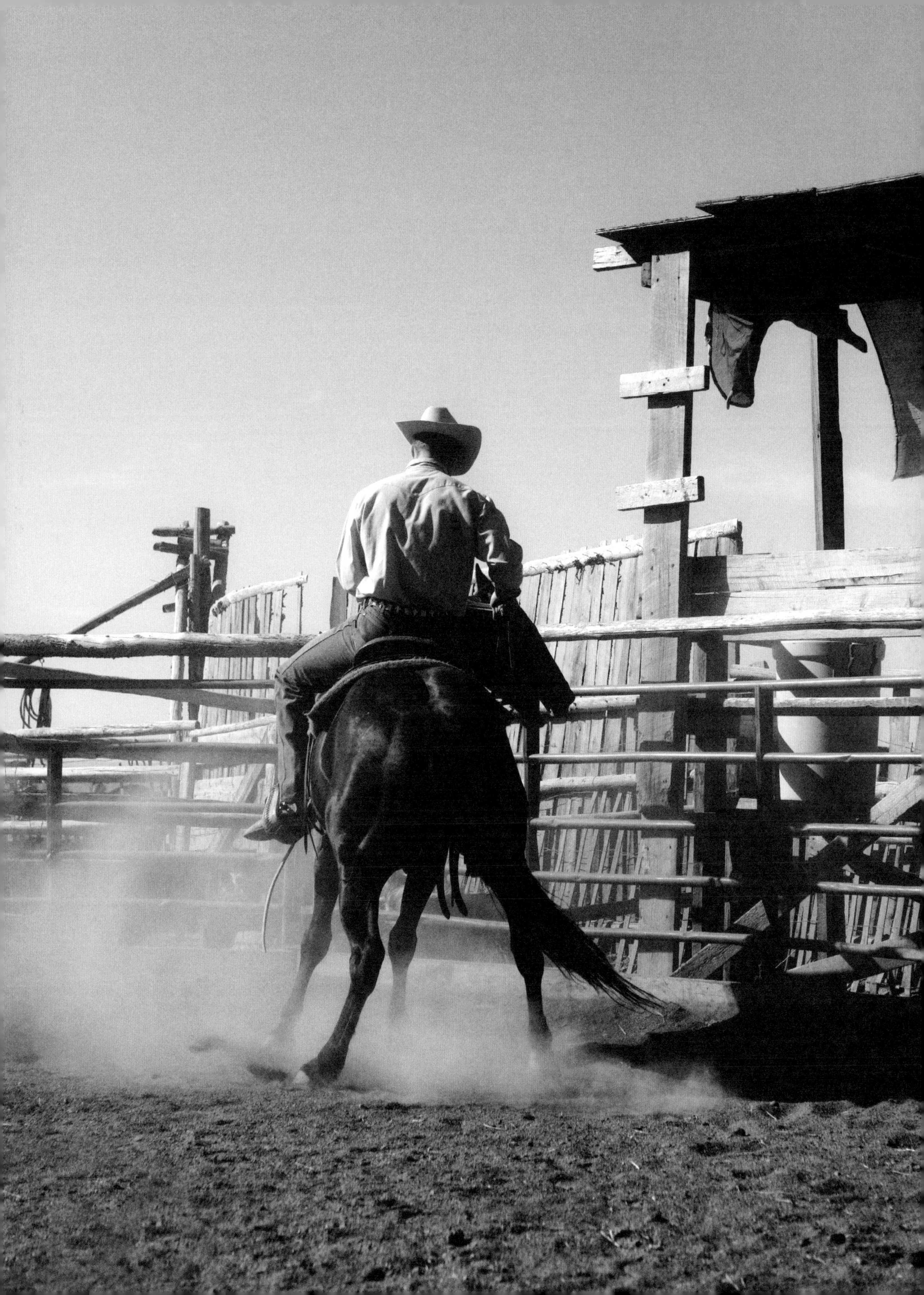

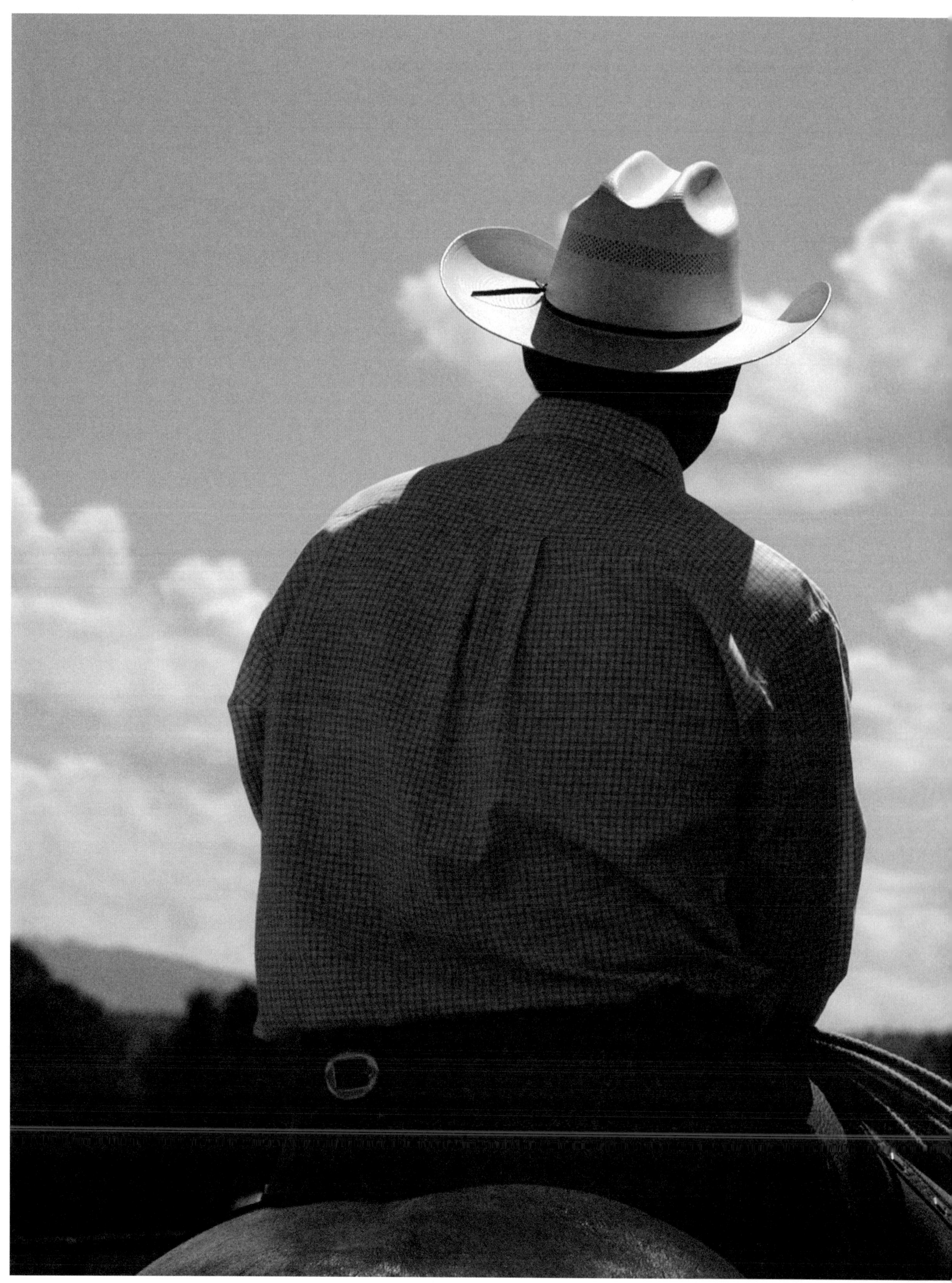

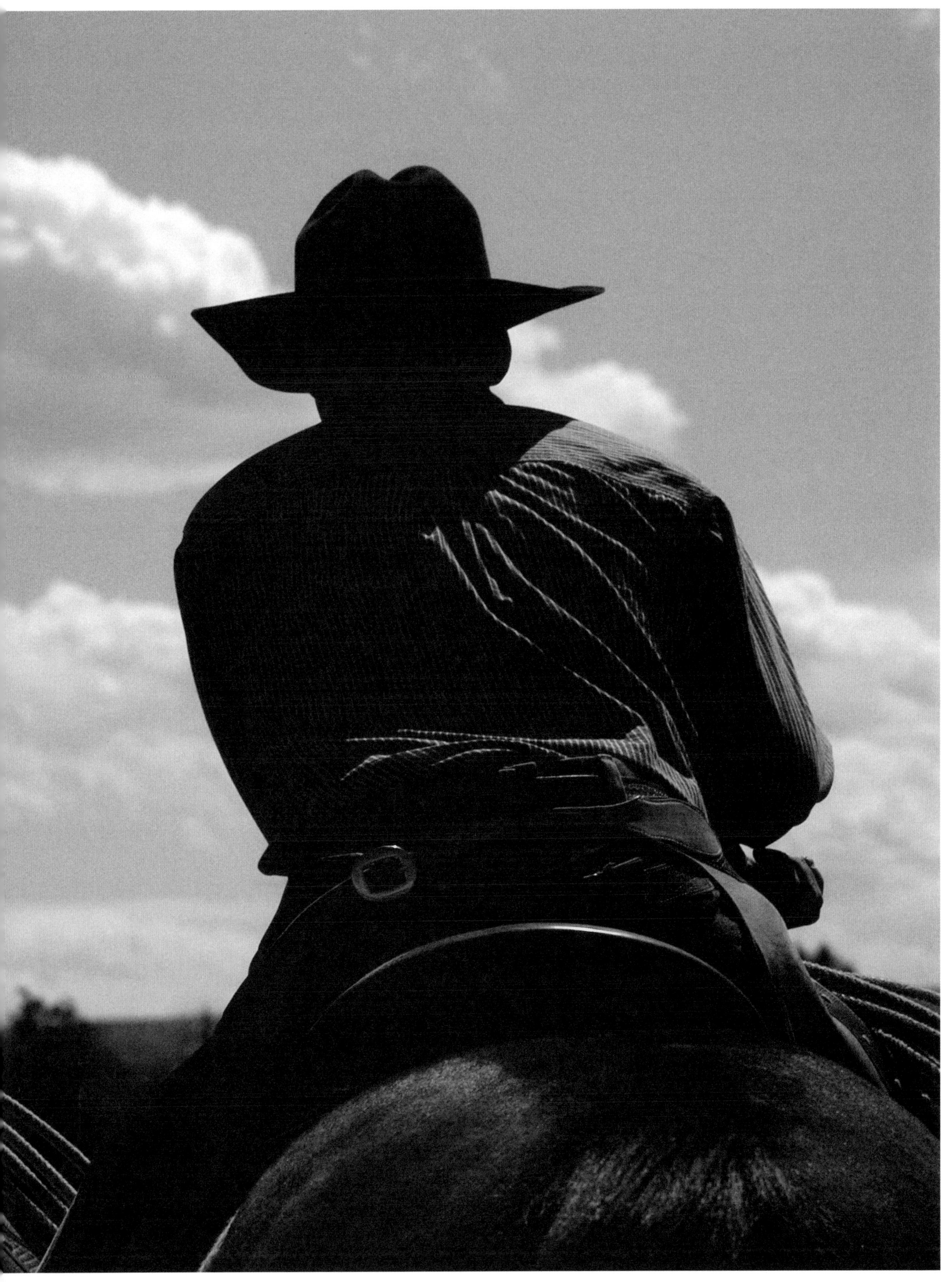

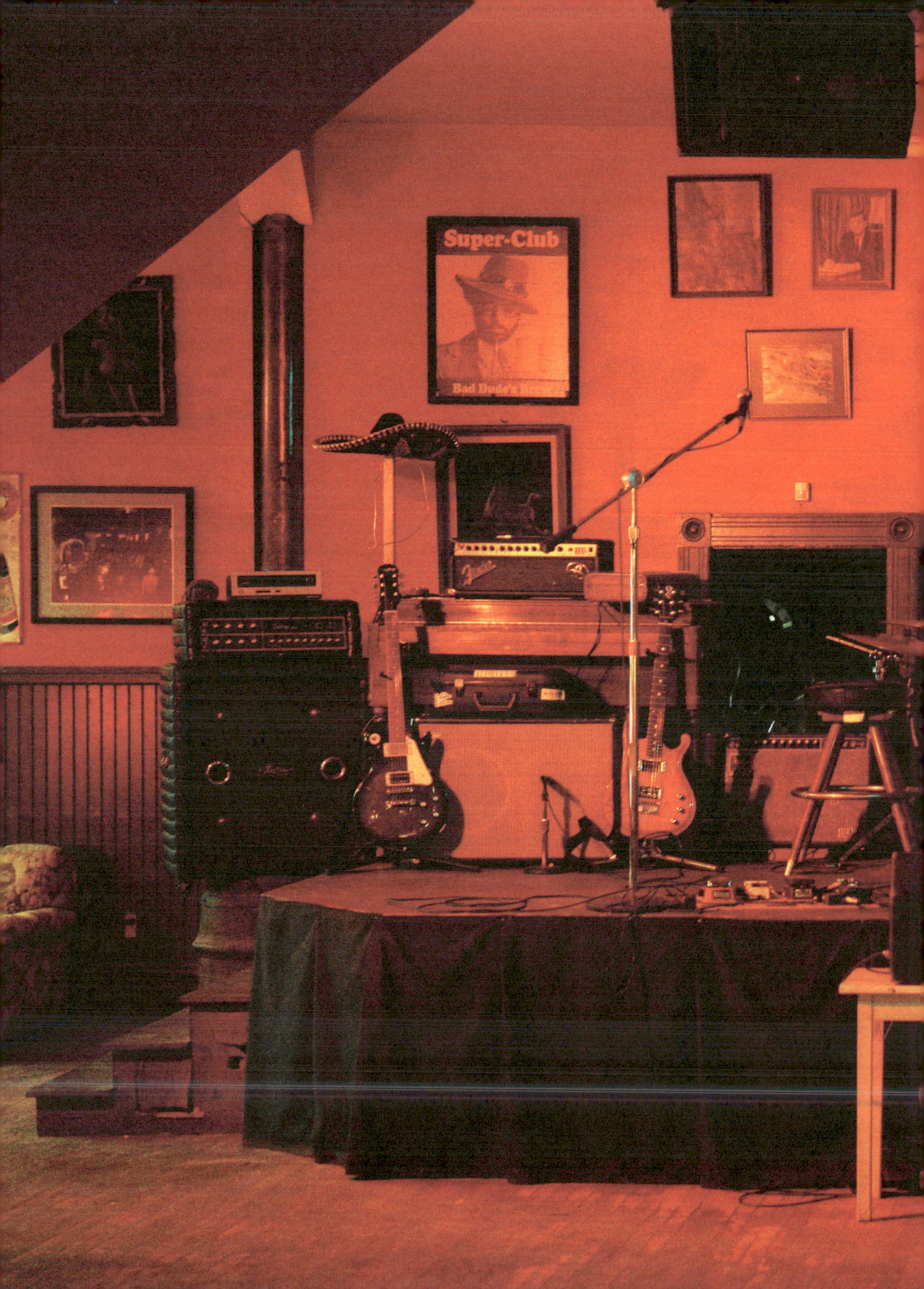
Super-Club

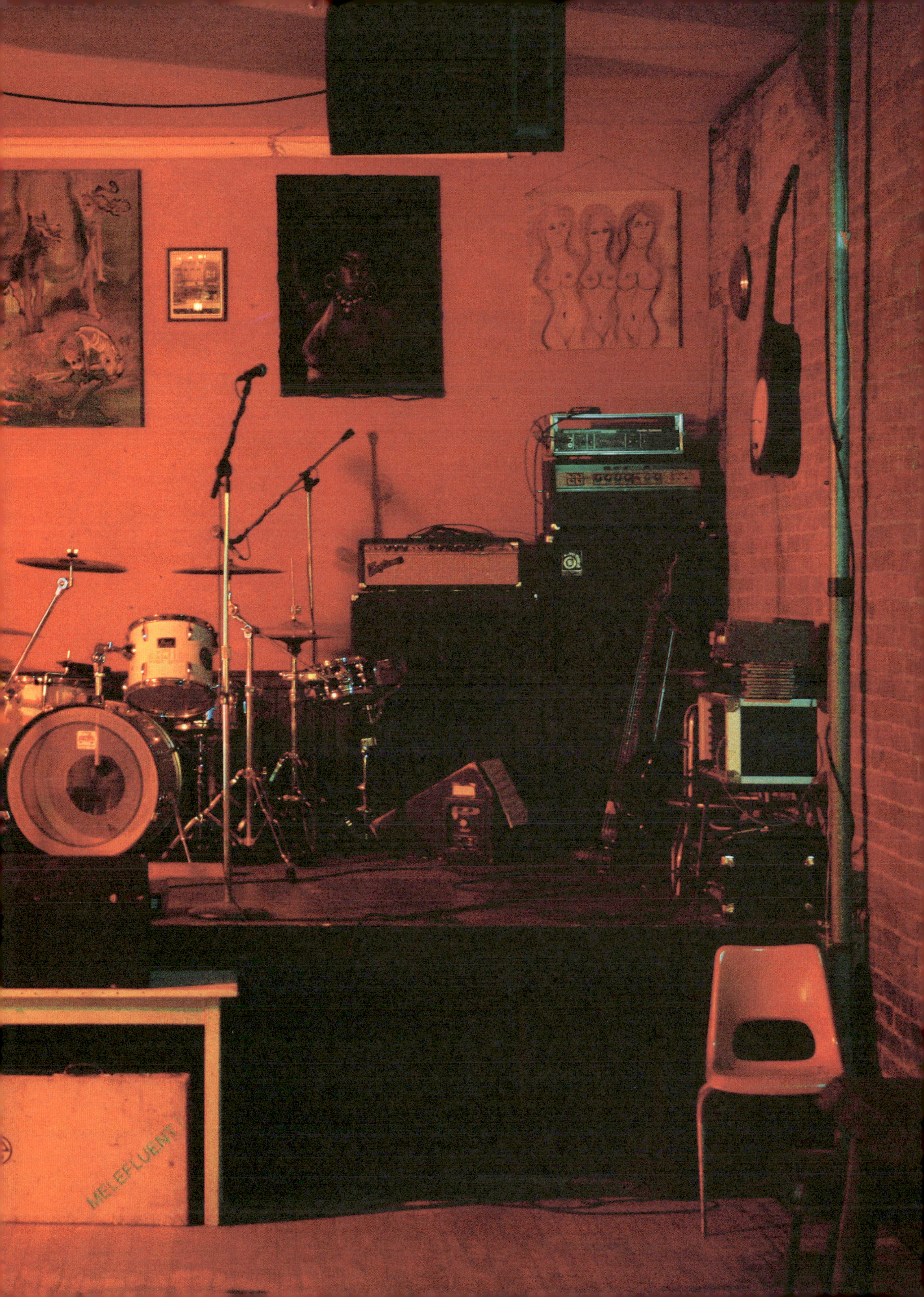
MELEFLUENT

FIRST EDITION
15 14 13 12 11 5 4 3 2 1

PUBLISHED BY
GIBBS SMITH
P.O. BOX 667
LAYTON, UTAH 84041

1.800.835.4993 ORDERS
WWW.GIBBS-SMITH.COM

DESIGNED BY RONNIE NILSSON
PRINTED AND BOUND IN CHINA

GIBBS SMITH BOOKS ARE PRINTED ON EITHER RECYCLED, 100% POST-CONSUMER WASTE, FSC-CERTIFIED PAPERS OR ON PAPER PRODUCED FROM SUSTAINABLE PEFC-CERTIFIED FOREST/CONTROLLED WOOD SOURCE. LEARN MORE AT WWW.PEFC.ORG.

LIBRARY OF CONGRESS CONTROL NUMBER: 2011924336

ISBN: 978-1-4236-2350-2

LARS STRANDBERG BEGAN PORTRAYING HIS FRIENDS IN MALMÖ, SWEDEN, WHEN HE WAS A TEENAGER. HE HAS SINCE WORKED INTERNATIONALLY AS A PHOTOGRAPHER, HIS WORK APPEARING BOTH IN BOOKS, MAGAZINES, NEWSPAPERS, EXHIBITIONS, AND ADVERTISING.

LARS ÅBERG IS A JOURNALIST AND THE AUTHOR OF A NUMBER OF NON-FICTION BOOKS WITH SWEDISH OR AMERICAN THEMES, INCLUDING TWO ABOUT NATIVE AMERICANS. HE HAS TRAVELED EXTENSIVELY IN THE U.S. SINCE THE 1970s AND VISITED 47 OF THE 50 STATES.

RONNIE NILSSON IS AN ART DIRECTOR WHO RUNS HIS OWN GRAPHIC DESIGN FIRM OUT OF A RENOVATED OLD FARMHOUSE ON THE SOUTH COAST OF SWEDEN. HE HAS DESIGNED A SERIES OF BOOKS, ONE OF WHICH WAS NAMED SWEDISH COOKBOOK OF THE YEAR.

THANK YOU

PATRICIA BERG AND ELIZABETH VAN CLEEF FOR REVIEWING THE TEXT.
JONAS NILSSON FOR HANDLING THE PREPRESS PROCEDURE.
MEG GLASER FOR CONNECTING THE DOTS OUT WEST.